Zion & Bryce Canyon

NATIVE PARKS

NATIONAL PARKS

D1026194

Arches National Park
p194

Moab
p204

Around Bryce Canyon National Park
p130

Bryce Canyon National Park
p108

Capitol Reef National Park
p160

Canyonlands National Park
p176

Around Zion National Park
p82

Zion National Park
p46

Grand Staircase-Escalante National Monument
p136

Around Grand Staircase-Escalante National Monument
p151

THIS EDITION WRITTEN AND RESEARCHED BY

Greg Benchwick, Carolyn McCarthy, Christopher Pitts

PLAN YOUR TRIP

ON THE ROAD

SAND DUNE ARCH P199

PHILIP LEE HARVEY / GETTY IMAGES ©

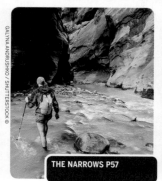

THE NARROWS P57

GALYNA ANDRUSHKO / SHUTTERSTOCK ©

PETER KUNASZ / SHUTTERSTOCK ©

Contents

FIERY FURNACE P198

Welcome to Zion & Bryce Canyon National Parks

If you think you've seen every possible hue of sandstone, the rising or setting sun over Utah's national parks will show you otherwise.

Canyons & Red Rocks

Perhaps nowhere else in the Southwest can compete with southern Utah when it comes to the sheer number of geological works of art. Soaring pinnacles and arches, dizzyingly deep canyons and rainbow-colored rocks are all par for the course. This is where the bones of the earth – and the powerful natural processes that shape them – are laid bare. Take the time to observe the different-colored layers stacked one upon the other: Kayenta, Navajo, Temple Cap, Carmel. These are snapshots of the planet's distant past, and an amazing opportunity to take in the work of 240 million years in a single glance.

Outdoor Adventures

There's no better way to get a feel for this red-rock wonderland than by having some fun. Serious fun. Whatever your sport, there's a good chance that Utah sets a pretty high standard. Hikes lead to majestic freestanding arches, secret oases, desert labyrinths and exposed traverses across narrow fins. Canyoneers rappel into the earth's wrinkles to explore dark, mystical passageways filled with adventure. Moab's slickrock trails set the standard for mountain biking decades ago, while desert spires and mighty big walls are the envy of rock climbers around the world.

Scenic Drives & Lookouts

Though southern Utah's majestic parklands are hardly drive-by attractions, scenic roads abound. In fact, they're an essential part of your journey here in canyon country, whether you're driving, cycling, riding the park shuttles in Zion and Bryce, or negotiating a teeth-rattling, nerve-wracking 4WD road in the rugged backcountry. And if there are moments when you feel as if you've seen that view in a Hollywood film, it's because you probably have.

Beyond the National Parks

You could spend weeks immersed in the national parks and monuments. But then you'd be missing out on some of the most memorable places, from arty, alternative-minded towns like Moab to Native American tribal lands and sites where prehistoric denizens made their mark. Detours are always worthwhile here, whether for an earthy plate of organic, farm-fresh food or to capture another top-of-the-world vista. Local state parks (Snow Canyon, Goblin Valley) and wilderness areas (Paria Canyon-Vermilion Cliffs) deserve consideration, as does off-the-grid Cedar Mesa. Take our suggestions as starting points for your own sojourn.

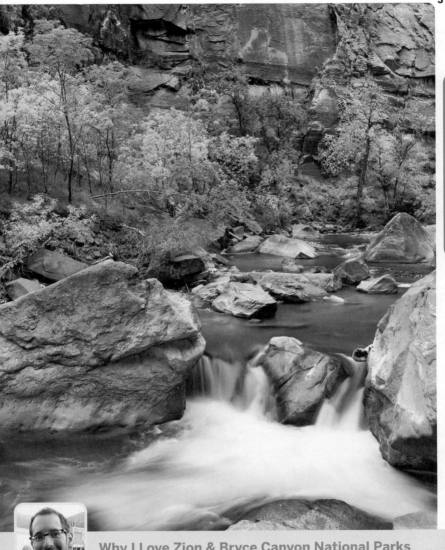

Why I Love Zion & Bryce Canyon National Parks

By Christopher Pitts, Writer

I love the prickly pear's hot-pink blooms, the tenacity of crimson paintbrush draped across a rock face. I love exploring canyons: listening to echoes of water – sometimes light and joyous, sometimes rumbling and ominous – or just tracing its ancient passage along the smooth, rippling walls. I love how a place that seems so barren is in fact so full of wonder. It's much like life itself: from afar it might appear tough and unforgiving, but take the time for a closer look and you'll find that each moment has its own special beauty.

For more about our writers, see p288

Above: Virgin River (p57), Zion Canyon

Zion & Bryce Canyon National Park

Capitol Reef National Park
Admire the Milky Way's
silver arc (p160)

Mcgill

Ely

Humboldt
National
Forest

Mount
Moriah
Wilderness

Delta

NEVADA

Currant
Mountain
Wilderness

Preston

Baker

Garrison

Great Basin
National
Park

*Sevier Lake
(dry)*

UTAH

Desert Range
Experimental
Station

Red Canyon
Saddle up and ride the
Wild West (p122)

Cove Fort

Fremo
Ind
State Pa

Milford

Beaver

Bryce Canyon
Hike the unreal Fairyland
Loop (p112)

Minersville

*Little
Salt Lake*

The Narrows
Wade the river that carved
Zion (p57)

Panaca

Modena

Parowan

Cedar City

Angels Landing
Chain-assisted climb to
heaven (p54)

Enterprise

Pine Valley
Mountain
Wilderness

Alamo

NEVADA

Central

Veyo

*Snow Canyon
State Park*

Leeds

Zion
National
Park

Glendale

Mt Carme
Junction

Las Vegas
Pre- or post-trip
decadence (p98)

Rockville

St George

Coral Pink
Sand Dunes
State Park

Kana

Colorado City

Fredonia

Virgin River

Mesquite

*Kaibab-Paiute
Indian
Reservation*

Moapa

*Moapa River
Indian
Reservation*

Hanging Gardens
Zion's lush oases of
desert life (p52)

**Paria Canyon-Vermilion
Cliffs Wilderness Area**
Home of the Wave (p159)

Dry Lake

*Lake
Mead*

Las Vegas

Lake Mead
National
Recreation Area

Grand Canyon
National
Park

Colorado River

0 100 km
N
0 50 miles

Nephi

Price

Uintah & Ouray IR

Willow Creek

Fishlake National Forest
Oak City

Uinta NF

Arches National Park
Find your way in the
Fiery Furnace (p198)

Scipio

Sevier Bridge Reservoir

Ephraim

Huntington

Gunnison

Palisade State Park

Manti-La Sal National Forest

Thompson Springs

Fillmore

Salina

Fishlake National Forest

Emery

Green River

Richfield

Muddy Creek

Moab
Southern Utah's capital
of adventure (p204)

Arches National Park

Fishlake National Forest
Burrville

Fish Lake

Goblin Valley State Park

Moab

Marysvale

Dead Horse Point State Park

Piute Reservoir

Caineville

Hanksville

Canyonlands National Park

La Sal Junction

Otter Creek Reservoir

Torrey

Capitol Reef National Park

Glen Canyon National Recreation Area

Circleville

Dixie National Forest

Colorado River

Monticello

Dixie National Forest

Escalante River Canyon

Boulder

UTAH

The Needles

Dark Canyon Wilderness

Red Canyon

Escalante

Calf Creek Recreation Area

Lake Powell

Natural Bridges National Monument

Bryce Canyon National Park

Cannonville

Blanding

Paria River

Escalante River

Canyonlands National Park
Impenetrable wilderness,
desert adventure (p176)

Grand Staircase-Escalante National Monument

Glen Canyon National Recreation Area

Lake Powell

San Juan River

Bluff

Goosenecks State Park

Glen Canyon City

Mexican Hat

Paria Canyon-Vermilion Cliffs Wilderness Area

Page

Monument Valley Navajo Tribal Park

Dinnehotso

Jacob Lake

Marble Canyon

Navajo National Monument

Rock Point

Kaibab National Forest

Bitter Springs

Horseshoe Bend

Kaibito

ARIZONA

Kayenta

Navajo Indian Reservation

Round Rock

Highway 12
Utah's prettiest drive (p153)

Canyoneering
Clamber through the earth's
wrinkles at Dry Fork (p142)

Grand Canyon North Rim

Hopi Reservation

Oraibi Wash

Chinle

Zion & Bryce Canyon National Parks'
Top 15

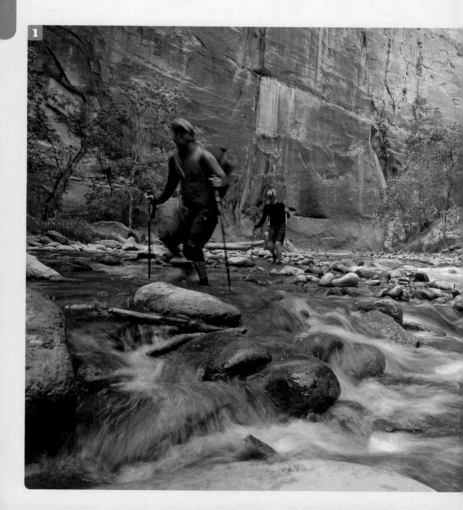

1

The Narrows

1 One of Utah's most famous back-country routes is this remarkably fun hike down the Virgin River (p58). It's deceptively easy at first, but once you hit the confluence with Deep Creek you'll be glad you brought that walking stick. By day two you'll be wading through chest-deep pools, the echoes of the rushing water growing louder and the dark canyon squeezing tighter until you reach Wall Street, where the sheer sandstone buttresses shoot up a neck-craning 1500ft. No permit? No worries: day hikers can get wet too.

Canyoneering

2 Canyoneering is that perfect combination of adventure, problem-solving, unsettling beauty and commitment. And indeed, it's that last element that gives the sport its particular thrill – for once you rappel into a serious canyon, there is generally only one way out. Luckily, the remarkable diversity of chasms in Utah means that you don't always need a rope or wetsuit to find yourself in some hidden corner of the earth. Get a taste at Escalante's Dry Fork (p142), which contains three nontechnical slots all within walking distance of one another. Below: Peek-a-Boo canyon (p143)

BEN COOPER / GETTY IMAGES ©

WESTEND61 PREMIUM / SHUTTERSTOCK ©

JORDAN SIEMENS / GETTY IMAGES ©

Mountain Biking Moab

3 Moab is one of the mountain-biking capitals of the world, where the desert slickrock surrounding the town makes a perfect 'sticky' surface for knobbly tires. Challenging trails ascend steep bluffs, twist through forests and slam over 4WD roads into the wilds of canyon country. And you'll surely redefine adventure after treading the roller-coaster rock face of the Whole Enchilada (p205). There's a reason why some Moab hotels have a shower for bikes. One trip and you'll be hooked.

Fairyland Loop

4 The sorbet-colored, sandcastle-like spires and hoodoos of Bryce Canyon pop like a Dr Seuss landscape. Though the smallest of Utah's national parks, this is perhaps the most immediately visually stunning, particularly at sunrise and sunset when an orange wash sets the otherworldly formations ablaze. Search for the perfect panoramic photo op from the Rim Trail, or let your imagination work overtime on the aptly named Fairyland Loop (p112), an all-day foray that gets up close and personal with wildly shaped hoodoos and ancient bristlecone pines.

Fiery Furnace

5 Eroded over millions of years, Arches' namesake formations elegantly defy gravity and struggle against the passage of time. A hike through the desert to Delicate Arch – the unofficial state symbol – is de rigueur for any first-time visitor, but if you want to walk on the wild side, sign up for a guided tour through the sandstone labyrinth known as the Fiery Furnace (p198). It's composed of giant fins and spectacularly narrow canyons – you'll be scrambling your way through one of the most improbable natural mazes on the planet.

5

Angels Landing

6 The climb to Angels Landing (p54) in Zion Canyon is among the most memorable day hikes in Utah, if not North America. The 5-mile trail hugs the face of a towering cliff, snakes through a cool canyon and climbs up Walter's Wiggles (a series of 21 sharp switchbacks) before finally ascending a narrow, exposed ridge – where steel chains and the encouragement of strangers are your only friends. Your reward after reaching the 5790ft summit? A lofty view of Zion Canyon, and some unreal photos of your vertigo-defying adventure.

GEIR OLAV LYNGFJELL / SHUTTERSTOCK ©

6

PHOTO BY MIRKO LIU / GETTY IMAGES ©

Stargazing

7 The American West is known for its star-studded nights, but few destinations can compete with Capitol Reef's views of the heaven-spanning Milky Way. If you want to watch for shooting stars from your sleeping bag or contemplate the possibility of life in distant galaxies, this is certainly the spot: Capitol Reef (p160) is one of the last preserves of natural darkness in the USA, with over 7500 stars visible to the naked eye. Evening stargazing programs are held here and in Bryce Canyon; the latter also hosts moonlit hikes.

Climbing

8 There's no sport quite like rock climbing. From a distance it appears to be a feat of strength, but balance, creativity, technical know-how and a Zen-like sangfroid are all parts of the game. Clinging by your fingertips 1000ft up on one of Zion's internationally renowned big walls? Not the place to lose your cool. Experts dream of tackling the cracks at Indian Creek or the desert towers of Castle Valley, while beginners can get in on the action via a guided climb, learning the basics outside Moab (p214) or Springdale. Top right: Indian Creek (p214)

Driving Highway 12

9 No American vacation is complete without a road trip, and there's no stretch of Utah asphalt more compelling than Hwy 12 (p153). Stretching from Capitol Reef in the northeast to Bryce and Red Rock Canyon in the west, this byway traverses 124 remote miles, passing desert slickrock, colossal domes, photogenic buttes and cool forests of aspen and fir. Take a 4WD detour along Burr Trail Rd, stop in Boulder for a bite at Hell's Backbone Grill, and remember to take it slow as you traverse razor-thin Hogback Ridge.

Canyonlands

10 If Arches is Red Rock 101, then Canyonlands (p176) is graduate school. Those looking for desert adventure, deep quiet or a long, challenging backpacking trip will find it in the park's vast, impenetrable acres of arid wilderness. Distant mesas and sidewinder-like canyons, carved out by the mighty Colorado and Green Rivers, are visible from overlooks on the Island in the Sky, while more remote districts – the Needles, Horseshoe Canyon and the Maze – beckon backcountry veterans, on foot, bike or raft.
Below top: Mesa Arch (p182)

Las Vegas

11 As you awake from your in-flight nap – rested, content, ready for red-rock inspiration – here comes Vegas (p98) on the horizon, like a showgirl looking for trouble. As you leave the airport and glide under the neon of her Strip, she puts on a dazzling show: dancing fountains, a spewing volcano, the Eiffel Tower. Her most dangerous charms lie in the gambling dens – seductive lairs where the fresh-pumped air and bright colors share one goal: separating you from your money. Step away if you can for fine restaurants and dazzling entertainment from Cirque du Soleil.

PLAN YOUR TRIP ZION & BRYCE CANYON NATIONAL PARKS' TOP 15

Rafting

12 Once the mercury starts to rise, nothing beats a fun day on the water to stay cool. And lucky for you, epic river trips (p211) abound outside Moab. If you're just looking for a lazy float, rent a canoe or kayak on the Green River. Ready to dial up the excitement a notch? The Colorado River's Westwater Canyon could be your go-to choice. The pick of the bunch, however, has to be a multiday trip through Canyonlands to legendary Cataract Canyon, the hardest stretch of white water in Utah. Above top: Green River (p213)

Horseback Riding

13 What, come out West and not ride a horse? Saddle up, pardner! Several outfitters can get you on horseback (p122) for rides in Red Canyon, a former hideout of Butch Cassidy, while another takes you into Bryce Canyon's hoodoo country. Grand Staircase-Escalante and Capitol Reef are other options with superb scenery. Nor will Moab outfitters and ranches disappoint; they can take you into the desert or mountains, and some trips combine horseback riding with river running – not at the same time, naturally. Above bottom: Bryce Canyon

Landscape Photography

14 Every park has its superlative viewpoints: Canyonlands alone could form its very own top 10 list, Goblin Valley's surreal formations enchant those in the know, while few places can match the majesty or contrasting colors of Zion. If you had to pick just one spot for photography, however, the Wave (p159) – a mesmerizing swirl of red and white layers, seeming to ripple across the slickrock with all the sensuousness of flowing water – might be the winner, encapsulating all that is visually sublime in canyon country. Above top: The Wave (p159)

Hanging Gardens

15 If the Utah sun has you feeling as shriveled as a raisin, you're going to find these lush desert oases all the more remarkable. Fed by mesa-top precipitation that has slowly percolated down through sandstone over the course of millennia, these vertical gardens appear where dripping seeps exit shaded canyon walls, forced outward by a layer of harder rock. Look for scarlet monkey flowers, mosses, golden columbines, maidenhair ferns and purple violets clinging marvelously to the rock face. Zion (p52) has some lovely examples.

Need to Know

For more information, see Survival Guide (p255)

Entrance Fees
Zion $30 per car; Bryce Canyon $30 per car; Arches $25 per car

Number of Visitors
(2014) Zion 3.2 million; Bryce Canyon 1.75 million; Arches 1 million

Year Founded
Zion 1909; Bryce Canyon 1923; Arches 1929

Money
ATMs in Springdale and Zion Lodge (Zion); Panguitch, Bryce Canyon City (Bryce Canyon); Torrey (Capitol Reef); Moab (Arches).

Cell Phones
Minimal to nonexistent cell-phone coverage throughout most parks.

Driving
Zion: Shuttle bus only in the main canyon; parking limited. Bryce: Shuttle bus (free); parking but limited for RVs. Arches: parking limited.

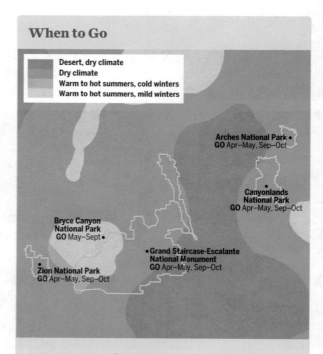

When to Go

Desert, dry climate
Dry climate
Warm to hot summers, cold winters
Warm to hot summers, mild winters

Arches National Park GO Apr–May, Sep–Oct

Canyonlands National Park GO Apr–May, Sep–Oct

Bryce Canyon National Park GO May–Sept

Grand Staircase-Escalante National Monument GO Apr–May, Sep–Oct

Zion National Park GO Apr–May, Sep–Oct

High Season
(May–Aug)

➡ Summer temperatures can soar above 100°F (38°C) and park traffic is at maximum capacity.

➡ July and August afternoon thunderstorms bring relief, but also create flash floods.

Shoulder
(Mar, Apr & Sep–Nov)

➡ Spring is pleasant but unpredictable. At higher elevations, snow can linger into May or June.

➡ Fall is ideal: September is still hot, but days are clear, rivers remain warm, and leaves begin to change.

Low Season
(Dec–Feb)

➡ Businesses have shorter hours or close altogether, but the peace and quiet make it a great time to visit.

➡ Winters are generally mild at low elevations; expect snow and road closures at higher elevations.

Useful Websites

National Park Service (www.nps.gov) Current information on national parks, trip planning.

Recreation.gov (www.recreation.gov) Camping reservations on federal lands.

Utah.com (www.utah.com) Utah's Office of Tourism; lots of free info.

Lonely Planet (www.lonelyplanet.com/usa/southwest/utah) Destination tips, bookings, Thorn Tree travelers' forum and more.

Utah State Parks (www.stateparks.utah.gov) Information on accommodation and activities in the state parks.

CUSA (www.canyoneeringusa.com) Excellent resource for Utah canyoneering routes.

Important Numbers

Emergency	☏ 911
Country code	☏ 1
International access code	☏ 011
Road conditions	☏ 511
Directory assistance	☏ 411

Exchange Rates

Australia	A$1	$0.76
Canada	C$1	$0.80
Euro zone	€1	$1.61
Japan	¥100	$0.80
Mexico	MXN10	$0.64
New Zealand	NZ$1	$0.71
UK	£1	$1.52

For current exchange rates see www.xe.com.

Daily Costs

Budget:
Less than $100

➡ Tent or RV camping: $15–$40

➡ Self-catering, cafe meals: $15–$25

➡ Gas and entrance fees: $15–$25

➡ Economy car rental: $30

Midrange:
$100–$250

➡ Mom-and-pop hotels, budget chains: $50–$150

➡ Diners, local restaurants: $25–$50

➡ Gas, entrance fees, activities: $15–$50

➡ Standard car rental: $45

Top End:
More than $250

➡ Upscale hotels, B&Bs: from $150

➡ Upscale restaurants: $50–$75

➡ Gas, entrance fees, activities: $15–$100

➡ SUV rental: $60

Opening Dates

All of Utah's national parks are open year-round, 24 hours a day. In winter, some roads will be impassable and some services reduced or closed. Most campsites are open year-round.

Park Policies & Regulations

Bicycles Generally permitted on park roads, but not on trails.

Campfires You may not gather wood in the park; campfires only permitted in designated sites; when fire danger is high, no campfires permitted anywhere.

Driving Unless otherwise posted, the maximum speed limit in parks is 35mph.

Pets Generally not permitted on trails, in the backcountry or in park buildings.

Trail Etiquette & Safety Stay on the trail and do not take shortcuts. Do not throw rocks. Take only pictures and leave only footprints.

Wildlife & Cultural Artifacts Feeding wildlife is prohibited, as is touching or defacing cultural artifacts and sites.

Getting There & Around

Most travelers to Utah arrive by air or car. Major airports include Las Vegas and Salt Lake City; Denver and Phoenix are manageable but further away.

Car & RV Traveling with your own vehicle is the easiest and most rewarding way to explore the national parks. Car and RV rental is best in large cities such as Las Vegas or Salt Lake.

Bus Signing on to a bus tour such as Adventure Bus or Green Tortoise is the next best option to your own wheels. Greyhound serves several towns and cities in the state, but there is no public transportation to any national park in Utah.

Train Amtrak operates two major routes through the area (Chicago–San Francisco/Los Angeles). Use them to reach the region, but not for touring.

Shuttle A handful of private shuttles connect parks with large towns, such as St George–Zion. Zion and Bryce Canyon both operate a free shuttle route within park boundaries.

For much more on **getting around**, see p268

If You Like...

Hiking

A wonderland of soaring sandstone cliffs, surreal hoodoos and 120 million years of geological history on display – Utah is a paradise for hikers of all levels.

Angels Landing Zion's iconic ascent – with precipitous drop-offs and chains to cling to – was cut into the cliffs in 1926. (p54)

Fiery Furnace Take a guided tour of the third level of hell in this devilish maze of rock and stone. (p198)

The Narrows An incredible in-the-river experience, hiking and wading 16 miles down Zion's most impressive canyon. (p58)

Navajo Loop Trail Descend through a pastel canyon of towering hoodoos for a short but challenging and otherworldly hike. (p114)

Chesler Park Head into the Utah wilderness for a long tramp past desert wonderment. (p186)

West Rim Two-day backpacking trip from the high plateaus down to the canyon floor, with plenty of solitude and big views. (p55)

Hickman Bridge Cruise up from Capitol Reef's Fremont River to this gorgeous natural bridge. (p164)

Canyoneering & Climbing

Squeezing your way through the twists and turns of a dark slot canyon or ascending a sheer, multipitch spire above the desert floor are just some of the adrenaline-fueled ways to gain a new perspective on the planet.

The Subway High on Zion's must-do list: swim and rappel your way to one of the park's most impressive geological formations. (p63)

Keyhole An excellent beginner's canyon, with thrills, watery chills and the occasional spill packed into a short highlight-reel route. (p71)

Dry Fork Slot Canyons Explore these sandstone slot canyons for an exquisitely sculpted landscape. (p142)

Cohab Canyon Ascend Capitol Reef's Waterpocket Fold for secret slot canyons and amazing views. (p165)

Castle Valley Challenge your way up Castleton or one of the other iconic towers. (p214)

Indian Creek The best crack climbing on earth tests you with vertical lines in a sea of sandstone. (p214)

The Maze Go beyond the tourist track in Canyonlands' forsaken district. (p191)

Scenic Drives

As amazing as Utah's national parks are, sometimes it's the drive between them you remember most.

Highway 12 Utah's most stunning stretch of highway winds through canyons, desert slickrock and alpine forest. (p153)

White Rim Road Take on one of America's most iconic 4WD adventures. (p189)

Arches Scenic Drive Cruise for views of balanced rocks, delicate arches and the La Sal Mountains. (p202)

Highway 14 The back road from Bryce to Zion climbs up to 10,000ft, passing Cedar Breaks National Monument along the way. (p97)

Colorado River Scenic Byway Follow the serpentine route of the Colorado River, stopping for canyon hikes near the Fisher Towers. (p210)

Mountain Biking

The scenic slickrock playground outside Moab turned Utah into a mountain-biking mecca decades ago.

Slickrock De rigueur intro to riding near Moab, this ride takes you on a roller coaster of descents, curves and cliffside lung-busting climbs. (p205)

The Whole Enchilada An all-in-one descent that takes you to some of Moab's most distinctive riding features. (p205)

White Rim Road Go multiday on one of the continent's best mountain-bike tours. (p189)

JEM Trail Fast and furious single-track in the desert; beginner friendly. (p83)

Gooseberry Mesa Technical slickrock fun with views back toward Zion. (p83)

Cycling

If you prefer a smooth, fast ride or just want to have some two-wheeled fun on a cruiser, try out these classics.

Zion Canyon Shuttle your bike up to the Temple of Sinawava and coast back to the visitor center amid spectacular scenery. (p68)

Red Canyon to Bryce Canyon Link two gorgeous parks with fiery hues of sculpted sandstone on this dedicated bike path. (p132)

Capitol Reef Head along the scenic drive for cool river views and plenty of sunshine. (p168)

Snow Canyon State Park Cycle from St George through red-rock scenery out to this gem of a park. (p93)

Dramatic Views

Southern Utah is an unfurling tableau of sweeping panoramas that will defy your camera's wide-angled lens.

Observation Point Intensely rewarding hike to the top of Zion Canyon's cliffs, looking out over Angels Landing. (p56)

Grand View Point (p188) Take in the immensity of the Colorado Plateau at this Canyonlands overlook.

Top: Walter's Wiggles (p54), Angels Landing
Bottom: Prairie dogs (p127)

PLAN YOUR TRIP IF YOU LIKE...

Landscape Arch Hike far into the backcountry for mind-blowing photo ops at this sandstone arch. (p198)

Dead Horse Point State Park Best views of the Colorado River, like, ever. (p190)

Bryce Canyon Rim Trail There's no need to climb as the flat rim trail provides soaring views of hoodoos and bristlecone forests. (p115)

Timber Creek Overlook Take in 270-degree views of finger canyons, scrubby plateaus, knobby buttes and Arizona on the distant horizon. (p67)

Cedar Breaks National Monument Wildly eroded natural amphitheater where sculpted cliffs and hoodoos glow like neon tie-dye. (p97)

Native American Cultural Sites

Observe the traces of the Native Americans who have lived here throughout the centuries, from the Ancestral Puebloans and Fremont people to the Ute, Navajo, Pueblo and Southern Paiute.

Parowan Gap Unusual petroglyphs date back as far as the Fremont people and are some of the oldest etchings in the region. (p97)

Newspaper Rock Take a read through history at this ancient media hub. (p191)

Horseshoe Canyon Enjoy the evocative and expressionistic petroglyphs at Utah's top spot. (p192)

Anasazi State Park Museum Offers up fascinating artifacts from the Coombs site, dating back to 1130. (p154)

Water Adventures

The desert may be arid, but water plays a critical role in shaping the landscape here. Ride the rapids or float along in an inner tube while contemplating its importance.

Green River Look to the sky as you paddle flatwater stretches of the Green River. (p213)

Cataract Canyon Take on one of America's hallmark stretches of white water as your rip down a canyon through Class IV and V rapids. (p213)

Lower Calf Creek Falls Swim in the emerald pool beneath this ribbon-like cascade. (p141)

Willis Creek A great family-friendly slot hike that follows a flowing creek – wear water shoes or sandals. (p143)

Virgin River Grab an inner tube to beat the summer heat with a float downstream in Springdale. (p83)

Pool Parties Vegas pool clubs are another example of Sin City–style decadence. (p106)

Film Locations

From glowing red buttes to scrubby desert plains to the lights of Vegas, the landscape glows with undeniable cinematic appeal.

Kanab This area as been popular with Hollywood since the 1920s. Everybody from John Wayne and Clint Eastwood to Charlton Heston (Planet of the Apes!) and several Lone Rangers have appeared against this classic Western backdrop. (p156)

Las Vegas Bad boys and their hijinks keep Sin City on the big screen in cult hits like The Hangover and Ocean's Eleven. (p98)

Grafton This 19th-century ghost town was the location of the bicycle scene in Butch Cassidy and the Sundance Kid. (p83)

Moab & Around Directors of Thelma & Louise and 127 Hours shot their most dramatic scenes in nearby Canyonlands and Dead Horse Point parks. (p190)

Moab Museum of Film & Western Heritage Discover the storylines that have made this area a cinematographer's dream. (p205)

Wildlife

With the exception of scurrying lizards, wildlife in the desert tends to be fairly secretive, particularly during the blazing midday heat of summer. That said, if you look closely enough, you can find some unique creatures.

California Condors Biologists recently confirmed a condor couple – the nation's largest bird – was raising a chick in a Zion nest, the first-ever documented occurrence in Utah. (p73)

Desert Tortoises A desert tortoise can live for up to 80 years and go for a year without drinking. They live in the Mojave Desert, which intersects with the Colorado Plateau at Zion. (p79)

Bighorn Sheep Depicted in rock art throughout the centuries, herds of bighorn sheep still inhabit the rocky terrain of Canyonlands and Capitol Reef. (p248)

Gila Monsters & Roadrunners Some unusual inhabitants rule the roost in sandy Snow Canyon State Park. (p93)

Prairie Dogs This threatened species, essential for a healthy ecosystem, is making a comeback in Bryce. (p127)

Month by Month

TOP EVENTS
....

Sundance Film Festival, January

Utah Shakespeare Festival, June–October

Western Legends Roundup, August

Moab Music Festival, September

Moab Folk Festival, November

January

January is particularly slow and much of the tourism infrastructure surrounding the parks shuts down, but for nature lovers the peace and quiet can make for a fabulous visit.

☆ Sundance Film Festival

It may not be in southern Utah, but this is nonetheless the state's most famous event (www.sundance.org/festivals). Aspiring filmmakers, actors and half of Hollywood gather for a week of cutting-edge film in Park City.

🏃 Winter Bird Festival

Birders gather in St George for three days of walks, lectures and kids' activities.

February

Lovers of snow and winter sports should check out high-altitude destinations such as Bryce Canyon, Cedar Breaks and the Brian Head ski resort.

🏃 Bryce Canyon Winterfest

Cross-country ski tours, ski archery, snowshoe races and lots of other snow-based activities and clinics. Held over Presidents' Day weekend in mid-February.

March

March is spring-break season in the US. Hordes of college students and families with young kids are out exploring the Southwest's national parks. This can be a surprisingly busy time; reserve accommodations and figure on unpredictable weather.

🏃 Skinny Tire Festival

Four days of great cycling trips outside Moab in early March. Ride through Arches, along the Colorado River and to Dead Horse Point and back.

🏃 Jeep Safari

The week before Easter, about 2000 Jeeps and thousands more people overrun Moab in the year's biggest event (www.rr4w.com). Register early; trails are assigned.

April

The weather starts to warm up, but is still hard to gauge with wind, rain and snow alternating with wonderfully pleasant sunny days hitting temperatures in the 70s and 80s (20s Celcius). Budding cottonwoods and blooming flowers brighten the landscape.

◉ Wildflower Viewing

Depending on rainfall and elevation, spring (April and May) is wildflower season in the desert. Check www.desertusa.com for wildflower bloom reports at your favorite national and state parks.

June

School's out for the summer! High season for road-tripping families is beginning and the blistering desert heat index is gradually inching up toward seasonal highs.

☆ Utah Shakespeare Festival

The play's the thing in Cedar City, where visitors can enjoy a dramatic Shakesperience (www.bard.org), with Tony Award–winning performances, literary seminars and educational backstage tours from late June to October.

✶ Bryce Canyon Astronomy Festival

Some 7500 stars are visible to the naked eye at Bryce, and even more are on display during this festival when the Salt Lake Astronomical Society breaks out some huge telescopes.

☆ Groove Fest

Cedar City's long weekend music fest (www.groove festutah.com) in late June jams with folksy and funky sounds.

July

Summer is in full swing with annual Fourth of July barbecues across the country. Despite 100+°F (38+°C) temperatures, this is one of the busiest months for most Utah parks. Beat the heat by scheduling activities for the early morning or late afternoon, or head to higher elevations.

✶ Independence Day

Cities and towns across the region celebrate America's birth with rodeos, parades,

music and fireworks on July 4.

🏃 Bryce Canyon Half Marathon

A wildly popular distance run through the park, starting at Ruby's Inn and ending in Cannonville (https://bchm.jit.su).

☆ Neil Simon Festival

American plays staged mid-July to mid-August (www.simonfest.org) in Utah's festival town, Cedar City.

🏃 Moonshadows in Moab

Bike out to Dead Horse State Park for sunset and then return to Moab by moonlight (www.moon shadowsinmoab.com).

🏃 GeoFest

Join park rangers in Bryce Canyon for a weekend of guided hikes, family-friendly geology programs, bus tours with a geologist, evening programs and other activities.

August

Hotels and campgrounds are booked up and it's still off-the-thermometer hot, although afternoon thunderstorms bring some relief – as well as flash floods.

✶ Western Legends Roundup

Kanab lives for the annual Western Legends Roundup (www.western legendsroundup.com) in late August. There are

concerts, gunfights, cowboy poetry, dances, quilt shows, a film festival and more. Take a bus tour to all the film sites, or sign up for a Dutch-oven cooking lesson.

✶ Garfield County Fair

This 75-year tradition in Panguitch hosts live bands and features parades, classic car shows, barbecues, livestock sales and rodeos for an entire week.

September

It's back to school for the kids, which means crowds begin to lessen. Fall is a particularly nice time to visit – weather is slightly cooler though the water is still warm, making it a good time to explore river canyons.

✶ Dixie Roundup

St George's mid-September weekend full of Western fun, including a parade and rodeo.

☆ Moab Music Festival

Each September, world-class classical, traditional and jazz musicians converge on the red-rock landscape around Moab for spectacular open-air concerts (www.moabmusic fest.org).

☆ Zion Canyon Music Festival

One weekend in late September is filled with an eclectic lineup of bands, with everything from flat-pickers to alternative rock (http://zioncanyonmusic festival.com).

October

Lingering warm weather and less traffic makes this a particularly nice month to visit. Look for golden aspens at higher elevations.

🏃 St George Marathon

This highly acclaimed marathon takes over the town of St George (www.stgeorgemarathon.com), attracting 7400 runners from all 50 states and some 20,000 spectators. The route is regularly rated one of the country's most scenic.

November

The low season is beginning and some hotels and restaurants have shuttered up for the winter. The long Thanksgiving weekend sees a final burst of visitors to the region's parks.

☆ Moab Folk Festival

Folk music and environmental consciousness combine. This November festival is 100% wind-powered, venues are easily walkable and recycling is encouraged (www.moabfolkfestival.com). Big-name singer-songwriters take top billing.

Top: Stars on display during the Bryce Canyon Astronomy Festival
Bottom: Sundance Film Festival (p21)

Itineraries

 The Grand Circle

See the best of Utah's parks, with possible detours to the Grand Canyon and Monument Valley.

Start off your trip with a bang in **Las Vegas**, but move on to **Zion National Park** by the second night so you can get an early start the next morning. See the highlights that day; the next morning hike Angels Landing and spend an afternoon in East Zion. Base yourself for the next two nights in **Kanab**, and detour for panoramic overlooks at the **Grand Canyon's North Rim**. Travel north to say hello to hoodoos in **Bryce Canyon National Park** and **Red Canyon**. Begin your drive down scenic Hwy 12, basing yourself in **Escalante** or **Boulder**, and squeeze through the slot canyons of **Grand Staircase-Escalante National Monument**. Continue down Hwy 12 to crack the geologists' code and go fruit-picking in the orchards of **Capitol Reef National Park**. Drive to **Moab** and spend three days in **Arches**, **Canyonlands** and on the mountain-bike trails around town. It's a 6½-hour drive back to Vegas on the interstate or, if you want to take the scenic route, nine hours via cinematic **Monument Valley** in Arizona.

A Week in Moab

Make the most of a week in the Moab area, visiting Arches and Canyonlands, interspersed with all the adventure sports for which the region is known. If you only have a long weekend, stick to Arches, Island in the Sky and a final day either mountain biking, climbing, canyoneering or rafting.

On your first day visit **Arches National Park**, following our one-day itinerary (p28). On your second day, load up with plenty of water and drive south to Canyonlands' **Island in the Sky**, a 6000ft flat-topped mesa. Follow the Grand View Point Scenic Drive, picnic at the White Rim Overlook and try out some of the day hikes in the area. On the way back to Moab, stop at **Dead Horse Point State Park** (time it for sunset), taking in the spectacular views of the horseshoe bend of the Colorado River some 2000ft below. Day three is devoted to the **Needles** area of Canyonlands, named for the giant spires that rise from the desert. Hikes are longer here, and experienced backpackers will want to consider an overnight trip on the Chesler Park Loop (also doable in a long day). Devote day four to quintessential **Moab**: mountain biking. Good trails include Dead Horse Point for novices, Klondike Bluffs for intermediate riders and the famed Slickrock Trail for the hardcore who have already broken a bone or two.

Scale back the adventure on day five and take a leisurely drive up into the aspens and firs of the high country on the **La Sal Mountain Loop Road**; picnic at Warner Lake. Alternatively, explore another of Moab's scenic byways, such as Potash Rd, where you'll find petroglyphs, dinosaur tracks and climbers. Day six, get up early to take a full-day river trip; reserve well in advance to avoid disappointment. White-water lovers will gravitate toward **Westwater Canyon** (Class III and IV). If you don't like navigating rapids, take a leisurely canoe, kayak or float along flatwater stretches. Also consider an overnight trip – this will give you a chance to experience Canyonlands' epic Cataract Canyon (Class V) on a high-speed raft. On your last day, make it special and sign up for a canyoneering or rock-climbing trip out in the desert, or take a horseback ride in the La Sal Mountains.

ED FREEMAN / GETTY IMAGES ©

Top: Virgin River and the Watchman (p52), Zion Canyon

Bottom: The Navajo Loop Trail (p114) through Bryce Canyon

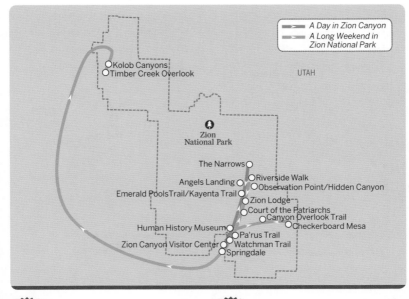

Legend:
- A Day in Zion Canyon
- A Long Weekend in Zion National Park

Map labels: Kolob Canyons; Timber Creek Overlook; UTAH; Zion National Park; The Narrows; Riverside Walk; Angels Landing; Observation Point/Hidden Canyon; Emerald Pools Trail/Kayenta Trail; Zion Lodge; Court of the Patriarchs; Canyon Overlook Trail; Checkerboard Mesa; Human History Museum; Pa'rus Trail; Zion Canyon Visitor Center; Watchman Trail; Springdale

1 DAY A Day in Zion Canyon

One day in Zion? It's not much, but a ride on the shuttle and a willingness to get your feet wet will give you a feel for this unique landscape.

Start early at the park's **visitor center** to get oriented and browse the introductory signage outside. Hop on the free shuttle, stopping off at Zion's **Human History Museum**. Ride the shuttle all the way up-canyon to the Temple of Sinawava. Follow the **Riverside Walk** and, if you're ready to get wet, plunge into the Virgin River and continue up the **Narrows** until your stomach begins to grumble. Picnic on the riverbank or catch the shuttle heading back down-canyon and have lunch beneath the giant cottonwood tree outside **Zion Lodge**. Hike the **Emerald Pools Trail** in combination with the quieter **Kayenta Trail**. Hop back on the shuttle, stopping at the **Court of the Patriarchs**. Hop off at Canyon Junction and follow the **Pa'rus Trail**, ideally around sunset. Alternatively, climb the peaceful hilltop **Watchman Trail**, which starts near the visitor center. Head back to **Springdale** for a hearty dinner and a peek at a gallery or two.

3 DAYS A Long Weekend in Zion National Park

A long weekend is more like it: you'll be able to hit all the highlights as well as get off the beaten track.

On your first day, follow our one-day itinerary and explore **Zion Canyon**. Day two, get an early start on the hike up to **Angels Landing**, which will probably take most of the morning. Alternatively, try less-crowded hikes like **Observation Point** or **Hidden Canyon**, both starting from Weeping Rock. After a picnic with high-altitude views, return to your car and drive Hwy 9 through the Zion–Mt Carmel Tunnel to East Zion and **Checkerboard Mesa**. There's no end to the exploring here: go off-trail and wander the slickrock, or hike the short but fun **Canyon Overlook Trail**. Return to **Springdale** for dinner.

On day three, sign up for a canyoneering trip with a local outfitter, or head to the more remote **Kolob Canyons** up I-15. Explore the magnificent finger canyons, hiking up the Taylor Creek Middle Fork to an old cabin or two. Have lunch on the trail before continuing on to the magnificent **Timber Creek Overlook** at the end of the road.

PLAN YOUR TRIP ITINERARIES

1 DAY A Day in Bryce Canyon

Let your imagination run wild as you visit the planet's epicenter of hoodoos – unusual 'fairy chimneys' shaped by erosion. With a day to spare, tack on the Fairyland Loop hike or a visit to Mossy Cave.

See the free film and pick up information at the **visitor center**. Drive Bryce Canyon Scenic Drive all the way out to **Rainbow Point**. Hike the short **Bristlecone Loop Trail**, with its awesome vistas and ancient trees. Return along the Scenic Drive, stopping at the major sights along the way. Grab lunch at **Bryce Canyon Lodge** or snacks at the general store. Head to **Sunset Point** to glimpse the towering eroded hoodoos of Bryce Amphitheater. Descend into the canyon on the **Navajo Loop** and/or **Queen's Garden Trail**. Head down to **Inspiration Point** and **Bryce Point** by car or shuttle. Stroll along the **Rim Trail** and watch the light play on the hoodoos. Alternatively, drive to **Paria View** to watch the sunset. To really escape the crowds, detour out to serene, largely untrammeled **Fairyland Point**.

1 DAY A Day in Arches National Park

Small in size but packed with over 2000 natural arches, this is a great park to explore, with plenty of opportunities to wander beyond the main sights for once-in-a-lifetime views of an enthralling geological process.

Get up early to beat the heat and stop at the **visitor center**. Take the park's **Scenic Drive**, which passes all the major sights. Walk among sandstone monoliths on the **Park Avenue Trail**, best in the morning. Don't miss the viewpoint turnout where you can spy on the **Three Gossips**. Gawk at **Balanced Rock**, then stroll beneath natural arches off **Windows Road**. Pause for 360-degree views and a geology lesson at **Panorama Point**. Visit famous **Delicate Arch** at road's end; have a tailgate picnic afterward. With advance reservations, you can take a ranger-guided hike in the **Fiery Furnace**. With more energy to burn, hike to more arches from the **Devils Garden**. For solitude and sunsets, take Salt Valley Rd out to the **Klondike Bluffs**. Spend the evening eating, drinking, shopping and wandering around downtown **Moab**.

Orderville Canyon (p58), Zion National Park

Activities

This is why you've come to Utah. Labyrinthine canyons, red-rock spires, moonlit desert arches and slickrock playgrounds. It doesn't matter if you're a couch potato or hardcore thrill-seeker equipped with a GoPro. Grab a bike, rope or paddle and get out there and have fun.

Desert Etiquette

The desert is an exceedingly fragile environment, easily damaged by feet, tires and fires, and slow to heal.

Stay on the trail, whether hiking, cycling or driving. If it's muddy, either be willing to get dirty or don't go – it's better than creating wider, braided trails.

If there is no trail, stay on slickrock, gravel or sand; never step or ride on plants or cryptobiotic soil.

Pack it in, pack it out: bring resealable plastic bags to contain trash and toilet paper.

Protect all water sources and riparian areas: camp 200ft from any water, never wash yourself or dishes in creeks or springs and use minimal or no soap.

Backcountry fires are usually prohibited.

Never touch, move or take any cultural or archaeological artifacts.

Hiking & Backpacking

Hiking is the main and most accessible activity in the national parks and can be done at any time of year. Walks can be as short or long as you like, but remember this when planning: you need to be prepared. The wild desert may be unlike anything you have ever experienced, and designating certain parcels as 'national parks' has not tamed it.

The weather is extraordinary in its unpredictability and sheer force. The summer sun is blazing hot, sudden thunderstorms can drop enough water in 10 minutes to create deadly flash floods, while ferocious windstorms can rip or blow away your poorly staked tent...all the way back at camp.

Number one on your packing checklist is water: a gallon (3.8L) of water per person per day is the recommended minimum in hot weather. Sun protection (hat, sunblock and sunglasses) is also vital. While the danger of dehydration and heat exhaustion is obvious enough, don't forget that violent downpours and strong winds can cause temperatures to quickly plummet. Always consider a waterproof shell and even a warm layer outside of summer.

After the elements, getting lost is the next major concern. Most day hikes are well signed and visitors are numerous, but nevertheless you should always take some sort of map. If you plan on going into the backcountry, definitely take a topographic (topo) map and a compass. You can pick up detailed maps in most visitor centers. All travelers, solo or not, should always remember the golden rule: let someone know where you are going and how long you plan to be gone.

When to Hike

Though southern Utah is a year-round destination, variations by location and season are extreme. As the majority of parks, monuments and other hiking destinations are in the desert, spring and fall are often the best times to hike. Summer – the height of tourist season – can be the worst, as temperatures routinely top 100°F (38°C). One smart summertime strategy is to hike the big canyons only very early or late in the day, planning your hike for the side that will be in shade.

Elevation also plays a factor. At over 8000ft, Bryce Canyon's rim stays a bit cooler, as do other spots in the mountains. However, in the fall certain roads and trails at higher elevations may be closed until April, May or even into June, and some canyon hikes are not safe in spring, when runoff from snowmelt can dangerously raise water levels. If you're planning on hiking the Narrows in Zion Canyon in April or May, for example, you'll need to check the river flow online to ensure that levels are low enough.

Day Hikes

The majority of hikes in the region are day hikes, taking anywhere from 20 minutes to eight hours. On steep trails that lead from canyon floors to rims, or vice versa, a general guide is that it takes twice as long to ascend as to descend. For people who want to test themselves, or who don't have time for a full hike, it's always possible to tackle just the first few miles of a day or backcountry hike.

Backcountry Hikes

People can and do spend weeks hiking in the southern Utah desert, but it's something to build up to, once you get to know the place better. Backcountry hikes in the area lean toward the easier ones, usually involving one to three nights out. When you're ready for more, park rangers and local outfitters can help you find new challenges. In general, Zion, Bryce Canyon and Capitol Reef offer a good selection of easy to moderate backpacking trips, while Canyonlands and Grand Staircase-Escalante are famous for their difficulty.

The most important consideration on any backcountry hike is water. Will there be any on your route, and of what quality and quantity? Many blue squiggles marked on topo maps are not rivers at all, but washes, only flowing during a rainstorm or with spring runoff. Always check with rangers or knowledgeable locals before trekking into the unknown.

See p256 for more information on what to pack.

Canyoneering near Moab (p214)

Canyoneering

Canyons can be secret, mystical destinations, with an eerie, unsettling beauty that sometimes gives the feeling that you're wandering the sacred ruins of an ancient civilization – although the smooth, scalloped walls and strange, sculpted dimples and pockmarks aren't the creations of any human culture, but the echoes of a much older visitor: water.

The thrill of squeezing yourself into a dark narrow slot, rappelling over the lip of a 70ft chute or swimming across a cold subterranean pool is obvious enough. The real question isn't whether or not you want to go, but rather what sort of experience you are looking for. For many people, a nontechnical hike is a perfect intro, and if you're short on time or don't have the gear, a guided canyoneering trip or intro course may be the solution. For others, nothing short of full-on immersion will do.

For the latter group, a solid understanding of technical skills – how to tie knots, set up an anchor, use a rappelling device, unsnag a stuck rope and so on – is required but, unlike rock climbing, you don't need years of practice (though the recent flood of inexperienced canyoneers has been largely responsible for an increase in the number of rescues at Zion and elsewhere). Rappelling is a particularly easy way to put yourself into situations you may not be able to get out of, especially if you get hurt. Talk to any local guide, and they'll immediately tell you the number one rule of canyoneering: no jumping (this is in stark contrast to European canyoning). Jumping is among the leading causes of injury in the Utah wilderness.

Canyoneers must also be especially mindful of flash floods and high water levels (wetsuits are required for some routes, regardless of the season). Being inside the cogs and wheels of earth's geological machinery is very cool – until they switch on. Always check the day's flash-flood forecast before you go out.

Canyoneering in Zion

Zion and its environs are the sport's epicenter in southern Utah – there are over 30 routes in the area. Before attempting

Hiking through the Virgin River in the Narrows (p57), Zion National Park

any of the park's canyoneering routes unaided, take a basic skills course. If you need to rent equipment, such a course is obligatory for liability reasons. The most famous routes for beginners are the **Subway** and **Keyhole Canyon**. **Orderville Canyon** is another classic, which dumps you out in the Narrows. Canyoneers with more experience and the necessary technical skills can tackle **Mystery Canyon**, which also drops dramatically into the Virgin River. If you don't want to bother with the gear, explore **Hidden Canyon** instead.

Southern Utah's Other Canyons

You'll find more fantastic slot canyons along the Escalante River and Hole-in-the-Rock Rd in Grand Staircase-Escalante National Monument. Routes include canyons for all skill levels, with or without gear, but getting lost is fairly easy, so consider going with a guide. The Paria Canyon-Vermilion Cliffs Wilderness Area is another awesome place for experienced canyoneers to explore, whether you're looking for the pre-

mier 16-mile **Buckskin Gulch** challenge or an epic five-day canyoneering adventure through Paria Canyon to Lee's Ferry, Arizona (permit required). Ask outfitters in Moab about more slot canyons in eastern Utah, including the wonderland of the **San Rafael Swell**, northwest of Moab off I-70, just west of the town of Green River.

Canyoneering Guides & Outfitters

In addition to recommended outfitters, the American Canyoneering Association (ACA; www.canyoneering.net) offers lots of information online, from technical forums and canyoneering primers to guide referrals. ACA also runs a multitude of certification courses across southern Utah.

For detailed route descriptions, browse CUSA (www.canyoneeringusa.com).

Canyoneering 1, 2 and *3* by Steve Allen are three top-notch guidebooks that cover southern Utah, particularly Grand Staircase-Escalante National Monument and the San Rafael Swell. *Zion: Canyoneering*, by Tom Jones, is an excellent guide to the Zion area.

Cycling in Zion National Park (p71)

Mountain Biking & Cycling

The fat-tire crowd already knows about Moab, a mountain-biking mecca for decades. The original **Slickrock Bike Trail** is there, among many others. If you're a novice rider, try the **Bar-M Loop**. For slickrock virgins who have mountain-biking experience, the **Klondike Bluffs Trail** awaits. When the summer sun is baking the desert lowlands, riders can escape to the cool forests of the La Sal Mountains outside town, where the **Moonlight Meadow Trail** is a high-altitude downhill challenge, or the flat single track of the **Intrepid Trail** at Dead Horse Point State Park.

What mountain bikers might not know is that southwest Utah offers equally good trails in places outside St George and Zion, including at Gooseberry Mesa and Hurricane Cliffs (**JEM Trail**), and on national forest land in Red Canyon, west of Bryce Canyon. Even though mountain biking is prohibited on national park trails, it's permitted on dirt roads. In Canyonlands, Island in the Sky's **White Rim Road** and the labyrinth of 4WD roads in the Maze are awesome experiences, as is **Cathedral Valley Loop** in Capitol Reef and backcountry roads in Grand Staircase-Escalante. All mountain bikers should observe desert conservation guidelines, particularly rules about staying on-trail.

Road cycling the paved scenic drives in Zion, Bryce Canyon and Capitol Reef is an excellent way to take in the parks' sights. The steeper, longer and more challenging paved roads in Arches and Canyonlands are best left for experienced cyclists in good shape. Recreational cycling paths are uncommon in southern Utah, with the notable exception of the St George area. The **Snow Canyon Loop** is the longest of the area trails (18 miles) connecting the town with the state park. Shorter paths are

EXTREME SPORTS

Need a thrill? Try these:

➡ Climb **Prodigal Sun**, **Space Shot** or one of Zion's other big walls (p72).

➡ Through-hike the **Subway** (p63) in Zion.

➡ Raft **Cataract Canyon** (p213) on the Colorado River.

➡ Four-wheel drive **Elephant Hill** (p190) in Canyonlands' Needles district.

➡ Mountain bike Moab's famous **Whole Enchilada Trail** (p205).

➡ Backpack the **Narrows** (p58) of the Virgin River.

➡ Canyoneer and backpack **Buckskin Gulch** (p159) in Paria Canyon.

➡ Skydive out of an airplane in **Moab** (p215).

Top: Rappelling at Cassidy Arch (p166), Capitol Reef National Park

Bottom: Mesa Arch (p182), Canyonlands National Park

CULTURA EXCLUSIVE / BEN PIPE PHOTOGRAPHY / GETTY IMAGES ©

Zion's **Pa'rus Trail** and the **Red Canyon Bike Path**, on US Forest Service land outside Bryce Canyon.

You'll find outdoor outfitters and bicycle shops offering rentals and guided trips outside all of the national parks. If you want to rent a mountain bike, expect to pay $35 to $40 for a full day, plus $12 for a car rack.

Rock Climbing

If Dr Seuss designed a rock-climbing playground, it would look a lot like this: a surreal landscape filled with enormous blobs, spires, soaring cliffs and canyon walls in kaleidoscopic colors. Some of the country's best rock climbing lies in southern Utah, though many routes are for moderate to

TIPS FOR SHUTTERBUGS

Nothing is more disappointing than coming home from the desert and uploading your digital photos or getting your rolls of film developed to find dozens, if not hundreds, of washed-out horizons, with tiny friends and family squint-smiling in the distance.

You're not alone. Even the best photographers can't get the whole desert in their pictures. But you can improve the quality and composition of your photos, whether your camera is a top-shelf digital masterpiece or a disposable throwaway.

➡ If you have a digital camera, bring extra batteries and a charger; the instant gratification of your LCD preview screen will run the battery down fast.

➡ For print film, use 100 ASA film for all but the lowest light situations; it's the slowest film and will enhance resolution. Color slide film is the best, though it's more expensive.

➡ A zoom lens is extremely useful; most SLR cameras have one. Use it to isolate the central subject of your photos. A common composition mistake is to include too much landscape around the person or feature that's your main focus. Sacrifice background for foreground, and your photos will be more dramatic and interesting.

➡ Morning and evening are the best times to shoot. The same sandstone bluff can turn four or five different hues throughout the day, and the warmest hues will be at sunset. Because of the way a camera reads color (as grays), underexposing the shot slightly (by a half-stop or more) can bring out richer details in red tones.

➡ When shooting red rocks, a warming filter added to an SLR lens can enhance the colors of the rocks and reduce the blues of overcast or flat-light days. You can achieve the same effect on any digital camera by adjusting the white balance to the automatic 'cloudy' setting (or by reducing the color temperature).

➡ As a rule, don't shoot into the sun or include it in the frame; shoot what the sunlight is hitting. This is especially important when photographing people, who will turn into blackened silhouettes with the sun behind them. On bright days, move your subjects into shade for close-up portraits.

➡ A tripod is useful for low-exposure dusk shots but is cumbersome on hikes.

➡ Some digital cameras have waterproof cases that are worth the investment for canyoneers and river runners.

➡ That endless horizon? Move people out of the way and shoot it at sunset's last gasp. Check the weather report for sunset times, as well as when the moon rises. If you're traveling during a full moon, it can be fairly easy to arrange yourself in front of an iconic arch at dusk for that million-dollar shot.

For an in-depth regional photography guide, *Photographing the Southwest, Volume 1: Southern Utah* by Laurent Martres will take you around the national parks and off the beaten path.

Falls at Pine Creek Canyon (p71), Zion National Park

expert climbers. Zion is famous for big-wall climbs, while the St George area, particularly Snow Canyon State Park, offers dozens of shorter bolted sport routes. You'll find great climbing in Arches, Canyonlands and Capitol Reef, although restrictions apply. Several popular routes for all abilities await near Moab: Indian Creek is known for its premier sandstone cracks, while Castleton and other desert towers offer superb multipitch adventure. Outdoor outfitters in Moab and Springdale offer rock-climbing classes for beginners and sell climbing gear.

Climbing in summer can get exceptionally hot. When the air temperature reaches 100°F (38°C), the cliff face could top 115°F (46°C), and the rocks hold the heat all night. Spring, fall and even winter are better times to climb; if you do climb in summer, start early in the morning. Some parks enforce seasonal route closures to protect nesting or breeding wildlife. All parks prohibit power drills, discourage excess bolting and ask climbers to use subdued colors for hangers and slings. Ask at park visitor centers about the latest regulations and permits, which are usu-ally required for overnight bivouacs. Even if you don't need a permit, stop by Zion's backcountry desk, where the rangers and volunteers are often climbers themselves, full of great local tips and advice.

Horseback Riding & Pack Trips

Canyon Trail Rides runs horseback and mule rides at Zion (p72), Bryce Canyon (p122) and the Grand Canyon's North Rim. One- and two-hour rides and half-day trips cost from $40 to $80 per person. Some rides are offered year-round, although the famous Grand Canyon trips are only available from mid-May to mid-October. You'll need to make reservations in advance in high season. Children must be at least seven years old for two-hour rides, and at least 10 for half-day rides. The weight limit is 220lb (100kg) per rider fully dressed.

Several outfitters can get you on horseback for rides in Red Canyon, in Dixie National Forest west of Bryce Canyon, as

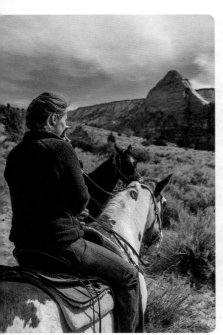

Horseback riding, Zion National Park (p71)

tional Forest and Paria Canyon in Grand Staircase-Escalante National Monument. Trips usually depart in spring and fall.

Four-Wheel Driving

Southern Utah boasts dirt roads aplenty, and a 4WD vehicle is useful on all of them. The region also has many dirt roads – some of which are legendary – that are only manageable via 4WD. Yet if there's one thing that can get the inexperienced into trouble faster than a static canyoneering rope, it's a 4WD vehicle. A rental 4WD is not a magic bullet; sometimes it's just a means for getting as far away from help as possible.

Before heading into the desert, know the capabilities of your vehicle. If you don't have the winches and experience to free a stuck vehicle, don't take chances on unknown roads. And before heading out, get current road and weather conditions from visitor centers and public lands information offices. GPS is delightful, but it's useless in a muddy wash with a storm coming. Expect that 4WD roads may be muddy and inaccessible for at least a day or two after even light rains, so wait until the road thoroughly dries out to tackle it. In winter, many 4WD roads in southern Utah may be impassable. If you've never driven back roads in Utah before, consider taking a guided tour first – it's a good reality check.

Remember, nothing ruins the desert's fragile cryptobiotic soil – which holds the

well as around Capitol Reef and into Grand Staircase-Escalante starting from Boulder and Kanab. Moab outfitters and ranches will take you into either the desert or the La Sal Mountains.

Red Rock Ride (☑435-679-8665; www.red rockride.com) offers week-long all-inclusive guided horseback trips visiting Zion, Bryce Canyon and the Grand Canyon's North Rim, Red Canyon in the Dixie Na-

---

COOL ESCAPES

It's the desert – you know it's gonna be hot. To beat the heat, escape to the following:

➡ Swimming holes on the Virgin River

➡ The Narrows of Zion Canyon

➡ High-elevation Cedar Breaks National Monument

➡ Pine Valley Mountains outside St George

➡ Calf Creek Recreation Area, especially Lower Calf Creek Falls

➡ Creeks winding through Capitol Reef National Park

➡ The shady pioneer-planted orchards of Fruita, in Capitol Reef National Park

➡ Moab's lofty La Sal Mountains

➡ Lazy float trips or white-water rafting near Moab

Rafting in Cataract Canyon (p213) on the Colorado River

entire ecosystem together – faster than car tires, and a single off-road joyride leaves harmful scars that can last decades.

Water Sports

Rafting & Canoeing

Folks with white-water fantasies should head directly to Moab. The main rafting season runs from April to September (jet-boating season lasts longer), with peak water flow usually occurring in May and June. Whatever your skill level, outfitters in Moab stand ready to provide everything you might need, from rental equipment, permits and shuttles to guided tours and lessons.

Moab offers a number of river trips, from family-friendly floats and mellow flatwater canoe trips to daredevil rapids-rafting and jet-boating tours. For the calmest trips, rent equipment and paddle the upper portion of the Green River through **Labyrinth Canyon**, starting from the town of Green River, or the **Daily**, aka

Fisher Towers, a section of the Colorado River alongside Hwy 128.

More adventurous trips through Canyonlands National Park require a permit, and the easiest way to get one is to join a guided trip. **Stillwater Canyon** is a calm section of Green River that allows you to float through the park. Just past the confluence of the Green and Colorado River is **Cataract Canyon**, the region's ultimate challenge when it comes to technical white water.

For a shorter white-water rafting excursion, try **Westwater Canyon** for a one-day trip.

Swimming & Tubing

Zion's **Virgin River** is the best option for swimming. While generally shallow and cold, it does offer lots of swimming holes and warms up just enough later in summer to enjoy a dip. Tubing is prohibited within the park, but outfitters in Springdale rent inner tubes for local floats in summer, unless water levels are too low. You'll find more summer swimming holes along creeks in **Capitol Reef**, as well as at **Calf**

Sledding in Dixie National Forest (p123)

Creek Recreation Area, where families can splash around and take a break from Grand Staircase-Escalante's dusty 4WD tracks.

Winter Sports

While destinations at lower elevations, like the floor of Zion Canyon, only rarely see significant snowfall, higher up there's often enough snowpack for some serious fun.

Cross-Country Skiing & Snowshoeing

Several spots offer cross-country skiing and snowshoeing. Among the most popular is Bryce Canyon, which features 10 miles of cross-country trails atop the canyon's rim, plus 20 additional miles in the surrounding Dixie National Forest. During winter, park rangers offer guided snowshoe hikes, with free snowshoes loaned to participants. Otherwise, you can rent showshoes and skis at Ruby's Inn, which also offers winter sleigh and horseback rides and snowmobiling tours outside the park. For the most fun in the snow, show up for the Bryce Canyon Winterfest, held annually in mid-February, featuring outdoor sports clinics, tours, ski races and competitions, as well as snow sculptures and sledding.

If you have your own skis, cross-country skiing is popular in the mountains east of Cedar City along Hwy 14, particularly the scenic amphitheater rim at Cedar Breaks, where a volunteer-staffed seasonal yurt lets you warm up with a cup of hot cocoa.

The La Sal Mountains outside Moab feature great snowshoeing and cross-country skiing and even a hut-to-hut system. Outdoor outfitters in Moab rent equipment, sell maps and cold-weather gear, and can arrange self-guided overnight trips.

Downhill Skiing

The only downhill skiing in the region is at Brian Head, northwest of Zion. While no big hitter, it's still respectable with 65 trails, four terrain parks and two lifts on Navajo Mountain and Giant Steps Mountain, which both summit over 10,000ft. The winter sports season usually runs from December to mid-April, when it offers opportunities for skiing, snowboarding, tubing and more. Rental equipment, lessons, outdoor clothing and gear shops, dining and lodging are all available at the full-service resort.

And even if they're not in southern Utah, it would be criminal not to mention the state's big resorts, like Deer Valley, Park City, Snowbird and Alta, which boast some of the best snow in the country.

Ski Utah (www.skiutah.com) has updated snow reports, detailed statistics and helpful travel info and deals for skiing statewide, including at Brian Head and around Bryce Canyon.

Plan Your Trip
Travel with Children

Southern Utah's national parks feature inconceivable landscapes that seem like one ginormous playground, with wild rock formations to clamber upon, canyons to squeeze into, creeks to splash in and a variable level of adventure that can be easily tailored to every family's needs.

Best Regions for Kids

Zion
Particularly good for families, with free shuttle buses, great ranger programs, river access and all levels of hikes and adrenaline-piqued activities.

Moab
Moab is awash in things to do: mountain biking, lazy river floats, white-water rafting and guided rock climbing. Arches is fabulous for families while Canyonlands appeals to adventure-loving teens.

Bryce
Kids will love finding resemblances in the hoodoos; a free park shuttle makes navigation hassle-free. Also astronomy programs, guided full-moon hikes and horseback rides.

Grand Staircase-Escalante
Rugged Escalante is suited to teens with some outdoors experience, though adventurous youngsters will also enjoy squeezing through slots.

Capitol Reef
Earn a junior geologist badge at the Ripple Rock Nature Center followed by a visit to pick-your-own-fruit orchards.

National Parks for Kids

The desert can be a magical experience, though expect it to be relatively physical and hands-on. Make sure to budget for some special activities – canyoneering, horseback riding, rafting and the like – in order to break up the time spent driving, posing for family photos at scenic viewpoints and (not again!) hiking.

Parents will often find themselves trying to balance risk and reward: how much room should you be giving your children to climb around and explore this amazing place, and when should you be stepping in to ensure their safety? Planning a ranger-led walk or a guided activity early on in your trip can be a good opportunity for kids to learn responsible behavior from a local expert, rather than the in-one-ear-out-the-other warnings of Mom and Dad.

Junior Ranger Programs

All of southern Utah's national parks offer junior ranger programs (www.nps.gov/learn), which focus on do-it-yourself activity books that kids can complete to get a special certificate and the all-important junior ranger badge. Of course, there's no age limit, and even adults can learn something and have fun doing the activities with their kids. For younger children, easier activity sheets may be available.

Most parks have free ranger-led educational activities and short walks in peak season. Evening family programs, scheduled after dinner, are usually a hit.

Also look for nature centers. In summer Zion offers a drop-off junior ranger program at the Zion Nature Center, where kids join instructor-led activities, hikes and games. Capitol Reef has its own Ripple Rock Nature Center, which hosts ranger-led programs for kids; borrow a free activity backpack for families here or at the main visitor center. Canyonlands also lets families borrow activity-based 'Explorer Packs.'

Children's Highlights

Hiking

➡ **Zion** Easy destinations include the hanging gardens of Emerald Pools and Riverside Walk. More challenging walks include the Narrows, Hidden Canyon and the famously exposed climb up to Angels Landing. (p52)

➡ **Snow Canyon State Park** Explore the desert landscape, with petrified sand dunes, real sand dunes and ancient lava tubes to climb into. (p93)

➡ **Bryce Canyon** Descend into the canyon on Queen's Garden Trail. (p112)

➡ **Grand Staircase-Escalante National Monument** Better suited for older kids; hike to Lower Calf Creek Falls or try squeezing into the slot canyons on Willis Creek. (p143)

➡ **Capitol Reef** Spot petroglyphs along Capitol Gorge and pass giant domes and a towering arch at Hickman Bridge. (p164)

➡ **Arches** Most of the classic hikes here are family friendly, including Landscape Arch, Delicate Arch and Sand Dune & Broken Arches. (p98)

➡ **Canyonlands** Pass an abandoned cowboy camp at Cave Spring or watch for passing condors at Grand View Point. (p183)

➡ **Goblin Valley State Park** Melted rock formations turn into goblins before your eyes. (p175)

Cycling & Mountain Biking

You can rent bikes and car racks in several park gateway towns.

➡ **Zion Canyon Scenic Drive** A fun bike ride in reverse; when you get tired, just hop on the park shuttle (maximum two bicycles per bus). (p68)

➡ **Pa'rus Trail** In Zion Canyon, this is one of the few park trails open to bikes. (p52)

➡ **Bryce Canyon** Paved recreational cycling path running west of Bryce to Red Canyon. (p122)

➡ **Capitol Reef** Head along the scenic drive for cool river views. (p168)

➡ **Bar-M Loop** If older kids want to go off-road, try this mountain-bike trail outside Moab. (p205)

➡ **Snow Canyon State Park** You can bike down the main road or take a gravel 'mountain-bike' trail through the desert. (p93)

Horseback Riding

Note that the minimum age for kids is usually seven or 10 years old. Trips range from one hour to full-day treks.

➡ **Canyon Trail Rides – Zion** Ride on the Sand Bench Trail along the Virgin River. (p72)

➡ **Canyon Trail Rides – Bryce** Short trips to the canyon floor or a half-day ride through dramatic hoodoos. (p122)

➡ **Red Canyon Trail Rides** Ride on private and public lands outside Bryce. (p122)

➡ **Scenic Rim Trail Rides** Head out to Thunder Mountain and other Red Canyon spots. (p133)

➡ **Hell's Backbone Ranch & Trails** Perfect for starring in your own Western. (p155)

➡ **Hondoo Rivers & Trails** Long-running guide service offering Capitol Reef–area rides. (p168)

➡ **Red Cliffs Lodge** Gorgeous scenery north of Moab in Castle Valley. (p214)

Museums & Historical Sights

➡ **Frontier Movie Town & Trading Post** Western movie sets, costume shop and mock gunfights in Kanab. (p156)

➡ **Children's Museum** Fun hands-on museum in St George; best for ages two to 10. (p90)

➡ **Dinosaur Discovery Site** Huge collection of fossilized tracks outside St George. (p90)

➡ **Best Friends Animal Sanctuary** Animal lovers will adore this rescue center, one of the largest in the country: take a tour, spend the night or volunteer. (p156)

DEHYDRATION

One important thing to remember is that children are particularly vulnerable to the heat; they dehydrate faster than adults, and symptoms can turn severe more quickly. Make sure they drink plenty of water at regular intervals, and to keep salts from being flushed out of the body when it is particularly hot, add a pinch of sea salt or electrolyte powder to drinking water. A wide-brimmed hat, sunglasses and sunscreen are absolutely essential.

➡ **Petroglyphs** Native American sites abound in southern Utah, but locations are not always advertised – ask at visitor centers for more info.

➡ **Bryce Museum** Displays dioramas of over 800 animals from around the world and live fallow deer, as well as Indian artifacts, and butterfly and giant-bug exhibits. (p132)

Water Sports

Never enter a creek or river if there is a chance of a flash flood. Storms can be miles away and completely out of sight; check the day's forecast and remain vigilant.

➡ **Zion** Wade in the Virgin River, hike part of the Narrows or float downstream on a tube when water levels are high enough. (p83)

➡ **Moab** Canoe or raft down the Colorado or Green Rivers outside of town. Guides run both flatwater and white-water trips. (p211)

➡ **Capitol Reef** Both Pleasant Creek and Sulphur Creek offer delightful spots for wading. (p168)

Planning

Traveling with children, especially during summer in southern Utah, means taking it easy. The hot sun, dry climate and occasionally high altitude can quickly turn into sunburn, dehydration and fatigue. Break up long car journeys with frequent stops; be realistic and try not to jam too much activity into the day. Remember that the best times for outdoor activities in summer are early in the morning or late afternoon.

Also keep in mind that most of southern Utah's park gateway towns do not have large supermarkets or chain stores. Plan ahead and stock up on supplies for babies and toddlers at the start of your trip in urban areas like St George, Las Vegas or Salt Lake City.

Lodging & Camping

Hotels and motels typically offer rooms with two beds, which are ideal for families. Some have cribs and rollaway beds, sometimes for a minimal fee. Ask about suites, adjoining rooms and appliances such as microwaves and refrigerators. Some hotels offer 'kids stay free' deals for children up to 12, and sometimes up to 18. Many B&Bs do not allow children, so ask before booking.

No trip to Utah's national parks would be complete without at least one night in a tent – most kids love it. Make sure you look for a campground that has designated fire rings so that you can have the obligatory campfire and trip-highlight s'mores. Seasonal fire restrictions in the West are very serious and not all campgrounds allow fires, so do some research ahead of time. If you do plan on camping, note that you won't be alone. Campsites are much harder to find than hotel rooms, particularly in national parks. Reserve ahead of time to avoid spending hours fruitlessly searching for an open site. Most parks have at least one first-come, first-served campground; if you can marshal the troops to hit the road early enough, show up around 8am, wait for somebody to leave and cross your fingers you get there first. If you don't mind primitive sites, ask rangers about free dispersed camping on nearby BLM (public) land.

HIKING TIPS

➡ Start the day with an educational ranger activity – you can then leverage the desire to show off new-found knowledge into a hike.

➡ Most younger children are not goal-oriented when hiking, and trying to reach a destination can cause no end of frustration for everyone. Pack a picnic, find some shade and plan on letting the kids climb on rocks, run after lizards, scoop up sand or play in a stream indefinitely.

➡ Many of the most famous hikes are physically demanding, but not impossible for older children. If you plan on tackling a harder hike, make sure you start with a few easy warm-ups so you can first get used to the desert environment.

➡ Bring some kid gear: binoculars, an inexpensive digital camera, compass and an appropriately sized daypack will up the fun level.

➡ Older children might be interested in geocaching (www.geocaching.com), an outdoor 'treasure hunt' using a GPS device.

➡ Sandstone is notoriously brittle and flaky; watch for loose rocks on the trail, when scrambling over boulders and especially near cliff edges.

Plan Your Trip
Travel with Pets

It's only natural to want to explore the great outdoors with your pet, but you'll want to ensure they stay healthy and safe. Expect to encounter a lot of restrictions in national parks; state parks are a better bet if you want to spend the day on the trail together.

Park Regulations

Pets are allowed in southern Utah's national parks, but under a lot of restrictions (exceptions are made for service animals). Pets aren't allowed on any trails (Zion's Pa'rus Trail is the lone exception), at scenic viewpoints or in the backcountry. Remember that these rules are in place to protect the park's flora and fauna, and also to keep your pet from getting hurt.

Pets are not allowed on any park shuttles. They *are* allowed in national park campgrounds and outside of cars on main roads. Dogs must remain on a 6ft-long leash and be accompanied by a person at all times. If you leave your dog tied up unattended at a park campground, you'll be cited by rangers. Pets may be left alone inside RVs during the day (keep those windows open!), but they may not be left in cars; summer temperatures can quickly become lethal.

Some of southern Utah's national parks are located near kennels, where dogs and cats can be boarded for a day or overnight, including in Springdale (p76), Bryce Canyon City and Moab. Contact park visitor centers and tourist information offices for more referrals, including to local veterinarians. If you're spending a long day in the car, vets recommend stopping at least every two hours to let your dog pee, stretch its legs and have a long drink of water.

Hotel Policies

Costs

Expect extra accommodation costs of anywhere from $10 to $50 per night. Some hotels might make you put down a hefty credit-card deposit when checking in.

Weight & Breed Restrictions

Some hotels will not take pets weighing more than 40lb, or accept what they call 'aggressive' breeds (eg pit bulls, rottweilers). You may be able to obtain a waiver if you contact the hotel in advance, however.

Call Ahead

To avoid any unpleasant surprises, call in advance to check a property's pet policies, especially at independently owned lodgings.

Chains

Best Western is one of the most dog-friendly of the chains, often with no weight limits. Motel 6 and La Quinta typically charge no extra fees.

44

PLAN YOUR TRIP TRAVEL WITH PETS

Dog-Friendly Areas

In Grand Staircase-Escalante National Monument, Utah's state parks, national forests and Bureau of Land Management (BLM) lands, dogs are usually allowed on hiking trails and in the backcountry, except in specially designated wilderness areas. That said, think twice before taking your pets on desert hikes in the summer – excruciatingly hot sand can burn tender paws – and always bring a water bowl. If you're camping, you'll need extra blankets year-round, as desert nights can be cold even after scorching summer days.

Outside the parks, southern Utah can be a pet-friendly travel destination, as long as you pay attention to a couple of rules. Don't immediately tie your dog up outside the first restaurant or cafe that you see. Instead, ask about local laws, to avoid ending up with a ticket. Some shops do allow dogs (often they'll post a note on the door or window saying so), or they might have a water bowl for customers' four-legged friends waiting outside.

In southern Utah, Kanab is easily the most pet-friendly town. It's home to Best Friends Animal Sanctuary (p156), a no-kill rescue center that's become famous for rehabilitating Michael Vick's pit bulls and for being featured on the popular National Geographic TV show *DogTown*. Many hotels and even a few restaurants allow dogs, while Willow Canyon Outdoor (p158) sells outdoor gear for your four-legged friend. Moab is another pet-friendly town, with dog-friendly hiking trails like Corona Arch, Negro Bill Canyon and Fisher Towers.

You won't see too many dogs in Las Vegas but the city has dozens of doggy day-care, canine spa and boarding facilities; contact the city's tourist information office or your hotel concierge for referrals. Otherwise, you'll likely have the best luck getting your dog a bed at one of the budget chains – Motel 6 has multiple locations, including near the Strip.

Horse Trails & Equestrian Facilities

You can bring horses, mules and burros into most of southern Utah's national parks, including Zion, Bryce Canyon, Capitol Reef and Canyonlands. Usually private stock are limited to specially designated trails and/or dirt roads. Stock may not be allowed at all during spring thaws and other periods when they could cause excessive trail damage. In canyon areas, watch out for descents that are steep, rocky and treacherous. Stock must be fed certified weed-free hay for at least 48 hours prior to their trip. Day rides in the national parks usually don't require permits (except in Canyonlands), but overnight backcountry trips do. Maximum group size is usually six to 12 animals. Consult each national park's website or call their visitor center or backcountry desk directly for updated regulations regarding private stock.

Throughout much of southern Utah, Dixie National Forest offers excellent riding opportunities with some trails open to horses and miles of dirt roads, as well as specially designated horse camps. Only certified hay is allowed within the forest. Some tour companies and pack-trip outfitters allow customers to bring along their own stock – be sure to ask when making reservations.

If you're traveling with a horse, only a few lodgings will accept your four-legged friend. These include Sandcreek RV Park (p174) and **Cowboy Homestead Cabins** (☑888-854-5871; www.cowboyhomestead cabins.com; Hwy 12, 3 miles south of Torrey; cabins $89-99; 🐾🐴) in Torrey, outside Capitol Reef. Horse-boarding facilities in southern Utah include **Lit'l Bit Ranch** (☑435-899-9655; http://litlbitranch.org; 2550 E Hwy 89) in Kanab and Red Cliffs Adventure Lodge (p214) in Moab.

On the Road

Zion National Park

Best Hikes

➜ The Narrows (p58)

➜ Angels Landing (p54)

➜ Emerald Pools (p52)

➜ Hidden Canyon (p56)

➜ The Subway (p63)

➜ West Rim Trail (p55)

Best Experiences

➜ Canyoneering (p72)

➜ Backpacking the Narrows (p58)

➜ Hanging Gardens (p52)

➜ Mountain biking (p71)

➜ Exploring East Zion (p77)

Why Go?

From secret oases of trickling water to the hot-pink blooms of a prickly pear cactus, Zion's treasures turn up in the most unexpected places. That's not to say that the soaring majesty of 2000ft sandstone cliffs won't leave you awestruck, but it's the finer details that really make Zion stand apart. You don't need to be an amateur photographer to enjoy all that the park has to offer, however – though it is likely you'll fill up your memory card with pictures by trip's end.

Whether you're capturing the play of shadows along the canyon walls, sharing the satisfaction of pulling over the final ledge of Angels Landing, admiring the echoes of water in the curves of a slot canyon or wading knee-deep in the adventure-fueled fun of the Narrows, Zion will continue to leave you breathless, every step of the way.

Driving Distances (miles)

	Bryce Canyon National Park (Park Entrance)	Grand Canyon North Rim (Park Entrance)	Kolob Canyons (Park Entrance)	Las Vegas	Springdale
Grand Canyon North Rim (Park Entrance)	145				
Kolob Canyons (Park Entrance)	110	140			
Las Vegas	260	250	150		
Springdale	85	110	40	160	
Zion National Park (Springdale Entrance)	85	100	40	160	1

Note: Distances are approximate

Entrances

Zion encompasses roughly 148,000 acres of land, though the vast majority of visitors head straight for Zion Canyon, the park's main attraction. Zion Canyon is closest to the south (main) entrance, outside the town of Springdale on Hwy 9. This supremely scenic highway continues 11.5 miles east through the park and the Zion–Mt Carmel Tunnel to the east entrance, where visitors from Bryce and other Utah parks will likely arrive. The park has two other entirely separate access points: Kolob Terrace Rd, which climbs from the town of Virgin over 4000ft up to the canyon-top area west of the main canyon, and Kolob Canyons, 40 miles (one hour) northwest of the main canyon, reached via I-15.

DON'T MISS

Zion's unique landscape has to be seen to be believed – it may be smaller than the Grand Canyon, but in a way this makes it easier to handle, with perspectives that are both monumental and yet still manageable at the same time. Hop on the **shuttle** (p78) for the best park overview, as it transports you the length of the main canyon.

Check out the oasis-like hanging gardens at the **Emerald Pools** (p52) or **Weeping Rock** (p54), where plants like scarlet monkey flowers and golden columbine grow from shaded seeps, clinging to the canyon walls.

Adventure lovers will want to make the white-knuckle climb up to **Angels Landing** (p54), the park's legendary vertigo-inducing trail up the canyon walls and out across a narrow fin of sandstone, with precipitous dropoffs nearly 1500ft down to the canyon floor.

Equally famous is the hike down – or up – the Virgin River, known as **the Narrows** (p58). Wading through chest-deep water with your backpack hoisted overhead and sheer walls closing in makes this a quintessential Zion experience.

If you prefer an even tighter squeeze, then Zion's slot canyons are a must. **Hidden Canyon** (p56) is a good intro as you won't need any gear; other descents like Keyhole (p71), Mystery (p71) and the **Subway** (p63) all require rope, harnesses and wetsuits.

When You Arrive

➡ Zion National Park is open 24/7 year-round. Park passes can be purchased at the south (main) and east entrance stations and at Kolob Canyons visitor center. Remember to hold on to your receipt if you are traveling to both the Zion Canyon and Kolob Canyons.

➡ If you are traveling between the south and east entrances and have a vehicle over 11ft 4in tall or 7ft 10in wide, you will need to pay an additional RV tunnel escort fee.

WHY 'ZION'?

One of the park's first Mormon settlers called the canyon 'Little Zion,' referring to it as a place of refuge. The original Paiute name was Mukuntuweap, meaning 'straight-up land.'

ZION NATIONAL PARK

Fast Facts

➡ **Entrance fee (valid 7 days)** vehicle/motorcycle/cyclist $30/25/15

➡ **Total area** 148,000 acres

➡ **Elevation range** 3660–8700ft

➡ **Average July temperature** 100°F (38°C)

➡ **Age of water seeping into the Emerald Pools** 12,000 years old

Reservations

Only one campground in Zion, Watchman, takes reservations. Consequently, you'll have to book months ahead if you want a guaranteed spot. Likewise, if you plan on backpacking or canyoneering, you should reserve your permits three months in advance.

Resources

➡ **Zion National Park** (www.nps.gov/zion)

➡ **Zion Natural History Association** (www.zionpark.org)

➡ **Zion Canyoneering Routes** (www.canyoneeringusa.com)

➡ **Cedar Breaks National Monument** (www.nps.gov/cebr)

Zion National Park

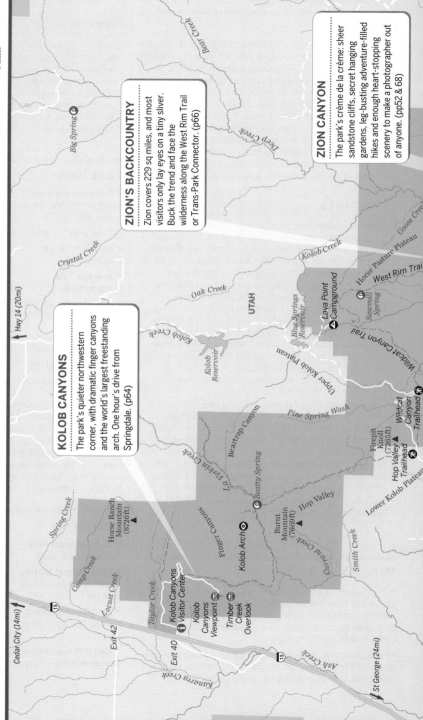

ZION'S BACKCOUNTRY

Zion covers 229 sq miles, and most visitors only lay eyes on a tiny sliver. Buck the trend and face the wilderness along the West Rim Trail or Trans-Park Connector. (p66)

KOLOB CANYONS

The park's quieter northwestern corner, with dramatic finger canyons and the world's largest freestanding arch. One hour's drive from Springdale. (p64)

ZION CANYON

The park's crème de la crème: sheer sandstone cliffs, secret hanging gardens, leg-busting adventure-filled hikes and enough heart-stopping scenery to make a photographer out of anyone. (pp52 & 68)

KOLOB TERRACE ROAD

Little-visited road that ascends a canyon-top landscape of cinder cones, ponderosa forest and solitary peaks. Access backcountry routes or climb down into the famous Subway canyon. (p72)

SOUTHWEST DESERT

Eyeball-melting hot in summer, but the forgotten desert landscape here can be fascinating out of season, particularly in winter. (p77)

EAST ZION

Go off-trail across desert slickrock, descend technical slot canyons with a rope and wetsuit, or hike to lookouts high above the main canyon floor. (p60)

Mt Carmel (12mi); Hwy 89 (12mi)

East Entrance

Checkerboard Mesa (6670ft)

Nippletop (6715ft)

Zion-Mt Carmel Tunnel

Watchman Campground

Patanangawi Canyon

East Fork Virgin River

Shanes Creek

South Creek

UTAH

Eagle Crags (6263ft)

Horse Valley

Wire Valley

Smithsonian Buttes (6200ft)

Goosberry Mesa

Grafton Wash

Grafton (ghost town)

Rockville

Zion Park Blvd

Springdale

9

Huber Wash

Zion Canyon Visitor Center

South Campground

Human History Museum

Canyon Junction

South Entrance

Court of the Patriarchs

East Temple (7709ft)

Zion Canyon Scenic Dr

Deertrap Mountain (6739ft)

Great White Throne (6744ft)

Zion Lodge

The Sentinel (7157ft)

The West Temple (7810ft)

Seestair Wash

Zion National Park

Cougar Mountain

South Guardian Angel (7140ft)

West Rim Trail

Angels Landing (5990ft)

The Narrows

Temple of Sinawava (4418ft)

Observation Point

Weeping Rock

Zion Ponderosa Ranch Resort

Virgin River

Clear Creek

Mt Carmel Junction

9

Right Fork North Creek

Left Fork Trailhead

Right Fork Trailhead

North Creek

Northgate Peaks (7200ft)

North Guardian Angel (7395ft)

Grapevine Wash

Black Wash

Smith Mesa

Dry Creek

Kolob Terrace Rd

Virgin

Virgin River

I-15 (13mi); St George (22mi)

9

La Verkin Creek

ZION NATIONAL PARK

HIKING IN ZION NATIONAL PARK

NAME	START LOCATION	DESCRIPTION
Angels Landing (p54)	Grotto	Legendary Zion hike traversing a rock fin with precipitous drop-offs and chain-assisted scrambles
Cable Mountain Trail (p61)	Zion Ponderosa Ranch Resort	A mesa-top jaunt that ends at a historic cable works overlooking Zion Canyon
Canyon Overlook (p60)	East of Zion–Mt Carmel Tunnel	A quick, elevated hike through canyon alcoves to panoramic vistas
East Mesa Trail (p61)	Zion Ponderosa Ranch Resort	Wanders through upcountry woods and then descends to incredible Observation Point views
Emerald Pools & Kayenta Trails (p52)	Zion Lodge	Popular series of trails leads up to three pools, hanging gardens and trickling waterfalls
Grotto Trail (p53)	Zion Lodge	Shady, even trail that connects Zion Lodge with the Grotto picnic grounds
Hidden Canyon Trail (p56)	Weeping Rock	Trace a trail carved into the cliff face to reach a gem of a hanging canyon
La Verkin Creek Trail to Kolob Arch (p65)	Lee Pass	Backcountry hike along a desert river to views of a giant arch
The Narrows: Bottom Up (p57)	Temple of Sinawava	A Zion icon: hikers walk, wade and swim up the Virgin River through spectacular canyon scenery
The Narrows: Top Down (p58)	Chamberlain's Ranch	A backcountry in-the-river experience, swimming and hiking through the park's most famous canyon
Northgate Peaks Trail (p62)	Wildcat Canyon trailhead	A pine-and-meadow trail leads to a lava outcrop; option to summit an easy peak
Observation Point (p56)	Weeping Rock	Strenuous hike climbs steeply, traversing a hanging chasm before reaching a rewarding overlook
Pa'rus Trail (p52)	Zion Canyon Visitor Center	A paved, pet-, wheelchair- and bike-friendly path meandering along the river in lower Zion Canyon
Riverside Walk (p57)	Temple of Sinawava	An end-of-the-canyon trail follows the Virgin River past hanging gardens, weeping seeps and waterfalls
The Subway (p63)	Wildcat Canyon trailhead	Adventure-filled canyoneering route to the famous Subway formation
Taylor Creek Middle Fork (p64)	Kolob Canyons Rd	Creekside trail passes historic cabins en route to the natural amphitheater of Double Arch Alcove
Timber Creek Overlook (p67)	End of Kolob Canyons Rd	A short trail to 270-degree views of Kolob's finger canyons and the varied landscape beyond
Trans-Park Connector (p66)	Lee Pass	Linking strenuous and varied trails allows backpackers to span Zion, northwest to southeast
Watchman Trail (p52)	Zion Canyon Visitor Center	A short ascent leads to fine views; great at sunset
Weeping Rock Trail (p54)	Weeping Rock	Hanging gardens and falls that sometimes seep, sometimes weep, lay at the end of a short hike
West Rim Trail (p55)	Lava Point trailhead	Backcountry trail affords primo views while descending from Zion's high country to the canyon floor

 Views Great for Families Waterfalls Rock Climbing 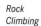 Flush Toilets

DIFFICULTY	DURATION	DISTANCE	ELEVATION CHANGE	FEATURES	FACILITIES
difficult	3-4hr	5.4 miles	1488ft		
moderate	3hr	7.2 miles	250ft		
easy-moderate	45min	1 mile	163ft		
moderate	3hr	6.4 miles	500ft		
easy-moderate	1-2½hr	1.2-2.6 miles	400ft		
easy	15min	0.5 miles	35ft		
moderate-difficult	2½-4hr	2.4 miles	850ft		
difficult	8hr-2 days	14-23 miles	800ft		
difficult	up to 8hr	up to 10 miles	334ft		
difficult	2 days	16 miles	1220ft		
easy-moderate	2hr	4.4 miles	110ft		
difficult	5hr	8 miles	2150ft		
easy	1-1½hr	1.7 miles	50ft		
easy	1½hr	2 miles	100ft		
technical	7hr	9.5 miles	1850ft		
moderate	3hr	5 miles	450ft		
easy	30min	1 mile	100ft		
difficult	4 days	36.3 miles	4000ft		
easy-moderate	1½-2hr	2.7 miles	368ft		
easy	15-30min	0.5 miles	100ft		
difficult	2 days	14.5 miles	3600ft		

 Drinking Water   Backcountry Camping   Public Transportation to Trailhead   Swimming

🚶 DAY HIKES

Zion has a fantastic diversity of hikes, from 15-minute excursions to hanging gardens to multiday quad-burning trips through sinuous river canyons and up relentless switchbacks that ascend the canyon walls. Though each area of the park offers hiking opportunities, the lion's share of trails depart from Zion Canyon and are only accessible via the park shuttle (see the Zion Canyon Scenic Drive, p68). These front-country trails are generally well signposted, paved and crowded.

Zion Canyon

These trails are listed here according to the order you'll encounter them on the shuttle, beginning with the visitor center and ending with the Narrows.

🚶 Pa'rus Trail

Duration 1–1½ hours

Distance 1.7 miles one way

Difficulty Easy

Start Zion Canyon Visitor Center

Finish Canyon Junction

Nearest Town Springdale

Transportation Zion Park Shuttle

Summary A paved, wheelchair-, dog- and bike-friendly trail that meanders beside and across the Virgin River, passing the South Campground and the Human History Museum.

Starting at the visitor center, the Pa'rus (*pah-roos*, meaning 'bubbling waters' in Paiute) is one of Zion's busiest thoroughfares. Paved, wheelchair accessible and open to both bikes and dogs (leashed only), it's a pleasant stroll along the Virgin River and across the open canyon floor.

Here the widely spread canyon walls are stately and majestic rather than awesome and overpowering. The trail is the perfect place to contemplate the Towers of the Virgin, the Streaked Wall, Bridge Mountain and the Watchman. Four footbridges along the way crisscross the river, and numerous dirt paths lead down to the water where you can play. You can exit at the Human History Museum shuttle stop, or continue to trail's end, the Canyon Junction shuttle stop. There's little shade, so dress appropriately.

🚶 Watchman Trail

Duration 1½–2 hours

Distance 2.7 miles

Difficulty Easy–moderate

Start/Finish Zion Canyon Visitor Center

Nearest Town Springdale

Transportation Zion Park Shuttle

Summary The sunset trail of choice in Zion Canyon; ascend a mere 368ft to a short loop that provides fine views of the park's mountainesque formations.

Don't be put off by the name; you're not climbing the monumental Watchman spire, but overlooking it. Wait until the midday heat has waned, then start off across the road from the visitor center on the same trailhead as Pa'rus. At first a dusty path along the Virgin River, the trail gently ascends to a small canyon at the base of Bridge Mountain. Continue your ascent on several long switchbacks past moderate drop-offs to the top of a foothill, where the trail emerges to wide views. The pungent scent of sagebrush and spring blooms of prickly-pear cactus make this an enjoyable ramble.

At the end a 0.3-mile loop trail skirts the foothill, leading to several prime overlooks of the Towers of the Virgin and the town of Springdale. Rising alone to the south you'll see the ragged Eagle Crags. The angular Watchman is the last formation to catch the fading light of sunset; bring a flashlight or headlamp for the return hike.

🚶 Emerald Pools

Duration 1–2½ hours

Distance 1.2 miles round trip

Difficulty Easy–moderate

Start/Finish Zion Lodge

Nearest Town Springdale

Transportation Zion Park Shuttle

Summary An extremely popular trail leads to a series of bucolic ponds, stunning desert-varnished rocks and a beautiful example of Zion's hanging gardens.

Short and sweet, this is a superb introduction to Zion's unique ecology. Regardless of your hiking ability or age, it's worth finding time to explore this area opposite the Zion Lodge.

From Zion Lodge, cross the road and bridge to get to the trailhead. The gradually rising trail leads to the **Lower Emerald Pool**, though it's not the pool that's the attraction but rather the refreshing water sprays cascading over the sandstone lip above. Wildflowers dot the wall of the hollowed-out alcove along the trail, seeming to subsist on nothing at all. Even when packed with admirers, it still feels like a secret oasis.

If that was enough walking for you, this is a good spot to turn around. Otherwise, follow the dirt trail up as it ascends 150ft to the **Middle Pool** that feeds the waterfalls below. A separate trail used to lead here directly from the trailhead, but it has since been decommissioned.

From here, a steep, rocky half-mile spur leads to the **Upper Pool**. This is the loveliest grotto of all, surrounded by the impossibly sheer skirts of Lady Mountain. If you're lucky, you'll get to watch the canyon wren at

play. But please stay out of the ecologically sensitive water.

ALTERNATIVE ROUTE: KAYENTA TRAIL
One you've backtracked down, you could return to Zion Lodge the way you came. But we recommend continuing in the opposite direction, northwest on the Kayenta Trail. This path affords spectacular views down-valley. Expect to be picking your way among rocks along the mile-long trail before you descend to the Grotto picnic grounds and shuttle stop. Following this route would bring the hike's total distance to 2.6 miles.

🚶 Grotto Trail

Duration 15 minutes
Distance 0.5 miles one way
Difficulty Easy
Start Zion Lodge
Finish Grotto shuttle stop

Zion Canyon – Day Hikes

Nearest Town Springdale

Transportation Zion Park Shuttle

Summary A short walk through the trees beneath the canyon wall en route from the lodge to a picnic table in a grove of leafy cottonwoods.

If you don't feel like picnicking with the masses on the lawn of Zion Park Lodge, grab your sandwich and take this easy-peasy stroll through the trees to the **Grotto** picnic area and shuttle stop. A tiny old brick building there was the first Zion NP visitor center and is now an artist retreat. Terrain is unpaved and unsuitable for wheelchairs.

🚶Angels Landing

Duration 3–4 hours

Distance 5.4 miles round trip

Difficulty Difficult

Start/Finish Grotto shuttle stop

Nearest Town Springdale

Transportation Zion Park Shuttle

Summary The most well known of Zion's canyon hikes ascends 1000ft before the main attraction – a razor-edge traverse and a final 488ft elevation gain on the chain-assisted scramble to the top. Grippy shoes are a must.

'How far did you get?' is the question asked every morning at coffee shops all over Springdale, as hikers compare notes on Angels Landing. This strenuous hike is not just a physical challenge, but a mental one for those with a fear of heights. While some will find this trail too unnerving to finish, adventure lovers will have a blast – the exposed scrambling and unrivaled panoramas ensure that Angels Landing lives up to the hype. By all means, start as early as possible. Not only to avoid the heat, but because the number of people on the trail by noon causes frequent bottlenecks at the narrowest, chain-assisted sections. Not sure if you're willing to brave it? Check out the national park's virtual 'eHike' at www.nps.gov/zion /photosmultimedia/virtualtour.htm.

At the trailhead across the road from the Grotto picnic area, bear right. From here to Scout Lookout, you're tracing part of the West Rim Trail. At first the trail meanders along the desert floor, then ascends gradually but relentlessly, becoming steeper as you begin climbing long, paved switchbacks up the canyon wall. The last switchback crosses beneath a rock overhang. Beyond it, the trail levels out, running deep into the narrow, slightly cooler **Refrigerator Canyon**.

Once through the canyon, you'll ascend a few more switchbacks before reaching **Walter's Wiggles**, one of the park's engineering marvels. This set of 21 short, steep stonework zigzags is named after the early superintendent of Zion who imagined them. You emerge atop **Scout Lookout** at a sandy bench with a pit toilet and a turnoff for the West Rim.

If you've made it this far, you should really continue at least the next 70ft or so to see the incredible views. To do so, you'll have to brave the first part of the scary stuff – a **cliff-face climb** using carved-out footfalls and anchor-bolted chains. Afterwards, you get your first good look at **Angels Landing**. Seeing the thin saddle you have to cross – with some 1000ft of precipitous drop-offs on either side – stops many in their tracks. Once across, the last half-mile of the 'trail,' such as it is, gets much steeper and rockier. Chains are bolted into the rock for much of the way. Trail's end, a sloping 30ft-wide flat rock surface at the top, is abundantly clear. Sit and take in the stunning 360-degree view of nearly all of Zion Canyon. You've earned it.

SIDE TRIP: WEST RIM TRAIL

If you want to make a day of it, escape the crowds or avoid the vertigo, try out the West Rim Trail. From Scout Lookout you can follow it into a landscape of surrealistic domes, desert wildflowers and sulfur-streaked rock. It's 6 miles round trip up to and back from the canyon rim and **Cabin Spring**, and the latter half is a real quad-burner, with another 1000ft of climbing. You don't have to go the whole way, though – a simple half-mile in will provide you with plenty to admire and photograph, and often in complete solitude.

🚶Weeping Rock Trail

Duration 15–30 minutes

Distance 0.5 miles round trip

Difficulty Easy

Start/Finish Weeping Rock shuttle stop

Nearest Town Springdale

Transportation Zion Park Shuttle

Summary Cool even in summer, a short-but-steep climb leads to an impressive alcove and hanging garden with water that sometimes seeps, sometimes weeps.

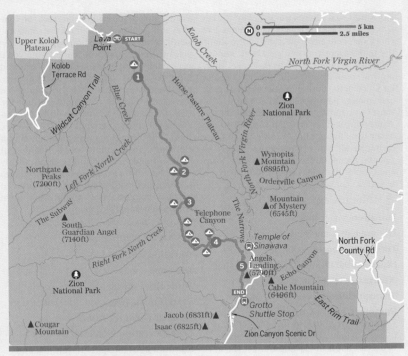

Overnight Hike
West Rim Trail

START LAVA POINT TRAILHEAD (KOLOB TERRACE RD)
END GROTTO SHUTTLE STOP
LENGTH 14.5 MILES; 2 DAYS

Starting on a high plateau, climbing down past Angels Landing, this is Zion's most popular backcountry trail. Permits are issued with campsite reservations; four are available online, while the rest are for walk-ins. Get info on which springs are running, as these are your only water sources and will affect how much water you will need to carry. The trailhead may be inaccessible in winter and early spring.

Arrange a hiker shuttle (p79) up to Lava Point trailhead, about 21 miles north of Virgin on Kolob Terrace Rd. There's a primitive campground here. The trail descends the Horse Pasture Plateau gently for about 5 miles. After the first mile, you'll reach the spur trail to the seasonal **1 Sawmill Spring** and campsite 9.

The first big view west opens up at around 4 miles, across the valley of the Left Fork of North Creek. A mile or so further you'll descend into the grassy meadows of **2 Potato Hollow**, where a spur leads to a good-sized

(seasonal) spring. If it's running, this is the best place to get water and a shady spot for lunch. Campsites 7 and 8 are located here.

The hike up and out is a bit of a workout, with increasingly dramatic views. After about 2 miles, you'll reach the junction with the **3 Telephone Canyon Trail**, a shorter route to West Rim or Cabin Spring (and access point for the technical Telephone Canyon), but don't take it. The next 2-mile stretch is incredible and the primary reason for this trail's enduring popularity. Campsites 3 through 6 are spread along this edge of the mesa; reserve one if you can. It can get windy, so bring rope for your tent, and never build a campfire.

Soon the trail descends steeply to the Grotto. **4 Cabin Spring** (also known as West Rim) is a major junction. From there, short spur trails lead to the spring (a trickle, though usually running) and campsite 2. Telephone Canyon connects here; campsite 1 is not far along it.

About 12.5 miles from Lava Point, you get to **5 Scout Lookout** and the junction for Angels Landing. Beyond the junction, it's a 2-mile drop to the canyon floor and a shuttle ride back to the visitor center.

For a trail that's over almost before it's begun, this one is surprisingly memorable. The enormous, cool alcove at trail's end contains the park's largest hanging garden and an incredible amount of plant diversity. Interpretive signs identify and provide context for much of the flora along the way. The popular, mostly paved trek climbs 100ft (some stairs) to a romantically framed view of the White Throne and Zion Canyon. When the water is really running, it forms a veil from above; in all temperate seasons, expect to get a bit damp. In winter the weep can form giant icicles that may cause trail closure.

Hidden Canyon Trail

Duration 2½–4 hours

Distance Minimum 2.4 miles

Difficulty Moderate–difficult

Start/Finish Weeping Rock shuttle stop

Nearest Town Springdale

Transportation Zion Park Shuttle

Summary Exposed panoramas await as you trace a trail carved into the cliff face to reach a gem of a canyon. You'll need to ascend 850ft in elevation to get there, though.

Get here early enough and you might have this cool hanging canyon all to yourself. Often overlooked by visitors en route to more well-known trails, Hidden Canyon is a great first-time canyoneering experience. There are no technical aspects to this hike, but if you enter deep enough into the canyon, you'll be presented with several fun, problem-solving challenges that require rock scrambling and route-finding skills.

Just getting to the canyon is something of an adventure. The initial ascent up a series of switchbacks is steep but mercifully short – definitely start early in the day while this section is in the shade. After passing the turnoff for Observation Point, the trail continues to climb, skirting a cliff face with vertiginous views as it winds around toward the mouth of the canyon. Chains are bolted into the rock at the most exposed points: although not as extreme as the Angels Landing trail, make use of these handholds – from the thin ledges, it's nearly 1000ft straight down.

Soon after you'll reach a series of pools and a (usually dry) waterfall, which mark the entrance to Hidden Canyon itself.

With rippled red-and-cream rock on one side and a steep gray slab on the other, the sandy confines here beg for exploration. As you proceed deeper into the canyon, you'll pass shady pockets of maidenhair ferns and false Solomon's seal, while bigtooth maples stretch upwards, their brilliant green leaves contrasting marvelously with the rich ochers of the sandstone walls. Eventually you'll come to a small standing arch: from here the trail requires a fair amount of climbing up and around rock falls and giant boulders, and it can become a game of sorts to see how far you can go before having to turn back. A word of caution: only proceed if you're comfortable climbing back down what you originally came up.

Observation Point

Duration 5 hours

Distance 8 miles

Difficulty Difficult

Start/Finish Weeping Rock shuttle stop

Nearest Town Springdale

Transportation Zion Park Shuttle

Summary An intensely rewarding, and strenuous, hike to some of the best views in the park. In the course of 4 miles, the trail climbs switchbacks and crosses a canyon to reach an Angels Landing overlook.

Yeah, we know, you want to climb Angels Landing. That's great, but don't overlook Observation Point: fewer people, an incredible hanging-chasm canyon, and the best views in the park at day's end. Be warned though, this is one of the most difficult day hikes in Zion, rising 2150ft in total. Bring plenty of water and food. You have two choices: start really early so that the initial challenging mile of switchbacks is sheltered from the sun, or make it a late-afternoon hike so the steepest ascent, out of Echo Canyon, lies in blessed shade. The trail is paved all the way to the mesa top, where it becomes dirt and later sand.

Starting from the Weeping Rock stop, the first half-mile of the trail is the same as for Hidden Canyon, ascending long, steep, leg-burning switchbacks. After you branch left at a signed junction, the switchbacks continue for another half-mile until you make a turn north and enter Echo Canyon, a beautiful hanging chasm. Here the trail levels out briefly, hugging the serpentine cliff as the water-eroded chasm yawns below. The sculptural walls close in to almost arms' length. Towering above, the flat face of Cable Mountain is truly a sight to behold. After the canyon floor rises, you're trekking through a sandy wash that turns into a bowl and, before you realize it, you're climbing again. In spring, purple penstemon and crimson paintbrush flowers dot the slickrock crevices; lizards skitter about year-round.

At the 2-mile point, you reach a junction with the East Rim Trail, which also leads to Cable and Deertrap Mountains. After this, a long series of tough switchbacks draw you up the mountain. The trail is exposed to a long drop, but it's wide – no chains necessary. That plus having a mountain on one side makes it much less dizzying than the Angels Landing ascent. After about a mile, you'll reach the mesa top, and the trail is fairly level as it skirts the rim. Bear left at the signed junction with the East Mesa Trail.

For the final half-mile, you'll traverse a sandy piñon-juniper forest to **Observation Point**. From this perch at 6508ft, you can peer 600ft down to the knife-edge of Angels Landing and 2150ft to the Virgin River – an incredible perspective of an iconic hike. The raven's-eye view down the canyon also includes a nice perspective of Red Arch Mountain. To the west, you're level with white Cathedral Mountain as the whole Zion world seems to spread out before you.

Observation Point has some great views, but climbing up from the canyon floor requires serious stamina. An alternative is to actually make a descent to the Point from the East Mesa Trail (p61). According to one ranger, that's the 'sneaky' way.

Riverside Walk

Duration 1½ hour

Distance 2 miles

Difficulty Easy

Start/Finish Temple of Sinawava

Nearest Town Springdale

Transportation Zion Park Shuttle

Summary A popular paved path follows the river at the end of the canyon, accessing seeps, hanging gardens and wading spots – a must on any visit to Zion.

Shadowed from the slanting sun by towering walls, this fun walk parallels the slippery cobblestones of the **Virgin River** and is a kids' favorite. Interpretive signs explain the geology and ecology of the corridor, and various mini-spur trails lead to the river itself. The water is a great place to play, though it can be be chilly. Starting from the **Temple of Sinawava** at the end of Zion Canyon Rd, the crowded trail also serves as a feeder for the Narrows hike.

Look up and around when you set off; the canyon walls around Temple of Sinawava are popular rock-climbing sites. From the start, the pavement undulates up and down over roots and in and around water-carved alcoves. Park literature describes the walk as 'wheelchair accessible with assistance'. We think someone fairly strong would have to be doing the pushing; strollers work fine though. The paved trail ends where the **Narrows** begin, at a raised cul-de-sac with benches. Steps leads down to a rocky fan at the river's edge. Wear shoes you don't mind getting wet; you may not be able to resist the river, which beckons all – even those not hiking further up-canyon.

The Narrows: Bottom Up

Duration up to 8 hours

Distance up to 10 miles (including Riverside Walk)

Difficulty Difficult

Start/Finish Temple of Sinawava

Nearest Town Springdale

Transportation Zion Park Shuttle

Summary Sometimes a bit more of a swim than a hike, as the Virgin River *is* the trail. You'll be in the water the majority of the way upstream through this impressive canyon.

Hiking through a fast-flowing river in knee- to chest-deep water, the canyon walls seem to grow and press in on you: this is arguably *the* quintessential Zion experience. Although some hikers will want to do the full overnight trip beginning at the top (p58), if you hike up from the bottom, you don't need a permit and you can still reach the narrowest and most spectacular section. If you trek the entire 5 miles to Big Springs (as far as day hikers are allowed), you'll outpace most of the daytrippers – but don't underestimate the distance, this is a long way to hike upstream!

Preparation and timing are the keys to a successful Narrows adventure. Always, and we mean always, check conditions with a ranger before hiking. Find out what the day's flash-flood forecast is and make sure you're aware of the dangers (p276). When the river is running more than 150 cubic feet per second (sometimes the case during spring runoff) the Narrows is closed. Runoff depends on the amount of winter snowfall: some years there is little change in the water level, other years the Narrows may be closed in April, May or June. Outside of summer, wet- or drysuits may be necessary. For more on what to bring, see p87.

The 'trail' begins at the end of the **Riverside Walk**, where you enter and start following the river. Around the first bend is **Mystery Falls**, the exit point for Mystery Canyon. You may catch canyoneers on their last rappel here. As you hike, each alcove, bowl, hollow, crack and arch seems its own secret place. Ravens glide low over the water, and you can sometimes hear waterfalls spilling down from inside the rock.

It's about 2.5 miles to the junction with **Orderville Canyon**, which is another popular canyoneering route. If you have time and energy, don't miss the side trip up the smaller and narrower Orderville. It's possible to follow the canyon half-a-mile upstream to a waterfall, beyond which you'll need a permit. (There are several small falls before this; you'll know you've reached the main one when you see a park service sign or by the simple fact that it is impassible to most.) However, there is an admission price of sorts to the canyon: about a quarter-mile upstream is a small pool that you'll need to swim across to continue on.

Past Orderville Canyon is the famous **Wall Street**, where the sheerness, nearness and height of the cliffs shatter whatever remains of your perspective. After this section, the canyon opens slightly again, the water gets periodically deeper (usually requiring swimming in places), and fellow hikers thin out.

After the 4-mile point, you'll negotiate a series of huge boulders, and the canyon, though gorgeous, becomes somewhat less otherworldly. At 5 miles you come to **Big Springs**, a fern-fringed rush of water much larger than anything so far. Here day hikers are required to turn around.

While it can take up to eight hours to do the full round-trip to Big Springs, set aside a minimum of five hours so you'll at least have time to reach Wall Street. Don't forget you also have to hike the Riverside Trail back to the Temple of Sinawava.

Overnight Hike
The Narrows: Top Down

START CHAMBERLAIN'S RANCH (EAST ZION)
END TEMPLE OF SINAWAVA
LENGTH 16 MILES ONE WAY; 2 DAYS

If there's one route that's made Zion famous, it's the wade down the Virgin River through a 1000ft sheer gorge known as the Narrows. Soaring walls, scalloped alcoves and wading through chest-deep pools with your backpack lifted over your head make it truly memorable. Overnight camping is far and away the best experience, though you can hike from the top in one *very* strenuous, long day (90 minutes' drive from Springdale to Chamberlain's Ranch, up to 12 hours' hiking). Remember that the most difficult sections are at the end of the hike, when you'll be the most tired; we don't recommend this unless you have ironman stamina and have done the hike before. You can also day hike the Narrows from the bottom (p57), the most popular approach and the only one that doesn't require a permit.

The Narrows permits are some of the most sought-after in the park and are attached to campsites, except for through hikers. Only 40 permits per day are issued: six campsites are available online; the other six are reserved for walk-ins at the Wilderness Desk. Permits are not issued any time the river is flowing more than 120 cubic feet per second, so this hike may be closed at times between March and June. The optimum time to hike is late June through September. Flash floods are not uncommon in late summer, when, again, the park may close the route (for more on flash floods, see p276). Outside of summer, wet- or drysuits are often necessary, as hypothermia is a real danger. The Wilderness Desk carefully tracks weather, and Springdale outfitters rent all the appropriate gear (p87). A summer-season checklist includes a walking stick, canyoneering shoes and neoprene socks, nylon clothing, extra fleece layers, bug spray and at least one dry bag, in addition to all the usual camping gear. Overnight hikers are required to use human-waste disposal (WAG) bags, which are given free to permit holders.

The trail begins at Chamberlain's Ranch, on the east side of the park, 90 minutes' drive from the south entrance. This is a one-way hike, so make reservations for a hiker shuttle (p79), unless you have two cars and drivers. Shuttles usually leave Springdale at 6:30am; a second may leave around 9am if there are enough people. Past the ranch gate, a dirt road leads to the river, where you'll find an NPS trailhead marker.

The first day is the quietest, the flowing water and undulating walls casting a mesmerizing spell. The first 3 miles are out of the river and the least interesting – power through so you can spend more time with the fun stuff, exploring side canyons and taking photographs. Once you see ❶ **Bulloch's Cabin**, an old homestead about an hour from the trailhead, you'll know that soon enough, the trail becomes the river. The ❷ **Narrows**, about 3½ hours into the hike and near the park boundary, is an early highlight and provides a taste of what's to come.

From here the hike is quite photogenic, with the canyon walls gradually coming closer together. A little over four hours from the trailhead, you'll reach a log-jam ❸ **waterfall** that appears impassable. Upon closer

inspection you'll soon pick out the trail that skirts around to the left. Depending on what time you started, this could be a good lunch spot.

❹ **Deep Creek** is the first major confluence, doubling the river's volume. In the subsequent 2-mile stretch, expect secretive side canyons and faster water, sometimes waist deep and involving swims. Almost six hours from the trailhead is ❺ **Kolob Creek** (generally dry), an interesting side canyon to explore. This area is the location of the 12 overnight campsites, each on a sandy outcrop far from the others.

On day 2 you'll pass ❻ **Big Springs**, a good place to fill water bottles. After this are the 5 miles open to day hikers and plenty of deep pools and fast-moving water. In 2 miles you'll reach well-known ❼ **Wall Street**, certainly one of the most memorable parts of all of Zion. Save some energy for ❽ **Orderville Canyon**, a narrow side canyon that is lots of fun to explore. Orderville is about three hours downstream from Big Springs; you can follow it upstream for a half-mile. From here your company will steadily increase until you're just one of the crowd on the ❾ **Riverside Walk** (p57).

East Zion

The following trails start on the east side of the Zion–Mt Carmel Tunnel, on Hwy 9. Note that these are the official trails; for more information on getting off the beaten track in East Zion see p77.

Canyon Overlook

Duration 45 minutes

Distance 1 mile

Difficulty Easy-moderate

Start/Finish East of Zion–Mt Carmel Tunnel

Nearest Town Springdale

Transportation Private

Summary A convenient stop off Hwy 9, Canyon Overlook is a relatively quick hike that rewards with fun desert scrambling and ends in a much-photographed panoramic vista.

Although this is not a particularly strenuous hike, the slickrock terrain is somewhat rugged, with exposed ledges and a pretty rocky trail – most kids will enjoy this one, though grandparents may be relatively less enthused.

At the east end of the Zion–Mt Carmel Tunnel, park and cross the road to the trailhead near the tunnel ranger booth. (If the small lot is full or if you're coming from Mt Carmel, park in the overflow lots 100yd east of the tunnel.)

After an initial staircase ascent, the trail clings to the cliff walls, passes beneath overhangs sheltering hanging gardens, and bridges over sheer drops. Peer into the dark, narrow recesses below as you cross **Pine Creek Canyon**, a favorite technical canyoneering route.

After you cross the slickrock, you'll arrive at the final sweeping **Canyon Overlook**, with views of lower Zion Canyon and the West Temple, Altar of Sacrifice and the Sen-

East Zion – Day Hikes

tinel. The Great Arch, visible from the west side of the tunnel, is directly below you, though you won't be able to see it.

🚶East Mesa Trail

Duration 3 hours

Distance 6.4 miles

Difficulty Moderate

Start/Finish Zion Ponderosa Ranch Resort, Beaver Rd

Nearest Town Springdale

Transportation Private

Summary The sneaky, backcountry approach to Observation Point. The trail starts off a 4WD road on the east side of Zion and traverses upcountry ecosystems before dropping down to the overlook.

It feels deliciously like cheating to wander through the woods and then descend (500ft elevation change overall) to Observation Point instead of hiking 2500ft uphill from Zion Canyon (p56). Either way, you get some of the park's best perspectives.

Getting to the trailhead requires navigating a dirt road for the last few miles, but most vehicles should be fine as long as there is no rain. Finding it may be an issue, though. First drive to Zion Ponderosa Ranch Resort (p76), 5 miles north up North Fork Rd; the turnoff is 2.5 miles east of the park's east entrance. Once you've arrived a the ranch, you'll want to continue north on dirt roads to the trailhead. You should take a topo map, and don't be shy about asking for directions at the ranch's front desk.

The first 2 trail miles meander through open stands of tall ponderosa pines, which may show signs of periodic park-prescribed burns. In May and June, keep an eye out for showy upcountry wildflowers. To the right you'll see canyon views open up in the distance before you get to the cairns marking Mystery Canyon. Take a short detour up the slickrock to the right to overlook the white, fingerlike canyons stretching out below.

From there the main trail turns southwest and starts gradually descending, with glimpses of Echo Canyon on your left and Zion Canyon on your right. Further descent down slickrock and loose stones, shaded by juniper and piñon, leads past some sandy sites and to the Observation Point spur at 3 miles. Sharing the last 0.2 miles of the trail with so many other people can be jarring.

But just think how much easier it was for you to get here.

🚶Cable Mountain Trail

Duration 3 hours

Distance 7.2 miles

Difficulty Moderate

Start/Finish Zion Ponderosa Ranch Resort, West Pine Rd

Nearest Town Springdale

Transportation Private

Summary An upcountry hike through ponderosa pines leads to your choice of Zion Canyon overlooks. Best of all, you'll encounter few fellow hikers on this trail, which is long but has little elevation change.

Seeking solitude? The route to Cable Mountain is an easy way to escape the crowds, and for those who want to make a long day of it, it can be combined with a hike to Deertrap Mountain. Even in season, you may not see a soul. Both are mainly plateau hikes that end at staggering viewpoints over Zion Canyon.

Like the East Mesa Trail, you'll first need to drive to Zion Ponderosa Ranch Resort (p76). Enter the ranch, and in half a mile, turn left at the signed junction for Cable Mountain onto Buck Rd. After 0.6 miles, turn left at an unsigned junction, and in 100yd turn right onto West Pine Rd. In half a mile, this road dead-ends at the fence for the national park. There is no parking area; try not to block the gate.

The clear dirt trail starts by threading through ponderosa pine forest, and in a quarter-mile passes a signed junction with a trail to Echo Canyon. After ascending for a steady half-mile through scrub forest, you'll reach a signed junction with the East Rim Trail. A mile further bear northward at the signed turnoff for Cable Mountain (Deertrap Mountain is another 2 miles straight on from this point).

The trail soon tops out and descends a final mile to the historic cable works, once used to haul down lumber. The wooden structure is rickety; don't climb on it. Instead, enjoy the panorama, overlooking the Big Bend of the Virgin River and the Oxbow containing Angels Landing. On a clear day you can see north to pink cliffs and Cedar Breaks National Monument (p95).

Kolob Terrace Road

Most of the trails along the scenic road that bisects the park are considered backcountry or technical routes, but Northgate Peaks is one notable exception.

🚶Northgate Peaks Trail

Duration 2 hours

Distance 4.4 miles

Difficulty Easy–moderate

Start/Finish Wildcat Canyon trailhead, Kolob Terrace Rd

Nearest Town Springdale

Transportation Private

Summary An overlooked canyon-top gem: traipse through meadows and pine forest to reach a lava outcrop with a view of 7000ft-plus peaks.

Looking for a cool retreat on a hot summer day? Starting at 6500ft makes a big temperature difference. And since this area sees so little traffic, this pleasant trail remains largely uncrowded. The trailhead is located about 16 miles north of Hwy 9 on Kolob Terrace Rd. The dirt path starts at the end of the parking area.

For about a mile, you'll wander through an open meadow of sage and scrub. At the first junction, stay straight, following the sign for the West Rim Trail. (The Wildcat Connector Trail branches right and connects with the Hop Valley Trail). A hundred yards further, look for the signed Northgate Peaks Trail junction and turn right. The ponderosa pines, manzanita and wildflowers (June through early July) are a welcome rest for rock-weary eyes. You soon crest a rise to a final Y junction. Here, the trailhead for the famous canyoneering route, the Subway, branches left. Keep going straight.

Kolob Terrace Road – Day Hikes

The aptly named White Cliffs tower to the east as you gently ascend and descend to a **lava-rock outcrop** at trail's end – a good perch to admire the stunning terrain. On either side, seemingly close enough to touch, are the pale, crosshatched Northgate Peaks. Front and center is **North Guardian Angel**, with an arch so deep it's more of a cave. Framed amid these in the distance is the heart of Zion Canyon, including the East and West Temples and Deertrap Mountain, on the East Rim.

SIDE TRIP: EAST NORTHGATE PEAK
Although the Northgate Peaks trail officially ends at the outcrop, summiting **East Northgate Peak** (on the left) provides fantastic 360-degree views and is a fun way to extend the hike if you're game. A fairly clear social trail extends down from the lava outcrop to the base of the peak; follow this until you reach the slickrock. From here, ascend the rocky north face up to the vegetated area, after which you'll be able to follow cairns the rest of the way. It's much easier than it appears from afar, though it is certainly steep and you should be comfortable doing off-trail scrambling.

Looking south from the summit (left of North Guardian Angel Peak), you'll be able to pick out a shadowy cleft on the canyon floor – this is the upper part of the Subway.

All in all, figure on anywhere between one to two hours to get up to the top and back. Note that you can also climb the **West Peak**, though this is a Class 3 route with loose rock and some serious exposure. It is not recommended unless you have mountaineering or rock-climbing experience.

The Subway

Duration 7 hours

Distance 9.5 miles one way

Difficulty Technical

Start Wildcat Canyon trailhead

Finish Left Fork trailhead

Nearest Town Springdale

Transportation Private or hiker shuttle

Summary A unique tunnel-like rock on this canyoneering route makes it the park's most photographed backcountry feature. The fun-filled trail requires up to five rappels and descends more than 1800ft, often in water.

Though the left fork of North Creek – better known as the Subway – is technically a canyoneering route, we've included a basic description here because of its incredible popularity. The whole sculpted canyon is full of surprises, beauty and camera-worthy moments, including the curving walls that form the tunnel-like Subway formation, and hard-to-find dinosaur tracks. Along the way, the creek – the only trail – tumbles scenically over low slickrock ledges, collects in deep pools, gives way to boulders and meanders in and out of the streambed. You'll be swimming, scrambling, rappelling, sliding on your butt and whatever else you have to do to continue on.

This is unquestionably the hardest backcountry permit to get (p67), involving an advance lottery system. If you can't get a permit for the technical top-down route, consider trying to hike it from the bottom up; a permit is also required, but it is somewhat easier to obtain. While the Subway is easy by canyoneering standards – four or five short rappels of 20ft or less – you still need to know what you're doing; people do get hurt here every year. Seek technical advice, get a good map and all the gear you'll need (including a wetsuit outside of summer), and arrange a hiker shuttle. The one-way trail starts at the Wildcat Canyon trailhead, about 16 miles north of Hwy 9 on Kolob Terrace Rd.

At first, the route follows the Northgate Peaks Trail. Once you get to the signed spur to the Subway, the real adventure – and route-finding – begins. You parallel, then cross the wooded **Russell Gulch** to an amazing bowl of **sculpted rock**. After about 2 miles and continuous deep, downhill scrambles and clefts in the rock face, you'll finally reach the left fork of North Creek.

From here, you enter the streambed. After your first rappel, the canyon narrows and you find yourself faced with your first swim through a long corridor filled with icy water. From here it's one obstacle after another, culminating with the famous **bowling ball chockstone** and the final 15ft rappel, **Keyhole Falls**. Just after Keyhole Falls is where you'll find the eerie **Subway** tunnel.

After passing through the Subway, you'll begin the lower portion of the hike. Although not as spectacular as the first half, there is still plenty to take in here. Two photogenic **waterfalls** and a set of **dinosaur prints** are the highlights. Eventually the valley begins to open up and vegetation becomes more desert-like, with yucca and prickly pear beginning to dot the trail. This is your cue to start looking for the exit trail on the right-hand side of the creek: if you go into autopilot and just wander along the streambed without paying attention, you can easily miss the sign indicating the way out – an all-too-frequent occurrence.

From here, the steep trail climbs sharply up before it reaches the volcanic rock of the plateau and meanders to the Left Fork trailhead parking lot. Figure on one to two hours to climb out of the canyon.

ALTERNATE ROUTE: BOTTOM UP

Although the approach is long and the trail not quite as spectacular as the top-down route, there's no arguing that the Subway and Keyhole Falls are awesome destinations – anywhere else and this hike would be a highlight. As you start and finish at the Left Fork trailhead, you won't need a shuttle; you will need a permit, however.

When you're descending from the trailhead, make sure to follow the cairns; if you find yourself walking through a dry wash at any time, you've probably missed the turnoff somewhere and should retrace your steps until you find it. Likewise, take note of where the trail enters the canyon floor as you'll need to find it on your way back out.

From the bottom of the canyon, simply follow the creek until you reach the Subway. You'll be hiking in ankle- to knee-deep water most of the time, so dress appropriately.

Kolob Canyons

Zion's northwest section, about 40 miles from Springdale, includes only three maintained trails. Want a challenge? Also consider day hiking La Verkin Creek Trail.

Taylor Creek Middle Fork

Duration 3 hours
Distance 5 miles
Difficulty Moderate
Start/Finish Kolob Canyons Rd
Nearest Town Cedar City
Transportation Private

Summary A refreshing trip that crisscrosses Taylor Creek, passing through juniper, sage and piñon to get to two historic cabins. The real payoff is at the end: views of Double Arch Alcove, a natural amphitheater.

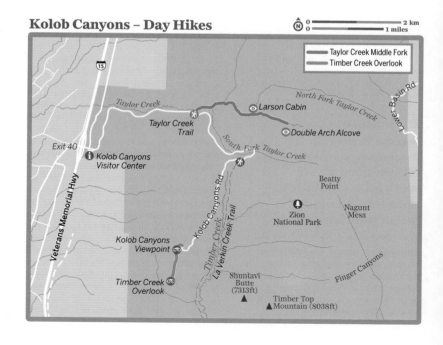

Kolob Canyons – Day Hikes

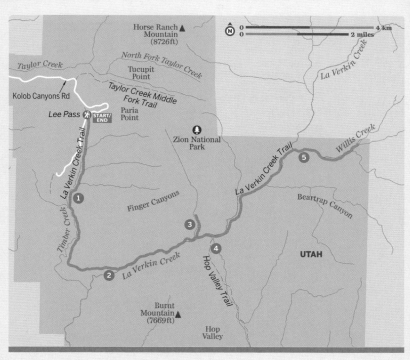

⬥ Overnight Hike
La Verkin Creek Trail to Kolob Arch

START/END LEE PASS (KOLOB CANYONS)
LENGTH 14–23 MILES, 8 HOURS TO 2 DAYS

Hiking along Timber, La Verkin and Willis Creeks is lovely in spring (late April to May) and fall (September and October). Early summer, biting goat flies can hound hikers and high-season temperatures are discouraging. It's a strenuous day hike due to length, sand and elevation changes (800ft overall); an overnight is easier and allows time to explore the recommended Willis Creek area. Permits are issued with campsite reservations; six are available online, while the remaining seven are for walk-ins. Day hikers do not need a permit.

The trailhead is just south of the Lee Pass parking area on Kolob Canyons Rd. For the first 2 miles or so, you descend an open ridge with fine views of the finger canyons. Eventually, you'll skirt the spire of ❶ **Shuntavi Butte** and descend more steeply through piñon-juniper forest along Timber Creek.

The trail then turns east to the north bank of ❷ **La Verkin Creek**, a permanent, vigorous stream lined with the most convenient camp-sites (numbers 4 through 10 are closest). The trail is sandy and slow going here. Ponderosa pines provide shade.

After about 6.25 miles, follow the signed Kolob Arch Trail turnoff. The half-mile ❸ **Kolob Arch Spur** is as far as day hikers should travel. Some scrambling and route finding is required. When you reach a sign advising against further travel up-canyon, look high on the west wall for Kolob Arch. Though its 310ft opening may be the largest in the world, the distant arch is so dwarfed by massive walls that it at first seems strangely anticlimactic. Spend some time watching the sun cloak the rock in ever-shifting shadows, however, and it soon makes a satisfying destination after all.

Just beyond the spur lies the signed junction for the ❹ **Hop Valley Trail**, which you can use as part of the Trans-Park Connector. Past this, La Verkin Creek Trail continues for 4.5 miles, steadily narrowing, then turning up ❺ **Willis Creek**, a steep defile with towering sheer walls that open up near the park boundary. Don't leave the park limits, as private-property owners have been known to run off stray hikers.

Overnight Hike
Trans-Park Connector

START LEE PASS (KOLOB CANYONS)
END GROTTO SHUTTLE STOP
LENGTH 36.3 MILES; 4 DAYS

The most popular way to traverse Zion is to hike northwest to southeast. Always check with rangers when planning, and bring detailed topo maps. There's very little water along this route, so you may need to carry quite a bit. Generally reliable springs can be found along La Verkin Creek, Wildcat Canyon and on the West Rim Trail. Spring is your best bet for water, while fall brings spectacular colors. Summer is hot, and parts of the trail may be closed because of snow December through March. You will likely need a hiker shuttle, and to arrange permits via campsite reservations for the La Verkin Creek Trail and the West Rim Trail.

Day 1 follows the ① **La Verkin Creek Trail** (p65), which begins off Kolob Canyons Rd. Campsites 7 through 12 are all reasonably close to the next leg and are good choices to spend the night. Rest up because day 2 covers a lot of ground – over 15 miles in total and some significant elevation gain.

Begin by heading head south on the 6.7-mile ② **Hop Valley Trail**, which climbs up about 1000ft to a scenic open canyon and long, hot, sandy stretches, emerging at ③ **Kolob Terrace Road**. The 3.4-mile ④ **Wildcat Connector Trail** links Hop Valley with the 4.7-mile ⑤ **Wildcat Canyon Trail**. Together, the Wildcats comprise an uneven ascent of another 1000ft. Lava Point Campground (p76) and Sawmill Spring (on the West Rim Trail) are the usual campsites of choice.

Day 3 is somewhat less strenuous, with a gradual descent along the canyon top and a total distance of only 7 to 10 miles along the ⑥ **West Rim Trail** (p55). The ideal spot to spend the night is in campsites 3 through 6, which provide fabulous views.

Your last day follows the West Rim Trail steeply down into the canyon, past ⑦ **Angels Landing** (p54), and then down again to emerge at the Grotto shuttle stop in Zion Canyon. The hardcore can actually extend this hike another day to climb up out of the canyon along the East Rim Trail (10 miles, 2000ft elevation gain), finishing at the east entrance.

From the start at a parking lot mid-scenic drive, the path quickly drops down stairs and sand to creek level; the overall elevation change is 450ft. From there trail and water interweave like strands of DNA. Pay attention; in places, informal spurs obscure the main trail. Though the creek is small, expect to get a little wet and muddy, and maybe harassed by bugs.

After about a mile, you come to the 1930 **Larson Cabin** and a sign identifying the Taylor Creek Trail. As the trail enters a **finger canyon** between Tucupit and Paria Points, the walls narrow, and your steady as-

cent grows steeper still. A mile further **Fife Cabin** appears. It, like its predecessor, is too fragile to enter; respect the chicken wire on the windows and doors. The last half-mile leads to **Double Arch Alcove**, where the seep-stained red rock glows and echoes with dripping water and swirling wind. It's a cool, refreshing break before your return trip.

🚶Timber Creek Overlook

Duration 30 minutes
Distance 1 mile

WILDERNESS PERMITS

Permits are required for all overnight backpacking trips, all through-hikes of the Virgin River (the Narrows top hike) and the Left Fork (the Subway bottom-up), and any canyoneering or climbing routes requiring ropes. The best way to secure these permits is online (www.nps.gov/zion/planyourvisit/permits.htm); however, for each trip a certain number of walk-in permits are also available. Permit fees (which are in addition to the online reservation fee) are $15 for one to two hikers, $20 for three to seven hikers, and $25 for eight to 12 hikers. Note that the group size limit for most trails is 12 people; for technical canyons it is generally six people. If you are taking a backpacking trip, your permit will be arranged together with your campsite reservation.

Online Permits

Online permit/campsite reservations cost $5 and can be made up to three months in advance (permits become available on the 5th day of each month, so, for example, for a June permit you could begin the process April 5). Permits remain available online until 5pm the day before your trip, unless all spots have been taken. Note that a reservation is not the permit itself, which you must pick up *in person* at the Zion Wilderness Desk or the Kolob Canyons Visitor Center. If you plan on applying for a lot of backcountry permits (eg you'll be canyoneering for several days in a row), it's best to become a **Zion Express Member**, which allows you to obtain your permits online rather than having to pick each one up in person. Membership is free and lasts for three years.

Note that the two most popular backcountry permits, the Subway and Mystery Canyon (both technical routes), have special rules from April through October. Rather than reserve your permit directly, you must instead submit an advance lottery application on which you can request three possible dates for your trip. Applications are submitted three months in advance and cost $5. If any spaces remain open after the lottery, they will become available online. Note that the reservation fee is not the permit fee; these are paid separately.

Last-Minute Drawings

If all online permits for a technical canyoneering route have already been booked, you can apply online for a last-minute drawing. Last-minute drawings open up one week before the desired date; the drawing is held two days before the trip date at 1pm.

Walk-In Permits

About one-third of all permits remain reserved for walk-in visitors the day before or the day of a trip. Out of season you shouldn't have too much trouble getting a permit this way. However, trying to get a next-day walk-in permit on a busy weekend can be like trying to get tickets to a rock concert; lines form outside the Wilderness Desk by 6am. Any campsites or routes that are not reservable online can only be obtained as a walk-in permit.

Difficulty Easy

Start/Finish End of Kolob Canyons Rd

Nearest Town Cedar City

Transportation Private

Summary A short dirt trail to a promontory with 270-degree views of canyons and mountains. The track gets a bit steep and rocky, but unless the elevation affects you, it isn't difficult.

The shortest of the Kolob Canyons hiking options provides a chance to stretch your legs at the end of the scenic drive, but it's not the best of the park's overlooks. Remember that you're above 6300ft here, so the elevation may wind you more than the 100ft ascent. Start at the end of Kolob Canyons Rd; about 100yd along the trail, you'll find picnic benches nestled beneath the Gambel oaks and junipers. The view at trail's end encompasses the ragged, fingerlike Kolob Canyons to the east and the flat mesas of the Lower Kolob Plateau to the south. From here, Zion Canyon is a wispy haze, unrecognizable as the mighty trench and inspiration of majestic homilies that it is.

OTHER ACTIVITIES

Besides hiking, the most popular activity in Zion is canyoneering – a world-class experience. There are also opportunities for cycling, horseback riding and wading/swimming. It is *not* a successful spot for anglers.

Note that classes and ranger-led programs are available too.

Canyoneering

If there's one sport that makes Zion special, it's canyoneering (also known as canyoning). Rappelling over the lip of a sandstone bowl, swimming icy pools, tracing a slot canyon's sculpted curves, staring up at a ragged gash of blue sky – canyoneering is beautiful, dangerous and sublime all at once. Zion's slot canyons are the park's most sought-after backcountry experience and you should reserve your permits far in advance.

Don't be discouraged if you lack the necessary equipment or experience; beginners can join the fun too. The easiest way is to take a guided trip from any of the outfitters in Springdale (p83). While these trips won't

Driving Tour
Zion Canyon
Scenic Drive

START SOUTH ENTRANCE
END TEMPLE OF SINAWAVA
LENGTH 6.2 MILES ONE WAY; 45 MINUTES

The premier drive in the park leads between the towering red-rock cliffs of Zion's main canyon and accesses all the major front-country trailheads. If you only have time for one activity in Zion, this is it – combined with a few of the hikes along the way. Note that most of the road is actually closed to private cars from March through October; you'll be traveling aboard the excellent park shuttle instead of self-driving.

Leaving from the visitor center, the first stop is the ❶ **Human History Museum**, where a 22-minute film introduces the park. The exhibits here cover the geology and human history of Zion Canyon. The building itself was erected on the site of an original Mormon homestead settled by the Crawford family. Outside the museum, interpretive signs point out the park's tallest sandstone cliffs, including the West Temple (7810ft) and the Towers of the Virgin.

Just past the museum on Hwy 9 are a few turnouts that overlook the Streaked Wall. In spring, with binoculars, scan the rim for nesting peregrine falcons. Officially, the scenic drive begins where you turn north, and cars are restricted, at ❷ **Canyon Junction**. This stop marks one end of the Pa'rus Trail, which follows the Virgin River downstream to the visitor center.

Continuing up the canyon, you'll pass the Sentinel Slide on the left. About 7000 years ago, a big chunk of the cliff face sloughed off and blocked the water flow, turning the canyon into a big lake. The water eventually carved its way through the blockage and carried on. The slide became active again in 1995, when it covered the road and trapped tourists at the Zion Lodge for three days, and again in 1998 when the road washed away. It's been properly reinforced now, but you'll notice that the rock looks a lot more loose and crumbly here than in other areas.

Next, the ❸ **Court of the Patriarchs** stop fronts the shortest trail in the park, a 50yd staircase of a walk uphill to a view of the namesake peaks. Named by a Methodist minister in 1916, from left to right are Abraham, Isaac and Jacob, while crouching in front of Jacob is Mt Moroni (named for a Mormon angel). Though many people skip it, even the road-level view is nice, especially at sunset.

Ahead on your right, **4 Zion Lodge** (p75) houses the park's only cafe and restaurant. The lodge was first built in the 1920s, but burned down in 1966. The grassy front lawn – shaded by a cottonwood tree – is a favored place for a post-hike nap. Across the road from the lodge is the corral for horseback rides and the trailhead for the Emerald Pools.

The **5 Grotto** (p53), barely a half-mile north, is a large, cottonwood-shaded picnic area with tables, restrooms and drinking water. From the picnic area, the Grotto Trail leads south to Zion Lodge. Across the road from the picnic area, the West Rim Trail leads north toward Angels Landing. Those who'd rather admire Angels Landing than climb it should stroll the first flat quarter-mile of the West Rim Trail to a stone bench for the perfect vantage.

Make sure you spend some time at **6 Weeping Rock** (p54). There's a lot to see at this bend in the river, a great example of an 'incised meander.' Pause to admire Angels Landing, the Organ, Cable Mountain, the Great White Throne and looming Observation Point. A short detour up the bucolic Weeping Rock Trail to a sheltered alcove and hanging garden is a worthwhile driving diversion. Two other great trails are accessed from here: the chain-assist Hidden Canyon Trail and the Papa Bear of workouts, Observation Point.

There are no trailheads at **7 Big Bend**, but rock climbers get out here on their way to some of Zion's famous walls. Others just soak up the view, which is a different vantage of the features seen from Weeping Rock. It's a good place to bring binoculars and scan the skies for California condors.

If you're using the shuttle, the only way to the next two sights is to walk. As you continue north, on a ledge up to the right look for a reconstructed granary. Although ancient Native American in origin, it was rebuilt in the 1930s by the Boy Scouts. After about a half-mile, you get to **8 Menu Falls**, so-named because it was pictured on Zion Lodge's first menu cover. The multilevel deck with overlook is the most popular place to get married in the park. From there it's easier to backtrack to Big Bend shuttle than to hoof it all the way up to the last stop. The canyon narrows near the cliff face that forms a natural amphitheater known as the **9 Temple of Sinawava**, at the road's end. Across the road the rock called the Pulpit does indeed look a bit like a giant lectern. From here you can take the popular Riverside Walk to the ultimate Zion experience, the Narrows.

Driving Tour
Zion–Mt Carmel Highway (Highway 9)

START SOUTH ENTRANCE
END EAST ENTRANCE
LENGTH 12 MILES ONE WAY; 45 MINUTES
TO 2 HOURS WITH STOPS

As far as Zion's scenic drives go, Hwy 9 certainly rivals the main canyon, with a series of magnificent overlooks followed by a landscape of multicolor slickrock, culminating at Checkerboard Mesa. You can start this drive at either the south (main) entrance or, if you're coming from Bryce Canyon or elsewhere, the east entrance near Mt Carmel.

If you begin at the south entrance, follow the main road about 1.5 miles into the park, passing the ❶ **Human History Museum**, until you reach Canyon Junction, where the Zion Canyon drive splits off from the highway. Follow the highway east, climbing up a series of six tight switchbacks. This picturesque stretch offers superb views both back to the main canyon and ahead to the Great Arch. Make sure to stop at one of the turnouts before you get to the engineering marvel that is the ❷ **Zion–Mt Carmel Tunnel**.

At the time of its completion, the 1.1-mile tunnel was the longest in the USA. During the three years of construction (from 1927 to 1930), more than 146 metric tons of dynamite were used to move 72,000 cubic yards of stone. Much of it was thrown out of the six 'galleries' you see as you drive through; the remainder was used to fill in the roadway below.

At the tunnel's east entrance is a small parking lot and the trailhead for the ❸ **Canyon Overlook** (p60), which leads to the top of the canyon wall you were just admiring. After a second, smaller tunnel, don't miss the numerous turnouts providing access to the slickrock. There are no official trails in this area, but it's rewarding to simply wander around.

After about 3.5 miles, you get your first glimpse of Checkerboard Mesa, a huge sloping face of beige slickrock, etched with horizontal cross-bedding layers and vertical stress fractures caused by countless freeze-thaw cycles.

It's another mile to the official ❹ **Checkerboard Mesa viewpoint**, your last must-see stop. About a quarter-mile further on is the east entrance, marking the park boundary.

actually be inside park boundaries, the canyons in the immediate area are every bit as beautiful and exciting. Expect to spend roughly $180 per person (two-person minimum, if you're solo you'll pay closer to $330); options include family, regular and more extreme adventure trips. Gear and transportation are included.

Otherwise, if you're eager to strike off on your own, take a course instead. Courses cover all the basic knowledge you'll need – setting anchors, rappelling, problem-solving – and allow you to rent gear the day after so you can explore famous routes like the Subway or Keyhole on your own. Expect to spend from $150 to $200 per person (two-person minimum); some courses include gear rental in the price. For liability reasons, outfitters will *not* rent you any gear unless you've taken a course first.

There are dozens of fantastic canyons in the Zion area, the most popular technical route being the Subway (p63). Get a guidebook (Tom Jones' *Zion Canyoneering* is a good one) or look online at www.canyoneeringusa.com or http://climb-utah.com for more information.

Keyhole Canyon   CANYONEERING
Off Hwy 9 east of the Zion–Mt Carmel Tunnel, Keyhole is a gem of a narrow slot that drops down two 20ft rappels and into a cold pool swim. Local outfitters describe it as the route that offers the most bang for your buck. Relatively short, it's a great beginners canyon. It requires 100ft of rope and a wetsuit even in summer.

Orderville Canyon   CANYONEERING
Orderville Canyon, accessed off North Fork Rd on the park's east side, is another classic beginners route and has the added bonus of feeding into the Narrows at the canyon's end. You'll need 60ft of rope, a wetsuit outside of summer and a permit. Experienced canyoneers can turn this one into a full day by starting in Birch Hollow above Orderville. Hiker shuttle necessary.

Mystery Canyon   CANYONEERING
Mystery Canyon lets you be a rock star: the last rappel drops into the Virgin River before admiring crowds hiking the Narrows. It's accessed off Zion Ponderosa Ranch roads in East Zion; ask rangers for more information. Advance lottery permit required; hiker shuttle necessary.

FLASH FLOODS

If you plan on entering a slot canyon or the Narrows, make sure you check the daily flash-flood forecast at the visitor center or with the national weather service before you go. Even when the weather seems clear, you should watch for signs of a flash flood (p276) as a storm upstream can still lead to flooding. A September 2015 afternoon downpour raised the volume of water in Keyhole Canyon from 55 cubic ft per second to 2,630 cubic ft per second in 15 minutes, resulting in the deaths of seven canyoneers. Late summer is the primary season for floods, but they can happen at any time of year.

Pine Creek Canyon   CANYONEERING
A popular route with moderate challenges and rappels of 50ft to 100ft, Pine Creek has easy access from near the Canyon Overlook Trail in East Zion. A backcountry permit and wetsuit are required.

Cycling

In the park, cycling is only allowed on the Zion Canyon Scenic Drive (p68) and on the Pa'rus Trail (p52), both of which are very pleasant and popular. In fact, the lack of cars from April through October makes cycling a great way to see the canyon. We recommend that you shuttle your bike up to the Temple of Sinawava and then bike Zion Canyon Scenic Drive going downhill. Being under your own steam allows you to stop at turnouts where the shuttle doesn't. Do note that the park requires that you pull over and let shuttles pass. In practice this is not really much of an inconvenience and it keeps the majority of park visitors on the road, so be courteous.

Mountain biking is prohibited in the park, but there are other public land trails nearby. For more information on local trails or to arrange a rental, head to one of the bike shops in Springdale (p83).

Horseback Riding

Horses are allowed on most trails in the backcountry, though you'll need your own horse. Permits are not required for day trips;

maximum group size is six animals. The only overnight stock camp is on the Hop Valley Trail, off Kolob Terrace Rd.

Canyon Trail Rides   HORSEBACK RIDING
(☑ 435-679-8665, 435-772-3810; www.canyon rides.com; 1hr/half-day trips $40/80; ☺ Mar–Nov) Zion's official horseback-riding concessionaire operates across from Zion Lodge. Ride on the Sand Bench Trail along the Virgin River. There's a minimum age of seven/10 for the one-hour/half-day trip.

Rock Climbing

Zion Canyon contains some of the most famous big-wall climbs in the country, including Moonlight Buttress, Prodigal Sun, Touchstone and Space Shot. These are epic multipitch climbs that draw the best of the best for their challenge and beauty. However, there's not much for beginners or those who like single-pitch sport climbs. If you're interested in trying out rock climbing, you

---

WORTH A TRIP

DRIVING KOLOB TERRACE ROAD

Even in season you'll see relatively few other cars on this subtly scenic high-plateau road, where striking rock formation views alternate with pastoral rangeland. It's free to drive Zion's narrow waist, but if you do stop to picnic or hike, be ready to show your park pass or entrance receipt to rangers. There are no services up here besides some pit toilets at trailheads – the road is 22 to 33.5 miles long one way, so make sure you have a full tank of gas before starting out. The upper reaches of the road close due to snow from winter through spring.

In the tiny burg of Virgin, just shy of 14 miles west of Zion's south entrance, turn north off Hwy 9 onto Kolob Terrace Rd – keep your eyes peeled as this road is very easy to miss! A quarter-mile past the technical Grapevine trailhead is the turnoff for **Smith Mesa Road**. This well-graded dirt road (passable to cars when dry, impassable to all when wet) leaves the park after a mile as it winds along the top of Smith Mesa. The first few miles are worth the detour for the views back toward Tabernacle Dome, South Guardian Angel and Cougar Mountain. Back on Kolob Terrace Rd, past the Smith Mesa turnoff is the **Left Fork trailhead**, the end point for the popular canyoneering route called the Subway.

From there you start ascending until you're 3000ft above where you started. The white and red Navajo sandstones you see at eye level up here are the same as those seen at the top of Zion Canyon. A series of turnouts offer views of Spendlove and Fire-pit Knolls, cinder cones that are reminders of the volcanism that once dominated this region. About 13 miles from Hwy 9, the **Hop Valley trailhead** takes off across sandy rangeland toward the park's Kolob Canyons section. This point in the road is also about as far as snowplows go in winter.

Three miles past Hop Valley is the Wildcat Canyon trailhead, the start of the **Subway** (p63) and the **Northgate Peaks Trail** (p62). Just past this turnoff is one of the largest scenic turnouts along the road, with benches.

Some 21 miles from Hwy 9, you reach the junction for the graded gravel road to **Lava Point**. Don't make this journey without visiting the point, 1.8 miles further on. At 7890ft, this one-time fire lookout (the tower was removed in 2000) is one of Zion's highest and best vantage points. A virtual diorama of the park spreads before you, with views south to Arizona on clear days. There's also a six-site primitive **campground** (p76) here, and pit toilets. A half-mile further on you reach the trailhead for the **West Rim Trail** (p55).

Lava Point is a good place to turn around. However, you can continue along Kolob Terrace Rd to the **Kolob Reservoir**, 33.5 miles north of Hwy 9. It's a popular spot with local anglers and also offers free dispersed camping. Beyond the reservoir, the road reverts to dirt and continues 20 miles further to Hwy 14, outside Cedar City. Lingering snow and runoff make this stretch wet and hazardous through late June. If you plan on going this way, check road conditions with the visitor center first.

can sign up for a class or trip with a Springdale outfitter (p83).

If you are climbing, note that day climbs in Zion do not require a permit, though all overnights and bivouacs do.

Kids' Activities

With its can't-lose combo of rushing water, giant boulders to climb on and a landscape that looks like the backdrop for any number of fantasy novels, Zion is sure to keep children entertained. Do note that some of the more spectacular hikes require an arduous initial climb off the valley floor, so have your bag of tricks ready to keep everyone entertained. Also remember that some of the activities in Zion have a real element of danger; don't attempt anything beyond your children's ability levels, and if you're starting to feel anxious, don't hesitate to turn around.

From late May through late August, Zion National Park offers a series of children's programs for various age groups. Many are based at Zion Nature Center (Map p84; ☑435-772-3256; South Campground, off Hwy 9; ⊙1-7pm late May-Aug) FREE, but some take place at Zion Lodge or on trails. You might hunt for animal habitats along the Virgin River or hear stories about the life of the first pioneer settlers in the area. For schedules, check online (www.nps.gov/zion) or in the summer park newspaper.

Year-round, children aged six to 12 can earn a badge and become a Junior Ranger by completing the activity-filled *Junior Ranger Handbook* ($1) available at both visitor centers and the Human History Museum. If you have a little one under five, pick up the free Junior Ranger Helper Activity Sheet so they can earn a pin. The bookstores also sell *Zion Canyon Adventure,* a fun and informative illustrated 'guidebook' to the park.

Outside of these programs, wading in the Virgin River along Riverside Walk or the Pa'rus Trail is a good bet; in Springdale, tubing (p83) can make for a fun way to cool down. Teenagers will definitely enjoy the adventure involved in Zion's premier hikes such as the Narrows, Angels Landing or Hidden Canyon.

Springdale outfitters also offer canyoneering and rock-climbing trips tailored to meet family needs.

IT'S A BIRD, IT'S A PLANE, IT'S A CONDOR!

With a wingspan of up to 10ft, the endangered California condor is the largest feathered flyer in North America. In the past decade, captive-bred birds released around the Grand Canyon have moved north. In 2014, biologists confirmed that a couple were raising a chick in a Zion nest – the first ever documented occurrence in Utah. Condors seem to like to circle above Angels Landing and other tall park features. The Big Bend shuttle stop is a good vantage point from which to look for them, and they have also been spotted around Lava Point. Bring binoculars. Condors are basically big vultures, and they can be hard to differentiate from the common variety. To identify the real thing, look for all-black wings with a triangle of white at the tip underneath, visible when they fly.

Tours & Classes

From fascinating geological forces to extreme desert flora and fauna, there's a lot to learn around Zion National Park. The wide variety of ranger-led activities are a great place to start. Daily talks (more frequent June through August) at the Human History Museum (⊙9am-7pm late May-early Sep, 10am-5pm Mar-late May & early Sep-Nov, closed Nov-Feb) cover topics such as the survival of species in the desert and the culture of the area's ancients. Guided hikes explore topics like the power of water and indigenous plant life along some of the most popular trails, including Emerald Pools and Riverside Walk. Occasionally, evening programs are held at Watchman Campground and Zion Lodge, and Kolob Canyons hosts limited talks and walks of their own. Visitor centers post lists of each week's programs and a schedule is available online at www.nps.gov/zion.

Ride Along With A Ranger   DRIVING TOUR

(www.nps.gov/zion; Zion Canyon Visitor Center; ⊙May-Oct) FREE The entertaining, ranger-led Zion Canyon shuttle tour (90 minutes) makes stops not on the regular route. It's a great nonhiking alternative for those with limited mobility. Reserve up to three days in advance at the visitor center.

Zion Canyon Field Institute   TOUR
(☑435-772-3264, 800-635-3959; www.zionpark.
org; programs $45-85) Explore Zion by moon-
light, take a wildflower photography class,
investigate Kolob Canyons' geology or help
clean up the Narrows. All courses and tours
include some hiking.

🛏 SLEEPING

Zion itself has just one lodge and a few basic
campgrounds, which generally fill up from
mid-March through November. The majority of visitors sleep in Springdale (p85), just
outside the park's south entrance. If you
are tent camping, be forewarned that there
are not a lot of great sites in the immediate area; many campsites are essentially RV
parking lots.

Zion Canyon

Just inside Zion's south entrance are the
park's two main campgrounds, Watchman
and South. Both are adjacent to the visitor
center. Neither has showers, laundry facilities or a general store; these are available in
Springdale. There is a maximum stay of 14
days from March through November. Up to
two vehicles and six people are allowed per
site. If you show up at the end of the day and
the campgrounds are marked full, it's worth
asking if Watchman has any overflow sites
(no-show reservations).

CAMPGROUNDS IN & AROUND ZION NATIONAL PARK

CAMPGROUND	LOCATION	DESCRIPTION
Point Supreme Campground (p98)	Cedar Breaks	Cedar Breaks National Monument campground. Beautiful but remote; 1hr from Kolob Canyons.
Cedar Canyon (p97)	Cedar City area	Closest campground to Cedar City.
Duck Creek Campground (p97)	Hwy 14	Pine-shaded sites at a blissfully cool 8400ft, east of Cedar City. Water; no showers, no hookups. Remote.
Lava Point Campground (p76)	Kolob Terrace Rd	Tiny, primitive NPS ground high in the upcountry. Tents only, no water. One hour from Springdale.
Pine Valley Recreation Complex (p94)	St George area	Escape the heat in the mountain wilderness an hour north of St George.
Snow Canyon State Park Campground (p94)	St George area	Fabulous red-rock formations but little shade. Hot showers, water and electrical hookups. One hour from Springdale.
South Campground (p75)	Zion Canyon	Top choice in Zion. No electricity, no showers. First-come, first-served only.
Temple View RV Resort (p91)	St George	Attracts St George snowbirds who live here all winter. One hour from Springdale, lots of services. Not for tents.
Watchman Campground (p75)	Zion Canyon	Top choice in Zion. Some electric hookups, no showers.
Zion Canyon Campground & RV Resort (p85)	Springdale	Crowded, friendly Springdale site with pool and river access. Full hookups, hot showers, wi-fi. Convenient to Zion.
Zion Ponderosa Ranch Resort (p76)	East Zion	Upcountry mesa-top camping at activity-oriented ranch. Wi-fi, showers. 45 minutes from Springdale.
Zion River Resort (p87)	Virgin	Fancy RV campground with 70ft pull-throughs and river sites. Loads of amenities. Convenient to Zion; not great for tents.
Zion Mountain Trading Post (p76)	East Zion	East-side campground convenient to the park. Showers, laundry and full hookups.

 Drinking Water *Flush Toilets* *Ranger Station Nearby* *Great for Families* *Wheelchair Accessible*

Watchman Campground
CAMPGROUND **$**

(Map p84; ✆ reservations 877-444-6777; www.recreation.gov; Hwy 9, Zion National Park; tent sites $20, RV sites with hookups $30; ☉ year-round; 🐾) Towering cottonwoods provide fairly good shade for the 184 well-spaced sites at Watchman (95 have electricity), located south of the visitor center. Sites are by reservation (six months in advance) and you should book a minimum several months ahead, otherwise it's unlikely you'll get a spot. Fire grates, drinking water, RV hookups and flush toilets; no showers. Sites along the river cost $4 extra.

South Campground
CAMPGROUND **$**

(Map p84; ✆ 435-772-3256; Hwy 9, Zion National Park; tent & RV sites $20; ☉ year-round; 🐾) The South Campground sits north of the visitor center beside the busy Pa'rus Trail. The 127 campsites are entirely first-come, first-served, so show up before 9am for the best chances of finding an open site. The South Campground has no electrical hookups for RVs; generator use is allowed from 8am to 10am and 6pm to 8pm. There is a dump station, however.

Zion Lodge
LODGE **$$**

(✆ 888-297-2757, 435-772-7700; www.zionlodge.com; Zion Canyon Scenic Dr; cabin/r/ste $204/210/270; ❄@🛜) We love the stunning red-rock cliffs on all sides, and the coveted location in the middle of Zion Canyon (along with the red permit that allows you to drive to the lodge in shuttle season). But be warned: today's reconstructed lodge is not as grand as other national-park lodges

NUMBER OF SITES	ELEVATION	OPEN	RESERVATIONS AVAILABLE?	FACILITIES
25	10,350ft	Jun-Sep	yes	
13	8100ft	late May–Sep	yes	
87	8400ft	mid-May–Sep	yes	
6	7900ft	Jun-Oct	no	
55	6900ft	mid-May–Sep	yes	
29	3200ft	year-round	yes	
127	3940ft	year-round	no	
260	2800ft	year-round	yes	
184	3940ft	year-round	yes	
200	3898ft	year-round	yes	
18	6500ft	Mar-Nov	yes	
122	3552ft	year-round	yes	
22	5000ft	year-round	yes	

  Dogs Allowed (On Leash)   *Grocery Store Nearby*   *Restaurant Nearby*   *RV Dump Station*

IS ZION FIDO-FRIENDLY?

We can't say that Zion is the canine-friendliest park in the area. Dogs are only allowed on one trail, the Pa'rus, and perhaps because of that, few motels in the area allow pets. If you want to take your furry friend hiking, you can try the Bureau of Land Management (BLM) land south of Rockville; the small Springdale River Park also allows dogs. But honestly, you have more hiking options in Grand Staircase-Escalante National Monument, and lots of Kanab hotels put out the doggie welcome mat. So you might want to head that way.

About 4 miles west of Zion Canyon, **Doggy Dude Ranch** (☑435-772-3105; www.doggyduderanch.com; 800 Hwy 9; daycare/overnight $21/28) will keep your canine friend overnight. They provide large outdoor play areas with kiddie pools and they walk dogs big and small twice a day.

(the 1920s original burned down in 1966). Nevertheless, you'll need to reserve months in advance.

East Zion

Although not technically in the park, East Zion offers both a closer proximity to Bryce and Escalante and a higher elevation, meaning cooler temperatures in summer.

Zion Ponderosa Ranch Resort   LODGE **$**
(☑435-648-2700, 800-293-5444; www.zionponderosa.com; N Fork Rd, off Hwy 9; tent sites per person $11, RV sites $52, cabins $79-179; @🕾🕾) Families love this activity-rich ranch occupying 4000 acres east of Zion. Driving to Springdale takes about 45 minutes, but two trails lead directly from here into the park. You may never leave the property since you can bike, canyoneer, play sports and eat three meals a day here (packages available). Comfy cabins, sleeping up to six, share spotless bathroom facilities. Showers are available for all.

Zion Mountain Trading Post   CAMPGROUND **$**
(☑877-290-5756; http://zionrv.com; Hwy 9; tent sites $19, RV sites with hookups $29-39) If you're simply looking for a place to pitch your tent, this isn't a bad spot. Sites are more spacious here than in the RV parks around Springdale; public showers and laundry are new additions. It is close to the road though, and there's not much shade. It's located just outside Zion's east entrance.

Zion Mountain Ranch   CABINS **$$**
(☑866-648-2555, 435-688-1039, campground 435-648-3302; www.zmr.com; Hwy 9; cabins from $166; 🕾@) Six different cabin types and a

variety of larger lodges are available at this luxury ranch. Buffalo roam (and appear on the dinner menu), though if you're looking to completely unplug, note that it is a bit closer to the highway than might be expected. The rustic farm-to-table **restaurant** (lunch $15-20, dinner $20-45) offers the only gourmet dining in East Zion, and various activities, including horseback riding and fly fishing, can be arranged through the resort. It's located about 3 miles from Zion's east entrance.

Kolob Terrace Road

Kolob Terrace Rd is not the most convenient location, but you will certainly escape the crowds up here. There is free dispersed camping on public land along the road on the way up; stop by the BLM office (p93) in St George for a map and tips on where to go (you cannot camp on private land or in the national-park boundaries).

Lava Point Campground   CAMPGROUND **$**
(Lava Point Rd, Zion National Park; ☺ Jun-Oct) **FREE** Six first-come, first-served park sites 35 miles up Kolob Terrace Rd at 7900ft (one hour from the main entrance). Pit toilets, no water.

Kolob Canyons

There are no accommodations in this part of the park; most people stay in or around Cedar City. If you're camping, however, you may be able to get a backcountry site on the La Verkin Creek Trail (minimum 2-mile hike).

EATING

Zion Lodge has the only in-park dining. Most visitors bring a picnic or eat in Springdale (p88).

Castle Dome Café   CAFE **$**
(Zion Canyon Scenic Dr, Zion Lodge; mains $5-9; ⊙6:30am-5pm Mar-Oct) This counter-service cafe serves sandwiches, pizza, salads, Asianish rice bowls and ice cream. A beer garden serving local suds is located on the patio from May through mid-October.

Red Rock Grill   AMERICAN **$$**
(☎435-772-7760; Zion Canyon Scenic Dr, Zion Lodge; breakfast & sandwiches $6-15, dinner $16-30; ⊙6:30-10am, 11:30am-2:30pm & 5-9pm Mar-Oct, hours vary Nov-Feb) Settle into your replica log chair or relax on the big deck with magnificent canyon views. Though

---

ZION: OFF THE BEATEN PATH

In season, when the Zion Park Shuttle is standing-room only, popular trails can be a great place to meet travelers from around the world. But you do have choices if you want to get away from them all.

Outside of summer, you can explore the area of Zion known as the **Southwest Desert**. Rarely visited, there are two hikes here, the Chinle and the unofficial Coalpits Wash. Six campsites are located 5.5 miles in. Access is off Hwy 9, just south of Springdale on the north side of the road.

Perhaps the best option of all, however, is to do some **slickrock hiking**. East of the Zion–Mt Carmel Tunnel, anyone with a sense of adventure will be tempted to park at every turnout along the way and start scrambling around (do remember to stay on the rock though, and not step on the fragile cryptobiotic soil). Some trails end after 50ft; others traverse the desert slickrock for miles. It's easy to find some very narrow slots here, which you can peer down into from the top, and indeed, some classic canyoneering routes such as **Keyhole** (p71) and **Pine Creek Canyon** (p71) and are located back this way. While there are few official trails in East Zion, here are a few unofficial destinations to give you some ideas of what's out there. Remember that it can get very hot here, so bring plenty of water, a hat and sunscreen, and don't hike at midday in summer.

Many Pools This trail follows an open wash up the hillside, beginning with a string of dry cascades and lovely pools, some of which hold some interesting critters (such as tadpoles) depending on the water level and season. You can follow the wash up through the slickrock for about a mile, until you eventually reach the mouth of a canyon.

To get here, park at the first major turnout east of the second (small) tunnel on Hwy 9; it's about a mile away. The wash is on the other side of the road from the parking lot, but it's not immediately visible. You'll either need to hike over a small hill heading slightly east, or cross under the road using the tunnel to the east, which will put you directly on the path.

Shelf Canyon This is a fun little scramble to a secret canyon just east of the main tunnel. Short and sweet, it involves lots of low-grade bouldering and is definitely not for casual hikers. As you follow the canyon further back it gets increasingly narrow, eventually ending in a cave-like formation filled with narrow ledges that you can clamber up.

To get here, park at the overflow lot just east of the main tunnel on the north side – ie, not the lot with the bathrooms. From here you'll need to figure out how to get into the drainage (walk up the road a bit) and then it's up, up and away.

Nippletop Hiking up Nippletop (6715ft) is a great way to experience Zion's east-side wilderness. The hike is relatively short (3 miles round trip) and only ascends about 1500ft – steep, but not too steep. The summit is Class 3 (exposed but nontechnical), though, so you should only attempt this if you have climbing or mountaineering experience.

While spotting the Nipple shouldn't prove too difficult, finding the trail can be tricky, so it's recommended you study trip reports online together with a topo map in order to orient yourself before you go. The turnout for Nippletop is 1.9 miles east of the second (smaller) tunnel.

the dinner menu touts its sustainable-cuisine stance for dishes like roast pork loin and flatiron steak, the results are hit-or-miss. Dinner reservations recommended. Full bar.

❶ Information

If you plan to do any serious hiking or exploring, a good map is essential. National Geographic (www.natgeomaps.com) puts out a colorful, waterproof *Trails Illustrated* map (No 214) for Zion. The less snazzy park map from Zion Natural History Association (www.zionpark.org) also gets the job done. Both are available at park visitor centers.

In an emergency, call ☑ 911 or ☑ 435-772-3322 for national park rangers.

Zion Canyon Visitor Center (Map p84; ☑ 435-772-3256; www.nps.gov/zion; Hwy 9, Zion National Park; ⊘ 8am-7:30pm late May-early Sep, 8am-5pm rest of year) Several rangers are on hand to answer questions at the main visitor center; ask to see the picture binder of hikes to know what you're getting into. Find out about ranger-led activities here.

Zion Natural History Association (www.zionpark.org) runs the excellent visitor center bookstore and has a good online book selection for advance planning.

Zion Wilderness Desk (☑ 435-772-0170; www.nps.gov/zion; Zion Canyon Visitor Center; ⊘ 7am-7:30pm late May-Sep, 8am-4:30pm rest of year) Provides backcountry trail and camping information and permits. Some permits available online.

Kolob Canyons Visitor Center (☑ 435-586-0895; www.nps.gov/zion; Kolob Canyons Rd,

Zion National Park; ⊘ 8am-7.30pm late May-Sep, to 5pm rest of year) A small visitor center in the Kolob Canyons section of the park.

❶ Getting Around

SHUTTLE BUSES

How you get around Zion depends on the season. Between spring and fall (roughly mid-March to October), private vehicles are not allowed on Zion Canyon Scenic Dr. The park operates two free, linked shuttle loops. The **Zion Park Shuttle** makes nine stops along the canyon, from the main visitor center to the Temple of Sinawava (a 45-minute trip). The **Springdale Shuttle** makes six regular stops and three flag stops along Hwy 9 between the park's south entrance and the Majestic View Lodge in Springdale, the hotel furthest from the park. You can ride the Springdale Shuttle to Zion Canyon Giant Screen Theatre and walk across a footbridge into the park. The visitor center and the first Zion shuttle stop lie on the other side of the kiosk.

The propane-burning park shuttle buses are wheelchair-accessible, can accommodate large backpacks, and carry up to two bicycles or one baby stroller. Schedules change, but in high season park shuttles generally operate from 6am to 9:15pm, every five to 15 minutes on average.

PRIVATE VEHICLE

Although the majority of the main canyon is closed to private vehicles for much of the year, you can always drive Hwy 9, which traverses the park between the south and east entrances, via the **Zion–Mt Carmel Tunnel**. Note that parking near the south entrance is limited: there

---

SACRIFICE ROCK

Spend a week in Zion and you may not realize that ancient peoples had much of a presence here. The National Park Service does its best to protect and preserve the natural and cultural resources under its care, but when it comes to the rock art and ruins left by ancestral inhabitants, there's only so much they can do. The **South Gate Petroglyphs**, aka 'Sacrifice Rock,' are a case in point. The handful of intriguing designs and animals are a few steps from the road near the south entrance. What strikes visitors most, however, is not the petroglyphs themselves, but the overwhelming amount of modern graffiti surrounding them. 'Jayrod' may indeed rock, but did he need to let everyone know right here, for all eternity?

So you'll understand if Zion rangers do not advertise rock-art locations, and ruins are strictly off-limits. Ask a general, 'I've heard there are petroglyphs in the park?' and you'll get a purposely obtuse, 'Yes, I've heard that too,' in response. There is at least one other rock-art site close to a road. If you do your research and ask a specific question, the rangers can answer. But please remember to regard all ancient sites as you would a museum. These locations are both priceless artifacts and spiritual sites for the modern-day tribes whose ancestors created them.

SLOW: DESERT TORTOISE CROSSING

One of the most endangered park residents is the tortoise, which inhabits the Mojave and Sonoran Deserts. Though slow moving, a desert tortoise can live for up to 80 years, munching on wildflowers and grasses. With its canteen-like bladder, it can go up to a year without drinking. Using its strong hind legs, it burrows to escape the summer heat and freezing winter temperatures, and also to lay eggs. The sex of the hatchlings is determined by temperature: cooler for males, hotter for females.

Disease, predation and shrinking habitat have decimated the desert tortoise population. They like to rest in the shade, including under parked cars, so take a quick look around before driving away. They are often hit by high-speed and/or off-road drivers. If you see a tortoise in trouble, call a ranger. Do not pick it up, as a frightened tortoise may often pee on what it perceives to be an attacker, possibly leading to it dying of dehydration before the next rains come.

are parking lots at the main visitor center, the Human History Museum and Canyon Junction, but you shouldn't count on finding a spot unless you show up early. It's generally easier to find parking in Springdale and then take the shuttle to the park.

If you have an RV or trailer that is 7ft 10in wide or 11ft 4in high or larger and you plan on taking the Zion–Mt Carmel Tunnel, you must pay a permit fee of $15 since vehicles this big need both lanes. The fee is good for two trips. Between April and October, rangers are stationed at the tunnel from 8am to 8pm daily; at other times, ask at the entrance stations. Vehicles prohibited at all times include those more than 13ft 1in tall or more than 40ft long.

HIKER SHUTTLES

Outfitters offer hiker shuttles to one-way and hard-to-reach backcountry trailheads, including the Narrows (Top Down) on the east side of the park and the Subway access in the west. Rates per person start around $37; reservations are always required.

Zion Adventure Company (435-772-1001; www.zionadventures.com) The only outfitter that runs a daily shuttle service.

Red Rock Shuttle & Tours (435-635-9104; www.redrockshuttle.com) By reservation only; also offers tours.

Zion Rock & Mountain Guides (435-772-3303; www.zionrockguides.com) By reservation only.

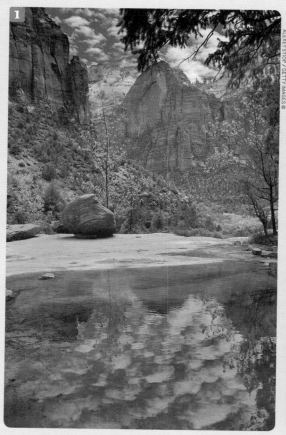

ALEXEY STIOP / GETTY IMAGES ©

JUSTIN REZNICK PHOTOGRAPHY / GETTY IMAGES ©

1. Emerald Pools (p52)
This popular Zion Canyon trail passes pools, grottoes and hanging gardens.

2. Watchman Trail (p52)
A short walk along the Virgin River takes hikers to a series of stunning overlooks.

3. Canyoneering (p68)
Rapelling into Zion's slot canyons is a sought-after backcountry experience.

4. The Narrows (p57)
Sometimes as much a swim as a hike, this trail follows the Virgin River though Zion Canyon..

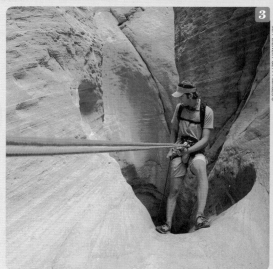

JEFF DIENER / GETTY IMAGES ©

Around Zion National Park

Best Places to Stay

➡ Under the Eaves Inn (p86)

➡ Desert Pearl Inn (p87)

➡ Seven Wives Inn (p91)

Best Places to Eat

➡ Whiptail Grill (p89)

➡ Riggatti's Wood Fired Pizza (p92)

➡ Painted Pony (p93)

➡ Centro (p96)

Why Go?

You may be tempted to speed out of Vegas with your foot on the gas and Zion firmly in your sights – after all, the park is less than three hours away via the interstate. But once you cross the state line, consider slowing down to explore the vast wilderness that surrounds you: Snow Canyon State Park, St George and Cedar Breaks National Monument are all worthy detours, with their own superb vistas and an array of fun activities, including mountain biking, cycling, climbing and cross-country skiing.

Even if time is short, it's likely you'll be based outside the park anyway, unless you've got a coveted park campsite. As far as towns go, Springdale is the pick of the bunch, with easy access and a range of accommodations and restaurants. For something a bit more off the beaten path, consider sleepy Cedar City for Kolob Canyons access, or idyllic Glendale, perfectly situated in between Zion, Bryce and Kanab.

When to Go
Zion National Park

May–Aug	Sep–Nov	Dec–Apr
Soaring heat; rains increase the risk of flash floods in July and August.	Clear, warm days; festivals in Cedar City and St George.	Snow at higher elevations; some trails may be closed.

Springdale

POP 548 / ELEV 3898FT

When the cottonwoods are budding against the red cliffs, Springdale is the perfect little park town, though more frequently it's a bottleneck of traffic entering Zion National Park. The main drag – well, the only drag – features eclectic cafes, galleries and restaurants touting local produce and organic ingredients. Many residents were drawn here for the surroundings, but you will occasionally run into a lifelong local who thinks they're 'just rocks.'

⦿ Sights

Grafton Ghost Town   GHOST TOWN

The freely accessible Grafton ghost town, outside Rockville, achieved its 15 minutes of fame in 1969 as the setting for the bicycle scene in *Butch Cassidy and the Sundance Kid*. Originally settled in 1859, the town never amounted to much. A restored 1886 school and church, a well-maintained cemetery and some pioneer cabins remain. In Rockville, 3.5 miles west of Springdale, take Bridge Rd north; cross the bridge and turn right on Grafton Rd. After half a mile follow the main road, which bears left and becomes gravel. A mile further, bear right at the sign. After another 2 miles, you'll pass the cemetery on your left, then drive a quarter-mile further to the ghost town. Park at the red gate.

La Verkin Overlook   VIEWPOINT

West of Virgin on Hwy 9, before La Verkin, a 1.5-mile gravel-and-dirt road leads south to La Verkin Overlook. Stop for a fantastic 360-degree view of the surrounding 40 sq miles, from Zion to the Pine Valley Mountains. Trails lead along the ridge above the Virgin River. This is a great sunset perch.

🏃 Activities

Mountain Biking

The area around Zion has a handful of heart-pumping mountain-bike trails through the desert – these are wicked-fun rides. The two most famous trail systems are the **JEM Trail** – fast singletrack through desert scrub along the canyon rim – and **Gooseberry Mesa**, a more technical slickrock route similar to what you'll find in Moab (and not for beginners). Note that Gooseberry Mesa access is rugged; you don't absolutely need high-clearance 4WD, but it is recommended. Further afield, the area around St George is another good spot for road and

mountain-bike trails. Ask at the bike stores for maps and more information. Zion Adventure Company also runs bike tours.

Zion Cycles   MOUNTAIN BIKING

(☑435-772-0400; www.zioncycles.com; 868 Zion Park Blvd; half-/full-day rentals from $28/38, car racks from $12; ⊙9am-7pm Feb-Nov) Next to Zion Mountain School, this is the most helpful bike shop in town, with lots of info on local trails and tandem, road and mountain-bike rentals. No tours.

Bike Zion   MOUNTAIN BIKING

(☑435-772-0320; www.bikingzion.com; 1458 Zion Park Blvd, Zion Rock & Mountain Guides; half-/full-day rental $25/35, car racks from $12; ⊙8am-8pm) Zion Rock's on-site sister cycle shop; has a variety of rentals and does tours. We never saw anyone in the store, so best call ahead.

Tubing

Tubing is prohibited within Zion but is quite popular outside the park. From Memorial Day through Labor Day, Zion Adventure Company and Zion Outfitters (p85) rent out river tubes ($17 per day), unless the water level is too low (or too high). The float stretches about 2.5 miles, and lasts from 90 minutes to two hours depending on the water flow. Good river play places include **Springdale River Park**, and from the campground at Zion Canyon Campground & RV Resort (p85).

Spa

Deep Canyon Adventure Spa   SPA

(☑435-772-3244; www.deepcanyonspa.com; 428 Zion Park Blvd, Flanigan's Inn; 1hr treatments from $99) After a hard day's hike, the river-stone massage will be your muscles' new best friend.

☞ Tours & Outfitters

If you're eager to try out canyoneering or rock climbing but don't have the gear or necessary experience, stop in at one of the following outfitters to sign up for a trip or a course. All outfitters offer half-day, full-day, family and adventure-level tours. Outfitters with storefronts also offer gear rental for the Narrows (wetsuits, drysuits, neoprene booties, etc). There are also a few off-road 4WD tours available.

Zion Adventure Company   ADVENTURE SPORTS

(☑435-772-1001; www.zionadventures.com; 36 Lion Blvd; canyoneering day from $177; ⊙8am-8pm Mar-Oct, 9am-noon & 4-7pm Nov-Feb) The main outfitter in town and certainly the most organized. The focus is on renting gear for the Narrows, but it also offers a good selection of canyoneering and climbing trips and courses. Solo travelers looking to bring the price down for guided trips by hooking up with others should try here first. Canyoneering and camping equipment for sale.

Zion Mountain School ADVENTURE SPORTS
(☎435-633-1783; www.guidesinzion.com; 868 Zion Park Blvd; canyoneering day from $175; ☺8am-8pm Mar-Oct, hours vary Nov-Feb) Local outfitter located behind the Zion Noodle Company, offering gear rental, courses and guided trips. It has public showers ($5).

Springdale

0 — 500 m
0 — 0.25 miles

Zion Rock & Mountain Guides ADVENTURE SPORTS
(☑435-772-3303; www.zionrockguides.com; 1458 Zion Park Blvd; canyoneering day $195; ⊗8am-8pm Mar-Oct, hours vary Nov-Feb) More down-to-business than other outfitters, and especially good for sporty types. Guides have a good reputation, though the in-store service is hit-or-miss.

Zion Outfitters ADVENTURE SPORTS
(☑435-772-5090; http://zionoutfitter.com; 95 Zion Park Blvd; bike/tube rentals from $25/17; ⊗7:30am-8pm Mar-Oct, hours vary Nov-Feb) Ideally located at the park entrance, this is the smallest of the outdoor stores. Handy for cruiser bikes, tube rentals and other gear. It also has public showers ($5).

Mild to Wild Rhino Tours ADVENTURE TOUR
(☑435-216-8298, 866-964-7961; www.mildtowild rhinotours.com; adult/under 12yr $135/65) Drive it yourself with Mild to Wild Rhino Tours. Guides teach you to use the four-seat, open-air Yamaha Rhino utility vehicle and then lead you around BLM lands like Gooseberry and Little Creek Mesa. The 'wild' option is if their experts drive while you ride.

Zion Outback Safaris ADVENTURE TOUR
(☑866-946-6494; www.zionjeeptours.com; adult/child under 12yr $60/45) Backroad 4WD tours in a 12-seat modified truck.

🛏 Sleeping

Springdale has a good selection of midrange to boutique hotels, upscale chains and smaller B&Bs, plus one campsite. Just 4 miles southwest is Rockville, which has a further selection of cheaper B&Bs. Note that many of the area B&Bs do not serve breakfast, but instead provide guests with a restaurant voucher in town, in order to cater to those who want an early start. If you're looking for cheaper lodging, you'll need to head to Hurricane (pronounced 'Her-uh-kin'), 22 miles west, with all the usual motel chains.

Springdale

Zion Canyon Campground & RV Resort CAMPGROUND $
(☑435-772-3237; www.zioncamp.com; 479 Zion Park Blvd; tent/RV sites with hookups $35/45; @🛜🕸🐾) Water and tubing access at this 200-site campground are just across the Virgin River from the national park. Attached to the Quality Inn Motel; shared amenities

SMITHSONIAN BUTTE BACKCOUNTRY BYWAY

Stratified buttes, slickrock pinnacles and balancing rocks are all part of the attraction on this challenging 9-mile backcountry drive. Though rated for regular passenger vehicles, the road is not well maintained – ruts can be giant and a high-clearance 4WD vehicle is preferable. In Rockville turn south on Bridge Rd and cross the river. The road will veer before you get to the left-hand turn for Smithsonian Butte Rd. (Follow signs to the right and you'll reach Grafton Ghost Town; p83).)

Start your trip counter here. Once you turn south, you'll be winding your way up with **Wire Valley** on your right and **Horse Valley** on the left: this initial 1-mile ascent is locally known as Cry Baby Hill and is the steepest and hardest part of the drive. The raggedly eroded formation to the southeast is **Eagle Crags**. Make sure to look around as you ascend. About a mile up the road the first panorama of Zion National Park formations unfolds; stop along the way to look at the other angles that follow. At 4.5 miles, the road to **Gooseberry Mesa**, a premier mountain-biking destination, branches off to the right. Shortly after, you're rounding **Smithsonian Butte** on BLM land to your left, in an area where petroglyphs have been found. The drive is almost over as you descend onto a plain and into **Apple Valley**. From there Hwy 59 leads toward Hurricane in one direction, and Arizona in the other.

include a heated pool, laundry, camp store, playground and restaurant. It's mainly for RVs, though it can be a handy backup for tent campers if you can't get a spot in the park. Not all sites have shade. Pets in RVs only.

Zion Park Motel   MOTEL **$**
(☑435-772-3251; www.zionparkmotel.com; 865 Zion Park Blvd; r from $94; ❋☎❄) It's a wonder what a coat of paint can do for old wood-paneled rooms. Microwaves and minifridges are the main perks at this family-owned and central budget option.

★**Under the Eaves Inn**   B&B **$$**
(☑435-772-3457; www.undertheeaves.com; 980 Zion Park Blvd; r incl breakfast $95-185; ❋☎) From colorful tractor reflectors to angel art, the owners' collections enliven every corner of this quaint 1930s bungalow. The fireplace suite is huge; other character-filled rooms are snug. Hang out in the arts-and-crafts living room or on Adirondack chairs and swings in the gorgeous gardens. The best room is the upstairs suite with clawfoot tub. Local restaurant coupon for breakfast.

Canyon Vista Suites B&B   B&B **$$**
(☑435-772-3801; www.canyonvistabandb.com; 897 Zion Park Blvd; ste incl breakfast $149-179; ❋☎) All the homey comfort of a B&B, coupled with the privacy of a hotel. Individual entrances lead out from Southwestern or Old World–esque rooms onto a wooden porch or a sprawling patio and lawn with river access. Breakfast coupons; hot tub on-site.

Red Rock Inn   B&B **$$**
(☑435-772-3139; www.redrockinn.com; 998 Zion Park Blvd; cottages incl breakfast $169-209; ❋☎) Five romantic country-contemporary cottages spill down the desert hillside, backed by incredible red rock. Enjoy the full hot breakfast (egg dish and pastries) that appears at the door either on the hilltop terrace or your private patio. One suite features an outdoor hot tub.

Novel House Inn   B&B **$$**
(☑435-772-3650, 800-711-8400; www.novelhouse. com; 73 Paradise Rd; r $139-159; ❋) Incredible detail has gone into each of the author-themed rooms: Rudyard Kipling has animal prints and mosquito netting, and a pillow in the Victorian Dickens room reads 'Bah humbug.' Breakfast coupons; hot tub.

Zion Canyon Bed & Breakfast   B&B **$$**
(☑435-772-9466; www.zioncanyonbandb.com; 101 Kokopelli Circle; r incl breakfast $115-190; ❋☎) Deep canyon colors echo the scenery and over-the-top Southwestern styling. Everywhere you turn there's another gorgeous red-rock view framed perfectly in an over-sized window. Full gourmet breakfasts and mini-spa.

Canyon Ranch Motel   MOTEL **$$**
(☑435-772-3357, 866-946-6276; www.canyon ranchmotel.com; 668 Zion Park Blvd; r $109-169; ❋☎❄) Small, cottage-like buildings surround a shaded lawn with redwood swings, picnic tables and a small pool at this 1930s motor-court motel. Rooms are thoroughly modern; apartments have kitchenettes.

Quality Inn Zion Park MOTEL **$$**
(☎ 435-772-3237, 877-424-6423; www.zioncamp.
com; 479 Zion Park Blvd; r from $130; @ 🛜 🐾)
Good-value rooms with microwave and
fridge at this Quality Inn, renovated in 2014.
It's adjacent to the campground.

Driftwood Lodge HOTEL **$$**
(☎ 888-801-8811, 435-772-3262; www.driftwood
lodge.net; 1515 Zion Park Blvd; r $159-229; ❄️ 🛜
🐾 🐾) Rich textures and dark leathers mold
the upscale style of thoroughly remodeled
rooms at this eco-minded lodging. Some of
the contemporary suites have pastoral sunset views of field, river and mountain beyond. Has an expansive pool on the grounds.
Breakfast included.

Flanigan's Inn HOTEL **$$**
(☎ 800-765-7787, 435-772-3244; www.flanigans.
com; 428 Zion Park Blvd; r from $189, ste from $279;
❄️ 🛜 🐾) Rejuvenate your spirit by indulging
in a seaweed and mineral mud wrap, walk-
ing the hilltop meditation labyrinth and
sinking into your king-size bed in front of
a crackling fire. Suites are deliciously plush
with vaulted ceilings, bold color schemes
and tasteful art; most sleep up to six. Stand-
ard rooms vary, so check out a few first.
There are also two villas.

Cliffrose Lodge HOTEL **$$**
(☎ 435-772-3234, 800-243-8824; www.cliffrose-
lodge.com; 281 Zion Park Blvd; r $200-219, ste from
$269; ❄️ 🛜 🐾) Kick back in a lounge chair
or take a picnic lunch to enjoy on the five
gorgeous acres of lawn and flower gardens
leading down to the river. High-threadcount
linens and pillow-top mattresses are among
the upscale touches. Suites sleep up to six
and feature full kitchens. This is a good
high-end choice for families.

★**Desert Pearl Inn** HOTEL **$$$**
(☎ 888-828-0898, 435-772-8888; www.desertpearl.
com; 707 Zion Park Blvd; r incl breakfast from $229;
❄️ @ 🐾) How naturally stylish: twig sculp-
tures decorate the walls and molded metal
headboards resemble art. Opt for a spacious
riverside king suite to get a waterfront patio.
The most sophisticated design in town and
popular with hip Angelenos.

Rockville & Around

Zion River Resort CAMPGROUND **$**
(☎ 435-635-8594, 888-822-8594; www.zionriver
resort.com; Hwy 9, Virgin; tents $43, RVs $49-62,
cabins $95-259; ⊙ year-round; @ 🛜 🐾) The
massive RV resort outside Virgin, 12 miles
west of Springdale, caters to upscale big rigs
with long pull-throughs and phone and cable
hookups. There are only a handful of tent

HIKING THE NARROWS: DO YOU NEED THE GEAR?

All outfitters in town feature a Narrows rental package, which generally includes some
combination of canyoneering shoes, neoprene socks, hiking stick and a wet- or drysuit.
But if you find yourself balking at the price tag that comes with most of these packages
($23 to $53 depending on the season), the next thought that pops into your head will
probably be, 'Do I really need all this stuff anyway?' This is a fair question to ask, and the
answer depends largely on your own experience, current river conditions and how far
you plan on going. The short answer is that you don't need anything in the package – you
will see people in all sorts of attire trying to hike the Narrows, some of which is quite
comical – but what you are wearing will greatly influence your comfort level and thus
your overall enjoyment. To help you decide, remember the following:

➡ You are going to get wet, and when the water temperature is below 50°F (10°C),
hypothermia is a real danger.

➡ It is cooler and shadier in the Narrows than elsewhere in Zion.

➡ You will be walking through fast-moving currents on slippery rocks – a sturdy walking
stick is like having a third leg.

➡ If you are carrying electronics, you obviously don't want them to get wet.

If you're still unsure, go to an outfitter the day before and talk to both employees and
customers returning gear. Most hikers will be eager to share their opinions with you. For
the record, we did the overnight hike in mid-April. On the first day we left around noon
and wore no gear (just a swimsuit and closed-toed sandals) and were reasonably com-
fortable. On the second day, we awoke to 40-degree (4°C) weather and were waist-deep
in icy water by 8:30am. Needless to say, we were glad to have a drysuit!

THE ART OF THE CANYON

With such incredible natural surrounds, it's no wonder that so many artists find inspiration in the canyon. You'll see the results hanging all over town in Springdale: in restaurants, hotels and B&Bs. A number of galleries in town carry the work of various local photographers, painters and sculptors, including the big three photographers: David Pettit, David West and Michael Fatali. Gallery hours can be as mercurial as their owners. From north to south:

David J West Gallery (801 Zion Park Blvd; ⊙10am-9pm Tue-Sun Mar-Oct, to 8pm Nov-Feb) Iconic local-landscape photography; sells some photo gear.

De Zion Gallery (1051 Zion Park Blvd; ⊙10am-9pm Wed-Sun Mar-Oct) Large studio with many Utah artists represented.

Fatali Gallery (☑877-250-8848; http://fatali.com; 839 Zion Park Blvd; ⊙11am-8pm Thu-Mon) Otherworldly colors in sensational nature photography. Arguably the most impressive of Springdale's galleries.

LaFave Gallery (☑435-772-0464; www.lafavegallery.com; 1214 Zion Park Blvd; ⊙11am-6pm) Large collection of ceramics, jewelry, sculpture and paintings, but pride of place here goes to the work of local photographer David Pettit. Also sells signed prints.

Worthington Gallery (☑435-772-0291; 789 Zion Park Blvd; ⊙8am-7pm) Represents 20 different potters from across the Southwest.

---

sites and camping cabins (no linens). Quality shower rooms, coin laundry, barbecue pavilion, guest kitchen, heated pool, and game and media room are tops. Pets in RVs only.

Bunk House at Zion GUESTHOUSE $
(☑435-772-3393; www.bunkhouseatzion.com; 149 E Main St; s/d incl breakfast $80/95; 🛜) 🌿 Renewable energy use, recycled flooring and organic breakfasts help the ranch-style Bunk House at Zion stay green. Two rooms only; shared bathroom.

Desert Thistle Bed & Breakfast B&B $$
(☑435-772-0251; www.thedesertthistle.com; 37 W Main St; r incl breakfast $135-150; 🌡🛜🏊) A big backyard pool makes the romantic, modern Desert Thistle Bed & Breakfast a top choice on hot summer days. Rates include a breakfast voucher for use in Springdale.

✖ Eating

The closest chain supermarkets are in Hurricane, 22 miles west of Springdale. Note that many places in town limit hours or close entirely from December through February.

Café Soleil CAFE $
(205 Zion Park Blvd; mains $6.50-12; ⊙7am-4pm; 🛜🌿) The food is every bit as good as the free-trade coffee. Try the Mediterranean hummus wrap or giant vegetable frittata; pizza and salads too. It's a good spot to grab sandwiches for hiking. Breakfast served till noon.

Oscar's Cafe SOUTHWESTERN $
(www.cafeoscars.com; 948 Zion Park Blvd; mains $12-18; breakfast $6-12; ⊙8am-9pm) From green-chile laden omelets to pork *verde* burritos (with a green salsa), expect big servings of Southwestern spice. There's also smoky ribs, garlic burgers and beer on tap. The Mexican-tiled patio with twinkly lights (and heaters) is a favorite hang-out in the evening. The breakfast is quite popular.

MeMe's Cafe CAFE $
(www.memescafezion.com; 975 Zion Park Blvd; breakfast & lunch $8-13, dinner $11-17; ⊙7am-9pm) For a coffee and sweet crêpes, make MeMe's your first stop of the day. It also serves paninis, quiches and salads, and, for dinner, beef brisket and pulled pork.

Park House Cafe CAFE $
(1880 Zion Park Blvd; breakfast $6-11; ⊙8am-2pm Mar-Oct; 🛜) Wake up as late as you like: Park House Cafe serves its Asiago bagel with egg and avocado – along with organic coffee and other breakfast items – until 2pm. It's a sweet little spot on the edge of town with an artsy vibe. Plans to serve dinner may be on the horizon.

Zion Deli DELI $
(866 Zion Park Blvd; sandwiches $8; ⊙9am-8:30pm) Sharing a space with a souvenir shop, this one-counter wonder turns out good sandwiches (including boxed lunches for the park), breakfasts, chocolates and ice cream, all to go.

Sol Foods Downtown
Supermarket
MARKET $

(☎435-772-3100; 995 Zion Park Blvd; ⏰7am-11pm Apr-Oct, 9am-8pm Nov-Mar) Springdale's grocery store has a decent selection, with plenty of variety, organic items and some camping-friendly meals. There's also a salad bar and deli with $6 sandwiches. Groceries are pricey, however.

Farmers' Market
MARKET $

(www.zionharvest.org; 1212 Zion Park Blvd; ⏰9am-noon Sat May–mid-Oct) Don't miss the farmers market in the Bit & Spur parking lot on Saturday morning.

★Whiptail Grill
SOUTHWESTERN $$

(☎435-772-0283; 445 Zion Park Blvd; mains $11-17; ⏰noon-9pm Mar-Nov; 🛜🍸) The old gas-station building isn't much to look at, but deep shade and fresh tastes abound: think gorgeous chile rellenos and *carne asada* (beef) tacos grilled to perfection. Desserts are rich with a kick. Outdoor patio tables fill up quick.

Spotted Dog
MODERN AMERICAN $$

(☎435-772-0700; www.flanigans.com; 428 Zion Park Blvd; breakfast $8, mains $13-24; ⏰7-11am & 5-9pm Mar-Nov) One of the more inventive top-end dining choices in Springdale, the Spotted Dog has a seasonal menu with a focus on regional specialties. Expect delicacies like Cedar Mountain lamb shank, wild game meatloaf and Rocky Mountain trout. Spacious dining areas plus two outdoor patios.

Flying Monkey
PIZZA $$

(☎435-772-3333; www.pizzainzion.com; 975 Zion Park Blvd; pizzas $12-16, mains $12-30; ⏰8am-9:30pm) Wood-fired goodness at great prices, though service is slow. Expect interesting ingredients like fennel and yellow squash on your roast veggie pizza or Italian sausage with the prosciutto on your oven-baked sandwich. Also serves breakfast.

Bit & Spur Restaurant
& Saloon
SOUTHWESTERN $$

(www.bitandspur.com; 1212 Zion Park Blvd; mains $13-28; ⏰5-11pm daily Mar-Oct, 5-10pm Thu-Sat Nov-Feb; 🛜) Sweet-potato tamales and chile-rubbed rib-eyes are two of the classics at this local institution. Inside, the walls are wild with local art; outside on the deck it's all about the red-rock sunset. Full bar.

Thai Sapa
ASIAN $$

(145 Zion Park Blvd; mains $10-27; ⏰noon-9:30pm) This mix of Thai, Chinese and Indian cuisine is your only Asian-cuisine option in town.

🍷 Drinking & Nightlife

Most of the restaurants serving dinner in town also have beer and wine on the menu. Only a select few have a full bar. If you just want a beer, remember you'll also have to order at minimum an appetizer (eg chips and salsa) per Utah state law. You can grab six-packs at Sol Foods supermarket.

★Deep Creek Coffee Co
CAFE

(932 Zion Park Blvd; ⏰6am-4pm; 🛜) The town's best coffee, with espresso drinks and fresh pastries ($3 to $6) daily.

Zion Canyon Brew Pub
BREWERY

(www.zionbrewery.com; 95 Zion Park Blvd; ⏰noon-9pm; 🛜) The local brewery has a killer location, with an outdoor patio that cozies up to the Virgin River and the park entrance. Nine varieties of suds are on tap, from Red Altar to Delusion Ale. It does have a full food menu, but all you really need are the pretzel sticks ($3) and you're good to go.

Jack's Sports Grill
SPORTS BAR

(☎435-772-3700; 1149 Zion Park Blvd; ⏰noon-10pm) Jack's has a full bar and serves pub grub (sandwiches, rice bowls and all-day breakfast; $9 to $16), but the real reason you're here is to catch the big game on one of the many big screens.

☆ Entertainment

OC Tanner Amphitheater
THEATER

(☎435-652-7994; www.dixie.edu/tanner; 300 Lion Blvd; adult/child $15/6; ⏰mid-May–Aug) Outdoor amphitheater surrounded by red rock; stages classical, bluegrass, country and other concerts and performances.

Zion Canyon Giant Screen Theatre
CINEMA

(www.zioncanyontheatre.com; 145 Zion Park Blvd; adult/child $8/6) Catch the 40-minute *Zion Canyon: Treasure of the Gods* on a six-story screen – it's light on substance but long on beauty. Also look for local outdoors documentaries and one Hollywood flick at 7pm ($2 extra).

❶ Information

There's no town information office; go to www.zionpark.com and www.zionnationalpark.com. The nearest full-service hospital is in St George.

Zion Canyon Medical Clinic (☎435-772-3226; 120 Lion Blvd; ⏰9am-5pm Tue-Sat Mar-Oct, shorter hours Nov-Feb) Walk-in urgent care.

Zion Park Laundry (865 Zion Park Blvd; per load $1.75; ⏰7am-10pm) Unstaffed laundromat on main street; soap available ($1).

ℹ Getting Around

PRIVATE VEHICLE

If you're staying in Springdale, it's definitely best to use the shuttle to get around as parking can be a real headache. If you're just passing through, arrive before 9am to secure a parking spot. In town you can park along the main road, but not in lots belonging to local businesses. Try the free park-and-ride lot across from the Majestic View Hotel if nothing is available; if all else fails, there is a **pay lot** (Lion Blvd; $10 per day) behind the Zion Adventure Company.

SHUTTLE

The free **Springdale Shuttle** makes six regular stops and three flag stops along Hwy 9 between the park's south entrance and the Majestic View Lodge in Springdale, the hotel furthest from the park. You can ride the Springdale Shuttle to the Zion Canyon Brewery and walk across a footbridge into the park. The visitor center and the first Zion shuttle stop lie on the other side of the kiosk. The shuttle operates from early spring through late fall, and runs from 7am to 9:30pm in summer, with slightly shorter hours in the shoulder seasons. You'll never wait more than 15 minutes for a bus.

St George

POP 76,817 / ELEV 2860FT

Nicknamed 'Dixie' for its warm weather and southern location, St George has long been attracting winter residents and retirees. Brigham Young, second president of the Mormon church, was one of the first snowbirds in the one-time farming community here. An interesting-if-small historic downtown core holds some interest, but it's the area outside of town, where you're quickly immersed in magnificent desert scenery, that's most appealing. Snow Canyon State Park is a great place to go cycling, rock climbing and hiking.

The abundant and affordable lodging make this an oft-used stop between Las Vegas and Salt Lake City – or en route to Zion National Park after a late-night flight. The town lies about 41 miles (up to an hour) from Zion National Park's south entrance and 33 miles (30 minutes) from the Kolob Canyons' entrance on I-15.

◉ Sights

Pick up a free, full-color, historic-building walking tour brochure at the visitor center. The intersection of Temple and Main Sts is at the heart of the old town center.

Dinosaur Discovery Site   MUSEUM
(www.dinosite.org; 2180 E Riverside Dr; adult/child under 12yr $6/3; ⊙10am-6pm Mon-Sat, 11am-5pm

Sun, shorter hours Oct-Feb) St George's oldest residents aren't retirees from Idaho, but Jurassic-era dinosaurs. Entry gets you an interpretive tour of the huge collection of tracks, beginning with a video. The casts were first unearthed by a farm plow in 2000 and rare paleontology discoveries, such as dinosaur swim tracks, continue to be made.

Brigham Young Winter Home   MUSEUM
(☑ 435-673-2517; 67 W 200 North; ⊙10am-6:30pm) FREE A tour of the Mormon leader's seasonal home and headquarters illuminates early town and experimental-farming history.

Jacob Hamblin Home   MUSEUM
(☑ 435-673-2161; Santa Clara Dr; ⊙9am-6:30pm) FREE For another evocative picture of the Mormon pioneer experience, head 5 miles north of town to Santa Clara and the 1863 Jacob Hamblin Home, where orchards still grow.

Children's Museum   MUSEUM
(www.sgchildrensmuseum.org; 86 S Main St; suggested donation $3; ⊙10am-6pm Tue-Sat) St George has plenty of 'No' signs: no touching this, no climbing that, no sitting here and definitely no skateboarding anywhere. So if the kids are starting to get a little antsy, let them loose here, where they can touch, climb and play to their heart's delight. It's best suited for ages two to 10.

Daughters of Utah Pioneers Museum   MUSEUM
(DUP; www.dupinternational.org; 145 N 100 East; ⊙10am-5pm, closed Wed & Sun) FREE Two floors packed full of pioneer artifacts, furniture, photographs, quilts, guns and so on.

Mormon Tabernacle   RELIGIOUS
(490 S 300 East; ⊙9am-dusk) Built in 1877, the red-brick Mormon Tabernacle hosts free music programs and tours.

🏃 Activities

Snow Canyon State Park (p93) is the best destination for hikers; mountain bikers will want to check out the Bearclaw Poppytrail singletrack through the desert just west of town. Other good mountain bike destinations include the JEM Trail and the Gooseberry Mesa Trail (p83). Road cyclists can follow popular bike paths all the way to Snow Canyon.

Being a retirement community, there are several golf courses to pick from. Find out more at www.stgeorgecitygolf.com.

Red Rock Bicycle Company MOUNTAIN BIKING
(☑ 435-674-3185; www.redrockbicycle.com; 446 W
100 S; mountain bikes per 24hr $50, car racks from
$15; ⊙ 9am-7pm Mon-Sat, 11am-5pm Sun) Rentals and servicing available.

Bicycles Unlimited MOUNTAIN BIKING
(☑ 435-673-4492; www.bicyclesunlimited.com; 90
S 100 East; mountain-bike rentals per 4hr/8hr/24hr
from $39/49/59, car rack $15-22; ⊙ 9am-6pm
Mon-Sat) Rentals available.

Desert Rat Outdoor Store OUTDOOR EQUIPMENT
(☑ 435-628-7277; www.thedesertrat.net; 468 West
St; ⊙ 9am-6pm Mon-Sat) This outdoor store
will outfit you for any activity and provide
area advice. Also sells all the gear you might
need.

Paragon Adventures ADVENTURE SPORTS
(☑ 435-673-1709; www.paragonadventure.com) Offerings from this popular outfitter range from
road or mountain-bike tours, rock climbing,
small-group canyoneering, interpretive hikes
and popular zip-line adventures.

✦✦ Festivals & Events

Dixie Roundup SPORTS
(☑ 435-628-8282) A mid-September weekend
full of Western fun, including a parade and
rodeo.

St George Marathon SPORTS
(www.stgeorgemarathon.com) This October event
takes over the town, attracting runners from
all 50 states.

🛏 Sleeping

St George offers the cheapest lodging near
Zion and has a plethora of generic motels,
some with rates that dip below $50 in the
off-season. Rates listed are for high season.

Campers should check out sites in Snow
Canyon State Park (p93). A bit further are
campsites at Red Cliffs Recreation Area
(near Hurricane), the Baker Dam Recreation
Area (north up Hwy 18) and the USFS campground in Pine Valley (p94).

Temple View RV Resort CAMPGROUND $
(☑ 800-776-6410, 435-673-6400; www.templeview
rv.com; 975 S Main St; RV sites with hookups $42;
@ 🛜 ⅏) The 260 sites at this cheek-by-jowl
lot accommodate RVs as long as 45ft. The
baking-hot tent spots are not recommended. Amenities include a rec room, business
center, swimming pool, gym, putting green,
cable hookups and wi-fi. It's not a top choice
as far as scenery goes, but it is a good Plan B
if the Zion sites are booked up.

Dixie Palm Motel MOTEL $
(☑ 866-651-3997, 435-673-3531; www.dixiepalms
motel.com; 185 E St George Blvd; r from $79;
❄ 🛜 ⅏) It may not look like much outside,
but regular maintenance and TLC put the
Dixie Palm at the head of the low-budget
pack. The 15 rooms have minifridges and
microwaves; a handful have full kitchens.

America's Best Inn & Suites MOTEL $
(☑ 800-718-0297, 435-652-3030; www.bestzion.
com; 245 N Red Cliffs Dr; r from $82; ❄ @ 🛜 ⅏)
Well positioned for fast out-of-town access
off I-15, this economic choice is also surprisingly quiet. Minifridges and microwaves
come standard in the tidy rooms. Coin laundry on property.

★ **Seven Wives Inn** B&B $$
(☑ 435-628-3737, 800-600-3737; www.sevenwives
inn.com; 217 N 100 West; r incl breakfast $99-199;
❄ @ 🛜 ⅏) Two 1800s homes and a cottage
feature lovely bedrooms and suites surrounded by well-tended gardens and a small pool.
The name is from settler times, when one of
the owners harbored fugitive polygamists (including one with seven wives) in the 1880s.
The cottage is pet-friendly.

Green Gate Village INN $$
(☑ 800-350-6999, 435-628-6999; www.greengate
villageinn.com; 76 W Tabernacle St; r incl breakfast
$119-199; ❄ 🛜 ⅏) Book a room or a whole
house from among nine historic buildings
brought together to make a historic village
of sorts, complete with a general store. Antiques such as white-iron beds and ornate
carved vanities figure prominently in all the
lodgings.

Best Western Coral Hills MOTEL $$
(☑ 435-673-4844, 800-542-7733; www.coralhills.
com; 125 E St George Blvd; r incl breakfast from $130;
❄ @ 🛜 ⅏) You can't beat being a block or two
from downtown restaurants and historic
sights. Waterfalls and spiffed-up decor set
this locally owned franchise apart.

Red Mountain Resort & Spa RESORT $$$
(☑ 877-246-4453, 435-673-4905; www.redmountain
resort.com; 1275 E Red Mountain Circle; retreats from
$205 per person; ❄ @ 🛜 ⅏) A Zen-chic sensibility pervades this low-profile adobe resort,
right down to the silk pillows that echo the
copper color of surrounding cliffs. Full meals,
guided hikes, spa services and yoga classes
are generally included, depending on the accommodation package. There's an additional
$25 resort fee. It's located 7 miles northwest
of town on Snow Canyon Pkwy.

St George

🍴 Eating & Drinking

⭐ **Riggatti's Wood Fired Pizza** PIZZA $
(📞435-674-9922; 73 N Main St; pizzas $8-18; ⊙11am-9pm Mon-Sat) With a fanatical local following, this tiny pizzeria is a boon for travelers searching for thin-crust pizzas with bubbling mozzarella and pesto. Grab one of the very few counter seats and save room for hot cinnamon sticks.

Thomas Judd's General Store ICE CREAM $
(76 Tabernacle St; ice cream from $2.69; ⊙9:30am-5:30pm Mon-Sat) Stop for a sweet scoop of ice cream or piece of nostalgic candy.

Bear Paw Cafe CAFE $
(75 N Main St; mains $6.50-10; ⊙7am-3pm) This homey cafe is St George's most popular breakfast spot. It also does lunch.

Bombay Cafe INDIAN $
(📞435-673-8888; http://bombaycafesg.com; 57 N 700 East; mains $8-12; ⊙11am-2:30pm & 5-9pm Mon-Sat) This tiny hole-in-the-wall is run by Pakistani batik artist Shazad Sheikh and his wife, Rabia. You'll find chicken tikka masala, daal chana, naan and other classic dishes alongside a small collection of handmade saris and scarves for sale.

Twenty-Five on Main CAFE $
(25 N Main St; mains $6.50-10; ⊙8am-9pm Mon-Thu, to 10pm Fri & Sat) A hip, modern cafe with sidewalk tables. Homemade cupcakes are not all it does well – check out the breakfast panini, warm salmon salad and pasta primavera, overflowing with veggies.

Xetava Gardens Cafe MODERN SOUTHWESTERN $$
(📞435-656-0165; www.xetavagardenscafe.com; 815 Coyote Gulch Ct; breakfast $7-12, lunch & dinner $11-18; ⊙9am-5pm Sun-Thu, 9am-9pm Fri & Sat; 🅿) We'd drive much further than 8 miles for the organic, locavore fare served here in a stunning red-rock setting. Expect small

St George

◎ Sights

◎ Activities, Courses & Tours

🛏 Sleeping

◎ Eating

◎ Drinking & Nightlife

plates (mahi cake), salads, ciabatta sandwiches, gyros and burgers.

★ **Painted Pony**　　　MODERN AMERICAN $$$
(☑435-634-1700; www.painted-pony.com; 2 W St George Blvd, Ancestor Sq; lunch $9-11, dinner $25-36; ☺11:30am-10pm Mon-Sat, 4-10pm Sun) Gourmet comfort food and great salads. At dinner you might choose juniper-brined pork chops; at lunch, meatloaf with a port-wine reduction and rosemary mashed potatoes.

George's　　　PUB
(http://georgescornerrestaurant.com; 2 W St George Blvd; ☺7am-midnight; 🛜) This central pub anchors historic Ancestor Sq. Local beers on tap and a reliable if unexcing menu; breakfast is also served.

☆ Entertainment

Two Friday evenings a month in summer the city screens family movies on the Town Square.

Tuacahn Amphitheater　　　THEATER
(☑800-746-9882, 435-652-3300; www.tuacahn. org) Ten miles northwest in Ivins; hosts

musicals in summer and other performances year-round.

ⓘ Information

Additional information is available at www. utahsdixie.com and www.sgcity.org.

Chamber of Commerce (☑435-628-1658; www.stgeorgechamber.com; 97 E St George Blvd; ☺9am-5pm Mon-Fri) The visitor center caters to relocating retirees, and has loads of city info.

Dixie Regional Medical Center (☑435-251-1000; www.intermountainhealthcare.org; 1380 E Medical Center Dr; ☺24hr)

St George Field Office (☑435-688-3200; 345 E Riverside Dr; ☺7:45am-5pm Mon-Fri, 10am-3pm Sat) Get interagency information on surrounding public lands: USFS, BLM and state parks. Topographic maps and guides available. Staff can also suggest where to camp for free on BLM land.

Utah Welcome Center (☑435-673-4542; http://travel.utah.gov; 1835 S Convention Center Dr, Dixie Convention Center; ☺8:30am-5:30pm) Statewide information 2 miles south of St George. There's a wildlife museum (think taxidermy) on-site with the same hours.

ⓘ Getting There & Away

Taxis ($15 to downtown) and all the big-chain car-rental companies are represented at the St George airport. Note that Las Vegas McCarran International Airport, 120 miles southwest, often has better flight and car-rental deals than Utah airports. Salt Lake City is 305 miles north.

Greyhound (☑435-673-2933; www.greyhound.com; 1235 S Bluff St) Buses depart from the local McDonald's en route to Salt Lake ($57, 5½ hours) and Las Vegas ($21, two hours).

St George Municipal Airport (SGU; www.flysgu.com; 4550 S Airport Parkway) Located 13.5 miles southeast of town.

St George Express (☑435-652-1100; www.stgeorgeexpress.com) Shuttle service to Las Vegas ($39, two hours) and Zion National Park.

Snow Canyon State Park

Gila monsters, roadrunners and desert tortoises populate a landscape of undulating slickrock and ancient lava flows in this popular state park. Snow Canyon (☑435-628-2255; http://stateparks.utah.gov; 1002 Snow Canyon Dr, Ivins; per vehicle $6; ☺day use 6am-10pm; 🐾) is a 7400-acre sampler of southwest Utah's famous land features, 11 miles northwest of St George. Easy trails – perfect for kids – lead to tiny slot canyons, petrified sand dunes, lava tubes and red-and-white

AROUND ZION NATIONAL PARK SNOW CANYON STATE PARK

domes. Summers are blazing hot: visit in early morning or come in spring or fall. The park was named after prominent Utah pioneers Lorenzo and Erastus Snow, not frozen precipitation, but for the record it does very occasionally snow here.

Hiking trails loop off the main road. **Jenny's Canyon Trail** is an easy 1-mile round-trip to a short slot canyon. Wind through a cottonwood-filled field and past ancient lava flows to a 200ft arch on **Johnson Canyon Trail** (2-mile round-trip). A 1000ft stretch of vegetation-free **sand dunes** serves as a playground for the kiddies, old and young, near a picnic area.

The best hike, however, is a loop that combines several different trails. Departing from the visitor center, follow the lovely **Hidden Pinyon** nature trail to the petrified sand dunes. From the top of the former dunes you descend to a 27,000-year-old lava flow via the Butterfly and **Lava Flow** trails – bring a headlamp to explore the lava tube along the latter. From here, follow the **West Canyon** trail south, returning to the visitor center by way of **Three Ponds**. The total distance is roughly 3.5 miles.

Cycling is popular on the main road through the park, a 17-mile loop from St George (where you can rent bikes). There's also great **rock climbing** in the park, particularly for beginners, with over 150 bolted and sport routes, plus top-roping.

Apart from during the unrelenting summer, the 29-site **campground** (800-322-3770; http://utahstateparks.reserveamerica.com; tent/RV sites with partial hookups $16/20;) is great, and so scenic. You can reserve one of the 22 bookable sites (14 with electrical and water hookups) up to four months in advance. There are showers and dump station available. Campers do not pay the park's day-use fee.

Pine Valley Mountain Wilderness Area

Mountains rise sharply in the 70-sq-mile **Pine Valley Wilderness Area** (435-652-3100; www.fs.usda.gov/dixie) in the Dixie National Forest, 32 miles northwest of St George off Hwy 18. The highest point, **Signal Peak** (10,365ft), remains snowcapped till July, and rushing streams lace the mountainous area. The St George Field Office provides information and free backcountry permits.

When the desert heat blurs your vision, Pine Valley offers cool respite. Most hikes here begin as strenuous climbs. The 5-mile round-trip **Mill Canyon Trail** and the 6-mile **Whipple Trail** are most popular, each linking with the 35-mile **Summit Trail**.

Pine Valley Recreation Complex (877-444-6777; www.recreation.gov; tent sites $15, RV sites no hookups $15-30; mid-May–Sep), 3 miles east of Pine Valley, has six pine-shaded campgrounds at 6900ft and 55 sites in total. They all have water but no showers or hookups; bring mosquito repellent.

Cedar City

POP 29,162 / ELEV 5850FT

This sleepy college town comes to life every summer when the Shakespeare Festival takes over. Associated events, plays and tours continue into fall. Year-round you can make one of the many B&Bs a quiet home base for exploring the Kolob Canyons section of Zion National Park or Cedar Breaks National Monument. At nearly 6000ft elevation, cooler temperatures prevail in Cedar City (even snowing occasionally in May) compared to Springdale or St George.

◉ Sights & Activities

Frontier Homestead State Park Museum   MUSEUM
(http://stateparks.utah.gov; 635 N Main St; admission $3; 9am-5pm Mon-Sat;) Kids love the cabins and brightly painted 19th-century buggies, as well as the garden full of old farm equipment to run through. Living history demos take place June through August.

Cedar Cycle   CYCLING
(435-586-5210; http://cedarcycle.com; 38 E 200 South; road/mountain-bike rental per day $29/39; 9am-5:30pm Mon-Fri, 10am-2pm Sat) After you rent a bike, the knowledgeable staff can point you to local trails.

✦ Festivals & Events

Utah Shakespeare Festival   THEATER
(800-752-9849, 435-586-7878; www.bard.org; Southern Utah University, 351 W Center St; tickets from $28) Southern Utah University has been hosting Cedar City's main event since 1962. From late June into September, three of the Bard's plays and three contemporary dramas take the stage. From mid-September into late October three more plays are presented – one Shakespearean, one dramatic and one musical. Productions are well regarded, but don't miss the extras, all free: 'greenshows' with Elizabethan minstrels, literary seminars dis-

cussing the plays, and costume classes. Back-stage and scene-changing tours cost extra.

Groove Fest MUSIC
(www.groovefestutah.com) A long weekend music fest in late June grooves with folksy and funky sound.

Neil Simon Festival THEATER
(www.simonfest.org) American plays staged mid-July to mid-August.

🛏 Sleeping

Anniversary House B&B $$
(☎800-778-5109, 435-865-1266; www.theanniversaryhouse.com; 133 S 100 W; r incl breakfast $99-144; ❋ 🔊 🐾) Remarkably comfortable rooms, a great-to-talk-to host and thoughtful extras make this one of our faves. Savor freshly baked cake and complimentary beverages in the mission-style dining room or lounge around in the landscaped backyard. Outdoor kennel available.

Cedar City

◎ Sights
1 Frontier Homestead State Park
   Museum.....................................C2

✪ Activities, Courses & Tours
2 Cedar Cycle..................................C4

🛏 Sleeping
3 Amid Summer's Inn......................C4
4 Anniversary House.......................C4
5 Big Yellow Inn.............................B4
6 Garden Cottage B&B....................C3
7 Iron Gate Inn..............................C3

✸ Eating
8 Centro..C3
9 Sonny Boy's BBQ.........................C3

🍷 Drinking & Nightlife
10 Grind Coffeehouse......................C3

Cedar City

Garden Cottage B&B B&B $$
(✆435-586-4919, 866-586-4919; www.thegarden cottagebnb.com; 16 N 200 W; r incl breakfast $119-129; ❄🖨) Romantic vines climb up the steep-roofed cottage walls, and in season a fantasia of blooms grows in encompassing gardens. If you like antiques and quilts, you're going to love Garden Cottage. The owner has done an amazing job displaying family treasures. No in-room TVs.

Amid Summer's Inn B&B $$
(✆888-586-2601, 435-586-2600; www.amidsum mersinn.com; 140 S 100 W; r incl breakfast $115-185; ❄@🖨) Tasteful additions have brought the guest-room count to 10 at this 1930s home-based B&B. Common areas and some rooms have a Victorian feel; others are more over-the-top trompe l'oeil fantasies. Accommodating hosts; great breakfasts.

Iron Gate Inn B&B $$
(✆800-808-4599, 435-867-0603; www.theiron gateinn.com; 100 N 200 West; r incl breakfast $119-149; ❄@🖨) With an on-site winery, this distinct 1897 Second Empire Victorian house features large, modern-luxury guest rooms, rambling porches and a big yard. Enjoy your breakfast on the large shady patio.

Big Yellow Inn B&B $$
(✆435-586-0960; www.bigyellowinn.com; 234 S 300 W; r incl breakfast $99-199; ❄@🖨) A purpose-built Georgian Revival inn with room to roam: dining room, library, den and many porches. Upstairs rooms are elegantly ornate.

BRIAN HEAD SKI RESORT

Did someone mention skiing in the desert? From Thanksgiving through April, snow bunnies come to test the closest slopes to Las Vegas. Advanced skiers might grow impatient with the short trails (except on a powder day), but there's lots to love for beginners and intermediates at Brian Head Resort (✆435-677-2035; www.brianhead.com; Hwy 143; one-day lift ticket adult/child $45/32), 35 miles northeast of Cedar City. Lines are usually short and it's the only resort in Utah within sight of red rock. Here's the lowdown: 1320ft vertical drop; base elevation, 9600ft; 640 acres and seven high-speed triple lifts. In summer, the mountain morphs into a premier cycling destination and fun zone for children (think climbing wall, trampoline, zip-lines etc).

Downstairs, the ground-floor walk-out rooms are simpler and a bit more 'country.' The owners also oversee several adjunct B&B properties and vacation rentals around town.

✗ Eating & Drinking

★ Centro PIZZA $
(✆435-867-8123; 50 W Center St; pizzas $10-15; ◷11am-10pm Mon-Sat) Serving wood-fired Neapolitan pizza and heaping bowls of fresh salad in a sleek atmosphere, Centro is a hub for hedonist appetites. Touches like hand-crushed tomato sauce and homemade fennel sausage up the ante. Though the wine list is basic, there's a good selection of brews. Good service.

Sonny Boy's BBQ BARBECUE $
(✆435-867-8010; 126 N Main St; sandwiches $7-9, mains $11-16; ◷11am-9pm Mon-Thu, to 10pm Fri & Sat) Locals love the piles of Texas-style, slow-smoked meat and fun side dishes such as fried pickles. Eat in or take out.

Rusty's Ranch House STEAK $$
(✆435-586-3839; http://rustysranchhouse.com; 2275 E Hwy 14; mains $13-26; ◷5-10pm Mon-Sat) Two miles east of town on Hwy 14, this steakhouse certainly has the nicest location in Cedar City. Expect moose and bison heads on the wall and all the steak, ribs and buffalo wings you can eat.

Grind Coffeehouse CAFE
(19 N Main St; ◷7am-6pm Mon-Sat; 🖨) Hang out with the locals and have a barista-made brew, a great hot sandwich ($6 to $10) or a big salad. Sometimes there's music on the menu.

❶ Information

Cedar City & Brian Head Tourism & Convention Bureau (✆800-354-4849, 435-586-5124; www.scenicsouthernutah.com; 581 N Main St; ◷8:30am-5pm Mon-Sat) Area-wide info and free internet use. A tiny **Daughters of Utah Pioneers Museum** (◷1-4pm Wed-Fri, 10am-4pm Sat) is located here.

Cedar City Ranger Station (✆435-865-3200; www.fs.usda.gov/dixie; 1789 N Wedgewood Lane; ◷8am-5pm Mon-Fri) Provides Dixie National Forest information and can advise on USFS campsites.

Valley View Medical Center (✆435-868-5000; www.intermountainhealthcare.org; 1303 N Main St; ◷24hr)

❶ Getting There & Away

Greyhound (✆800-231-2222; www.greyhound.com; 1495 W 200 North)

Highway 14

Scenic Hwy 14 leads 42 miles over the Markagunt Plateau, cresting at 10,000ft and offering awesome vistas of Zion National Park and Arizona to the south. This is essentially a backdoor route between Zion and Bryce or Escalante: it's not quite as stunning as Hwy 9, though it will be less crowded, and along the way you'll find several hiking trails, campgrounds and overlooks, as well as the main attraction, Cedar Breaks National Monument. Stop by the Cedar City Ranger Station for maps and information. Though Hwy 14 remains open all winter, you may want snow tires between November and April. The closest campsite to Cedar City is the pleasant USFS **Cedar Canyon** (☑877-444-6777; www.recreation.gov; Hwy 14; tent & RV sites without hookups $15; ☺late May-Sep; 🐾), located 11 miles east of town and 31 miles from Zion's Kolob Canyons entrance at an elevation of 8100ft.

Hiking and cycling trails past the Cedar Breaks National Monument turnoff on Hwy 14 have tremendous views, particularly at sunset. They include the short (less than a mile one way) **Cascade Falls** and **Bristlecone Pine Trail** and the 32-mile **Virgin River Rim Trail**. A signed turnoff 24.5 miles from Cedar City leads to jumbled lava beds.

Boating and fishing are the activities of choice at **Navajo Lake**, 25 miles east of Cedar City. You can rent canoes ($25) or motorboats ($80 to $175) or stay over in a historic 1920s cabin at **Navajo Lake Lodge** (☑702-646-4197; www.navajolakelodge.com; cabins $89-144; ☺May-Oct). The rustic lodgings include fireplaces and bedding, but no refrigerators.

Five miles further east, **Duck Creek Visitor Center** (☑435-682-2432; Hwy 14; ☺10am-5pm late May-early Sep) provides information for nearby trails and fishing in the adjacent pond and stream. Here at 8400ft, the 87 pine-shaded sites at **Duck Creek Campground** (☑877-444-6777; www.recreation.gov; Hwy 14; tent & RV sites without hookups $15-30; ☺mid-May-Sep; 🐾) are blissfully cool in summer. The ever-expanding log-cabin town at nearby **Duck Creek Village** (www.duckcreekvillage.com) has more services, including a couple of restaurants, realty offices, cabin-rental outfits, a laundromat and an internet cafe. The village area is big with off-road enthusiasts – ATVs in summer and snowmobiles in winter.

About 7 miles east of Duck Creek, a signed, passable dirt road leads the 10 miles to

---

WORTH A TRIP

PAROWAN GAP

People have been passing this way for millennia, and the **Parowan Gap** (www.blm.gov) FREE petroglyphs prove it. Look closely as you continue walking along the road to find panels additional to those signed – there are some particularly unusual etchings here. Archeoastronomers believe that the gap in the rocks opposite the petroglyphs may have been used as part of an ancient, astronomically based calendar. Cedar City's tourism office has colorful interpretive brochures explaining site details. It's located 21 miles north of town off Hwy 130.

Strawberry Point, an incredibly scenic overview of red-rock formations and forest lands.

Cedar Breaks National Monument

ELEV 10,300FT

Sculpted cliffs and towering hoodoos glow like neon tie-dye in a wildly eroded natural amphitheater encompassed by **Cedar Breaks National Monument** (☑435-586-0787; www.nps.gov/cebr; Hwy 148; 7-day pass per person $5; ☺late May-mid-Oct). The majestic kaleidoscope of magenta, salmon, plum, rust and ocher rises to a height of 10,450ft atop the Markagunt Plateau. The compact park lies 22 miles east and north of Cedar City, off Hwy 14. (There are no cedar trees here, by the way: early pioneers misidentified the evergreen junipers.)

This altitude gets more than a little snow, and the monument's one road, Hwy 148, is closed from sometime in November through at least May. Summer temperatures range from only 40°F to 70°F (4°C to 21°C); brief storms drop rain, hail and even powdery white snow. In season, rangers hold geology talks and star parties at the small visitor center. A free app (Cedar Breaks Scenic Drives) guides visitors with smartphones past nine waypoints.

No established trails descend into the breaks, but the park has five viewpoints off Hwy 148 and there are rim trails. **Ramparts Trail** – one of southern Utah's most magnificent trails – leaves from the visitor center. The elevation change on the 4-mile round-trip is only 400ft, but it can be tiring because of the overall high elevation. **Alpine Pond Trail** is a lovely, though less dramatic, 2-mile loop.

Once snow blankets the trails, the park is open to cross-country skiing and snow-mobiles (which must follow the groomed trail above Hwy 148). On weekends, volunteers staff a heated yurt where you can stop for hot chocolate and ski-trail information.

The monument's **Point Supreme Campground** (tent & RV sites without hookups $18; ⊙ Jun-Sep; 🏕) has water and restrooms; 10 of the 25 sites can be reserved. It's about an hour's drive from Zion's Kolob Canyons.

Glendale & Around

There's not much along the 10 miles of Hwy 89 between the junctions with Hwy 14 and Hwy 9, but it certainly is ideally located: you're within an hour's drive of Zion, Bryce, and Kanab, and two hours from the Grand Canyon's North Rim. You can also access Escalante via the town of Glendale. Across from the Historic Smith Hotel on Hwy 89, the rough-and-tumble **Glendale Bench Road** (300 N) takes off toward Johnson Canyon (paved) and Skutumpah (definitely not paved) roads (p146). A faded 'Glendale Bench' sign marks the intersection.

◉ Sights

Maynard Dixon Home & Studio   MUSEUM
(self-guided tour $10; ⊙10am-5pm Mar-Nov) In Mt Carmel, the *Architectural Digest*–noted Maynard Dixon Home & Studio is where renowned Western painter Maynard Dixon (1875–1946) lived and worked in the 1930s and '40s. Docent-led tours ($20) are by appointment only. Look for the house at mile 84 on Hwy 89, about 6 miles south of Glendale; it's easy to miss.

Thunderbird Foundation
for the Arts   ARTS CENTER
(☑435-648-2653; www.thunderbirdfoundation. com; 2200 S State St, Mt Carmel; ⊙10am-5pm Mar-Nov) Runs exhibits and artist retreats in adjacent spaces.

🛏 Sleeping & Eating

Historic Smith Hotel   B&B $
(☑435-648-2156, 800-528-3558; www.historic smithhotel.com; 295 N Main St, Glendale; r incl breakfast $79-89; 🅿🛜🐾) Fifty miles from Bryce and 26 miles to Zion, Glendale is a historic little Mormon town founded in 1871. Today there's an excellent B&B to draw you in. The six-room Historic Smith Hotel, c 1927, offers true rural hospitality. Pull up a

cozy quilt among the antiques in your room, bubble away in the whirlpool hot tub or roam the 2 acres of gardens and fruit trees (late summer, pick your own fruit).

Arrowhead Country Inn & Cabins   B&B $$
(☑888-821-1670, 435-648-2569; www.arrow headbb.com; 2155 S State St; r $79-119, cabins $129-269, both incl breakfast; 🅿🛜🅿🐾) The quilt-covered four-poster beds sure are comfy at Arrowhead Country Inn & Cabins. The east fork of the Virgin River meanders behind the inn and a trail leads from here to the base of the white cliffs. It's located 2.5 miles north of Mt Carmel Junction and Hwy 9. Two cabins are pet-friendly.

Best Western East Zion
Thunderbird Lodge   MOTEL $$
(☑800-780-7234, 435-648-2203; www.bestwest ernutah.com; cnr Hwys 9 & 89, Mt Carmel Junction; r $150-170; 🅿🛜🐾) The Navajo facade is just that; the rooms within are standard Best Western. A bit pricey for what it is, but could serve if you need a Plan B.

Wild Boar Bistro   AMERICAN $$
(☑435-648-2778; www.wildboarbistro.com; 305 N Main St, Glendale; lunch $8-12, dinner $14-26; ⊙11am to 9pm Tue-Sat) Next door to the Historic Smith Hotel, the Wild Boar Bistro conjures up an Old West spirit with its breezy wooden porch and outdoor sizzling grill.

Las Vegas

POP 603,488 / ELEV 2030FT
A blazing oasis of glitz and fantasy aiming to please, Las Vegas, with over 36 million visitors per year, delivers on its promises. The city demands a suspension of disbelief, so don't take it too seriously. A Bible-toting Elvis kisses a giddy couple that just pledged eternity in a drive-thru wedding chapel. A blue-haired granny pumps dollar bills into a slot machine while millions are lost in no-limit Texas Hold'em poker rooms. A porn star saunters by a nightclub's velvet rope. Blink, and you'll miss it. Sleep? Fuhgeddaboutit.

Then again, park travelers using Las Vegas as a jumping-off point may be more interested in the cheap flights and proximity to the great outdoors. Red Rock Canyon is just a fat-tire hop away, and even the Grand Canyon's South Rim is a doable day trip from the Strip.

◉ Sights

Roughly 4 miles long, the Strip, aka Las Vegas Blvd, is the center of gravity in Sin City.

The Stratosphere caps the north end and Mandalay Bay is at the south end, near the airport. Whether you're walking or driving, distances on the Strip are deceiving; a walk to what looks like a nearby casino usually takes longer than expected.

Downtown Las Vegas is north of the Strip and home to the city's oldest hotels and casinos: expect a retro feel, cheaper drinks and lower table limits.

The Strip

New York–New York   CASINO
(☎702-740-6969;   www.newyorknewyork.com; 3790 Las Vegas Blvd S; ⏰24hr) Opened in 1997, the mini-megalopolis of New York–New York features scaled-down replicas of the Big Apple's landmarks, such as the **Statue of Liberty** and a miniature **Brooklyn Bridge**, out front. Rising above are perspective-warping replicas of the Chrysler, Empire State and Ziggurat buildings. Wrapped around the hotel's flashy facade is the pièce de résistance: the **Big Apple roller coaster** (1 ride/day pass $14/25; ⏰11am-11pm Sun-Thu, 10:30am-midnight Fri & Sat; ♿), with cars resembling NYC taxicabs.

★**CityCenter**   LANDMARK
(www.citycenter.com; 3780 Las Vegas Blvd S) We've seen this symbiotic relationship before (think giant hotel anchored by a mall 'concept') but the way that this futuristic-feeling complex places a small galaxy of hypermodern, chichi hotels in orbit around the glitzy **Crystals** (www.crystalsatcitycenter. com; 3720 Las Vegas Blvd S; ⏰10am-11pm Sun-Thu, to midnight Fri & Sat) shopping center is a first. The uber-upscale spread includes the subdued, stylish Vdara (p103), the hush-hush opulent **Mandarin Oriental** (www. mandarinoriental.com; 3752 Las Vegas Blvd S) and the dramatic architectural showpiece **Aria** (☎702-590-7111; www.aria.com; 3730 Las Vegas Blvd S; ⏰24hr), whose sophisticated casino provides a fitting backdrop to its many drop-dead gorgeous restaurants.

Cosmopolitan   CASINO
(☎702-698-7000;   www.cosmopolitanlasvegas. com; 3708 Las Vegas Blvd S; ⏰24hr) Hipsters who thought they were too cool for Vegas finally have a place to go where they don't need irony to endure – or enjoy – the aesthetics of the Strip. Like the new Hollywood 'It' girl, the Cosmopolitan casino looks absolutely fabulous at all times. A steady stream of ingenues and entourages parades through the lobby, along with anyone else who adores contemporary art and design.

Planet Hollywood   CASINO
(www.planethollywoodresort.com; 3667 Las Vegas Blvd S; ⏰24hr) Lest you mistake that Planet Hollywood is to Hollywood what the Hard Rock is to rock 'n' roll, two steps into the casino will instantly clear up the difference. We're not sure what the inordinate number of scantily clad women gyrating on poles above the table games have to do with the movies but, if that's your thing, plunk down your cash on blackjack in the Pleasure Pit. The coolest movie stuff actually hangs in some of the most inconspicuous places, like by the elevators or in the hallways: go figure.

Paris Las Vegas   CASINO
(☎702-946-7000;   www.parislasvegas.com; 3655 Las Vegas Blvd S; ⏰24hr) Welcome to the City of Light, Vegas-style. This mini version of the French capital may not exude the true charm of Paris – it feels like a themed section of Disney World's Epcot – but efforts to emulate the city's great landmarks, including a 34-story Hotel de Ville replica and famous facades from the Paris Opera House and the Louvre, make it a fun stop.

Fountains of Bellagio   FOUNTAIN
(www.bellagio.com; Bellagio; ⏰shows every 30min 3-7pm Mon-Fri, noon-7pm Sat & Sun, every 15min 7pm-midnight daily; ♿) **FREE** With a backdrop of Tuscan architecture, the Bellagio's faux Lake Como and dancing fountains are the antithesis of the Mojave Desert – although the resort does use reclaimed water. The fountain show's recorded soundtrack varies, so cross your fingers that it will be Italian opera or Ol' Blue Eyes crooning 'Luck Be a Lady,' instead of country-and-western twang.

Caesars Palace   CASINO
(☎702-731-7110; www.caesarspalace.com; 3570 Las Vegas Blvd S; ⏰24hr) Despite recent upgrades that have lent the once-gaudy Palace a more sophisticated air, some of the resort's original features from the swinging '60s have survived. Out front are the same spritzing fountains that daredevil Evel Knievel made famous when he jumped them on a motorcycle on December 31, 1967 (and ended up with a shattered pelvis and a fractured skull. More than two decades later, his son Robby repeated the attempt – more successfully).

LINQ & High Roller   LANDMARK
(☎800-223-7277; www.thelinq.com; 3545 Las Vegas Blvd S; High Roller ride before/after 5:50pm $25/35; ⏰High Roller noon-2am daily) A mammoth open-air dining, entertainment and retail complex, the $550-million LINQ project has transformed what was once a lackluster stretch

Las Vegas Strip

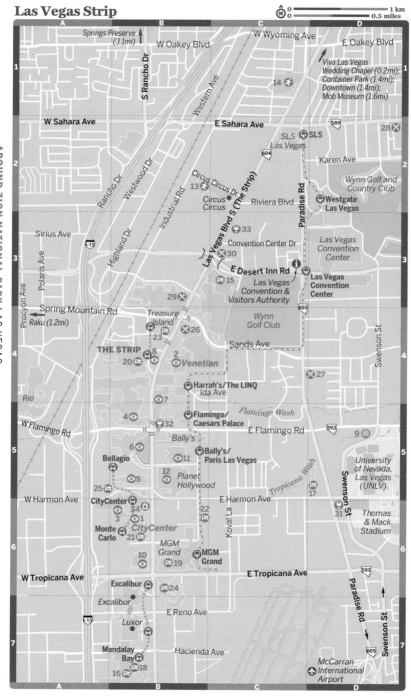

Springs Preserve (3.1mi)

W Oakey Blvd

W Wyoming Ave

E Oakey Blvd

Viva Las Vegas Wedding Chapel (0.2mi); Container Park (1.4mi); Downtown (1.4mi); Mob Museum (1.6mi)

W Sahara Ave

E Sahara Ave

SLS Las Vegas

Karen Ave

Wynn Golf and Country Club

Circus Circus Dr

Circus Circus

Riviera Blvd

Westgate Las Vegas

Las Vegas Blvd S (The Strip)

Sirius Ave

Las Vegas Convention Center

Convention Center Dr

E Desert Inn Rd

Las Vegas Convention & Visitors Authority

Las Vegas Convention Center

Spring Mountain Rd

Raku (1.2mi)

Treasure Island

Wynn Golf Club

Sands Ave

THE STRIP

Venetian

Harrah's/The LINQ

Ida Ave

Rio

Flamingo Wash

W Flamingo Rd

Flamingo/Caesars Palace

E Flamingo Rd

Bally's

University of Nevada, Las Vegas (UNLV)

Bellagio

Bally's/Paris Las Vegas

Planet Hollywood

W Harmon Ave

CityCenter

E Harmon Ave

Koval La

Tropicana Wash

Thomas & Mack Stadium

Monte Carlo

CityCenter

MGM Grand

MGM Grand

W Tropicana Ave

E Tropicana Ave

Excalibur

Paradise Rd

E Reno Ave

Excalibur

Luxor

Mandalay Bay

Hacienda Ave

Swenson St

McCarran International Airport

S Rancho Dr

Western Ave

Paradise Rd

Westwood Dr

Rancho Dr

Industrial Rd

Highland Dr

Polaris Ave

Procyon Ave

of the center Strip between the Flamingo and Quad casino hotels. Eclectic shops, buzzing bars, trendy restaurants, live-music venues and even a bowling alley line the pedestrian promenade, where you'll also find the **High Roller**, a 550ft-tall observation wheel.

Mirage Volcano   LANDMARK
(Mirage; ⊙shows 8pm-midnight; 🚹) **FREE** When the trademark artificial volcano erupts with a roar out of a 3-acre lagoon, it inevitably brings traffic on the Strip to a screeching halt. Be on the lookout for wisps of smoke escaping from the top, signaling that the fiery Polynesian-style inferno, with a soundtrack by a Grateful Dead drummer and an Indian tabla musician, is about to begin.

Venetian   CASINO
(🖉702-414-1000; www.venetian.com; 3355 Las Vegas Blvd S; ⊙24hr) The Venetian's regal 120,000-sq-ft casino has marble floors, hand-painted ceiling frescoes and 120 table games, including a high-limit lounge and an elegant no-smoking poker room, where women are especially welcome (unlike at many other poker rooms in town).

Viva Las Vegas
Wedding Chapel   WEDDING CHAPEL
(🖉800-574-4450, 702-384-0771; www.vivalasvegas weddings.com; 1205 Las Vegas Blvd S) Even if you're not contemplating tying the knot, it's worth a peek inside this little assembly-line wedding chapel of looooovvvee to see if anyone is getting married. The public is welcome to attend the themed weddings: kitschy as all get-out, too, they range from Elvis' 'Blue Hawaii' and 'Pink Caddy' to 'Twilight,' 'Gangster' and 'Gladiator' themes. Book ceremonies in advance.

Downtown & Off-Strip

★**Mob Museum**   MUSEUM
(🖉702-229-2734; www.themobmuseum.org; 300 Stewart Ave; adult/child 11-17yr $20/14; ⊙10am-7pm

Las Vegas Strip

Sun-Thu, to 8pm Fri & Sat; 🚌 Deuce) It's hard to say what's more impressive: the museum's physical location in a historic federal courthouse where mobsters sat for federal hearings in 1950–51, the fact that the board of directors is headed up by a former FBI Special Agent, or the thoughtfully curated exhibits telling the story of organized crime in America. In addition to hands-on FBI equipment and mob-related artifacts, the museum boasts a series of multimedia exhibits featuring interviews with real-life Tony Sopranos.

El Cortez
CASINO
(☎702-385-5200; www.elcortezhotelcasino.com; 600 E Fremont St; ☺24hr; 🚌 Deuce) Head to the unabashedly retro El Cortez, Vegas' oldest continuously operating casino, on the National Register of Historic Places. Going strong since 1941, it's one of the only carpet joints left where the slot machines are the real thing. If you hit the jackpot, you'll enjoy the clatter of actual coins – none of that newfangled paper-ticket nonsense.

National Atomic Testing Museum
MUSEUM
(☎702-794-5151; www.nationalatomictesting museum.org; 755 E Flamingo Rd, Desert Research Institute; adult/child 7-17yr $14/12; ☺10am-5pm Mon-Sat, noon-5pm Sun; 🚌202) Fascinating multimedia exhibits focus on science, technology and the social history of the 'Atomic Age,' which lasted from WWII until atmospheric bomb testing was driven underground in 1961 and a worldwide ban on nuclear testing was declared in 1992. View historical footage of atomic testing and examine southern Nevada's past, present and future, from Native American ways of life to the environmental legacy of atomic testing. Don't miss the cool museum shop near the ticket booth, a Nevada Test Site guard station replica.

Springs Preserve
MUSEUM, PARK
(☎702-822-7700; www.springspreserve.org; 333 S Valley View Blvd; adult/child 5-17yr $19/11; ☺10am-6pm; 🚹; 🚌104) On the site of the natural springs (which ran dry in 1962) that fed *las vegas* ('the meadows'), where southern Paiutes and Spanish Trail traders camped, and later Mormon missionaries and Western pioneers settled the valley, this educational complex is an incredible trip through historical, cultural and biological time. The touchstone is the Desert Living Center, demonstrating sustainable architectural design and everyday ecoconscious living.

Red Rock Canyon National Conservation Area
OUTDOORS
(☎702-515-5350; www.redrockcanyonlv.org; entry per car/bicycle $7/3; ☺scenic loop 6am-8pm Apr-Sep, to 7pm Mar & Oct, to 5pm Nov-Feb; visitor center 8am-4:30pm; 🚹) The startling contrast between Las Vegas' artificial neon glow and the awesome natural forces found here can't be exaggerated. Created about 65 million years ago, the canyon is more like a valley, with a steep, rugged red-rock escarpment rising 3000ft on its western edge, dramatic evidence of tectonic-plate collisions. A 13-mile, one-way scenic drive passes some of the canyon's most striking features, where you can access hiking trails and rock-climbing routes, or simply be mesmerized by the vistas.

🏃 Activities

Adventuredome
THEME PARK
(www.adventuredome.com; Circus Circus; per ride $5-8, day pass over/under 48in tall $30/17; ☺10am-6pm daily, later weekends & May-Sep; 🚹) Enclosed by over 8000 pink-glass panes, Circus Circus' indoor amusement park is packed with thrills. Must-rides include the double-loop, double-corkscrew Canyon Blaster and the gravity-defying El Loco that packs a whopping -1.5 Gs of vertical acceleration. Older kids get a rock-climbing wall, bungee-jumping area, mini golf and 4D special-effect 'ridefilms.' Clowns perform free shows throughout the day.

Stratosphere Tower
TOWER
(☎702-380-7777; www.stratospherehotel.com; Stratosphere, 2000 Las Vegas Blvd S; elevator adult/concession $18/15, incl 3 thrill rides $33, all-day pass $34; SkyJump from $110) The world's highest thrill rides await, a whopping 110 stories above the Strip. Big Shot straps riders into completely exposed seats that zip up the tower's pinnacle, while Insanity spins riders out over the tower's edge. Views from xScream are good, but the ride itself is a dud. If you want an adrenaline rush, save your dough for the SkyJump instead.

👉 Tours

Flightlinez Bootleg Canyon
OUTDOORS
(☎702-293-6885; www.flightlinezbootleg.com; 1644 Nevada Hwy, Boulder City; 2½hr tour $159) This thrilling aerial adventure is like zip-lining, but with a paragliding harness. Morning tours see the coolest temps, while late afternoon tours may catch sunset over the desert. Riders must weigh between 75lb and 250lb (fully dressed) and wear close-toed shoes.

Las Vegas Cyclery CYCLING
(☎702-596-2953; http://lasvegascyclery.com; 10575 Discovery Dr; bicycle rental per day $40-100; ⏰10am-7pm Mon-Fri, 9am-6pm Sat, 10am-4pm Sun) Rent high-quality road and mountain bikes in suburban Summerlin, 10 miles west of the Strip. Ask about guided cycling and mountain-biking tours of Red Rock Canyon.

🛌 Sleeping

Las Vegas room rates fluctuate wildly, ranging from mega-deals of $25 to over $300 on big weekends. Almost all hotels tack on a resort fee (from $20).

The Strip

New York–New York CASINO HOTEL $
(☎702-740-6969, 866-815-4365; www.newyork newyork.com; 3790 Las Vegas Blvd S; r Mon-Fri from $50, Sat & Sun from $110; P✳@☎☒) A favorite of college students, these decent digs are rather tiny (just what one would expect in NYC).

Treasure Island CASINO HOTEL $
(☎800-944-7444, 702-894-7111; www.treasureisland .com; 3300 Las Vegas Blvd S; r Mon-Fri from $50, Sat & Sun from $99; P✳@☎☒) Breezily renovated rooms are comfortable enough, although on-site dining and amenities are only so-so. Good value for the location.

Vdara HOTEL $$
(☎702-590-2111, 866-745-7767; www.vdara.com; 2600 W Harmon Ave; r Mon-Fri from $119 Sat & Sun from $179; P⊖✳@☎☒) 🖊 Cool sophistication, generously apportioned apartments and warm hospitality merge seamlessly at this nongaming, nonsmoking, all-suites hotel at CityCenter.

Tropicana CASINO HOTEL $$
(☎800-462-8767, 702-739-2222; www.troplv.com; 3801 Las Vegas Blvd S; r Mon-Fri from $75, Sat & Sun from $120; P✳@☎☒; 🚌Deuce) Keeping its tropical vibe going since the 1950s, the vintage Trop's multimillion-dollar renovation pays off with Miami-chic rooms painted in sunset hues.

Planet Hollywood CASINO HOTEL $$
(☎702-785-5555, 866-919-7472; www.planetholly woodresort.com; 3667 Las Vegas Blvd S r Mon-Fri from $59, Sat & Sun from $160; P✳@☎☒🐾) Ultra-contemporary rooms contain black lacquer furnishings, club chairs and plush beds with leather headboards.

Venetian CASINO HOTEL $$
(☎866-659-9643, 702-414-1000; www.venetian. com; 3355 Las Vegas Blvd S; ste Mon-Fri from $149,

Sat & Sun from $289; P✳@☎☒) Vegas' own 'Most Serene Republic' features huge suites with sunken living rooms and countless luxuries, from deep soaking tubs to pillow menus.

Caesars Palace CASINO HOTEL $$
(☎702-731-7110, 866-227-5938; www.caesarspalace .com; 3570 Las Vegas Blvd S; r Mon-Fri from $90, Sat & Sun from $125; P✳@☎☒🐾) Expect towers of oversized rooms with marble bathrooms, Nobu boutique hotel and the Garden of the Gods pool complex.

Mirage CASINO HOTEL $$
(☎702-791-7111, 800-374-9000; www.mirage. com; 3400 Las Vegas Blvd S; r Mon-Fri from $95, Sat & Sun from $130; P✳@☎☒) Remodeled rooms are delightfully contemporary, with bold color palettes, plush beds and geometrically patterned carpets.

Monte Carlo CASINO HOTEL $$
(☎800-311-8999, 702-730-7777; www.montecarlo. com; 3770 Las Vegas Blvd S; r Mon-Fri from $45, Sat & Sun from $105; P✳@☎☒) Literally the next best thing to CityCenter, this Euro-style hotel is more than just a poor man's Bellagio, and includes a lazy river ride.

MGM Grand CASINO HOTEL $$
(☎877-880-0880, 702-891-1111; www.mgmgrand. com; 3799 Las Vegas Blvd S; r Mon-Fri from $70, Sat & Sun from $140; P✳@☎☒) Vegas' biggest hotel, with high-end **Skylofts** (☎877-646-5638, 702-891-3832; www.skyloftsmgmgrand. com; MGM Grand; ste from $1000; P✳@☎☒), apartment-style **Signature** (☎877-727-0007, 702-797-6000; www.signaturemgmgrand.com; 145 E Harmon Ave; ste Mon-Fri from $95, Sat & Sun from $170; P✳@☎☒) suites and the Strip's most mammoth pool complex.

Mandalay Bay CASINO HOTEL $$
(☎877-632-7800, 702-632-7777; www.mandalay bay.com; 3950 Las Vegas Blvd S; r Mon-Fri from $105, Sat & Sun from $130; P✳@☎☒; 🚌Deuce) The upscale Mandalay Bay casino hotel, exclusive **Four Seasons** (☎702-632-5000; www.fourseasons.com/lasvegas; r Mon-Fri from $229, Sat & Sun from $289; P✳@☎☒) hotel and boutique **Delano** (www.delanolas vegas.com; P✳@☎☒) hotel offer variety at the Strip's southernmost resort.

Cosmopolitan CASINO HOTEL $$$
(☎855-435-0005, 702-698-7000; www.cosmopoli tanlasvegas.com; 3708 Las Vegas Blvd S; r/ste from $160/220; P✳@☎☒🐾; 🚌Deuce) Frequented by style-conscious clientele, the arty, cool Cosmo wins the contest for the Strip's hippest hotel rooms.

Encore
CASINO HOTEL **$$$**

(☑877-321-9966, 702-770-7100; www.wynnlas vegas.com; 3131 Las Vegas Blvd S; r Mon-Fri from $199, Sat & Sun from $249; [P][✳][@][⊚][≋]; [◲]Deuce) Newer than its sister resort Wynn, Encore offers similarly lavish yet even more spacious suites amid gorgeous surrounds.

Downtown & Off-Strip
Many off-Strip casino hotels offer free guest shuttles to/from the Strip.

El Cortez Cabana Suites
HOTEL **$**

(☑800-634-6703, 702-385-5200; http://elcortez hotelcasino.com; 651 E Ogden Ave; r Mon-Fri from $40, Sat & Sun from $80; [P][✳][@][⊚]) Across the street from the 1940s casino, mod suites decked out in mint green hide fab retro tiled bathrooms with walk-in showers.

South Point
CASINO HOTEL **$**

(☑866-796-7111, 702-796-7111; www.southpoint casino.com; 9777 Las Vegas Blvd S; r Mon-Fri from $45, Sat & Sun from $70; [@][⊚][≋]) Encompassing a cineplex, bowling alley and big rooms with comfy beds, this tidy casino hotel is flung south of the Strip, near an outlet mall.

Hard Rock
CASINO HOTEL **$**

(☑702-693-5000, 800-473-7625; www.hardrock hotel.com; 4455 Paradise Rd; r Mon-Fri from $45, Sat & Sun from $89; [P][✳][@][⊚][≋]) Sexy, over-sized rooms and HRH suites at this shrine to rock 'n' roll pull in the SoCal party crowd. Free Strip shuttles for guests.

Red Rock
CASINO HOTEL **$$**

(☑702-797-7777, 866-767-7773; www.redrock.sclv. com; 11011 W Charleston Blvd; weekday/weekend r from $95/140; [P][✳][@][⊚][≋]) At this upscale casino hotel, forget about the faraway Strip and spend your time outdoors by the resort pool or at nearby Red Rock Canyon.

✕ Eating

With so many stellar restaurants in town, we've listed just a few reliable favorites here. Reservations are always a good idea.

The Strip

Tacos El Gordo
MEXICAN **$**

(☑702-641-8228; http://tacoselgordobc.com; 3049 Las Vegas Blvd S; menu $2-10; ⊙9pm-3am Sun-Thu, to 5am Fri & Sat; [◲]Deuce, SDX) This Tijuana-style taco shop from SoCal is just the ticket when it's way late, you've got almost no money left and you're desperately craving *carne asada* (beef) or *adobada* (chile-marinated pork) tacos in hot, handmade tortillas. Adventurous eaters order the authentic *sesos* (beef brains), *cabeza* (roasted cow's head) or tripe (intestines) variations.

Stripburger
BURGERS **$**

(☑702-737-8747; www.stripburger.com; 3200 Las Vegas Blvd S, Fashion Show; menu $4-14; ⊙11am-11pm Sun-Thu, to midnight Fri & Sat; [◨]) This shiny silver, open-air diner in the round serves up all-natural (hormone-free etc) beef, chicken, tuna and veggie burgers, atomic cheese fries, thick milkshakes, buckets of beer and fruity cocktails, with elevated patio tables overlooking the Strip.

Earl of Sandwich
DELI **$**

(www.earlofsandwichusa.com; Planet Hollywood; menu $2-7; ⊙24hr; [◨]) Pennypinchers sing the praises of this super-popular deli next to the casino, which pops out sandwiches on toasted artisan bread, tossed salads, wraps and a kids' menu, all with quick service, unbeatable opening hours and some of the lowest prices on the Strip.

Village Street Eateries
INTERNATIONAL **$$**

(New York–New York; mains $5-20; ⊙7am-3am, restaurant hours vary; [◨]) The cobblestone streets of NYNY's Greenwich Village are bursting with budget options: authentic **Greenberg & Sons Deli**; **Broadway Burger Bar** for patties made with grass-fed beef sourced from a ranch in Uruguay; bargain slices from **Sirrico's Pizza**; **Chin Chin** for take-out-quality Chinese dishes and Japanese sushi; and **Gonzalez Y Gonzalez**, a tequila-soaked Tex-Mex cantina.

Lemongrass
ASIAN **$$**

Aria, CityCenter; mains $14-29, tasting menus $39-59; ⊙11am-2am; [✈][◨]) Visually high impact, this Thai and pan-Asian kitchen offers a satay bar and quasi-authentic soups, curries and noodle dishes, from *tom kha* chicken to drunken noodles with seafood. Use caution when ordering spice level 10 – it's mouth-searing.

Gordon Ramsay BurGR
BURGERS **$$**

(☑702-785-5555; www.gordonramsay.com; Planet Hollywood; mains $13-18; ⊙11am-midnight Sun-Thu, to 2am Fri & Sat) Even the special-effects window installation at the entrance looks like it's on fire at this hot, hot burger joint by the *Hell's Kitchen* chef. Open wide and bite into Gordon's 'farm burger' topped by duck-breast bacon, a fried egg and English cheddar cheese, with truffled parmesan fries and a caramel-toffee milkshake on the side. It's casual, but reservations help.

Bouchon
FRENCH **$$$**

(☑702-414-6200; www.bouchonbistro.com; Venezia Tower, Venetian; mains breakfast & brunch $12-26, dinner $19-51; ⊙7-10:30am & 5-10pm Mon-Fri, 8am-2pm & 5-10pm Sat & Sun) Napa Valley wunderkind Thomas Keller's rendition of a Lyonnaise bistro features a seasonal menu of French classics. The poolside setting complements the oyster bar (open 3pm to 10:30pm daily) and an extensive raw seafood selection. Decadent breakfasts and brunches, imported cheeses, caviar, foie gras and a superb French and Californian wine list all make appearances. Reservations are essential.

Jaleo
SPANISH, TAPAS **$$$**

(☑702-698-7950; www.jaleo.com; Cosmopolitan; shared plates $5-35; ☺noon-midnight; 🚗) The Vegas version of pioneering Spanish chef José Andrés' flagship restaurant in DC brings modern tapas to a light-hearted setting with a rustic-chic look: recycled wooden tables with mismatched chairs, whimsical glassware and colorful details left and right. Try the potent sangria and a few traditional small plates or more innovative tastes like gin-and-tonic Pacific oysters. Reservations essential.

Joël Robuchon
FRENCH **$$$**

(☑702-891-7925; www.joel-robuchon.com/en; MGM Grand; tasting menus $120-425; ☺5:30-10pm Sun-Thu, to 10:30pm Fri & Sat) The acclaimed 'Chef of the Century' leads the pack in the French culinary invasion of the Strip. Adjacent to the high-rollers' gaming area, Robuchon's plush dining rooms, done up in leather and velvet, feel like a dinner party at a 1930s Paris mansion. Complex seasonal tasting menus promise the meal of a lifetime – and often deliver.

Cut
STEAK **$$$**

(☑702-607-6300; www.wolfgangpuck.com; Grand Canal Shoppes at the Palazzo; mains $39-119; ☺5:30-10pm Sun-Thu, to 11pm Fri & Sat, lounge from 5pm daily) Peripatetic chef Wolfgang Puck strikes again and this time he's on fire – or 1200°F (650°C) in the broiler, to be exact. Modern earth-toned furnishings with stainless-steel accents and dried-flower arrangements complement a surprisingly smart menu, which dares to infuse Indian spices into Kobe beef and accompany Nebraska corn-fed steaks with Argentinean chimichurri sauce or Point Reyes blue cheese.

Restaurant Guy Savoy
FRENCH **$$$**

(☑702-731-7286; www.guysavoy.com; Augustus Tower, Caesars Palace; mains $80-110, tasting menus $120-350; ☺5:30-10:30pm Wed-Sun) With Strip-view picture windows, this exclusive dining room is the only US restaurant by three-star Michelin chef Guy Savoy. Both the culinary concepts and the prices reach heavenly heights. If you just want a small taste,

perhaps of artichoke black-truffle soup or crispy-skinned sea bass, sit in the Cognac Lounge for drinks and nibbles. Dinner reservations are essential.

Downtown & Off-Strip

Get off the Strip for more reasonable prices.

Container Park
FAST FOOD **$**

(☑702-637-4244; http://downtowncontainerpark.com; 707 E Fremont St; menu $3-9; ☺11am-11pm Sun-Thu, to 1am Fri & Sat; 🚌Deuce) With food-truck-style menus, outdoor patio seating and late-night hours, food vendors inside the cutting-edge Container Park sell something to satisfy everyone's appetite. When we last stopped by, the ever-changing line-up included **Pinche's Tacos** for Mexican flavors, **Pork & Beans** for piggy goodness, Southern-style **Big Ern's BBQ**, raw-food and healthy vegan cuisine from **Simply Pure**, and **Bin 702** wine bar.

Lotus of Siam
THAI **$$**

(☑702-735-3033; www.saipinchutima.com; 953 E Sahara Ave; mains $9-30; ☺11:30am-2:30pm Mon-Fri, 5:30-10pm daily; 🚗; 🚌SDX) Saipin Chutima's authentic northern Thai cooking has won almost as many awards as her distinguished European and New World wine cellar. Renowned food critic Jonathan Gold once called it 'the single best Thai restaurant in North America.' The strip-mall hole-in-the-wall place may not look like much, but foodies flock here. Reservations essential.

Firefly
TAPAS **$$**

(☑702-369-3971; www.fireflylv.com; 3824 Paradise Rd; shared plates $5-12, mains $15-20; ☺11:30am-midnight; 🚌108) Firefly is always packed with a fashionable local crowd, who come for well-prepared Spanish and Latin American tapas, such as *patatas bravas,* chorizo-stuffed empanadas and vegetarian bites like garbanzo beans seasoned with chili, lime and sea salt. A backlit bar dispenses the house specialty sangria – red, white or sparkling – and fruity mojitos. Reservations recommended.

Raku
JAPANESE **$$**

(☑702-367-3511; www.raku-grill.com; 5030 W Spring Mountain Rd; shared dishes $2-12; ☺6pm-3am Mon-Sat; 🚌203) At the place where LA chefs come to dine when they're in town, Japanese owner-chef Mitsuo Edo crafts small plates blossoming with exquisite flavors. You'll find yourself ordering just one more thing, again and again, from the menu of *robata*-grilled meats, homemade tofu and seasoned vegetables. Make reservations a few days in advance or angle for the tiny bar.

🍸 Drinking & Nightlife

Drinks are free while you're gambling in casinos; do tip your cocktail server.

The Strip

Level 107 Lounge   LOUNGE
(☎702-380-7685; www.topoftheworldlv.com; 2000 Las Vegas Blvd S, 107th fl, Stratosphere Tower; ☺4pm-4am) There's just no place to get any higher in Las Vegas – without the approval of an air traffic controller – than the lounge overlooking the revolving Top of the World restaurant. Come during happy hour (4pm to 7pm daily) for two-for-one cocktails, half-price appetizers and striking sunset views.

Fireside Lounge   LOUNGE
(www.peppermilllasvegas.com; 2985 Las Vegas Blvd S, Peppermill; ☺24hr; 🚌Deuce) Don't be blinded by the outlandishly bright neon outside. The Strip's most spellbinding retro hideaway awaits at the pint-sized Peppermill casino. Courting couples adore the sunken fire pit, fake tropical foliage and 64oz goblet-sized 'Scorpion' cocktails served by waiters in black evening gowns.

Chandelier Bar   COCKTAIL BAR
(Cosmopolitan; ☺24hr; 🚌Deuce) Towering high in the center of Cosmopolitan, this ethereally designed cocktail bar is inventive yet beautifully simple, with three levels connected by romantic curved staircases, all draped with glowing strands of glass beads. The 2nd level is headquarters for molecular mixology (order a martini made with liquid nitrogen), while the 3rd specializes in floral and fruit infusions.

Double Barrel Roadhouse   BAR
(www.sbe.com/doublebarrel; 3770 Las Vegas Blvd S, Monte Carlo; ☺11am-2am) With a Strip-view patio, this double-decker bar and grill anchors the new pedestrian district between the Monte Carlo and New York–New York casino hotels. Staff pour stiff house-made wine coolers into mason jars, cook up Southern comfort food and cheer the live rock bands on stage.

Double Down Saloon   BAR
(www.doubledownsaloon.com; 4640 Paradise Rd; ☺24hr; 🚌108) This dark, psychedelic gin joint appeals to the lunatic fringe. It never closes, there's never a cover charge, the house drink is called 'ass juice', and it claims to be the birthplace of the bacon martini. When live bands aren't terrorizing the crowd, the jukebox vibrates with New Orleans jazz, British punk, Chicago blues and surf-guitar king Dick Dale.

XS   CLUB
(☎702-770-0097; www.xslasvegas.com; Encore; cover $20-50; ☺9:30pm-4am Fri & Sat, from 10:30pm Sun & Mon) XS is *the* hottest nightclub in Vegas – at least for now. Its extravagantly gold-drenched decor and over-the-top design means you'll be waiting in line for cocktails at a bar towered over by ultra-curvaceous, larger-than-life golden statues of female torsos. Famous-name electronica DJs make the dancefloor writhe, while high rollers opt for VIP bottle service at private poolside cabanas.

Drai's   CLUB
(☎702-737-0555; www.drais.net; 3595 Las Vegas Blvd S, Cromwell; cover $20-50; ☺nightclub 10am-5pm Thu-Sun year-round, pool club 10am-7pm Fri-Sun usually May-Sep) Feel ready for an after-hours party scene straight outta Hollywood? Or maybe you just wanna hang out all day poolside, then shake your booty on the petite dancefloor while DJs spin hip-hop, mash-ups and electronica? This multi-venue club has you covered pretty much all day and night. Dress to kill: no sneakers, tank tops or baggy jeans.

Wet Republic   POOL CLUB
(☎702-891-3715; http://wetrepublic.com; MGM Grand; cover $20-40; ☺usually Mar-Sep, hours vary) Think of Wet Republic, the city's biggest 'ultra pool,' as a nightclub brought out into the sunlight. The mostly 20- and 30-something crowd in stylish swimwear show up for EDM tunes spun by megawatt DJs like Calvin Harris, fruity cocktails and bobbing oh-so-coolly around saltwater pools while checking out the bikini-clad scenery. Book ahead for VIP bungalows, daybeds and cabanas.

Downtown & Off-Strip

Downtown Cocktail Room   LOUNGE
(☎702-880-3696; www.thedowntownlv.com; 111 Las Vegas Blvd S; ☺4pm-2am Mon-Fri, 7pm-2am Sat; 🚌Deuce) With a serious list of classic cocktails and house-made inventions, this low-lit speakeasy is undeniably romantic, and it feels decades ahead of downtown's old-school casinos. The entrance is ingeniously disguised: the door looks like just another part of the wall until you discover the sweet spot you have to push to get in. Happy hour runs 4pm to 8pm weekdays.

Beauty Bar   BAR
(☎702-598-3757; www.thebeautybar.com; 517 Fremont St; cover free-$10; ☺10pm-4am; 🚌Deuce) Swill a cocktail or just chill with the cool kids inside the salvaged innards of a 1950s

New Jersey beauty salon. DJs and live bands rotate nightly, spinning everything from tiki lounge tunes, disco and '80s hits to punk, metal, glam and indie rock. Check the website for special events like 'Karate Karaoke.' There's often no cover charge.

Entertainment

Pro fighters, pop stars and Broadway musicals all find audiences in Vegas, as do over-the-top stage spectaculars like Cirque du Soleil. Buy discounted same-day show tickets at **Tix4Tonight** (✆ 877-849-4868; www.tix 4tonight.com; ⊙ usually 10am-7pm or 8pm), with multiple locations on and off the Strip.

Kà
THEATER

(✆ 800-929-1111, 702-531-3826; www.cirquedu soleil.com; MGM Grand; adult $69-150, child 5-12yr $35-75; ⊙ 7pm & 9:30pm Tue-Sat; ♿) Cirque du Soleil makes this sensuous story of imperial twins, mysterious destinies, love and conflict one of the Strip's hottest tickets. Instead of a stage, there's a $200 million grid of moving platforms elevating a frenzy of martial-arts-styled performances. Children under five years old are not allowed.

Joint
MUSIC, COMEDY

(✆ 888-929-7849; www.hardrockhotel.com; 4455 Paradise Rd, Hard Rock; most tickets $40-200; ☐ 108) Concerts at the Hard Rock's scaled-down music venue, holding just 4000 people, feel like private shows, even when rock royalty like the Red Hot Chili Peppers and David Bowie are in town. Intimate acoustic shows happen inside **Vinyl** lounge (cover charge varies, from nothing up to $40), off the main casino floor.

ⓘ Information

INTERNET ACCESS

At casino hotels, wi-fi is generally included in the resort fee (don't expect streaming-capable speeds) and there are generally internet kiosks with printers in lobbies ($5 minimum).

MEDICAL SERVICES

Harmon Medical Center (✆ 702-796-1116; www.harmonmedicalcenter.com; 150 E Harmon Ave; ⊙ 8am-8pm Mon-Fri) Discounts for uninsured patients; limited translation services available.

University Medical Center (UMC; ✆ 702-383-2000; www.umcsn.com; 1800 W Charleston Blvd; ⊙ 24hr) Southern Nevada's most advanced trauma center has a 24-hour ER.

Walgreens (✆ 702-739-9645; 3765 Las Vegas Blvd S; ⊙ store 24hr, pharmacy 8am-10pm,

clinic 9am-5:30pm) Has an in-store healthcare walk-in clinic.

MONEY

Every casino hotel and bank, and most convenience stores, have ATMs. Fees imposed by casinos for ATM transactions or foreign-currency exchange are much higher than at banks.

TOURIST INFORMATION

Las Vegas Convention & Visitors Authority (LVCVA; ✆ 702-892-7575, 877-847-4858; www. lasvegas.com; 3150 Paradise Rd; ⊙ 8am-5:30pm Mon-Fri)

USEFUL WEBSITES

Eater Vegas (www.vegas.eater.com) The latest news about Sin City's chefs and new restaurants. Posts a regularly updated list of the city's top 38 eateries.

Vegas.com (www.vegas.com) Travel information with booking service.

ⓘ Getting There & Around

AIR

Las Vegas is served by **McCarran International Airport** (LAS; ✆ 702-261-5211; www.mccarran. com; 5757 Wayne Newton Blvd; ☎), one of the USA's 10 busiest airports. Taxis to Strip hotels average $15 to $20 (cash only, plus tip); super-slow airport shuttle buses charge half as much. **Airport shuttles** (p93) also run to/from St George, Utah.

BUS

Long-distance **Greyhound** (✆ 702-384-9561; www.greyhound.com; 200 S Main St; ⊙ 24hr; ☐ SDX) buses arrive at the downtown **bus station** (BTC; ✆ 702-228-7433; www.rtcsnv. com; 101 E Bonneville Ave; ⊙ 24hr), near the Fremont Street Experience.

Two routes run 24/7 between the Strip and downtown: the double-decker Deuce, which stops more frequently, and the speedier SDX. A 24-hour pass for both is $8.

CAR

Major car-rental agencies are based at the airport's rent-a-car center, accessible via a free shuttle from outside the main terminal. Free self-parking and valet (tip $3 to $5) are available at most casino hotels. From Las Vegas, it's about a three-hour drive to Zion National Park via I-15 north to Hwy 9 east.

TAXI

It's illegal to hail a cab on the street. Look for taxi stands at casinos, hotels and shopping malls, or **call** (✆ 702-873-2000). Fares are metered; a lift from one end of the Strip to the other runs about $20, plus tip.

Bryce Canyon National Park

Best Hikes

➡ Fairyland Loop Trail (p112)
➡ Peekaboo Trail (p116)
➡ Navajo Loop Trail (p114)
➡ Queen's Garden Trail (p112)
➡ Rim Trail (p115)

Best Places to Stay

➡ Sunset Campground (p123)
➡ Bryce Canyon Lodge (p124)
➡ Bryce Canyon Resort (p125)

Why Go?

These sights are nothing short of otherworldly. Repeated freezes and thaws have eroded soft sandstone and limestone into a landscape that's utterly unique: sandcastle spires known as hoodoos, jutted fins, windows and deep narrows. Though it's the smallest of southern Utah's national parks, Bryce Canyon stands among the most prized.

Not actually a canyon, Bryce comprises the eastern edge of an 18-mile plateau. Its Pink Cliffs mark the top step of the Grand Staircase, a giant geologic terrace reaching to the Grand Canyon. Trails descend through 1000ft amphitheaters of pastel daggers into a maze of fragrant juniper and sculpted high-mountain desert.

High altitude means cooler temperatures than other Utah parks. Clean, dry air also means excellent visibility, reaching all the way into the Andromeda Galaxy 2.2 million light-years away.

Driving Distances (miles)

	Bryce Canyon National Park (Park Entrance)	Kenab	Moab	Panguitch	Tropic
Kanab	75				
Moab	275	320			
Panguitch	25	70	250		
Tropic	10	80	280	30	
Zion National Park (East Entrance)	75	30	315	65	80

Note: Distances are approximate

Entrances

The park's sole vehicle entrance is 3 miles south of Utah Hwy 12, via Hwy 63. The park gate is always open, though entrance booths are not staffed at night.

The entrance fee is $30 for a vehicle and $15 for a motorcycle, cyclist or pedestrian, valid for seven days.

Bryce Canyon is open 24 hours a day, 365 days a year.

Because of severe traffic issues, the park has implemented parking restrictions on RVs and trailer vehicles in high season. Those affected should check the park website for details on any restrictions between May and September.

Compared with the vast landscape that surrounds it, the park is relatively small, at 16 miles long and 4 miles across at its widest point.

DON'T MISS

➡ Best short canyon hike: Navajo Loop Trail (p114)

➡ Best colors: Bryce Amphitheater at sunrise (p120)

➡ Best long hike for solitude among the amphitheaters: Fairyland Loop Trail (p112)

➡ Most stunning hoodoos: Silent City from Inspiration Point (p121)

➡ Best overlooked sight: 1600-year-old trees on Bristlecone Loop Trail (p120)

➡ Best nightlife: night-sky programs offer stargazing with telescopes and expert insight (p123)

When You Arrive

➡ As you approach, tune your radio to AM 1590 for current general park information.

➡ The entrance booth distributes park brochures with a driving map and facilities information along with the park newspaper, the *Hoodoo*, which gives current information about opening hours, ranger-led activities, hiking trails, backpacking and shuttle information.

➡ Take advantage of the Bryce Canyon Shuttle, a free service that operates between Ruby's Inn and Bryce Point, with buses every 15 minutes between 8am and 8pm in high season.

➡ Hydration stations throughout the park offer free water-bottle refills.

➡ Backcountry permits for overnight travel are issued at the visitor center on a first-come, first-served basis.

PARK POLICIES & REGULATIONS

It's important you don't feed wild animals. Pets must be on a leash and are only allowed on paved surfaces (roads, parking lots, paved scenic overlooks and the Rim Trail between Sunset and Sunrise Points). They are not allowed on unpaved trails or in public buildings.

Fast Facts

➡ Area: 56 sq miles

➡ Elevation: 7894ft to 6600ft

➡ Average July temperatures: high 80°F (27°C), low 46°F (8°C)

➡ Oldest residents: the park's bristlecone pines are up to 1600 years old

➡ When to go: from May through September, the park's sole road and scenic overlooks can get crowded. For solitude, hike off-hours or seek less-traveled trails under the rim.

Reservations

Reservations may be made up to six months in advance for North Campground (RV reservations on 13 sites) and Sunset Campground (reservations on 20 tent sites). Otherwise, it's a first-come, first-served basis.

Resources

➡ **Bryce Canyon National Park** (www.nps.gov/brca)

➡ **Bryce Canyon Natural History Association** (www.brycecanyon.org)

Bryce Canyon National Park

BRYCE CANYON CITY

The free park shuttle starts at this village just outside the park, which also has ample lodging and dining services. (p124)

BRYCE AMPHITHEATER

The highest concentration of hoodoos in the park. Look out on Silent City; various paths twist to the canyon floor 1000ft below. (p120)

PARIA VIEW

This is the place for sunset photos, where hoodoos are set aflame by the last light. (p120)

Red Canyon (5mi); Hwy 89 (7mi); Panguitch (14mi)

Dixie National Forest

Bryce Museum

Red Canyon Bike Path

Bryce Canyon Pines

Bryce Canyon Pines Campground & RV Park

East Fork Sevier River

Bryce Canyon Resort

Tropic Ditch

Shuttle Parking & Boarding Area

Bryce View Lodge

Bryce Canyon Grand Hotel

Best Western Ruby's Inn

Pink Cliffs

Mossy Cave Trail

Mossy Cave

Shakespear Point

Tropic

Fairyland Canyon

Fairyland Point

Fairyland Loop Trail

Boat Mesa

Bryce Canyon

Bryce Creek

Hat Shop

Visitor Center

General Store

Rim Trail

Sunrise Point

Thor's Hammer

Silent City

Sunset Point

Bryce Canyon Lodge

Inspiration Point

Rim Trail

Bryce Point

East Creek

Blue Fly Creek

Right Fork Blue Fly Creek

Blue Fly Creek

Dixie National Forest

King Creek

King Creek Campground

Tropic Reservoir

Sheep Creek Connecting Trail

Paunsaugunt Plateau

Whitemn Bench

PEEKABOO LOOP TRAIL

A heady place for horseback riding is beneath the soaring Wall of Windows on this trail; one of few places horses are permitted in the park. (p116)

RAINBOW POINT

The end point of the park road looks out onto a vast landscape of sloping plateaus, tilted mesas and towering buttes, with trails. (p120)

Henrieville (3.6mi);
Escalante (34mi)

Cannonville

Peekaboo Trail

Grand Staircase
- Escalante
National Monument

Bryce Canyon
National Park

Pink Cliffs

Sheep Creek

Swamp
Canyon

Swamp Canyon Butte (8315ft)

Mud Canyon Butte (8330ft)

Noon Canyon Butte (8466ft)

Willis Creek

Horse
Mountain

Ponderosa Ridge

Squaw Creek

Swamp Canyon
Connectng Trail

Whiteman
Connecting Trail

Whiteman
Bench

Piracy
Point

Fairview
Point

Bridge Canyon

Deer
Mountain
(7830ft)

Under-the-Rim Trail

Bristlecone
Loop Trail

Rainbow Point

Riggs Spring Loop Trail

East Fork Sevier River

Natural
Bridge

Agua
Canyon

Ponderosa
Canyon

Black Birch
Canyon

Yovimpa Point

Agua Canyon
Connecting Trail

Skunk Creek

East Fork Sevier River

Dixie
National
Forest

Crawford Creek

History

Bryce Canyon borrows its moniker from an early pioneer who settled in the valley east of the park. In 1870 Ebenezer Bryce made the journey from Salt Lake City with other Mormon pioneers hoping to establish permanent settlements. During Ebenezer's five-year stint here, he surveyed the 10-mile-long Tropic Ditch, looking for a means to deliver water for crops and livestock. Today the ditch still provides water to the town of Tropic. The canyon behind Ebenezer's home was dubbed 'Bryce's Canyon.'

Forget romantic illusions. Bryce described his namesake canyon as 'a hell of a place to lose a cow.' Just gaze off the rim into a maze of hoodoos to understand just what he meant.

🏃 DAY HIKES

Bryce is a relatively small park and most trails are day hikes around and into Bryce Amphitheater, home to the highest concentration of hoodoos. Hikes range from easy walks on paved paths along the rim (with some stretches suitable for wheelchairs) to steep switchbacks up and down sometimes muddy, sometimes dusty, packed-earth trails. Further south or north on the plateau you won't see as many hoodoos – or as many people.

Loose rocks act like marbles under your feet; ankle injuries are extremely common and can ruin your trip. Always wear well-fitting hiking boots with ankle support, and lace boots all the way up.

Hikes are listed in the order of approach, starting from outside the park entrance and heading toward Bryce Point.

🏃 Fairyland Loop Trail

Duration 4–5 hours

Distance 8 miles

Difficulty Difficult

Start/Finish Fairyland Point

Nearest Towns Tropic, Panguitch

Transportation Private

Summary A great day hike and a good workout, with multiple elevation changes. Unlike Bryce Amphitheater, Fairyland is spared the crowds.

This trail begins at Fairyland Point and circles the majestic cliffs of flat-topped, 8076ft Boat Mesa, emerging on the rim near Sunrise Point. There are fewer hoodoos in this area. The last 2.5 miles of the loop follow the Rim Trail back to the trailhead. Note that the park shuttle doesn't stop at Fairyland.

This trail is difficult primarily because it meanders – in and out of the hoodoos, down into washes, up and over saddles etc. Carry plenty of water, and pace yourself.

From the point, the trail dips gradually below the rim – watch your footing on the narrow sections. To the south, Boat Mesa stands between you and views of the park. A short walk leads past ancient bristlecone pines, some clinging precariously to the ragged cliffs, their 1000-plus-year-old roots curled up like wizened fingers. Looping around hoodoos that rise like castle turrets and towers, the trail soon drops to the canyon floor and a seasonal wash. Much of the north-facing terrain here holds its snowpack until May, sometimes June.

At **Fairyland Canyon**, 600ft below your starting point, towers of deep-orange stone rise like giant totem poles. The trail rises and falls before traversing a ridge toward **Campbell Canyon**. As you walk beneath Boat Mesa's great cliffs, notice how the formation comes to a point like the bow of a ship – you'll quickly understand how it got its name.

Zigzagging up and down, the trail eventually reaches a seasonal wash on the floor of Campbell Canyon. Keep an eye out for **Tower Bridge**, which connects three spires to two windows. To reach the base of the formation, take the clearly marked dead-end spur from the wash. From Tower Bridge it's a 950ft climb in 1.5 miles to the Rim Trail, some of it strenuous. En route, to your left, look for the long, white **China Wall** and its little windows. A look back at Boat Mesa shows the changing vistas of canyon country.

🏃 Queen's Garden Trail

Duration 1–2 hours

Distance 1.8 miles

Difficulty Moderate

Start/Finish Sunrise Point

Nearest Towns Tropic, Panguitch

Transportation Park shuttle

Summary Good for kids, the easiest trail into the canyon makes a gentle descent over sloping erosional fins. It passes elegant hoodoo formations but stops short of the canyon floor.

The hike to Queen's Garden is not a loop, but an in-and-out hike. You can also add the

Queen's Garden Connecting Trail, part of the Navajo Loop–Queen's Garden Combination.

From Sunrise Point, follow signs to the trailhead off the Rim Trail. Views of the amphitheater as you descend are superb – a maze of colorful rock spires extends to Bryce Point, and deep-green pines dot the canyon floor beneath undulating slopes seemingly tie-dyed pink, orange and white. As you drop below the rim, watch for the stark and primitive bristlecone pines, which at Bryce are about 1600 years old (specimens in California are 5000 years old). These ancient trees' dense needles cluster like foxtails on the ends of the branches.

After a series of switchbacks, turn right and follow signs to Queen's Garden. The short spur from the main trail passes through a tunnel and emerges among exceptionally beautiful hoodoo castles in striking whites and oranges amid rich-green pines. After looping around a high wall and passing through two more tunnels, bear right and

follow signs to Queen Victoria. The trail's namesake monarch peers down from a white-capped rock, perched atop her throne.

Return to the rim or link with the Navajo Loop via the Queen's Garden Connecting Trail, which drops to the canyon floor.

🏃 Navajo Loop–Queen's Garden Combination

Duration 2–3 hours

Distance 2.9 miles

Difficulty Moderate

Start/Finish Sunrise Point

Nearest Towns Tropic, Panguitch

Transportation Park shuttle

Summary The most popular route in the park, and fairly gentle, it hits Bryce's signature features in a relatively short amount of time, despite the sometimes steep grade.

Bryce Canyon – Day Hikes

◉ N 0 ▬▬▬▬▬ 1 km
   0 ▬▬▬▬▬ 0.5 miles

Dixie National Forest

Entrance 🛈 Kiosk

63

Fairyland Point

Fairyland Canyon

Visitor Center 🛈

Boat Mesa

North Campground

China Wall

Tower Bridge

Sunrise Point

Bryce Canyon Lodge

Thor's Hammer

Bryce Canyon National Park

Sunset Point

Silent City

Bryce Canyon

Bryce Creek

Inspiration Point

63

Wall of Windows

Bryce Point

▬▬ Fairyland Loop Trail
▬▬ Navajo Loop Trail
▬▬ Navajo Loop–Queen's Garden Combination
▬▬ Peekaboo Loop Trail
▬▬ Queen's Garden Trail
▬▬ Rim Trail

Begin with Queen's Garden to avoid the steep descent through Wall Street (it does a number on ankles). Check ahead with rangers for trail-closure information, particularly after winter.

From Sunrise Point, follow the Queen's Garden Trail description. Follow signs for the Queen's Garden Connecting Trail, which descends to the garden of spires and follows the canyon floor.

Another advantage of taking this trail is time spent on the canyon floor, where tall pines provide shade and offer perspective on oversize hoodoos. The final push, a steep ascent through **Wall Street** and past the **Silent City**, is the more visually stunning of the two trails.

If Wall Street is closed due to rockfall, opt to ascend to the rim via the Two Bridges side of the Navajo Loop Trail.

Before you top out on the rim, detour right a short distance to see **Thor's Hammer**. Then stroll back to Sunrise Point along the Rim Trail, gazing into the canyon for yet another perspective on the hoodoos.

🏃 Navajo Loop Trail

Duration 1–2 hours

Distance 1.3 miles

Difficulty Moderate–difficult

Start/Finish Sunset Point

Nearest Towns Tropic, Panguitch

Transportation Park shuttle

Summary This sometimes-steep hike is short but spectacular. From the trailhead at Sunset Point, you drop right into the canyon beneath towering hoodoos that dwarf onlookers.

This popular trail passes alongside Thor's Hammer, the park's most famous rock formation; beneath Two Bridges, a pair of small water-carved arches; and through Wall Street, a narrow canyon with steep rock walls that reveal only a sliver of sky above. It's a steep ascent and descent, but the trail is clearly marked and fairly wide. Those in reasonably good shape won't have a problem. Rangers strongly recommend hiking it clockwise to avoid a steep descent through Wall Street, a notorious ankle-buster. To lengthen your hike by 30 minutes to an hour, you could also start at Queen's Garden Trail.

From the wide, fenced-in viewing area at Sunset Point, follow signs for the Navajo Loop. The trail drops immediately into a switchback, then forks about 100yd ahead. Take the left fork, which leads past **Thor's Hammer** down a long slope to the canyon

HIKING IN BRYCE CANYON NATIONAL PARK

NAME	START LOCATION	DESCRIPTION
Under-the-Rim Trail (p117)	Bryce Point	Bryce's premier backcountry hike passes few hoodoos but promises solitude
Peekaboo Loop Trail (p116)	Bryce Point	The greatest variety of terrain and scenery in Bryce; horses allowed
Rim Trail (p115)	Fairyland Point, Bryce Point or any rim trailhead	Canyon rim hike with stellar overlook of hoodoos
Fairyland Loop Trail (p112)	Fairyland Point	Long hike (away from crowds) leads past castle-like formations
Riggs Spring Loop Trail (p119)	Rainbow Point	This strenuous hike drops off the plateau's southern tip through three ecological zones
Queen's Garden Trail (p112)	Sunrise Point	Gentlest descent into the canyon on eroding fins, passing myriad hoodoos
Navajo Loop–Queen's Garden Combination (p113)	Sunrise Point	Most popular route in the park; hits Bryce's signature features
Navajo Loop Trail (p114)	Sunset Point	Short and steep but spectacular, with hoodoo views

 Wildlife Watching   *Views*   *Great for Families*

floor. Entering the canyon, you can follow the sign on your left to see **Two Bridges**.

At the canyon floor, turn right to continue the loop and ascend back to the rim. Sometimes closed due to rockfall (check ahead with rangers), **Wall Street** features 100ft walls which block much of the sunlight, keeping the canyon shady and cool. The giant Douglas fir trees towering between the walls are over 750 years old!

To the left of the Wall Street trail, the **Silent City** looms large. If the spur trail through the tunnel on your left is open, take a quick jaunt to look down on these eerie pinnacles. The trail finishes with a steep ascent and some 30 switchbacks that lead to the rim.

🚶 Rim Trail

Duration 2–3 hours

Distance 5.5 miles one way

Difficulty Easy–moderate

Start Bryce Point

Finish Fairyland Point

Nearest Towns Tropic, Panguitch

Transportation Park shuttle

Summary With great views, this trail hugs the canyon rim, stretching from the south end of Bryce Amphitheater at Bryce Point all the way to Fairyland Point, near the northern park boundary.

Sections of this trail are level, particularly between Sunrise and Sunset Points, where the path is paved and wheelchair accessible. Log rail fences mark vertical drop-offs in many places. In other spots you'll ascend moderately steep, wooded rises to seek shade beneath the pines, watch wildlife or soak up vibrant displays of spring wildflowers. The colors in the rock pop out most when lit by the morning or afternoon sun.

You can join the trail anywhere along its 5.5-mile route – just keep in mind that unless the shuttle is running or you arrange to be picked up, you'll have to walk back. If you plan on taking the shuttle, note that buses don't stop at Fairyland. You'll find restrooms and drinking water at Sunset Point, and the general store and snack bar (both open spring through fall) near Sunrise Point, the approximate midpoint of the hike. You can also duck into Bryce Canyon Lodge for lunch, restrooms and drinking water.

Remember that Bryce sits atop a sloping plateau. The north end of the Rim Trail is lower than the south end, so it's downhill from Bryce Point to Fairyland Point, though the trail rises and falls in a few spots,

BRYCE CANYON NATIONAL PARK DAY HIKES

DIFFICULTY	DURATION	ROUND-TRIP DISTANCE	ELEVATION CHANGE	FEATURES	FACILITIES
moderate-difficult	3 days	22.9 miles one way	1315ft	🦌 🔭	🚰 ⛺
difficult	3-5hr	5.5 miles	500-900ft	🔭	🚻 🚰
easy-moderate	2-3hr	5.5 miles one way	550ft	🔭 👫	🚻 🚰
difficult	4-5hr	8 miles	900ft	🔭	
difficult	4-5hr or overnight	8.8 miles	1675ft	🔭	🚰 ⛺
moderate	1-2hr	1.8 miles	320ft	🔭 👫	
moderate	2-3hr	2.9 miles	521ft	🔭 👫	
moderate-difficult	1-2hr	1.3 miles	521ft	🔭 👫	

 🚻 Restrooms   🚰 Drinking Water   ⛺ Backcountry camping

particularly in its climb from Sunrise Point to North Campground.

During the walk, you'll leave behind Bryce Amphitheater and arrive above Campbell Canyon and Fairyland Amphitheater. You'll find fewer formations at this end of the park, but giant Boat Mesa and its high cliffs rise majestically to the north.

From Bryce Point to Inspiration Point the trail skirts the canyon rim atop white cliffs, revealing gorgeous formations, including the Wall of Windows. After passing briefly through trees, it continues along the ridge top to the uppermost level of Inspiration Point, 1.3 miles from Bryce Point.

The leg to Sunset Point drops 200ft in 0.75 miles, winding its way along limestone-capped cliffs that yield to orange sandstone fins. Below the rim the Silent City rises in all its hoodoo glory; the lower you go, the higher the rock spires rise beside you.

At Sunset Point you may wish to detour along the Navajo Loop Trail for a taste of the canyon; you can reemerge on the Rim Trail further ahead by adding the Queen's Garden Connecting Trail. Otherwise, stay the course and look for Thor's Hammer as you continue the 0.5-mile stroll along a paved path to Sunrise Point – the most crowded stretch of trail in the entire park. Views are worth it.

Past Sunrise Point, crowds thin as the trail climbs 150ft toward North Campground. Fork left at the Fairyland Loop Trail junction, unless you'd like to follow the moderately difficult, 3-mile round-trip spur into the canyon (950ft elevation loss) to see the window-laced China Wall and Tower Bridge, twin arches between chunky rock spires. Otherwise, watch for these features from the Rim Trail.

Topping out near North Campground, the path ambles across gently rolling hills on the forested plateau before rejoining the canyon rim at Fairyland Point, 2.5 miles from Sunrise Point.

🏃 Peekaboo Loop Trail

Duration 3–5 hours

Distance 5.5 miles

Difficulty Difficult

Start/Finish Bryce Point

Nearest Towns Tropic, Panguitch

Transportation Park shuttle

Summary An ideal day hike, Peekaboo Loop Trail sees the most variety of terrain and scenery in Bryce, with 1500ft to 1800ft of cumulative elevation changes.

Access to this circular trail is via either the Navajo Loop or the Queen's Garden Connecting Trail. The following description starts from Bryce Point – if starting from Sunrise Point it's a 6.6-mile hike; from Sunset Point it's 5 miles.

The Peekaboo Loop Trail is also a horse trail, so expect to see occasional riders. They move slowly, so you'll have plenty of advance warning. Stock animals have right of way – step off the trail and let them pass undisturbed. If you don't want to navigate around horse droppings, consider another route. But views here are among the park's best, particularly of the Wall of Windows, the Silent City and the Fairy Castle. You'll also find shady spots to rest, a picnic area and pit toilets (the latter are on the loop, just west of its intersection with the connecting trail to Bryce Point).

This trail rises and falls many times; be prepared for a workout. If you're afraid of heights, be forewarned that in places you'll pass sheer drops, though the trail is comfortably wide enough for a horse.

From Bryce Point follow signs to the Peekaboo Connecting Trail, just east of the parking area. Bear left at the fork where you'll descend 1.1 miles down the connecting trail. You'll pass through mixed conifers, then swoop out along a gray-white limestone fin beneath the Bryce Point overlook. Further down the trail, hoodoo columns take on a bright-orange hue. After passing through a human-made tunnel, look for the Alligator in the white rock ahead. As you work your way down the switchbacks, watch for the Wall of Windows, which juts above bright-orange hoodoos atop a sheer vertical cliff face perpendicular to the canyon rim. The windows line the top of this wall.

At the loop trail junction, bear right. As you pass beneath healthy fir and spruce trees, you'll spot a few blackened snags. They're victims of electrical storms, not forest fires – the plateau's high elevation and isolated trees attract lightning. Also look for ancient bristlecone pines; an inch of these trees' trunks represents 100 years' growth.

Climbing a saddle, you'll rise to eye level with the hoodoo tops before dropping over the other side to the cluster of delicate red spires at Fairy Castle. Midway around, just past the turnoff for the Navajo Loop, the trail climbs again to spectacular views of the Silent City and passes beneath the

Cathedral, a majestic wall of buttresslike hoodoos. The rolling trail skirts the Wall of Windows, threads through a tunnel and switchbacks down. Notice the rapidly changing views as you pass the huge Wall of Windows. The trail turns west and climbs, then drops again amid more hoodoos. As you approach the Bryce Point trail, take the spur on your right to the lush green rest area near the horse corral for a cooldown or picnic before climbing out of the canyon.

🚶 OVERNIGHT HIKES

🚶 Under-the-Rim Trail

Duration 3 days

Distance 22.9 miles one way

Difficulty Moderate–difficult

Start Bryce Point

Finish Rainbow Point

Nearest Towns Tropic, Panguitch

Transportation Park shuttle

Summary Ideal for getting away from it all, this multiday hike skirts beneath cliffs, through amphitheaters and amid pines and aspens. Originally fire trails, these paths lack some of the drama of backcountry hikes elsewhere.

If you start at Bryce Point and end at Rainbow Point, you can hike the park's primary backcountry trail in two days, though three is recommended. In either direction you'll face a hefty ascent the last 3 miles. By hiking north to south, you'll have the sun at your back in the afternoon and Rainbow Point as the grand finale.

Running nearly the length of the park, the trail rises from the piñon juniper community (6600ft to 7000ft), through the ponderosa pine community (7000ft to 8500ft) to the fir-spruce community (8500ft to 9100ft), touching the rim only at the trailheads.

Descending from the scenic drive, four connecting trails link with the Under-the-Rim Trail, each near a backcountry campsite. These connecting trails allow hikers to approach any section as a day hike. Rangers can offer details on the connecting trails. You could also set up base camp at one of the sites and take day hikes in either direction. If you have the time, extend your trek south along the 8.8-mile Riggs Spring Loop Trail.

This is a one-way hike, so consider leaving a car at one or both ends. A shuttle service to Rainbow Point may be available; ask at the visitor center. Hitching is prohibited in the park, but hikers can sometimes catch rides back to Bryce Point without much difficulty.

Permits ($5 to $15, depending on the number of hikers in your party) are obtained at the visitor center between 9am and one hour prior to the center's closing time. You cannot place an advance order by phone or email, but you can make reservations in person up to 48 hours in advance. Campsites are assigned with the purchase of a backcountry permit. The maximum stay at any particular site is three nights.

Most backcountry trails are covered with snow from late October to March or April; even in May, snowpack sometimes obscures sections of trail. June and September are ideal times to hike, while in July and August you'll have to contend with thunderstorms. Mosquitoes are rare, but cedar gnats are annoying in early summer. In winter, backpackers must have an interview with the backcountry ranger to discuss hazards.

Under-The-Rim Trail

Beyond the usual safety preparations for hiking in the deserts of southern Utah, the primary concern is elevation. Take it slow until you're acclimated. For navigating, use the medium-scale National Geographic Trails Illustrated *Map of Bryce Canyon*. All water in the backcountry must be purified.

DAY 1: BRYCE POINT TO RIGHT FORK SWAMP CANYON CAMPSITE
4–6 HOURS, 10.5 MILES

From Bryce Point the trail descends steeply almost due east, then swings south. After 0.5 miles you'll wind down to a ridge, where the earth changes from gray to orange. Over the next 0.5 miles Rainbow Point comes into view above the ridge in the foreground.

As the trail traces a south-facing promontory, look north for a grand panorama of the Pink Cliffs. On the right (west) the Right Fork Yellow Creek forms a steep-sided drainage. Two miles in you'll pass the Hat Shop, its gray boulder caps perched atop spindly conglomerate stands. At the base of this descent, 2.8 miles from Bryce Point, is the Right Fork Yellow Creek campsite, a good spot in a clearing beside the creek, which runs all year.

From the campsite, follow the left (east) bank of the creek for half a mile, then cross it and bear south. Here the landscape is a semi-desert, with little shade and plenty of pungent sage growing in the sandy soil. As the trail turns west, you'll pass the Yellow Creek group campsite on the left. A quarter-mile beyond the campsite, you'll reach Yellow Creek. The trail follows the creek and climbs toward the Pink Cliffs at the head of the creek and Paria View, 1000ft above. The trail soon crosses the creek; cairns point the way.

Another 0.25 miles brings you to the Yellow Creek campsite, in plenty of shade beside the creek. It's a great spot to watch the sunset. From here you'll turn southwest up a short, steep hill. The trail undulates for about 2 miles, crossing a slope between two amphitheaters. After 1.5 miles the trail drops into Pasture Wash. Follow cairns to the south edge of the wash and look for a sharp uphill turn, where the trail visibly zigzags up and out of the wash. The view (north to south) of Swamp Canyon, Mud Canyon and Noon Canyon Buttes will reward your effort.

Descend into the valley to the junction with the Sheep Creek Connecting Trail, which climbs 2 miles to the scenic drive. A well-marked spur leads 0.5 miles south to the Sheep Creek campsite, its beauty second only to the Yellow Creek site; you can usually find water here.

From the junction, the trail climbs 150ft (crossing from the Sheep Creek amphitheater to the Swamp Canyon amphitheater) then descends into Swamp Canyon amid a stand of large quaking aspens. On the left (southeast), in a clearing among large ponderosa pines, is the Right Fork Swamp Canyon campsite; water is sometimes available in upper Swamp Canyon, 100yd north of the campsite.

DAY 2: RIGHT FORK SWAMP CANYON CAMPSITE TO NATURAL BRIDGE CAMPSITE
1½–2½ HOURS, 4.6 MILES

One hundred yards past the campsite is the junction with the mile-long Swamp Canyon Connecting Trail, which climbs north to the scenic drive. From the connecting trail junction, you'll climb steadily south, then turn west up switchbacks. Just beyond, at 8200ft, is the Swamp Canyon campsite. Although there's not much flat ground, and the site is near the trail, it's cool in summer. You'll sometimes find water 0.25 miles up the Whiteman Connecting Trail, which climbs 0.9 miles to the scenic drive.

Beyond camp the trail passes aspens and pines, then descends to the base of Farview Cliffs. From here you'll skirt Willis Creek for a mile until it turns southeast. You may find it difficult to distinguish the trail from other small creeks; bear south and west.

The trail ducks into Dixie National Forest for 0.25 miles, then curves sharply east to climb an eroded sandstone slope southwest of Willis Creek. At the top, the sandy trail snakes around the east edge of a promontory for gorgeous views of the Pink Cliffs.

Descend to a southern tributary of Willis Creek and continue 0.5 miles (you may need to cross several times if the water is running high) to the Natural Bridge campsite, which lacks water.

DAY 3: NATURAL BRIDGE CAMPSITE TO RAINBOW POINT
3–5 HOURS, 7.8 MILES

Half a mile out of camp, the trail traverses a sage meadow toward Agua Canyon. Crossing this canyon may prove tricky: on older topo maps, the trail turns slightly west and cuts straight across the canyon, but due to floods you now need to hike up the canyon 0.75 miles, then switchback up the canyon's south ridge. When in doubt, follow the cairns. The switchbacks are snowed under until late spring. Atop this ridge, the Agua Canyon Connecting Trail climbs 1.6 miles to the scenic drive.

From the connecting trail junction, you'll skirt a pink promontory, descend into Ponderosa Canyon, then zigzag up and down to South Fork Canyon. Just past the head of the canyon, you'll reach the **Iron Spring campsite** on your right; the east-facing ridge leaves little room to spread out. Amid a grove of aspens 600ft up-canyon (southwest) from the campsite, **Iron Spring** supplies year-round water. The turnoff for the spring lies 100yd north of the campsite.

The trail continues its undulating rhythm, dipping to cross both arms of Black Birch Canyon, where directional cairns are sometimes obscured by debris. After clambering over the lower slopes of a northwest-jutting promontory, you'll enter the southernmost amphitheater of Bryce Canyon's Pink Cliffs.

The trail traces the hammer-shaped ridge below Rainbow Point, climbing steadily and offering unsurpassed views. Ascend the final 1.5 miles up the back (south) side of the amphitheater to the rim. You'll cross the Riggs Spring Loop Trail just beneath the rim, 100yd east of the Rainbow Point parking lot. While the urge to peer over the rim is irresistible, use extreme caution, as the edges are unstable.

🏃 Riggs Spring Loop Trail

Duration 4–5 hours (or overnight)

Distance 8.8 miles

Difficulty Difficult

Start/Finish Rainbow Point

Nearest Towns Tropic, Panguitch

Transportation Park shuttle

Summary This tough trail loops from the tip of the Paunsaugunt Plateau, descending beneath the spectacular Pink Cliffs through spruce, fir and aspen, then through ponderosa pines to a desert habitat of sagebrush and scrub oak.

If you choose to do this hike over two days you will need a backcountry permit. Permits ($5 to $15, depending on the number of hikers in your party) are obtained at the visitor center between 9am and one hour before the center closes. You cannot place an advance order by phone or email, but you can make reservations in person up to 48 hours in advance. Campsites are assigned with purchase of a backcountry permit. The maximum stay at any particular site is three nights.

Make this loop clockwise, not counterclockwise; it's a safer way through steep terrain. Extend the hike to an overnight outing to ease your pace and soak up the solitude. Starting at Rainbow Point, follow the Bristlecone Loop Trail to the turnoff for the Under-the-Rim Trail and follow signs to the Riggs Spring Loop Trail.

The trail descends the Pink Cliffs onto the **Promontory**, a ridgeline that juts from the plateau in a sweeping arc south. Molly's Nipple rises to the southeast; Navajo Mountain is on the horizon 80 miles to the east-southeast.

After dropping off the Promontory along tree-lined slopes, you'll double back north for grand views of the Pink Cliffs, then descend to **Coral Hollow campsite**. This site lies beneath oak and pine trees 3.6 miles from, and 1200ft below, Rainbow Point; there's no water here.

From Coral Hollow you'll loop below Yovimpa Point on a gradual descent through pines to **Mutton Hollow**. **Riggs Spring campsite** (7480ft) sits amid pines at the base of this hollow. Of the three camps on this loop, this one is the most idyllic. You'll almost always find water at Riggs Spring, hemmed in by a log fence. This is the lowest point along the trail.

Onward, the increasingly steep trail climbs past towering ponderosa pines en route to **Yovimpa Pass**, which lies atop a plateau at 8360ft. The higher you get, the better the views of the approaching cliffs. Perched atop this plateau, the **Yovimpa Pass campsite** provides little shade but often has water.

The last 1.6 miles of the trail skirt the edge of the plateau through woods before rejoining the rim at **Yovimpa Point**. Breaks in the forest reveal views of the Grand Staircase and the hoodoos below Rainbow Point.

Riggs Spring Loop Trail

Driving Tour
Bryce Canyon Scenic Drive

DURATION 2 HOURS
DISTANCE 34 MILES
START/FINISH VISITOR CENTER
NEAREST TOWN TROPIC

Spanning the length of the park, this out-and-back route hits all the park highlights. Drive to the end point first to avoid left-hand turns into the lookouts.

The scenic drive winds south for 17 miles and roughly parallels the canyon rim, climbing from 7894ft at the visitor center to 9115ft at Rainbow Point, the plateau's southern tip at road's end. Snowstorms may close the road in winter. Check at the visitor center for current road conditions.

Head directly to Rainbow Point (a 35-minute drive from the visitor center), then stop at the scenic overlooks and turnouts as you return. Visit ❶ **Rainbow Point** via a short, paved, wheelchair-accessible path at the far end of the parking lot. The overlook offers a jaw-dropping glimpse of canyon country, with giant sloping plateaus, tilted mesas and towering buttes jutting above the vast landscape. On the northeastern horizon look for the Aquarius Plateau – the very top step of the Grand Staircase – rising 2000ft higher than Bryce.

At the other end of the parking lot another short, paved, wheelchair-accessible trail leads to ❷ **Yovimpa Point**, one of the park's windiest spots. The southwest-facing view reveals more forested slopes and less eroding rock. Look for Molly's Nipple, an eroded sandstone dome often mistaken for a volcano. Dipping below the horizon is the Kaibab Plateau, marking the Arizona border and the Grand Canyon.

Take the easy 1-mile ❸ **Bristlecone Loop Trail** from Rainbow Point. Yovimpa Point also offers a great tree-shaded picnic area.

Just north of mile marker 16, at 8750ft, the small ❹ **Black Birch Canyon** overlook shows precipitous cliffs roadside. It also offers your first up-close look at hoodoos – though modest ones. There are no trailheads here, only a small lookout.

Higher than the previous stop, ❺ **Ponderosa Canyon** offers long vistas like those at Rainbow Point. Below, note the namesake

giant ponderosa pines, some as tall as 150ft. This small amphitheater of hoodoos and burnt-orange cliffs is breathtaking, especially in morning light. If you're feeling ambitious, descend a stretch of the moderately strenuous ❻ **Agua Canyon Connecting Trail**, a lightly traveled, steep trail that drops past woods into a brilliant amphitheater of hoodoos before joining the ❼ **Under-the-Rim Trail**.

One of the best stops at this end of the park, the ❽ **Agua Canyon** viewpoint overlooks two large formations of precariously balanced, top-heavy hoodoos that could tip at any time. Note the precipitous drop-off at your feet. On the ridge above, distinct sedimentary lines stripe iron-rich red rock and white limestone.

The parking lot at ❾ **Natural Bridge** is the biggest since Rainbow Point, and with good reason: a stunning span of eroded, red-hued limestone juts from the edge of the overlook.

The stop at ❿ **Fairview Point** offers a grand view of the tree-studded rises and benches, giant plateaus, blue-hued mesas and buttes that extend from the skirts of Bryce into the Grand Staircase, as far as the eye can see. On clear days you can see 160 miles to Arizona's Black Mesas. A short walk among vanilla-scented pines leads to another overlook at ⓫ **Piracy Point**. There are toilets but no running water.

The overlook at ⓬ **Swamp Canyon** sits in a forested dip between two ridgelines that extend into the canyon. From the turnout you can take a short walk through the trees and descend slightly to towering pink-orange cliffs of crumbling limestone. Nature lovers like the variety of plant and animal life here; kids like the steep trail into the canyon. This is also the jumping-off point for the scenic ⓭ **Swamp Canyon Connecting Trail**.

Three miles north of Swamp Canyon, turn right and follow signs to the ⓮ **Paria View** viewpoint, 2 miles off the main road. This small overlook is for cars only – though it's reserved for cross-country skiers in winter, when the access road isn't plowed. This is *the* place to come for sunsets. Most of the hoodoo amphitheaters at Bryce face east and are best viewed at sunrise. The amphitheater here faces west toward the Paria River watershed.

If you make just one stop, make it ⓯ **Bryce Point**. You can walk the rim above ⓰ **Bryce Amphitheater** for awesome views of the Silent City, an assemblage of hoodoos resembling figures frozen in the rock. Be sure to follow the path to the actual point, a fenced-in promontory that juts over the forested canyon floor, 1000ft below. This rivals any overlook in the park for splendor and eye-popping color.

Bryce Point marks the beginning of the 5.5-mile **17** **Rim Trail** and the **18** **Peekaboo Loop Trail**. There's also a pit toilet.

At **19** **Inspiration Point** a short ascent up a paved path takes you to another overlook into Bryce Amphitheater. Inspiration Point sits lower than Bryce Point and provides much the same view, though the Silent City is most compelling from here. The hoodoos feel closer, and you can make out more details on the canyon floor. Inspiration Point is a great place to return for stargazing.

Views into Bryce Amphitheater at **20** **Sunset Point** are as good as they get, but don't expect solitude. It's at the core of the park, near campgrounds, the lodge and all visitor services. Aside from great views of the Silent City, this point is known for **21** **Thor's Hammer**, a big square-capped rock balanced atop a spindly hoodoo. This is the starting point for the **22** **Navajo Loop Trail**, the park's most popular hike, and you'll find restrooms, drinking water and picnic tables. Don't be fooled by the name of this point. Because it faces east, sunrises are better here than sunsets.

Marking the north end of Bryce Amphitheater, the southeast-facing **23** **Sunrise Point** offers great views of hoodoos, the Aquarius Plateau and the Sinking Ship, a sloping mesa that looks like a ship's stern rising out of the water. Keep your eyes peeled for the **24** **Limber Pine**, a spindly tree whose roots have been exposed through erosion, but which nonetheless remains anchored to the receding sand. Within walking distance or a one-minute drive are the Bryce Canyon General Store, drinking water, restrooms, picnic tables and a snack bar; head north toward the campground on the loop road.

End your driving tour at the visitor center or head to Fairyland Point. To reach the point, drive a mile north of the entrance gate, then a mile east of the main road. Fairyland is a less-visited spot with wooded views north toward the Aquarius Plateau. Here you can see hoodoos at all stages of evolution, from fin to crumbling tower, and start the Fairyland Loop Trail.

OTHER ACTIVITIES

Cycling

The park is in the process of building a multi-use path. Several companies lead bicycle tours in and around Bryce, including **Backroads** (☑800-462-2848; www.backroads.com; 6-day trip from $2498), **Rim Tours** (☑435-259-5223, 800-626-7335; www.rimtours.com; half-day from $90) and **Western Spirit Cycling** (☑435-259-8732, 800-845-2453; www.westernspirit.com; 6-day trip $1395).

Horseback Riding

There are no overnight backcountry tours within the park. All outfitters have a limit of 220lb for riders.

To bring your own horse to Bryce, coordinate with Canyon Trail Rides. Contact the park for regulations. There are no backcountry campgrounds suitable for stock animals.

Canyon Trail Rides   HORSEBACK RIDING
(☑435-679-8665; www.canyonrides.com; Bryce Canyon Lodge; 2hr/half-day tour $60/80) The national park's only licensed outfitter operates out of the park lodge. You can take a short, two-hour trip to the canyon floor or giddy-up for a half-day through the dramatic hoodoos on Peekaboo Trail.

Red Canyon Trail Rides   HORSEBACK RIDING
(☑800-892-7923, 435-834-5441; www.redcanyontrailrides.com; Hwy 12, Bryce Canyon Pines; 1hr ride $40; ☺Mar-Nov) Ride for as little as a half-

SEE ANOTHER SIDE OF BRYCE

➔ See stars loud and clear through telescopes at the Astronomy Festival

➔ Bound the lip of Bryce Canyon at the Rim Run (www.rubysinn.com/run.html), an annual 5-mile running race held in August

➔ Join rock jocks examining Bryce's amazing formations during the Geofest geology festival

➔ Watch broncos buck at the Bryce Canyon Country Rodeo, near Ruby's Inn at 7pm in summer

➔ Ditch your flashlight and join a ranger for summer's cool moonlight hikes; reservation required

hour or as long as a whole day on private and public lands outside the park, including Red Canyon.

Watching Wildlife

Bryce Canyon is home to 59 mammal species, 11 reptile species, four amphibian species and more than 1000 insect species. As many as 175 bird species pass through annually, though large, highly adaptable ravens are among the few birds found year-round. If you're lucky, you might also spot California condors or a peregrine falcon. Keep an eye to the ground for the threatened Utah prairie dog. For more information, pick up books and wildlife charts at the visitor center, or visit www.nps.gov/brca/naturescience/animals.htm.

Ranger Programs

From early summer until fall, rangers lead rim walks, hikes amid the hoodoos, short geology lectures, evening programs, kids' ecology walks and astronomy talks, with telescopes. Check the *Hoodoo* newspaper or ask at the visitor center for current schedules, or visit the park website for general information.

If you time your visit to coincide with the full moon (and clear skies), don't miss the **moonlight hike**, a popular two-hour stroll among the hoodoos. A lottery for participation is held at the visitor center on the afternoon of the hike; treaded hiking boots are required.

Kids' Activities

When you arrive at the park, stop by the visitor center to pick up a **Junior Ranger Activity Guide**. Once kids complete certain activities, they can return to the visitor center to receive a badge from a ranger. The visitor center also sells coloring books specific to Bryce, as well as outdoor-related toys.

Winter Activities

In winter Bryce's rosy rock formations and pine forests wear a blanket of fresh powder. Though nighttime temperatures can drop below freezing for more than 200 consecutive nights, days are often mild and sunny, ideal for winter sports. Snowfall averages 100in per winter. Visitors become scarce, and the dry, light powder is perfect for snowshoeing and cross-country skiing.

Ten miles of Bryce's dedicated ski trails (ungroomed) connect with 20 additional miles of groomed trails through Dixie National Forest. Trail use in the national forest is free, though snowmobiles are also granted access, so keep watch for traffic. Rent skis, snowshoes and snow boots (half-day $7, full day $10) at **Ruby's Inn**; it also has trail maps. You can also ski from here.

When snow and staff are sufficient, rangers offer guided snowshoe hikes along the plateau top. Inquire at the visitor center.

Every Presidents' Day weekend, in February, the **Bryce Canyon Winterfest** is hosted at Ruby's Inn. In addition to races, there are free ski and photography clinics, kids' races and snow sculptures.

☆✷FESTIVAL & EVENTS

Astronomy Festival   ASTRONOMY
(www.nps.gov/brca/planyourvisit/astrofest.htm) Bryce Canyon's annual four-day Astronomy Festival in mid-June celebrates the exceptional viewing of the night skies at Bryce. It features talks, walks and stargazing with experts, the park's Astronomy Rangers and the Salt Lake Astronomical Society. A rocket-building workshop appeals to kids.

Bryce Canyon Winterfest   SPORTS
Early February. Includes everything from cross-country skiing and snowmobiling to archery and snow sculpting.

GeoFest   FAIR
Join park rangers for guided hikes, family-friendly geology programs, bus tours with a geologist, evening programs, as well as exhibits and family-oriented activities. Held in late July.

Bryce Canyon Half Marathon   SPORTS
(https://bchm.jit.su) A wildly popular distance run through the park in July, starting at Ruby's Inn and ending past Tropic in Cannonville.

⌸SLEEPING

The park is home to two campgrounds and a lodge. However, most visitors stay at lodgings just north or west of the park, or 11 miles east in the town of Tropic. If nearby lodgings are full, consider staying in or around Panguitch, 24 miles west of the park, or Kodachrome Basin State Park, 19 miles east.

DOG LODGING

Even picky pet-owners laud **Pawz** (☑435-691-3696; www.pawzdogz.com), a down-home kennel located in rural sagebrush country. Features include indoor dog beds and yards with pools. It's 5 miles out of Panguitch but doggie pickups are available in town with advance notice. There's both day camp and overnight options. Another acceptable option, **Canyon Park Animal Retreat** (☑435-679-8548; Tropic), is in Tropic, 11 miles east of Bryce.

Dixie National Forest, which surrounds Bryce Canyon, offers several campgrounds within a short drive of the park. For a complete list, visit www.fs.fed.us/dxnf (the Powell and Escalante ranger districts are closest to Bryce). The ranger stations in Panguitch and Escalante can provide maps and information.

In the Park

Bryce's two campgrounds are extremely popular. They have renovated bathroom facilities as well as recycling (at entrances).

Sunset Campground   CAMPGROUND $
(☑877-444-6777; www.recreation.gov; Bryce Canyon Rd; tent/RV site $15/30; ⊙Apr-Sep) Just south of Sunset Point, this 102-site campground offers more shade than North Campground but has few amenities beyond flush toilets. Inquire about availability at the visitor center, and secure your site early. Twenty tent sites can be reserved up to six months ahead. Loop A allows RVs, though it has few pull-through spots (generators are allowed 8am to 8pm). Loops B and C are reserved for vehicles under 20ft. Loop B offers less shade, while Loop C's sites vary widely in quality; for shade and privacy, try for sites on the outer ring.

North Campground   CAMPGROUND $
(☑877-444-6777; www.recreation.gov; Bryce Canyon Rd; tent & RV sites $30) Near the visitor center, this year-round trailside campground is enormous, with 101 sites with campfire rings. A short walk from the campground takes you to showers, a coin laundry and a general store. A fee-for-use sanitary dump station ($5) is available in summer months at the south end. RV reservations are available six months out. It's divided into

> **ⓘ ESSENTIALS: SUDS & SCRUBS**
>
> The showers and coin-op laundry facilities for Sunset Campground, in the park, are found at **Bryce Canyon General Store & Snack Bar** (p126). North of the park, **Ruby's Campground** offers coin-operated laundry; buy soap next door at the general store. It also has showers.

four loops. In summer Loops A and B are for RVs over 20ft only and provide many pull-through spots. Loops C and D accommodate vehicles less than 20ft. Loops A and B sit up high amid tall trees, while Loop C is closest to the canyon rim (sites 59 through 61 have canyon views, though little privacy). Loop D sits on a hill amid small to medium-size trees.

Bryce Canyon Lodge   LODGE $$
(☑ 435-834-8700,877-386-4383;www.brycecanyon forever.com; Hwy 63, Bryce Canyon National Park; r & cabins $208-256; ⊗ Apr-Oct; @ 🛜) Built in the 1920s, the main park lodge exudes rustic mountain charm, with a large stone fireplace and exposed roof timbers. Most rooms are in two-story wooden satellite buildings with private balconies. The walls prove thin if the neighbors are noisy. In the perfect woodsy setting, the the retro-cool Western cabins have gas fireplaces and creaky porches. No TVs. Wi-fi operates in parts of the main lodge.

Bryce Canyon City

The village of Bryce Canyon City is located just outside the park. Not an actual town, it is a growing tourist center with minimarts, outfitters, a gas station and hotels.

If you're unable to secure a reservation or don't arrive early enough to get a site in the park, you could spend a night at a Bryce Canyon City campground and return early in the morning to grab a spot in the park.

Except for a few notable exceptions, lodgings at Bryce are nothing special. Expect motel rooms with fiberglass tub-shower

CAMPGROUNDS IN & AROUND BRYCE CANYON

CAMPGROUND	LOCATION	DESCRIPTION	NUMBER OF SITES
North (p125)	Bryce Canyon, in the park	Large, private and forested, recycling bins, good amenities and direct trail access	101
Sunset (p125)	Bryce Canyon, in the park	Shady, few amenities, best for last-minute availability in the park	102
Bryce Canyon Pines Campground & RV Park (p125)	Bryce Canyon City	Convenient behind gas-station minimart but bare and lacking ambience	24
Ruby's RV Park & Campground (p125)	Bryce Canyon City	Packed with amenities, near the park entrance; little privacy	200
Pine Lake (p125)	Clay Creek	Lovely and private, trailside in pine forest with good amenities	37
KOA of Cannonville (p125)	Hwy 12, east of Tropic	Great for families, ample amenities include pool and roadside ambience	80
Red Canyon (p125)	Hwy 12, Red Canyon	Pretty and forested with basic amenities, popular with off-road vehicles (ORVs)	37
Red Canyon RV Park (p125)	cnr Hwys 12 & 89	Friendly roadside RV village, convenient but with little privacy	24
King Creek (p125)	USFS Rd 087, near Tropic	Woodsy and well maintained, near river, popular with (loud) ORVs	37

 Drinking Water   *Flush Toilets*   *Great for Families*   *Wheelchair Accessible*   *Dogs Allowed (On Leash)*

combinations and plastic drinking cups by the sink. A coffeemaker is a luxury. For more character, book a B&B in nearby towns. Rates drop in the fall and spring; most properties close in winter.

Bryce Canyon Pines
Campground & RV Park
CAMPGROUND $

(☏ 435-834-5441, 800-892-7923; www.bryce canyonmotel.com; Hwy 12; tent/RV sites $25/45; ☺ Apr-Oct) Across the street from the hotel, 4 miles west of the Hwy 12/63 junction, this campground sits behind a gas station and general store. The roadside location is convenient, but not exactly ambient. Showers are available for guests. Note that at 7700ft it can be windy and cold in spring.

Ruby's RV Park &
Campground
CAMPGROUND $

(☏ 866-878-9373, 435-834-5301; www.rubysinn. com; 1000 S Hwy 63; tent sites $30, tipis $40, RV sites with partial/full hookups $42/48, cabins $64; ☺ Apr-Oct; ⛺✨) This crowded campground, 3 miles north of the Bryce visitor center, has amenities including flush toilets, showers, drinking water, a coin laundry, electrical hookups, a dump station, restaurant, general store and a hot tub. Both double-bunk cabins and tipis use shared bathroom facilities. Bring your own sleeping bag. Though over-the-top commercial, it's nonetheless convenient. Online reservations and walk-ins accepted.

Bryce View Lodge
MOTEL $

(☏ 888-279-2304, 435-834-5180; www.bryce viewlodge.com; d $80; ☺ Apr-Oct; ⊖@⛺✨) Geared to budget travelers, these 130 standard rooms are decent, though smaller than Ruby's Inn and with fewer amenities. Guests enjoy free access to all the facilities across the street at Ruby's, including the pool and hot tub.

Bryce Canyon Resort
MOTEL $$

(☏ 800-834-0043, 435-834-5351; www.brycecan yonresort.com; cnr Hwys 12 & 63; r $145-189, cabins $175; ✳⛺✨✳) Four miles from the park, this is a great alternative. Remodeled rooms include newer furnishings and extra amenities, while economy rooms are standard. Some units have kitchenettes. Cottages have kitchenettes and sleep up to six. Pets are extra. There's also a heated outdoor swimming pool, small campground and restaurant.

BRYCE CANYON NATIONAL PARK SLEEPING

ELEVATION	OPEN	RESERVATION REQUIRED?	DAY FEE	FACILITIES
8000ft	year-round	early May-late Sep	free	
8000ft	late spring-fall	May-Sep	free	
7700ft	Apr-Oct	yes	NA	
8000ft	Apr-Oct	partial	NA	
7400ft	Jun-Sep	no	free	
6000ft	Mar-Dec	partial	NA	
8000ft	mid-May–Sep	groups only	$4	
6500ft	Apr-Sep	partial	NA	
8000ft	mid-May–Oct 1	no	$4-6	

 Grocery Store Nearby   *Restaurant Nearby*   *Pay-phone*   *Summertime Campfire Program*   *RV Dump Station*

RAILROAD DAYS

In the early 1920s, the Union Pacific Railroad saw dollar signs in starting tourism in the majestic but still-inaccessible canyons of southern Utah and northern Arizona. It built great lodges laden with modern comforts at the Grand Canyon, Zion, Cedar Breaks and Bryce Canyon. Trains reached Cedar City, where guests were shuttled via motor coach on a loop dubbed the Grand Circle Tour. Railroad brochures whetted travelers' appetites for Bryce, 'probably the most astonishing blend of exquisite beauty and grotesque grandeur ever produced by the forces of erosion. It is not to be described, however imperfectly, except in the language of fancy.' Today Bryce Canyon Lodge, the last of the original lodges, is the final remnant of the long-lost era of luxury rail travel in America.

Best Western Plus Bryce Grand Canyon Lodge HOTEL **$$**
(☑ 435-834-5700, 866-866-6634; www.brycecanyongrand.com; 30 North 100 East, Bryce Canyon City; d/ste incl breakfast $210/280; ⊙ Apr-Oct; ❋ @ ❄ ☒) New in 2009, this Best Western hotel is the best digs in this strip, with stylish, ample rooms featuring flatscreen TVs and a breakfast bar that spoils you for choice. Amenities include an outdoor swimming pool, fitness center and coin laundry.

Bryce Canyon Pines MOTEL **$$**
(☑ 800-892-7923, 435-834-5441; www.brycecanyonmotel.com; Hwy 12; r & cottages $115-190, ste $325; ⊙ Apr-Nov; ☒) If everything else is booked, check out this friendly motel, 4 miles west of the Hwy 12/63 junction. Standards are a bit dreary and outdated but deluxe rooms and cottages are smart. The restaurant is a favorite of locals. There's a small campground.

Best Western Ruby's Inn HOTEL **$$**
(☑ 435-834-5341, 866-866-6616; www.rubysinn.com; 1000 S Hwy 63; r $145-160, ste $220; ❋ @ ❄ ☒) A gargantuan motel complex with ample facilities, 1 mile before the park entrance. Standard rooms feature two beds, either queen or king size, coffeemakers and hair dryers. The sprawling property includes a grocery store with camping supplies, gas stations, a post office, coin laundry, pool and hot tub, showers, currency exchange, internet, and a liquor store (a rarity around here).

The tour desk can book helicopter tours and horseback riding. Ruby's also rents bicycles and all-terrain vehicles (ATVs). In summer there's a nightly rodeo (except Sunday); it's best to make reservations in high season.

✖ EATING

The food around Bryce isn't nearly as good as the scenery. Service may be poky, coffee watered-down and vegetables possibly limited to the speck of garnish alongside your chicken-fried steak. Particularly for vegetarians, it's worth traveling with a cooler of fresh fruit and vegetables.

In the Park

Bryce Canyon General Store & Snack Bar MARKET **$**
(Bryce Canyon Rd, nr Sunrise Point; dishes $3-9; ⊙ noon-10pm) In addition to foodstuff and sundries, the general store near Sunrise Point sells hot dogs, cold drinks, packaged sandwiches, chili, soup and pizza.

Bryce Canyon Lodge MODERN AMERICAN **$$$**
(☑ 435-834-5361; Bryce Canyon Rd; breakfast & lunch $10-20, dinner $18-35; ⊙ 7am-10pm Apr-Oct) While service may lag, meals deliver, with excellent regional cuisine ranging from fresh green salads to bison burgers, braised portobellos and steak. All food is made on-site and the certified green menu offers only sustainable seafood. The wine list is decent and, best of all, the low-lit room is forgiving if you come covered in trail dust.

Bryce Canyon City

Ruby's Inn General Store SUPERMARKET
(☑ 435-834-5341; Best Western Ruby's Inn, 1000 S Hwy 63; ⊙ 7am-10pm) Sells groceries with a considerable markup, plus sundries, clothing and camping supplies.

Bryce Canyon Pines Restaurant AMERICAN **$$**
(☑ 435-834-5441; www.brycecanyonmotel.com; Hwy 12; breakfast & lunch $5-14, dinner mains $12-24; ⊙ 6:30am-9:30pm Apr-Nov) This super-cute diner is classic Utah, with waitstaff that dotes, Naugahyde booths and even a crackling fire on cold days. Expect hearty plates of meat and potatoes, perfect BLTs and meal-size soups. While mains feel run-of-the-mill, locals come for towering wedges of homemade pie such as banana blueberry creme.

Best Western Ruby's Inn   AMERICAN $$
(📋435-834-5341; 1000 S Hwy 63; mains $8-34; ⏱6:30am-9pm) Ruby's operates two restaurants: a full-service dining room and buffet off the lobby, and an economical diner that serves pizza, burgers and fried food. Both deliver mediocre assembly-line cooking that's overpriced but convenient. For fresher food, order off the menu instead of the buffet. Expect a wait at dinner.

Cowboy Ranch House   AMERICAN $$$
(📋435-834-5100; cnr Hwys 12 & 63; mains $14-30; ⏱7-11am, 5-10pm) Part of Bryce Canyon Resort, this is a decent spot to grab a bite if you're hungry even before you get to the park. Expect classic American fare like flame-grilled steaks, trout and burgers, with some Mexican dishes and an emphasis on local farm providers. Breakfast is also available and there's a small sports bar.

Ebenezer's Barn & Grill   BARBECUE $$$
(📋800-468-8660; http://ebenezersbarnand-grill.com/bryce-canyon-dinner.html; 1000 S Hwy 63; dinner show $32-38; ⏱7pm mid-May–Sep) Kitschy but good-natured evening of country-and-western music with a big BBQ dinner (drinks not included). Options include salmon, steak, pulled pork or chicken served with beans and cornbread. Since it's wildly popular, reservations are necessary. It's run by Ruby's and located across the street.

ℹ Information

Due to Bryce's high elevation, some visitors may experience altitude sickness.

Bryce Canyon National Park Visitor Center
(📋435-834-5322; www.nps.gov/brca; Hwy 63; ⏱8am-8pm May-Sep, 8am-6pm Oct & Apr, 8am-4:30pm Nov-Mar) Check here for weather, hiking and road conditions and campground availability. Exhibits show plant, animal life and geologic displays and there's an excellent 20-minute orientation video. The park headquarters are here, as are first aid, phones and wi-fi in the lobby. Families can pick up Junior Ranger Activity Guides. Located adjacent to the entrance station.

Bryce Canyon Natural History Association
(📋435-834-4600; www.brycecanyon.org) A nonprofit that aids the park service with educational, scientific and interpretive activities. The association operates the bookstore, and staff answer questions in the visitor center. Its excellent online shop sells books, maps, videos, music and trip-planning packets tailored to individual traveler's needs.

ℹ Getting Around

Most people arrive at Bryce in their own car. In summer take advantage of the park's free shuttle buses, which stop at all of the major sights and trailheads.

Unless you're on an organized tour, the only way to get around the park from fall through spring is in a private vehicle. The park's main road is easily navigable and well maintained, with turnouts and parking areas clearly marked in the brochure you receive upon paying your fee. Posted speed limits in the park range from 25mph to 45mph. Rangers do give traffic tickets, so avoid speeding.

The closest gas stations are 3 miles north, in Bryce Canyon City. If you're towing a trailer, you are not permitted to take it to Bryce Point or Paria View. You can park it at the trailer turnaround lot in summer or the visitor center parking lot in winter. (If camping, you can leave the trailer at your campsite.)

Bryce Canyon National Park Shuttle (⏱8am-8pm late May-Sep) If you're traveling Bryce in summer, ride the voluntary shuttle into the park. The shuttle goes as far as Bryce Point; buses come roughly every 15 minutes, 8am to 8pm. A round-trip without exiting takes 50 minutes. Keep your admission receipt with you on the bus to avoid having to pay again if you return.

The free Rainbow Point bus tour hits the highlights daily at 9am and 1pm. Hikers can also take this bus to trailheads.

PRAIRIE DOGS

Although Utah prairie dogs once numbered in the billions across the West, a century of shooting and poisoning at the hands of ranchers drove them to near extinction by 1950. As a keystone species, the threatened animal is essential to the grassland ecosystem, improving soil quality, providing homes for other animals, prey and even maintaining meadow ecosystems. In 1974 scientists established a small prairie dog colony in the meadows at Bryce Canyon National Park and carefully monitored these small rodents (named 'dogs' by the Lewis and Clark Expedition for their barks). In March, as snows begin to melt, about 300 prairie dogs emerge from hibernation and begin a luxurious summer of calling, mating and fattening up on sweet grasses. Every June the park celebrates their continued presence with the Annual Utah Prairie Dog Day. The park asks that visitors stay out of the colonies and avoid the temptation to feed or pester the animals.

2

NEALE CLARK / GETTY IMAGES ©

3

BRAD MCGINLEY PHOTOGRAPHY / GETTY IMAGES ©

Navajo Loop Trail (p114)
s short but spectacular trail passes
heath towering hoodoos.

2. Inspiration Point (p116)
Climb the ridge to this gorgeous viewpoint
and look out over the hoodoo spires of
Silent City.

3. Bryce Canyon (p108)
Balloons drift over the spires, fins and cliffs
of Bryce Canyon National Park.

Around Bryce Canyon National Park

Best Places to Stay

➜ Buffalo Sage (p131)

➜ Red Brick Inn (p134)

➜ Cottonwood Meadow Lodge (p134)

➜ Red Canyon Campground (p133)

Best Places to Eat

➜ Stone Hearth Grille (p132)

➜ Café Adobe (p135)

➜ Henrie's Drive-in (p135)

Why Go?

If you're looking for a base for visiting Bryce Canyon National Park, towns include the farming community of Tropic and tourist-friendly, old-fashioned Panguitch, the gateway to Bryce Canyon.

This is Butch Cassidy country, where legends of the outlaw abound. He's said to have ridden the trails in scenic Red Canyon, past the red limestone towers where a hiking route is named for him today. The gunslinger's boyhood home can be visited in tiny Circleville.

This is a great place to go cycling: unlike Bryce Canyon, Red Canyon has both paved bike paths and mountain-biking trails.

When to Go
Bryce Canyon National Park

May–Aug
Moderately hot; afternoon thundershowers common in late summer.

Sep & Oct
Mild days; you'll still need a warm coat.

Nov–Feb
Very cold, with snow on the ground.

Tropic

POPULATION 521 / ELEVATION 6309FT

Founded in 1891 by Mormon pioneers, the tiny town of Tropic is a satellite to Bryce Canyon National Park, located 10 miles east of the park on Hwy 12. The farming community got its start with the creation of Tropic Ditch, which diverted water from Bryce Canyon to irrigate fields.

🏃 Activities

Mecham Outfitters   HORSEBACK RIDING
(📞435-679-8823; www.mechamoutfitters.com; Tropic; half-day $75) Long-time locally run outfitter leading highly recommended half- and full-day rides, including through slot canyons, in nearby Dixie National Forest and on Grand Staircase-Escalante National Monument lands.

🛏️ Sleeping

Bryce Pioneer Village   CABIN $
(📞435-679-8546, 800-222-0381; www.brycepioneervillage.com; 80 S Main St; tent/RV site $15/30, cabins $80, d $85-95; ❄️) On the edge of town in 14 acres of land, these cabins are standard and a little cramped. There's also an RV campground featuring full electrical hookup and showers included in the camping fee.

King Creek   CAMPGROUND $
(📞435-676-2676, group reservations 877-444-6777; www.fs.usda.gov/main/dixie/home; site $12; ⏰mid-May–Oct 1) Near Bryce's western boundary, 3 miles west of the Hwy 12/63 junction then 7 miles south via unpaved USFS Rd 087, this woodsy, well-maintained, first-come, first-served 37-site campground is adjacent to Tropic Reservoir and the Sevier River (bring bug spray). It's also popular with ATV riders (bring earplugs). Amenities include flush toilets, drinking water and a dump station.

KOA of Cannonville   CAMPGROUND $
(📞435-679-8988; http://koa.com/campgrounds/cannonville; Hwy 12; tent/RV site $31/45, cabin $70; ⏰Mar-Dec; 🚿❄️) Particularly good for families, it provides lots of amenities (flush toilets, drinking water, dump station, electrical hookups, spotlessly clean bathrooms and showers). It's 5 miles east of Tropic, and has 80 sites and cabins.

Pine Lake   CAMPGROUND $
(📞Escalante Ranger District 435-826-5400, group reservations 877-444-6777; www.recreation.gov; sites $11; ⏰Jun-Sep) In a pretty pine forest near a reservoir, 11 miles north of the Hwy 12/63 junction then 6 miles east on unpaved Clay Creek. Powerboats aren't allowed, but expect ATVs. Only groups may reserve. There's no trash collection and amenities are limited to vault toilets and drinking water.

★ Buffalo Sage   B&B $$
(📞435-679-8443; www.buffalosage.com; 980 N Hwy 12; d incl breakfast $120; ⏰May-Sep; ❄️🖥️) Perched on a hilltop with sweeping views, this comfortable B&B features ample country-style rooms with separate entrances. Guests can join the llama and goat that can be found relaxing here. There's a full breakfast that accommodates vegetarians.

Bryce Country Cabins   CABIN $$
(📞435-679-8643, 888-679-8643; www.brycecountrycabins.com; 320 N Main St, Tropic; cabins $99-149; ⏰Feb-Oct; ❄️🖥️) Friendly and family-run, these well-designed pine cabins are centered around an outdoor fire pit, perfect for stargazing around a bonfire. The only drawback is they're right on the main street. Deluxe cabins have cozy furniture and vaulted ceilings. Perks include TVs, coffeemakers, small porches and charm – it's among the best simple accommodations near Bryce.

Bullberry Inn   B&B $$
(📞800-249-8126, 435-679-8820; www.bullberryinn.com; 412 S Hwy 12, Tropic; r incl breakfast $115-130; 🖥️) Though the home dates only to 1998, this farmhouse-style inn serves up traditional Utah, down to the Bullberry jelly, a recipe that's been in the family for generations. The family gives a warm welcome and the country-cozy theme goes far – from ample log and bear themed rooms to a full country breakfast.

Bryce Trails B&B   B&B $$
(📞435-679-8700, 866-215-5043; www.brycetrails.com; 1001 W Bryce Way; r incl breakfast $115-180; ❄️🖥️) Reticent toward walk-ins, this tidy lodging nonetheless offers bright and slightly kitsch Western theme rooms, some with deck or Jacuzzi. It's located 1 mile from Main St.

Bryce Canyon Inn   INN $$
(📞435-679-8502, 800-592-1468; www.brycecanyoninn.com; 21 N Main St; r $84-90, cabin $129-140; ❄️🖥️) These immaculate, pine-scented, roadside rooms feature quilted beds and free continental breakfast. Cabins are tightly

spaced, but feature a refrigerator, coffee-maker and TV. There's also an on-site pizzeria and espresso bar.

Bryce Valley Inn INN $$
([phone] 435-679-8811, 800-442-1890; www.americasbestvalueinn.com; 199 N Main St; r $90-119; [icons]) These standard rooms in a boxy setting are competitively priced. Look online for discounts. Pets allowed with fee.

Stone Canyon Inn INN $$$
([phone] 866-489-4680,435-679-8611;www.stonecanyoninn.com; 1220 Stone Canyon Lane, Tropic; cabins $235-360; [icons]) In a Wild West setting of scrub hills backed by Technicolor sunsets, this stately stone-and-wood lodging offers adventure out the back door – stroll or bike to your heart's content. Cabins are spacious and luxuriously private, though trumped by the charm of the main house, where a restaurant was recently added. There's a Finnish sauna. It's 1.3 miles from Main St.

✗ Eating

Bryce Canyon Inn & Pizza AMERICAN $
([phone] 435-679-8888; 21 N Main St; mains $7-14; [clock]11am-9pm) If you want to keep it simple, this pizzeria is a solid bet for steak-and-cheese sandwiches or taco pizza. It's a well-scrubbed family locale and the pulse of Tropic. Hours vary seasonally.

Clarke's Grocery MARKET $
(121 N Main St, Tropic; sandwiches $5-8; [clock] 7:30am-8pm Mon-Sat, 2-8pm Sun) Tropic's only grocery store has a deli sandwich counter and homemade baked goods.

Clarke's Restaurant AMERICAN $$
([phone] 435-679-8383; 141 N Main St, Tropic; breakfast & lunch $4-15, dinner $14-25; [clock]7am-10pm; [icon]) A full-service American restaurant with outdoor deck seating. Portions are large though not very memorable. Beer and wine are available.

★Stone Hearth Grille MODERN AMERICAN $$$
([phone] 435-679-8923; www.stonehearthgrille.com; 1380 W. Stone Canyon Ln; mains $14-30; [clock]5-10pm) In a lovely rural setting staring out at the bluffs, this upscale lodge restaurant serves rib-eye steaks, quinoa-stuffed peppers and satisfying green salads alongside a decent wine list. It's the best dinner option in the area. The deck seating offers a heavy dose of romance.

Red Canyon

If you're heading to Bryce Canyon from the west, Red Canyon provides your first arresting view of magnificent rock formations. The canyon is aptly named – its iron-rich limestone towers are saturated a deep red. Legend has it that outlaw Butch Cassidy once rode trails in this area, and one of the toughest hiking routes (Cassidy Trail) bears his name.

◉ Sights

Bryce Museum MUSEUM
(www.brycewildlifeadventure.com; 1945 W Hwy 12; admission $8; [clock]9am-7pm Apr–mid-Nov) Displays dioramas of more than 800 animals from around the world, as well as live fallow deer, Indian artifacts, and butterfly and giant-bug exhibits. It also rents bicycles and ATVs and is a good location to start the nearby bike path. Call ahead to see if kid-size bikes are available. You can also rent a bike rack for your car.

✗ Activities

Red Canyon Trails HIKING
Several moderately easy hiking trails begin near the visitor center: the 0.7-mile (30-minute) Arches Trail passes 15 arches as it winds through a canyon; and the 0.5-mile (30-minute) Pink Ledges Trail winds through red-rock formations. For a harder hike, try the 2.8-mile (two to four hours) Golden Wall Trail; you can extend it to a 5-mile round-trip by adding Buckhorn Trail.

Thunder Mountain Trail MOUNTAIN BIKING
Unlike much of the region around Bryce, mountain-biking trails abound at Red Canyon. The best is the Thunder Mountain Trail: 5 miles of this loop trail are paved and suit families; the other 7.8 miles are strenuous and involve sand and switchbacks (start the ride toward Bryce to ride uphill on the pavement and downhill on the dirt). Be aware that horses share the trail.

Red Canyon Bike Path CYCLING
This recently built bike path currently runs 8.6 miles along Hwy 12 from Thunder Mountain trailhead to East Fork Rd. It's paved and perfect for families. There are plans to eventually extend the path all the way to Bryce.

Scenic Rim Trail Rides   HORSEBACK RIDING
(☑435-679-8761, 800-679-5859; www.brycecan-
yonhorseback.com; Ruby's Inn, 1000 S Hwy 63)
Guided horseback rides to Thunder Mountain and other Red Canyon locations. Based
at Best Western Ruby's Inn (p126).

🛏 Sleeping

It's a 20-minute drive from Red Canyon to
Bryce, and 10 minutes to Panguitch.

Red Canyon Campground   CAMPGROUND $
(☑435-676-2676; www.fs.usda.gov; Scenic Byway
12; tent & RV sites $15; ☺mid-May–Sep) One of
the best-maintained campgrounds in the national forest, Red Canyon has pretty hiking
trails and doesn't allow ATVs. Amenities include showers, flush toilets, drinking water
and a dump station. The 37 sites are first-
come, first-served. It's 10 miles west of the
Hwy 12/63 junction.

Red Canyon RV Park   CAMPGROUND $
(☑435-676-2243; www.reserveamerica.com; cnr
Hwys 12 & 89; sites $20; ☺Apr-Sep) If you can't
secure a site at the campground, try this
park, which also operates a small store.
Options include tent sites, RV hookups and
cabins. Cabins are micro-size, without private bathrooms.

ⓘ Information

Visitor Center (☑435-676-2676; Hwy 12;
☺9am-6pm Jun-Aug, 10am-4pm May & Sep)
Check out the excellent geologic displays and
pick up trail maps at the visitor center.

ⓘ Getting There & Away

Red Canyon is in the **Dixie National Forest
Powell ranger district** (see p135 for ranger
station details). It's on Hwy 12, 1.5 miles from
the Hwy 89 junction south of Panguitch, and 15
miles from Bryce Canyon.

Panguitch

POPULATION 1623 / ELEVATION 6666FT
Founded in 1864, Panguitch (pang-witch)
was traditionally a center for the local
ranching and lumber communities. Now
tourism is the number-one industry, drawing transplants from Las Vegas and California and slowly changing the old-fashioned
feel. Nonetheless, taxidermy is still common restaurant decor, and you can see locals on ride-on lawnmowers headed to the
mini-mart on Main Street.

> ## BUTCH BEFORE SUNDANCE
>
> In the wee town of **Circleville**, 28 miles
> north of Panguitch, stands the boyhood
> home of the gunslingin' bandit Butch
> Cassidy. The cabin, partially renovated
> but uninhabited, sits 2 miles south of
> town on the west side of Hwy 89. After
> the release of the film *Butch Cassidy
> and the Sundance Kid* (1969), reporters
> met the outlaw's sister, who claimed
> that Butch didn't die in South America
> in 1908, but circled back to visit.
>
> For more of all things Butch, check
> out Red Canyon, where one trail is
> named for the outlaw who rode the
> area.

Popular with passing travelers, the town
enjoys pleasant summer weather and is
crisscrossed by scenic byways – Hwy 89 to
the north and south, Hwy 143 to the west
and Hwy 12 to the east. Panguitch is the Garfield County seat and has long been the gateway to Bryce Canyon (24 miles to the east).

⊙ Sights

Nearby Red Canyon has gorgeous hiking
and many locals enjoy Panguitch Lake in
summer. Panguitch once hosted a brick fac-
tory and boasts a number of beautiful red-
brick houses.

🎉 Festivals & Events

Quilt Walk Festival   ART
(www.quiltwalk.org; ☺mid-Jun) The popular
Quilt Walk Festival honors pioneer history and also features historic home tours,
theater, tractor parades and a chocolate fair.

Panguitch Valley Balloon Rally   FAIR
(www.panguitchvalleyballoonrally.com) A huge
hot-air balloon festival featuring music and
family activities. Held in late June.

Garfield County Fair   STREET CARNIVAL
One of the most anticipated events of the
year, this 75-year tradition in late August
hosts live bands and features parades, classic car shows, barbecues, livestock sales and
rodeos for an entire week.

🛏 Sleeping

Panguitch and the area around the Hwy
89/12 junction (7 miles south) feature a good

AROUND BRYCE CANYON NATIONAL PARK PANGUITCH

selection of motels, budget and midrange accommodations. If you pull into town without a reservation, rates may be higher. Properties open in the off-season (November to March) reduce rates significantly. Motels that allow pets generally only keep a few pet-friendly rooms, best reserved in advance.

Camping

Hitch-N-Post
CAMPGROUND $
(☑435-676-2436; www.hitchnpostrv.com; 420 N Main St; tent/RV sites with hookups $19/32; 🗐🛠) Small lawns and trees divide RV spaces; tent sites are in a grassy field, but still have barbecue grills. RV wash and heavy-duty laundry on-site.

Panguitch KOA
CAMPGROUND $
(☑435-676-2225, 800-562-1625; http://koa.com/campgrounds/panguitch; 555 S Main St; tent/RV site $25/39; 🗐🛠🏊) Offers complete facilities, including a swimming pool. Showers cost $5 for nonguests.

Lodging

Panguitch House
B&B $
(☑435-899-0190, 435-676-2574; 259 E Center St; r incl breakfast $89; 🛠🗐) The nicely simple, new B&B rooms in this renovated red-brick home are an excellent alternative to a motel. The price is more than right and the friendly

---

hosts provide a big breakfast and advice on area adventures.

Canyon Lodge
MOTEL $
(☑800-440-8292, 435-676-8292; www.canyonlodgemotel.com; 210 N Main St; r $79-109; 🛠🗐) A little frayed around the edges, this clean 10-room motel has in-room refrigerators, microwaves and coffeemakers in addition to a picnic area with grill.

Purple Sage
MOTEL $
(☑435-676-2659, 800-241-6889; 132 E Center St; d $84; ☉Mar-Oct; 🛠🗐) Comfy, as motels go, and helpfully chatty too, this tidy motel slips in sweet extras such as pillow-top mattresses, new furnishings and coffeemakers. Pets may be allowed, check first in person.

★ Red Brick Inn
B&B $$
(☑435-690-1048; www.redbrickinn.com; 11161 N 100 West; d incl breakfast $130, ste $220; ☉Apr-Oct; 🛠🗐) Warm California native Peggy runs this 1919 charmer that once served as the town hospital. Rooms are cozy and comfortable, breakfasts are elaborate and outstanding, and stories abound. Chill out swinging in a garden hammock or pedaling a loan bike. Ask in advance about pets.

Grandma's Cottage
RENTAL HOUSE $$
(☑435-690-9495; www.grandmascottages.com; 90 N 100 West; 2-6 person rentals $100-160; ☉Mar-Nov; 🛠) Excellent for groups and families, these renovated cottages and homes around central Panguitch have been lovingly put together by a semiretired couple. Except for the studio cottage, the decor is nothing like grandma's. Think savvy and stylish. Themes vary – there's a 1960s hideout, a country cottage and a historic brick home, all with gorgeous touches and cable TV.

Some accommodations have cooking facilities and washer/dryer.

★ Cottonwood Meadow Lodge
LODGE $$$
(☑435-676-8950; www.brycecanyoncabins.com; Mile 123, Hwy 89; cabins & houses $165-295; ☉mid-April–Oct; 🗐) Dubbed 'Cowboy-licious' by a wizened ranch hand, this lodge delivers open-range dreams. Recycled from a Mormon saw town, this private ranch (2 miles south of Hwy 12, near Panguitch) occupies acres of tawny grass and tumbling sagebrush.

Cabins range from a rustic-chic bunkhouse with wooden-plank floors to stylish farmhouses with gleaming kitchens, blazing

---

THE QUILT WALK FESTIVAL

In quaint homes around Panguitch, quilters are working as feverishly as Penelope at the loom. This subculture owes its origin to history, when the settlers nearly perished in their first winter. With food scarce during the brutal winter of 1884, seven men set out on a 40-mile journey in a wagon pulled by oxen to find provisions. Impeded by deep snow, they would have perished but found that the quilts that they used to pray on also served to compact the snow. Panguitch legend has it that they completed the journey by laying quilts across the snow and walking over them.

They are now honored by the annual Quilt Walk Festival, a week-long event that has banished local hunger with tall stacks of pancakes offered post-tractor-pull. There are also races, parades, quilt shows and an art fair.

hearths and porch rockers. A trout pond stocked with browns and rainbows is in easy reach; otherwise there are miles of roads and open space for country walkers and mountain bikers. Lest they help themselves to the grass-raised beef on-site, pets are not allowed.

Eating & Drinking

Panguitch's dining scene doesn't have much variety.

★ Café Adobe   AMERICAN $
(16 N Main St, Hatch; mains $10-16; ⊘ 8am-8pm Mar–mid-Nov) Though it's not in Panguitch, it's worth the 15-mile trek south to Hatch to sample this spot's gourmet hamburgers, enormous salads and decadent homemade pies. Locals from the whole region congregate here.

Henrie's Drive-in   BURGERS $
(154 N Main St; burgers $4-7; ⊘ 11am-9pm Mar-Oct) Craving a deliciously greasy burger and fries? Look no further – and don't forget the strawberry milkshake.

Joe's Main Street Market   MARKET $
(10 S Main St) This is the town's main grocery store.

Cowboy's Smokehouse BBQ   BARBECUE $$
(95 N Main St; mains $15-32; ⊘ 4-8pm Tue-Wed, 4-9pm Thu-Sat) Sweet staff serve steaks and brisket with house-made sauce, but the food quality can be erratic. Portions are generous.

❶ Information

Powell Ranger Station (☑ 435-676-9300; www.fs.fed.us/dxnf; 225 E Center St; ⊘ 8am-4:30pm Mon-Fri) Dixie National Forest camping and hiking info.

Garfield County Tourism Office (☑ 800-444-6689, 435-676-1160; www.brycecanyon country.com; 55 S Main St; ⊘ 9am-5pm) Provides regional travel and event information.

Garfield Memorial Hospital (☑ 435-676-8811; 224 N 400 East; ⊘ 24hr) The park's nearest clinic and emergency room, 25 miles northwest of Bryce Canyon.

Police (☑ 435-676-8807; 45 S Main St)

Post Office (☑ 435-676-8853; 65 N 100 West)

❶ Getting There & Away

The main drag through town, Hwy 89, comes in on Main St from the north, then turns east on Center St. South of Center, Main becomes Hwy 143 leading to Panguitch Lake.

There are no scheduled bus, air or train services to Panguitch.

Grand Staircase-Escalante National Monument

Best Hikes

➡ Slot Canyons of Dry Fork/ Coyote Gulch (p142)

➡ Willis Creek (p143)

➡ Lower Calf Creek Falls (p141)

➡ Escalante River Natural Bridge (p140)

➡ Boulder Mail Trail (p144)

Best Drives

➡ Burr Trail (p145)

➡ Hole-in-the Rock Road (p145)

➡ Cottonwood Canyon Road (p147)

Why Go?

The largest park in the Southwest, Grand Staircase-Escalante National Monument (GSENM) features spectacular scenery in rough-cut wilderness. From the Grand Canyon floor, geological strata climb in staircase fashion 3500ft to Bryce Canyon and the Escalante River canyons. These rock layers tell 260 million years of history in a riot of color. The diversity of landscapes is astounding – pink dunes, white cliffs, red canyons, vast slickrock and undulating slot canyons.

The monument was established in 1996 by US President Bill Clinton in a controversial designation. Many ranchers and residents were concerned about losing access. Local legislators and mining interests were stymied. Environment activists appeared and conflicts ensued. Years later, federal versus local control is still a hot issue, though there is also recognition that the land needs, and deserves, some protection.

Driving Distances (miles)

	Boulder	Bryce Canyon National Park (Park Entrance)	Escalante	Grand Staircase-Escalante National Monument (Canonville Visitor Center)	Kanab
Bryce Canyon National Park (Park Entrance)	80				
Escalante	30	50			
Grand Staircase-Escalante National Monument (Canonville Visitor Center)	65	15	35		
Kanab	150	75	120	85	
Grand Canyon North Rim (Park Entrance)	215	145	190	155	70

Note: Distances are approximate

Entrances

There are no entrance stations; the monument is accessible 24/7. It encompasses three major geologic areas: the westernmost Grand Staircase, south of Bryce Canyon and west of Cottonwood Canyon Rd; central Kaiparowits Plateau, east of Cottonwood Canyon Rd and west of Hole-in-the-Rock Rd; and the eastern Escalante Canyons, southwest of the Burr Trail. In the north, scenic Hwy 12 skirts the boundary of GSENM, passing through the small towns of Escalante and Boulder.

In the south, Hwy 89 arcs east from the larger town of Kanab. Three unpaved roads cross the park between the highways, roughly north to south: Skutumpah and Johnson Canyon Rds, Cottonwood Canyon Rd and Smoky Mountain Rd. Hole-in-the-Rock Rd, a dead end, leads southeast from Hwy 12 toward Glen Canyon National Recreation Area. Partly paved Burr Trail crosses the monument's northeast corner from Boulder into Capitol Reef.

You'll need a free permit to car-camp or backpack overnight, available from any visitor center, information kiosk or major trailhead. Only Calf Creek Recreation Area carries a day-use fee.

DON'T MISS

GSENM is so big that it is conducive to multiple visits. Start with a hike near Boulder (Lower Calf Creek or Escalante Natural Bridge) and explore some of the slot canyons on Hole-in-the-Rock Rd. If you have time, drive the Cottonwood Canyon Rd toward Kanab and enjoy the solitude of its lesser-known hikes.

When You Arrive

→ Day use is generally free. Visitor centers in Escalante, Cannonville and Kanab offer free park bulletins and maps, and sell more detailed maps, like the USGS 7.5-quadrangles.

→ Fill up on water at visitor centers, since there is none at trailheads and most campgrounds.

→ Check with rangers at a visitor center about road conditions, the weather forecast and the type of vehicle suitable for the roads you plan to travel. Much of the park is on 4WD roads and clay surfaces become impassable when wet.

→ There is no comprehensive topo for the park but the National Geographic Trails Illustrated (www.natgeomaps.com) map No 710, *Canyons of the Escalante,* covers the northeast corner of the park.

PARK POLICIES & REGULATIONS

All vehicles must stay on designated roads, which are open to mountain bikes, cars, 4WDs, all-terrain vehicles (ATVs) and other off-highway vehicles.

Campfires in developed campgrounds are restricted to fire rings; elsewhere you're allowed to use a fire pan. Do not light fires at archaeological sites or in rock shelters or alcoves. Banned in Coyote Gulch, dogs are allowed elsewhere, often leashed.

Fast Facts

→ Total area: 2969 sq miles

→ Elevation: 4900ft

→ Average high/low temperature (at Escalante) in July: 91°F/55°F (33°C/13°C)

Reservations

While GSENM campgrounds do not accept reservations, the state park and private campgrounds do. Campers may wild camp on Bureau of Land Management land, following regulations and standard Leave No Trace ethics. Some popular hikes require permits based on a lottery system.

Resources

→ **Grand Staircase-Escalante National Monument** (www.blm.gov/ut/st/en/fo/grand_staircase-escalante.html)

GRAND STAIRCASE-ESCALANTE NATIONAL MONUMENT

Grand Staircase-Escalante National Monument & Aroun

ESCALANTE

The central GSENM hub, with adventure-tour operators aplenty and trails and roller-coaster back roads radiating in all directions. (p152)

COTTONWOOD CANYON ROAD

The best cross-monument drive is this dirt road linking the upper GSENM to its lower section, with striking rock formations that make for beautiful scenery and good canyon hikes. (p147)

KANAB

The southern hub of GSENM and a favorite location for Hollywood Westerns. (p156)

Junction (16mi);
Richfield (60mi)

Antimony

Dixie
National
Forest

Dixie
National
Forest

Old Escalante Rd

Bear Valley Rd

Sevier River

Dixie
National
Forest

Panguitch

East Fork Sevier River

UTAH

Red Canyon
Campground

Bryce Canyon
City

Tropic

Cedar Breaks National
Monument (24mi);
Cedar City (42mi)

Tropic
Reservoir

Bryce Canyon
National Park

Cannonville

Henrieville

Kodachrome
Basin State Park

East Fork Sevier River

Willis Creek

Bull Valley Gorge

Grosven
Arch

Lick
Wash

Paria River

Lower Hackberry Canyon

Cottonwood Canyon Rd

The Cockscomb

Wahweap Cr

Glendale

Pink Cliffs

Gray Cliffs

Grand Staircase

Zion National
Park East
Entrance
(12mi)

Kanab Creek

Skutumpah Rd

White Cliffs

Mt Carmel
Junction

Pahreah
(Ghost Town)

Former Paria
Movie Set

Best Friends
Animal
Sanctuary

Johnson Canyon Rd

Old Gunsmoke Set

Vermillion Cliffs

Paria Valley

Paria
Contact
Station

White House
Campground

Coral Pink Sand Dunes
State Park (22 mi);
Moccasin Mountain
Dinosaur Track
Site (31 mi)

Kanab

House Rock Valley Rd

Stateline
Campground

Coyote
Buttes
North

Paria Canyon -
Vermilion Cliffs
Wilderness Area

ARIZONA

Coyote Buttes
South

Kaibab Paiute
Indian Reservation

Fredonia

Pipe Spring National Monument (20mi);
North Rim Grand Canyon (80mi)

Torrey (18mi);
Capitol Reef NP
(60mi)

Boulder Creek

Hell's Backbone Rd

The Box

Pine Creek Rd

Box-Death
Hollow
Wilderness

Boulder

12

Circle Cliffs

● Anasazi State Park

Deer Creek
Campground

Burr Trail Rd

Notom-Bullfrog Rd

Waterpocket Fold

Strike Valley

Henry Mountains

Bullfrog Creek

BOULDER

This is alternative southern Utah, with
sustainable eateries, spa services and
a survivalist school. (p154)

Calf Creek
Recreation Area
& Campground

Long Valley

King
Bench

Capitol Reef
National Park

Escalante River
Natural Bridge

Escalante

Escalante
Petrified
Forest State
Park

Maverick Arch

Phipps Arch

Head of
the Rocks

Old Sheffield Rd
(Spencer Flats)

Harris Wash

Escalante Canyons

Escalante River

Circle Cliffs

Moody Creek

HIGHWAY 12

This National Scenic Byway links
several national parks in jaw-dropping
fashion; a highlight is the Hogback, a
narrow section between Boulder and
Escalante. (p153)

Devils Garden ●
Picnic Site

Twentyfive Mile Wash

Glen Canyon
National
Recreation Area

Smoky Mountain Rd

Straight Cliffs

Croton Canyon

Dry Fork

Coyote Gulch

Hole-in-the-Rock Rd

Fiftymile Bench

HOLE-IN-THE-ROCK ROAD

A dead end used by Mormon settlers
to lower wagons through the canyons.
Now famous for the short slot
canyons at Dry Fork and Devils
Garden. (p145)

Grand Staircase -
Escalante
National Monument

Last Chance Creek

Kaiparowits Plateau

Warm Creek

UTAH

Hole-in-the-Rock ●

Glen Canyon
National
Recreation Area

Navajo
Indian Reservation

Alstrom
Point

Navajo
Mountain
(10,388ft) ▲

Piute Creek Rd

PARIA CANYON-
VERMILION CLIFFS

This remote wilderness area features
some of the most stunning slickrock
you will see, plus long slot canyons
ideal for backpacking; highlights
include Wire Pass and Buckskin
Gulch. (p158)

Big Water

Wahweap
Marina

Lake
Powell

89

ARIZONA

Page (14mi)

🚶 DAY HIKES

🚶 Escalante River Natural Bridge

Duration 3 hours

Distance 4.4 miles

Difficulty Easy–moderate

Start/Finish Hwy 12, 15 miles east of Escalante

Nearest Town Escalante

Transportation Private

Summary The fairly flat, sometimes sandy trail crisscrosses the river six times before reaching a large natural bridge and arch beyond. Be prepared to get your feet wet.

If you want a level walk with dramatic scenery, you've found it. The Escalante River hike is not as demanding as Lower Calf Creek Falls and it allows (requires) you to play in the water. Park at the trailhead by the Hwy 12 bridge over the Escalante River, just west of the Calf Creek Recreation Area. Water sandals are best for the alternating sandy and wet conditions. Note that biting flies can be bothersome in early summer.

Descend and cross the **Escalante River**. Walk through cottonwoods then an exposed sagebrush and sand valley. Trees appear again when you get closer to the second river crossing, and the cliff walls close in before the third. After another full-sun stint,

Escalante Natural Bridge appears off to the left. The 130ft-high sandstone arch with a 100ft span is best viewed from the fourth crossing at 1.8 miles.

Continue, and look up and left for the rock alcove that has a small **granary ruin**. You'll ford the river three more times before you get to **Natural Arch** up on the skyline to the southwest. Note that this is the end for the day hike, but you can continue on this trail for a total of 15 miles and end up at a trailhead back in Escalante town.

🚶 Upper Calf Creek Falls

Duration 1½ hours

Distance 2.2 miles

Difficulty Moderate

Start/Finish Hwy 12

Nearest Town Boulder

Transportation Private

Summary A short, but steep and strenuous, trail down slickrock leads through a desert moonscape to an oasis. The two sets of pools and waterfalls at hike's end appear like a mirage.

Soaking your feet in a moss-covered pool while canyon wrens and mountain bluebirds dart about seems like an impossible dream when you first start your slickrock descent. The upper hike may not be as well known or dramatic as Lower Calf Creek Falls, but stick

HIKING IN GRAND STAIRCASE-ESCALANTE NATIONAL MONUMENT

NAME	START LOCATION	DESCRIPTION
Lower Calf Creek Falls (p141)	Calf Creek Recreation Area	A sandy, creekside canyon walk past Native American sites to a 126ft-tall waterfall and pool
Lower Hackberry Canyon (p143)	Cottonwood Canyon Rd	A pleasant hike through a deep, narrow gorge that's cooled by a shallow stream
Willis Creek (p143)	Cottonwood Canyon Rd	Accessible slot canyon that alternates between narrows and open sections along a seasonal creek
Boulder Mail Trail (p144)	Hell's Backbone Rd	Hearty wilderness hike following the historic Boulder–Escalante mail route through Box-Death Hollow
Slot Canyons of Dry Fork/ Coyote Gulch (p142)	Hole-in-the-Rock Rd	Drops steeply down slickrock to reach four sinuous slot canyons
Escalante River Natural Bridge (p140)	Hwy 12	A flat, sandy trail crisscrosses the river numerous times before reaching a large natural bridge
Upper Calf Creek Falls (p140)	Hwy 12	A short but strenuous trail down slickrock leads to falls and two sets of pools

  Views   Flush Toilets   Great for Families   Waterfalls

with it and you'll be rewarded with unexpected beauty. The quarter-mile unmarked dirt road to the trailhead is outside of Boulder, on the north side of Hwy 12 between mile markers 80 and 81.

Start at the rim, which overlooks all of **Calf Creek Canyon**, the **Straight Cliffs** beyond. From there the trail descends 550ft down steep white Navajo sandstone littered with dark volcanic boulders. Follow the cairns down until the incline levels off. The rock becomes more stratified and colorful just about the time you get a glimpse of treetops in the inner canyon to the west.

Shortly after, you'll come to a fork. Follow cairns down to the left and you'll reach the **lower pool** of the Upper trail – a vegetation-covered oasis beneath an 86ft waterfall. Follow the path up to the right for the **upper pools**, where water cascades through shallow potholes and ponds before falling over the rim. Take the time to explore both pools: swim if it's warm, look over the canyon edge and appreciate the isolation.

🚶Lower Calf Creek Falls

Duration 4 hours

Distance 6 miles

Difficulty Moderate

Start/Finish Calf Creek Recreation Area, Hwy 12, 14 miles east of Escalante

Nearest Town Escalante

Transportation Private

Summary The sandy track eventually follows a year-round running creek through a spectacular canyon before arriving at a 126ft waterfall, a joy on a hot day.

Lower Calf Creek Falls' beauty is no secret; this is easily the most heavily traveled trail in the entire monument. Its accessibility – right off Hwy 12 between Escalante and Boulder – makes it a perfect stopover. Though it doesn't climb much, the trail has long sandy stretches that can take a lot out of you. Carry plenty of water (available at the trailhead); the creek is not safe for drinking.

Park at the **Calf Creek Recreation Area** (day use $5) and campground, between mile markers 75 and 76 on Hwy 12. As you work your way toward the creek, you'll pass honeycombed rocks and Navajo sandstone domes, an 800-year-old Native American **granary**, a box canyon where calves were once herded (hence the name Calf Creek), **prehistoric pictographs** and lush green wetlands.

Past the last bend, the trail ends in an amphitheater of rock with a 126ft-tall **waterfall** with a thin stream cascading into a large pool. The sandy shore and extended knee-deep wading area, before the deeper drop-off, make this a favorite with families. Remember, the sandy walk out is as strenuous as the walk in, so pace yourself.

GRAND STAIRCASE-ESCALANTE NATIONAL MONUMENT DAY HIKES

DIFFICULTY	DURATION	ROUND-TRIP DISTANCE	ELEVATION CHANGE	FEATURES	FACILITIES
moderate	4hr	6 miles	250ft	🔭👨‍👩‍👧🏊	🚻💦
easy-moderate	2-3hr	3-6 miles	100ft		
easy-moderate	up to 3hr	up to 4.4 miles	300ft	🔭👨‍👩‍👧🏊	💦
difficult	2-3 days	16 miles one way	1800ft	🔭	🔺
moderate-difficult	3hr	4.5 miles	600ft	🔭🧗	🚻
easy-moderate	3hr	4.4 miles	200ft	🔭👨‍👩‍👧	🚻
moderate	1½hr	2.2 miles	600ft	🔭	🚻

 Rock Climbing   💦 *Swimming*   🔺 *Backcountry Campsite*

🚶Slot Canyons of Dry Fork/ Coyote Gulch

Duration 3 hours

Distance 4.5 miles

Difficulty Moderate–difficult

Start/Finish Dry Fork Rd, off Hole-in-the-Rock Rd

Nearest Town Escalante

Transportation Private

Summary A remote but popular Hole-in-the-Rock Rd hike leads to four different slot canyons, complete with serpentine walls, narrows and bouldering obstacles.

GSENM is famous for its sculpted slot canyons, spillways of brightly colored, weathered rock, and the four slots on this route are some of the most visited in the monument. Expect to encounter pools of water in some. From Hwy 12, drive 26 miles down Hole-in-the-Rock Rd to Dry Fork Rd (Rte 252), turn left, and drive 1.7 miles to the parking area, bearing left at all junctions.

From the parking area the route switchbacks steeply down the slickrock and you find yourself alternately sidestepping and

Grand Staircase – Day Hikes

Legend:
- Escalante River Natural Bridge
- Lower Calf Creek Falls
- Lower Hackberry Canyon
- Slot Canyons of Dry Fork/Coyote Gulch
- Upper Calf Creek Falls
- Willis Creek

pitching forward. An overabundance of willy-nilly rock cairns can lead you astray here. Look up and see where you're headed: toward the reddish-brown dirt hills with little vegetation to the north (leftish). You reach the bottom in **Coyote Gulch** wash. Follow it north, and when you emerge into an opening, **Dry Fork** slot canyon is immediately to the left (west). Dry Fork is often overlooked as not tight or physically challenging enough, but it's our favorite. You can walk for miles between undulating orange walls, with only a few small boulder step-ups.

Double back to Coyote Gulch and head downstream (east), keeping your eyes peeled for the first slot on the left, **Peek-a-Boo**. Even to get into this dramatic canyon, you have to climb up a 12ft handhold-carved wall (much easier if you're tall or not alone). From there the hanging slot tightens dramatically and passes under several arches. You may have to navigate some water, and scrambling is definitely required to the end point. Hikers have climbed up and over Peek-a-Boo to sneak up behind Spooky but it requires good orienteering skills, otherwise it's easy to get lost.

Retrace your steps to the main wash. A half-mile further downstream, veer left and hike through the sandy wash to **Spooky Gulch**, which is even narrower. The 0.3-mile slot is less technically challenging, but impassable for larger hikers. Turn back and return to the trailhead from here.

If you really want to lengthen your hike, you could continue to **Brimstone Gulch**; half a mile further.

🚶 Willis Creek

Duration up to 3 hours

Distance 4.4 miles round-trip

Difficulty Easy–moderate

Start/Finish Skumptah Rd, 6.9 miles southwest of Cannonville

Nearest Towns Cannonville, Escalante

Transportation Private

Summary A great little slot-canyon hike, accessible to young and old. Actually it's more like four little slot canyons, as you alternate between open and narrow sections.

Unlike most of GSENM's slot canyons, the cliffs around Willis Creek are light beige, not red – an interesting contrast to the oftentimes orange mineral stream flowing through it. The trail starts 3 miles south of Cannonville on Skumptah Rd (access via Cottonwood Canyon Rd). Easy access and an almost-level canyon floor make this a great family route.

Across the road from the parking lot, follow the well-worn path down the hill and proceed left, down-canyon. In less than five minutes the serpentine walls rise around you. There's no trail per se, you're just wandering from bank to bank following **Willis Creek**. Avoid drinking from the creek, there is sometimes horse manure about. The narrows open up after about half a mile, and this is where many people turn around. But you shouldn't.

Once you hike around, not slide down, the 11ft **pour off**, the canyon walls grow taller. At times cliffs tower 200ft above, only 6ft apart. Tight and narrow sections alternate until 2.2 miles along you reach the confluence with **Sheep Creek**, the end to this day hike.

🚶 Lower Hackberry Canyon

Duration 2–3 hours

Distance 3–6 miles

Difficulty Easy–moderate

Start/Finish Cottonwood Canyon Rd, 14 miles north of Hwy 89

Nearest Town Kanab

Transportation Private

Summary A pleasant hike through a cool gorge that flows with a shallow stream. Walk as much or as little as you like – Lower Hackberry continues for 26 miles.

This narrow gorge hike provides a welcome stretch for drivers on Cottonwood Canyon Rd. The marked trailhead takes about half an hour to reach from Hwy 89. From Cannonville and Hwy 12, the trailhead is 31 miles south. Wear long sleeves and pants to avoid deer flies in late spring.

Follow the dirt track to a typically dry wash. Past the corral you'll reach **Lower Hackberry Canyon**. Water often flows down the canyon, and many stream crossings are required, but it's not usually deep – normally a few inches. Wander as far as you like; the first few miles of the canyon are the most narrow and interesting. After a while, the canyon opens up; in early summer, clouds of gnats often choose this point to attack. Mostly only backpackers proceed from here.

🥾 OVERNIGHT HIKES

Boulder Mail Trail

🥾 Boulder Mail Trail

Duration 2–3 days

Distance 16 miles one way

Difficulty Difficult

Start Boulder landing strip

Finish Upper Escalante River trailhead

Nearest Towns Boulder, Escalante

Transportation Hiker shuttle

Summary A hearty wilderness hike following the historic Boulder–Escalante mail route around rugged Box-Death Hollow. Detouring into the slickrock wilderness area provides an interesting extra day's adventure.

The monument is a mecca for hardcore backcountry adventurers, but significant route-finding skills are required (GPS skills don't count). Be sure to carry 7.5-minute USGS maps. The BLM recommends using portable waste containers (available at the BLM in Escalante); in the future these will be mandatory. Talk to rangers before heading out, and don't take unnecessary risks. In addition to this epic trail, ask rangers about Coyote Gulch, off Hole-in-the-Rock Rd, and the Gulch, off Burr Trail Rd. Escalante River Natural Bridge day hike can also be stretched into a 15-mile trek.

A free permit is needed for overnight hikes, and can be picked up at any visitor center, information kiosk or trailhead register. Beware: poison ivy abounds along creek banks.

This historic trail was once the supply and mail route between Boulder and Escalante. Much of it is unmarked or follows cairns. Most people do the one-way trip in two days, but a third day allows you to do some cross-country wandering and further explore Death Hollow, a world of gullies, grottoes, spires and other slickrock wonders perched on the east edge of your route.

There are serious ups and downs along the trail. We recommend beginning at the **Boulder landing strip**, off Hell's Backbone Rd outside of Boulder at 6800ft, and ending at the Upper Escalante River trailhead, less than a mile outside Escalante at 5800ft. Arrange a hiker shuttle to and from, or just back to your car from the endpoint. The following description is general and is not meant to be your sole route guide; get detailed maps such as the USGS *Escalante,*

Calf Creek and Boulder Town quadrangles. Check with rangers for current conditions and descriptions.

The first leg takes you from the landing strip to Death Hollow (four to five hours, 5.5 miles). Don't start late: you'll want plenty of light for the final descent. A mile-long 4WD road leads from the parking lot to the sign marking the start of the Boulder Mail Trail and the flats atop New Home Bench. From there it's 450ft down to the **Sand Creek** drainage, where cottonwoods offer shade and there's water year-round. Then it's a 400ft trudge back up to the **Slickrock Saddle Bench** before making the precipitous 900ft drop into **Death Hollow**, a gorgeous, riparian canyon named for mules lost on the steep trip down. Death Hollow has several springs at the point where the Mail Trail traverses the canyon. Several campsites lie within 0.25 miles of where the trail meets the creek here; some of the best are 300yd downstream.

A strenuous 800ft ascent out of Death Hollow kicks things off on day two. The trail then crosses to a slickrock plateau, descends to the usually dry **Mamie Creek** and along and over a cracked sandstone formation resembling a giant cerebellum. At **Antone Flat** you come into open country, where a chalky-white slickrock draw may hold water in deep pockets.

After another 900ft slickrock descent, you climb down to **Pine Creek**. The creek's west bank is private, so follow its east bank to the **Escalante River**. To the west the canyon opens and the trail swings south through the brush, meeting a 4WD road and the Upper Escalante Canyon trailhead.

🚗 DRIVING

Check road conditions before entering the monument and note that high-clearance 4WD is recommended for some roads.

🚗 Burr Trail

Duration 3 hours

Distance 60 miles

Start/Finish Hwy 12, Boulder

Summary This paved route provides an intro to all park formations – cliffs, canyons, buttes, mesas and monoliths – in colors from sandy white to deep coral red. Sweeping curves and steep ups and downs add to the attraction.

The most immediately gratifying, dramatic drive in the area, the Burr Trail heads east from Boulder as a paved road, crosses GSENM's northeast corner and, after 30 miles, arrives at Capitol Reef National Park, where the road becomes loose gravel. This first section is quite a challenging road-bike ride, as well.

Once you enter the monument, it's not far to the two trailheads: the 7-mile-long **Deer Creek trail** and the 52-mile trek through **Grand Gulch**, popular with backpackers. Check with rangers for details on these spectacular hikes through riparian zones and red-rock desert. Deer Creek also has a tiny campground.

Just past the creek, the road enters **Long Canyon** beneath towering vertical slabs of red rock. At 11 miles look for an unmarked pullout on the road's left side. You'll see the opening for a side **slot canyon** north across a scrubby wash. Poke about the narrowing red-rock slot as far as you like.

Driving out of Long Canyon, stop at the crest for views beyond of the sheer **Circle Cliffs**, which hang like curtains above the undulating valley floor. Still snowcapped in summer, the **Henry Mountains** rise above 11,000ft on the horizon. **Wolverine Loop** is a 25-mile, 4WD road that circles south through an area riddled with scrubland, canyons and nearby cliffs. Several hiking trails lead off from there, and the area is popular with mountain bikers. Continuing on Burr Trail, you cross the **White Canyon Flat** plateau before the pavement ends and the road meets the giant, angled buttes of 100-mile **Waterpocket Fold** in Capitol Reef, the feature that blocked 19th-century settlers' passage west. Trailhead access to **Muley Twist Canyon** is nearby. Just ahead, the **Burr Trail Switchbacks** follow an original wagon route through the fold. You can continue onto **Notom-Bullfrog Road** and north to Hwy 24 or south to Glen Canyon. But if you plan to turn around and return to Boulder, first drive the switchbacks – the magnificence and scale of the landscape will blow your mind.

🚗 Hole-in-the-Rock Road

Duration 8–9 hours

Distance 114 miles

Start/Finish Hwy 12, 5 miles east of Escalante

Nearest Town Escalante

Hole-in-the-Rock Road

Summary A much-traveled, washboard-rough road follows the route of a historic wagon trail, providing access to area attractions and trails. Expect to be sucking at least a little dust behind other cars.

The history is wilder than the scenery along this dust pit of a road. From 1879 to 1880, more than 200 pioneering Mormons followed this route on their way to settle southeast Utah. When the precipitous walls of Glen Canyon on the Colorado River blocked their path, they blasted and hammered through the cliff, creating a hole wide enough to lower their 80 wagons through – a feat that is honored by the road's name today. The final part of their trail lies submerged beneath Lake Powell. History buffs should pick up Stewart Aitchison's *Hole-in-the-Rock Trail* for a detailed account.

The road is passable by ordinary passenger cars when dry, except for the last 7 miles, which always require 4WD. Even if you don't drive the entire route, at least visit the freely accessible Devils Garden, 12 miles in. Here rock fists, orbs, spires and fingers rise to 40ft above the desert floor. It's a sandy but fairly short walk from the parking lot to the formations. When climbing on, over and under the giant sandstone slabs, nature becomes your playground.

About 26 miles in, turn left for Dry Fork, with the most well-known slot-canyon day hikes on the road. While there are no facilities on the road, dispersed camping is permitted with a free backcountry permit. The last section of this road may be really rough, in which case you should park and walk the final half-mile to the trailhead parking lot.

The last 7 miles are so rugged, they can take almost as long to traverse as the first 50. The road stops short of the actual Hole-in-the-Rock, but hikers can trek out and scramble down past the 'hole' to Lake Powell in less than an hour. Sorry, no elevators for the climb back up.

Skutumpah & Johnson Canyon Roads

Duration 2½ hours

Distance 51 miles one way

Start Hwy 89, 9 miles east of Kanab

Finish Cannonville

Nearest Town Kanab

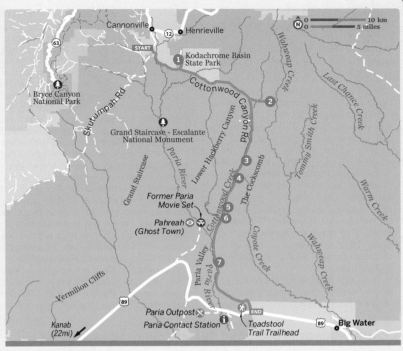

Driving Tour
Cottonwood Canyon Road

DURATION 3 HOURS
DISTANCE 46 MILES ONE WAY
START HWY 12, 34 MILES WEST OF ESCALANTE
FINISH HWY 89, 45 MILES EAST OF KANAB
NEAREST TOWNS ESCALANTE, KANAB

If you make only one of the three cross-monument drives, we suggest it be Cottonwood Canyon Rd, with its stunning geological sights, interesting hikes and ever-changing geography. The rough road is passable only when dry. Usually 2WD vehicles will do, but 4WD is never a bad idea.

The first 9 miles of road to ❶ **Kodachrome Basin State Park** are paved. Stop at the park to see a wonderland of red-rock spires, balancing rocks and mini-buttes. South from here, the road gets bumpy. After about 20 miles, and a short side detour, you'll reach the 90ft-high ❷ **Grosvenor Arch**. Follow the level sidewalk to stand beneath this rare yellow- and sand-colored stone double arch towering so far above. Definitely a Kodak moment. (Picnic tables and pit toilets available.)

The main road continues south, weaving in and among rock formations (look for the stark white pinnacles contrasting with red hoodoos, for example). You're traveling along the west side of the ❸ **Cockscomb**, a distinctive, long, narrow monocline caused by a fold in the earth's crust. ❹ **Cottonwood Narrows** is a worthwhile 1.5-mile hike through a sandstone slot canyon that takes about 1½ hours. There are signposted parking areas at both the north and south entrances.

Soon after, stands of cottonwoods appear in the wash on the right, and the rutted road rises along a narrow shelf.

❺ **Lower Hackberry Canyon** is another good day hike, right before ❻ **Yellow Rock**, a tough, steep but climbable light-hewn peak made of Navajo sandstone, with elaborate cross-bedding and fracture lines. It's 2 miles round-trip.

From there, interesting features abound as the landscape morphs from jagged rock into coal-colored dirt hills before the road reaches the pastoral ❼ **Paria Valley** and Hwy 89 beyond.

Summary A partially paved, partially dirt road crosses the monument beneath Bryce Canyon. En route it passes through the Vermilion, White, Gray and Pink Cliffs, the latter of which are particularly dramatic.

Together these two roads comprise the monument's westernmost route. Paved Johnson Canyon Rd trundles north for 16 miles to intersect Skutumpah (*scoot*-em-pah) Rd. This very rutted dirt route (4WD recommended, and sometimes required) continues for 35 miles to Cannonville on Hwy 12. Driving south–north provides the best perspective.

Start out in very scenic **Johnson Canyon**, which has distant views of the coral **Vermilion Cliffs**. About 6 miles along, you'll see the crumbling wooden buildings of the old **Gunsmoke set**, where the TV Western was filmed. They are on private property, but are easily visible from the road. Soon after, the landscape changes color as the **White Cliffs** appear to the east.

Those who don't have the time, or a proper vehicle, to tackle Skutumpah Rd could turn off at the junction onto the 15-mile **Glendale Bench Road**, a much easier 2WD dirt track that leads east to Glendale on Hwy 89.

Once on Skutumpah Rd, there are numerous old side roads, so pay attention and keep to the main road. Here the **Gray Cliffs** rise to the north and you pass through pastureland before reaching the trailhead for **Lick Wash**. It's 8 miles round-trip on this trail, turning around at Park Wash junction. Uneven stones line part of the way and it can be broiling hot in the canyon, but it's worth doing just the first section to see the scenery.

The road gets steep and rocky before **Bull Valley Gorge**. Stop at the wide spot in the road and walk left along the gorge rim; after about 50ft look back at the debris beneath the 'bridge' you're about to drive across. If you have good eyesight, or binoculars, you might make out a wheel or a window of the **1950s truck** that fell off the road and now forms part of the bridge base. Exploring the gorge itself requires rock-climbing skills.

Soon after, on the road north, is the trailhead parking lot (and pit toilet) for **Willis Creek**, an easy slot-canyon hike. The dramatic **Pink Cliffs** are the last thing you see

CAMPGROUNDS IN & AROUND GRAND STAIRCASE-ESCALANTE

CAMPGROUND	LOCATION	DESCRIPTION	NUMBER OF SITES
Deer Creek (p149)	Burr Trail Rd	Primitive campground near Boulder: creek, trees and red rock. No water, no hookups.	7
Escalante Petrified Forest State Park (p149)	Escalante Petrified Forest State Park	By a swimmable reservoir and forest outside Escalante, with showers, and electrical and water hookups. Interpretive trail.	22
Calf Creek (p149)	Hwy 12	Popular canyon ground near year-round creek and the monument's only marked trail. No showers.	14
Hitch'n Post (p149)	Kanab	Shady little rustic campground in the center of Kanab. Full hookups, pull-through sites and wi-fi.	17
Basin Campground (p149)	Kodachrome Basin State Park	Park service campground with well-spaced sites. Some shade; good hot showers.	26
Bryce View Campground (p149)	Kodachrome Basin State Park	New in 2015; sites have fire rings, vault toilet and water tap.	11
Stateline (p149)	Paria Canyon-Vermilion Cliffs Wilderness Area	An excellent primitive campground near Wire Pass trailhead. Shade, pit toilets and picnic tables; no water.	6
White House (p149)	Paria Canyon-Vermilion Cliffs Wilderness Area	Primitive campground at White House trailhead with pit toilets; no water, no trash collection. Tents only.	5
Coral Pink Sand Dunes State Park (p149)	Sand Dunes Rd	Near stunning pink dunes outside Kanab; can get windy, all-terrain-vehicle use noisy. Showers, no hookups.	22

Drinking Water   Flush Toilets   Ranger Station Nearby   Great for Families   Wheelchair Accessible before the sharp descent to the valley intersection with **Cottonwood Canyon Road**, just south of Cannonville.

OTHER ACTIVITIES

Outfitters in Escalante, Boulder and Kanab offer half-, full- and multiday guided treks into the monument. Horseback riding is available out of Boulder and Kanab; fly-fishing from Escalante.

Boulder Outdoor Survival School OUTDOORS (☎ 800-335-7404; www.boss-inc.com) Learn how to survive in this forbidding wilderness. The school operates seven-day and longer courses in GSENM in subjects including primitive living and hunter-gathering.

Cycling

Though the monument is laced with old ranching roads, such as **Wolverine Loop**, that could be used for mountain biking, the sport really hasn't caught on here.

Escalante Outfitters (p152) rents mountain bikes. For more on trails, look under 'Visitor Information', then 'Recreation Activities' on www.ut.blm.gov/monument. Road cyclists enjoy the challenging hills of paved **Burr Trail**. There are also cycling tours throughout the region.

🛌 SLEEPING

Free, dispersed backcountry camping – outside wilderness study areas – is widely available in the monument, but you need a permit. Pick one up at any visitor center, where you can discuss locations with rangers, or at major trailheads.

Outside the monument, campgrounds at Kodachrome Basin, Escalante Petrified Forest and Coral Pink Sand Dunes State Parks have running water and hot showers. Area towns are the only option for lodgings with walls.

In the monument's two campgrounds you have to pack out trash, but leashed pets are allowed. Both are first-come, first-served.

ELEVATION	OPEN	RESERVATION REQUIRED?	DAY FEE	FACILITIES
5800ft	mid-May–mid-Sep	no	$10	
5900ft	year-round	yes	$5	
5400ft	year-round	no	$15	
4900ft	year-round	yes	NA	
5800ft	year-round	yes	free	
5800ft	year-round	yes	free	
5040ft	year-round	no	free	
3000ft	year-round	no	free	
6000ft	year-round	yes	free	

 Dogs Allowed (On Leash)   Grocery Store Nearby   Restaurant Nearby   Pay-phone   RV Dump Station

GRAND STAIRCASE-ESCALANTE NATIONAL MONUMENT SLEEPING

Deer Creek Campground   CAMPGROUND **$**
(www.blm.gov/ut; Burr Trail Rd; tent sites $10;
⊘mid-May–mid-Sep) This campground, 6
miles southeast of Boulder, has few sites and
no water, but does have pit toilets. It sits beside a year-round creek beneath tall trees.

Calf Creek Campground   CAMPGROUND **$**
(www.blm.gov/ut; Hwy 12; tent & RV sites $15) Be-
side a year-round creek, this campground
is surrounded by red-rock canyons (hot in
summer) and has 14 incredibly popular,
nonreserveable sites. Drinking water is
available; there are no hookups. It's near the
trailhead to Lower Calf Creek Falls, 15 miles
east of Escalante.

❶ Information

Food, gas, lodging and other services are
available in Boulder, Escalante, Kanab and Cannonville. Note that most lodgings in the area are
entirely nonsmoking.

Interagency desks answer questions about all
area public lands: National Park Service (NPS),
US Forest Service (USFS) and Bureau of Land
Management (BLM).

Big Water Visitor Center (☑435-675-3200;
100 Upper Revolution Way, Big Water; ⊘9am-

5.30pm Apr-Oct, 8am-4.30pm Tue-Sat Nov-
Mar) Near Lake Powell.

Cannonville Visitor Center (☑435-826-5640;
10 Center St, Cannonville; ⊘8am-4:30pm Apr-
Oct) Five miles east of Tropic.

Escalante Interagency Office (☑435-826-
5499; www.ut.blm.gov/monument; 775 W
Main St; ⊘8am-4:30pm daily Apr-Sep, Mon-Fri
Oct-Mar) *The* source for information about area
public lands; jointly operated by the BLM, the
USFS and NPS.

Kanab Visitor Center (☑435-644-4680; 745
E Hwy 89, Kanab; ⊘7:30am-5:30pm) Park
headquarters in the Southwestern section.

❶ Getting Around

The only way to get around the monument is in a
private vehicle or on foot. Some unpaved roads
require a high-clearance 4WD. Note that most
off-the-lot SUVs and light trucks are *not* high
clearance.

Towns outside the park – Escalante, Boulder
and Kanab – have all services, including gas
stations and hiker shuttles. Escalante and Kanab
have one 4WD Jeep rental place apiece. However, it's cheaper per day to rent upon arrival in
Las Vegas.

---

❶ SAFETY OFF THE GRID

Please remember that Grand Staircase-Escalante National Monument is a remote
desert wilderness park with few services and flash-flood danger.

Always

➥ Check with a ranger about weather and road conditions before driving or hiking

➥ Keep your gas tank as full as possible; stations are few and far between

➥ Carry extra water and food in case of a breakdown

➥ Stop the car and wait for the storm to pass if it does start raining unexpectedly; roads
dry quickly, sometimes within 30 minutes

➥ Let someone know where you're going and when you plan to return if you're traveling
alone

➥ Take sun protection and a gallon of water per day when hiking in the desert

➥ For emergencies: 911 can work in remote areas even when your cell phone says 'no
service'

Never

➥ Attempt a 4WD road beyond your vehicle's capability

➥ Park in a wash; flash floods come suddenly

➥ Start a slot-canyon hike or long back-road drive when rain is imminent

➥ Remove or defile Native American artifacts or sites; it's against the law

➥ Walk on cryptobiotic crust

Around Grand Staircase-Escalante National Monument

Best Places to Stay

➡ Escalante Grand Staircase B&B (p153)

➡ Boulder Mountain Lodge (p155)

➡ Canyons Lodge (p157)

➡ Basin Campground (p152)

Best Places to Eat

➡ Hell's Backbone Grill (p155)

➡ Burr Trail Grill & Outpost (p155)

➡ Rocking V Cafe (p157)

➡ Kiva Koffeehouse (p155)

Why Go?

Highway 12 brings the vast majority of visitors to Grand Staircase, and as such you'll find the main visitor centers and services north of the national monument in the towns of Boulder and Escalante. Nearby Kodachrome Basin State Park features hiking and biking trails past petrified geysers and sandstone chimneys, but is best for pitching a tent – the campground here has showers, which definitely hit the spot after a day scrambling around in the dusty slots.

A full 120 miles from Escalante, at the southwest corner of Grand Staircase off Hwy 89, is cinematic Kanab, another good base for exploring the park and ideally situated between GSENM, Bryce, Zion and the Grand Canyon's North Rim. The remote Paria Canyon-Vermilion Cliffs wilderness area is a must for hardcore explorers and landscape photographers, with tough multiday canyoneering treks and a coveted hike to the world-famous Wave formation.

When to Go
Escalante

May–Aug	Mar-Jun, Sep & Oct	Nov-Feb
Temperatures soar, thought nights are cool, and traffic is busy.	Generally pleasant but often unpredictable weather.	Snow at higher elevations; canyons are bitterly cold.

Kodachrome Basin State Park

Petrified geysers and dozens of red, pink and white sandstone chimneys – some nearly 170ft tall – resemble everything from a sphinx to a snowmobile at **Kodachrome Basin** (☑ 435-679-8562; www.stateparks.utah. gov; off Cottonwood Canyon Rd; day use per vehicle $8; ☉day use 6am-10pm). The park lies off Hwy 12, 9 miles south of Cannonville and 26 miles southeast of Bryce Canyon National Park. Visit in the morning or afternoon, when shadows play on the red rock.

Most sights are along mountain-biking and hiking trails. The moderately easy, 3-mile round-trip **Panorama Trail** gives the best overview. Be sure to take the side trails to **Indian Cave**, where you can check out the hand prints on the wall (from 'cowboys' or 'Indians'?), and **Secret Passage**, a short hike through a narrow slot canyon. **Angel Palace Trail** (1-mile loop, moderate) has great desert views from on high. Red Canyon Trail Rides (p122), based near Bryce, offers horseback rides.

The 26 well-spaced sites at the reservable park service **Basin Campground** (☑800-322-3770; http://utahstateparks.reserveamerica. com; tent/RV sites $19/28) have showers, full hookups for RVs and shade from juniper trees. The new **Bryce View Campground** (site $16) has 11 reservable sites with fire rings, vault toilet and water tap.

The four **Red Stone Cabins** (☑435-679-8536; www.redstonecabins.com; cabin $109; ☉Mar-Oct; ✱🐾) are simple but cozy, with all the essentials (linens, microwave, minifridge and coffeemaker) and a king bed or two queens.

PARK RESOURCES

Paria Canyon-Vermilion Cliffs Wilderness (www.blm.gov/az/st/en/prog/blm_special_areas/wildareas/paria_vermilion.html)

Coral Pink Sand Dunes National Park (http://stateparks.utah.gov/parks/coral-pink)

Kodachrome Basin State Park (http://stateparks.utah.gov/parks/kodachrome-basin)

Escalante Petrified Forest State Park (http://stateparks.utah.gov/parks/escalante-petrified-forest)

The same family runs a little **camp store** (☉8am-6:30pm Sun-Thu, to 8pm Fri & Sat Apr-Oct).

Escalante

POPULATION 779 / ELEVATION 5600FT

Your gateway to the north side of the GSENM, Escalante is a mix of ranchers, old-timers, artists and post-monument-creation outdoors lovers. The town itself doesn't exude character, but a friendly selection of lodgings and restaurants make it a decent base camp. Numerous outfitters make this their base for hiking excursions, and you could, too. At the head of several park back roads, it's not far from the most popular GSENM hikes.

⊙ Sights & Activities

Hiking and driving in the monument are the main activities here. Reserve ahead to rent 4WD vehicles at **High Adventure Rentals** (☑435-616-4640; www.highadventurerentals.com).

Escalante Petrified Forest State Park   PARK
(www.stateparks.utah.gov; day use $8; ☉day use 8am-10pm) Two miles west of town, the centerpiece of this state park is a 130-acre lake. Hike uphill about a mile on an interpretive route to see pieces of colorful petrified wood, millions of years old. Follow another short interpretive trail for further examples. The sites at the campground are reservable; showers available.

⌃ Tours

Escalante Outfitters   ADVENTURE SPORTS
(☑435-826-4266; www.escalanteoutfitters.com; 310 W Main St; natural history tours $45; ☉7am-9pm) A traveler's oasis, this store sells area books, topographic maps, camping and hiking gear, and is attached to a cafe. Reputable guided hikes, fly-fishing, natural-history tours and mountain-bike rentals (from $35 per day) available.

Escape Goats   ADVENTURE SPORTS
(☑435-826-4652; www.escapegoats.us; day hike $100) Take an evening tour or day hike to dinosaur tracks, slot canyons and ancient sites. There's also fully catered backpacking trips (three days $750) including gear. Recommended.

Excursions of Escalante   ADVENTURE SPORTS
(☑800-839-7567; www.excursionsofescalante. com; 125 E Main St; full day from $150; ☉8am-

> **DON'T MISS**
>
> ## HIGHWAY 12
>
> Arguably Utah's most diverse and stunning route, **Highway 12 Scenic Byway** (www.scenicbyway12.com) winds through rugged canyonland, from near Capitol Reef southeast past Bryce Canyon – linking several national parks on a 124-mile journey. See how quickly and dramatically the land changes from wooded plateau to red-rock canyon, from slickrock desert to alpine forest, as it climbs over an 11,000ft mountain. Highlights include the switchbacks and petrified sand dunes between Torrey and Boulder. Also, the razor-thin Hogback Ridge between Escalante and Boulder is pretty stunning, too.
>
> Take time to stop at the many viewpoints and pullouts, especially at Mile 70, where the Aquarius Plateau lords over giant mesas, towering domes, deep canyons and undulating slickrock, all unfurling in an explosion of color. A bike lane, currently only around Bryce, is slated to expand further along Hwy 12.

6pm) For area canyoneering and climbing trips, Excursions is the best; it does hiker shuttles and guided photo hikes, too. Has an on-site cafe.

Rising DT Trail   HORSEBACK RIDING
(☑ 435-616-3045; www.escalantehorsetours.com; 3680 W Hwy 12) Dave Trainor offers recommended rides through GSENM.

🛏 Sleeping

**Escalante Outfitters Bunkhouse
Cabins**   CABIN **$**
(☑ 435-826-4266; www.escalanteoutfitters.com; 310 W Main St; tent sites 19, cabins $45; 🐾🐕) Pitch a tent or rent a rustic, but heated, teeny-tiny log cabin (linens included, shared bathroom, no air-conditioning) in a shady yard. Picnic tables and grills available.

**Escalante Petrified Forest
State Park Campground**   CAMPGROUND **$**
(☑ 800-322-3770; http://utahstateparks.reserve america.com; tent/RV sites $19/25; 🐕🐾) The 22-site, reserveable campground has water, picnic tables, firepits and restrooms with wonderfully hot showers. It's 2 miles northwest of town along Hwy 12. RV sites with hookups.

Rainbow Country Bed & Breakfast B&B **$**
(☑ 800-252-8824, 435-826-4567; www.bnb escalante.com; 586 E 300 S; r incl breakfast $79-114; 🐾🐕) Good trail advice and big home-cooked breakfasts. This split-level house on the edge of town is not flashy, just comfortable – with a big TV lounge (no in-room TVs), guest refrigerator and outdoor hot tub.

Circle D Motel   MOTEL **$**
(☑ 435-826-4297; www.escalantecircledmotel. com; 475 W Main St; r $74-99, cottage $125; 🐾🐕🐕) We love the little library of guide-

books and hiking information in the rooms. The friendly proprietor goes out of his way to accommodate guests at this partially updated, older motel. Room microwaves and minifridges are standard.

★ **Escalante Grand Staircase B&B** B&B **$$**
(☑ 435-826-4890; www.escalantebnb.com; 280 W Main St; d incl breakfast $140; 🐾🐕) A wonderful find, with eight spacious rooms with individual entrances, skylights and porches. Rooms feature landscape murals with Western motifs. Tom, the host, provides vast quantities of coffee and extensive trail information, with helpful binders with photos and directions.

Canyons B&B   INN **$$**
(☑ 435-826-4747, 866-526-9667; www.canyons bnb.com; 120 E Main St; d incl breakfast $140; ⊙Mar-Oct; 🐾🐕) A self-catered lodging with upscale cabin-rooms, with kitchenette use and porches surrounding a shaded terrace and gardens. Owners speak Russian and Spanish.

Slot Canyons Inn   INN **$$**
(☑ 435-826-4901, 866-889-8375; www.slotcanyons inn.com; 3680 W Hwy 12; r incl breakfast $169-219, cabin $309; 🐾@🐕) An architectural showpiece on the edge of the desert; upscale all the way.

> **THE HOGBACK**
>
> East of Calf Creek, between mile markers 78 and 80, Hwy 12 crosses the narrow Hogback Ridge, with precipitous drop-offs into seemingly bottomless canyons and rolling slickrock desert. There are no guardrails; pull off at designated turnouts.

✕ Eating

Griffin Grocery MARKET
(30 W Main St; ⊙8am-7pm Mon-Sat) The only grocery in town.

Escalante Mercantile Natural Grocery MARKET
(☑435-826-4114; 210 W Main St; ⊙9am-7pm Mon-Sat, 10am-5pm Sun) A well-stocked natural grocer, better with dry goods than produce.

Circle D Eatery AMERICAN $$
(475 W Main St; mains $9-19; ⊙7am-9:30pm, limited hours Nov-Feb) Attentive service and satisfying burgers, with local beef on fresh jalapeno buns and shoestring fries. Smoked meats are a specialty, but there are also pastas, salads and hearty breakfasts.

Esca-Latte Cafe & Pizza PIZZA $$
(310 W Main St; breakfast $3-6, pizza $12-22; ⊙8am-9pm Mar-Oct; 🛜) Espresso drinks and decent quick bites. There's granola and quiche at breakfast, and tasty homemade pizza and beer. Hikers will want to pack one of the monster cinnamon buns.

OFF THE BEATEN TRACK

4WD ADVENTURES

Looking for even more 4WD adventure than the cross-monument drives offer? You have alternatives.

Hell's Backbone Road Loops a gravel-strewn 48 miles off Hwy 12 between Boulder and Escalante. The original mule-mail route, it crosses the rugged Box-Death Hollow Wilderness area. The highlight is a single-lane track atop an impossibly narrow ridge.

Smoky Mountain Road A challenging, 78-mile, dirt-and-gravel road between Escalante and Big Water visitor center. It's passable by 4WD vehicle only (preferably with high clearance). The prime destination is Alstrom Point, 12.5 miles from Hwy 89, a plateau-top vantage with stunning views that include Lake Powell.

Old Sheffield Road (or Spencer Flats) Undulates for 3 sand-and-gravel miles through desert, slickrock formations and canyons. Some great backcountry camping is to be found out here too. The road leaves Hwy 12, 6 miles east of Escalante.

ⓘ Information

Cell-phone reception is spotty. For local info, see http://escalanteut.com. Services are limited from November through March.

Escalante Interagency Visitor Center
(☑435-826-5499; www.ut.blm.gov/monument; 755 W Main St; ⊙7:30am-5:30pm) Ask here about all public lands, trails, road conditions and camping.

Kazan Memorial Clinic (☑435-826-4374; 65 W Main St; ⊙9am-5pm Mon, Wed & Fri) Limited medical care; the closest hospital is in Panguitch.

Post Office (☑435-826-4314; 230 W Main St; ⊙7:15am-3:45pm Mon-Fri, 8:30am-noon Sat)

Wells Fargo ATM (250 W Main St; ⊙24hr)

Boulder

POPULATION 220 / ELEVATION 6675FT

Boulder is a tiny slice of heaven and a great base to explore the surrounding desert wilderness. Until 1940, this isolated outpost received its mail by mule – it's still so remote that the federal government classifies it as a 'frontier community.' Its diverse population includes artists, ecologists, farmers, cowboys and cowgirls. Though only 32 miles south of Torrey on Hwy 12, you have to traverse 11,317ft-high Boulder Mountain to get here. Note that pretty much all services shut down from November through March.

◉ Sights & Activities

Anasazi State Park Museum MUSEUM
(www.stateparks.utah.gov; Main St/Hwy 12; admission $5; ⊙8am-6pm Mar-Oct, 9am-5pm Nov-Apr) This petite museum protects the Coombs Site, excavated in the 1950s and inhabited from 1130 to 1175. The minimal ruins aren't as evocative as some in southeastern Utah, but it's well worth seeing the re-created six-room pueblo and excellent exhibits about the Ancestral Puebloan peoples. Get backcountry road updates and backcountry permits at a seasonal information desk staffed by rangers.

Dixie National Forest PARK
(www.fs.usda.gov/dixie) North of Boulder, the Escalante District of this 2 million-acre forest has trails and campgrounds, including a few up on Boulder Mountain.

☞ Tours

Earth Tours HIKING
(☑435-691-1241; www.earth-tours.com; Boulder; day tours from $110;) Choose from half- and

full-day area hikes and 4WD trips into the backcountry in and around Bryce, Escalante, Boulder Mountain and Capitol Reef. Keith will pick you up at your hotel in Torrey or Boulder.

Escalante Canyon Outfitters HIKING
(ECO; ☏435-691-3037, 888-326-4453; www.ecohike.com; 2520 S Lower Deer Creek Rd; ☉Mar-Nov) Started by cofounder of the Southern Utah Wilderness Alliance Grant Johnson, ECO has well-regarded multiday treks with a canyonland or archaeological-site focus.

**Hell's Backbone
Ranch & Trails** HORSEBACK RIDING
(☏435-335-7581; www.bouldermountaintrails.com; off Hell's Backbone Rd; half-day $105) Head across the slickrock plateau, into Box-Death Hollow Wilderness or up the forested mountain on two-hour to full-day horseback rides. Or perhaps you'd prefer a multiday camping trip or cattle drive?

🛌 Sleeping

Pole's Place MOTEL $
(☏435-335-7422, 800-730-7422; www.polesplaceutah.com; Hwy 12; r $76-85; ☉late Mar-Oct; ❄) Run by a fourth-generation local, this nicely kept motel has quiet, decent rooms without wi-fi. There are local menus and historical news clippings to peruse in each room. Limited TV.

★ Boulder Mountain Lodge LODGE $$
(☏435-335-7460; www.boulder-utah.com; 20 N Hwy 12; r $135-184, ste $310, apt $220; ❄ @ 🛜 ❄) Watch the birds flit by on the adjacent 15-acre wildlife sanctuary and stroll through the organic garden – Boulder Mountain Lodge has a strong eco-aesthetic. It's an ideal place for day-hikers who want to return to high-thread-count sheets, plush robes, spa treatments and an outdoor hot tub. The onsite Hell's Backbone Grill is a southern Utah must-eat.

Boulder Mountain Guest Ranch LODGE $$
(☏435-335-7480; www.bouldermountainguestranch.com; off Hell's Backbone Rd; r $80-115, cabins $115-125, tipi $55; ❄ 🛜) This giant log lodge is in a peaceful 160-acre wilderness with trails, a waterfall, and outfitter-led hikes and activities. Think rustic, with a happy hippie vibe. Bunk and queen rooms enjoy a communal atmosphere; out-cabins are more private. The dining room has chef-cooked meals at breakfast and dinners use garden produce.

DON'T MISS

KIVA KOFFEEHOUSE

Just past the Aquarius Plateau at Mile 73 on Hwy 12, you reach this singular coffee house (☏435-826-4550; www.kivakoffeehouse.com; Hwy 12, Mile 73; dishes $4-12; ☉8am-4:30pm Wed-Mon Apr-Oct), whose round structure was built directly into the cliffside. Floor-to-ceiling glass windows, separated by giant timber beams, overlook the expansive canyons beyond. Besides serving barista-brewed coffee and yummy baked goods, Kiva also rents two cushy hideaway rooms in Kiva Kottage (www.kivakoffeehouse.com/kottage.htm; r incl breakfast $190; 🛜), with whirlpool tubs and fireplaces – and the same stellar views.

🍴 Eating

Hills & Hollows Country Store MARKET $
(Hwy 12; ☉9am-7pm, gas 24hr; 🛜) Groceries and organic snacks available year-round, though hours may be limited November through February.

★ Hell's Backbone Grill MODERN AMERICAN $$
(☏435-335-7464; www.hellsbackbonegrill.com; 20 N Hwy 12, Boulder Mountain Lodge; breakfast $8-12, lunch $12-18, dinner $18-27; ☉7:30-11:30am & 5-9:30pm Mar-Nov) Earthy preparations of Southwestern dishes include gorgeous salads made from organic garden produce, and braised beef in rich preparations. While this restaurant, a pioneer in sustainable eating and mindfulness, has garnered regional fame, not all dishes are winners – the tofu is a dud. Breakfasts remain satisfying, and there are lunchboxes for hikers. Dinner reservations are a must.

**★ Burr Trail Grill
& Outpost** MODERN AMERICAN $$
(www.burrtrailgrill.com; cnr Hwy 12 & Burr Trail Rd; dishes $8-18; ☉grill 11:30pm-9:30pm, outpost 8:30am-6pm Mar-Oct; 🛜) These organic vegetable tarts and eclectic burgers (plus scrumptious homemade cookies and cakes) served here rival those of the more famous restaurant next door. We like the homey vibe here. It's worth browsing the Outpost art gallery, gift shop and coffeehouse.

ℹ Information

Most of the town's businesses close from November through March, when heavy snow sets in.

Boulder Interagency Desk (☑ 435-335-7382; Hwy 12, Anasazi State Park Museum; ⊙ 9am-5pm mid-Mar–mid-Nov) BLM and other public-land trail and camping information.

Boulder Tourism Information (www.boulderutah.com) Provides regional information.

Kanab

POPULATION 4410 / ELEVATION 4925FT

Vast expanses of rugged desert surround the remote outpost of Kanab. Don't be surprised if it all looks familiar: hundreds of Western movies were shot here. Founded by Mormon pioneers in 1874, Kanab was put on the map by John Wayne and other gunslingin' celebs in the 1940s and '50s. You can still see a couple of movie sets in the area and hear old-timers reminisce about their roles. In August, the Western Legends Roundup celebrates 'Utah's little Hollywood.'

Kanab sits at a major crossroads: GSENM is 20 miles away and Zion, Bryce Canyon, Lake Powell and Grand Canyon's North Rim just beyond. It makes a good base for exploring the southern side of GSENM and Paria Canyon-Vermilion Cliffs Wilderness.

👁 Sights & Activities

Parry Lodge HISTORIC SITE
(www.parrylodge.com; 89 E Center St; ⊙ movies 8pm Sat Jun-Aug) FREE Built in the 1930s, this hotel was movie central. Stars stayed here and owner Whit Parry provided horses, cattle and catering for the sets. There are nostalgic photos, and old Westerns play in a barn out back on summer Saturday nights.

> ### KANAB IN PICTURES
>
> The movie industry has harnessed the rugged wilds around Kanab since its early days. In the 1920s, film adaptations of Zane Grey novels were shot here. And in the '40s and '50s, dozens of Westerns were filmed in the area, including those by screen legend John Ford. John Wayne, Charlton Heston and Clint Eastwood all filmed here too. So did iconic TV shows *The Lone Ranger, Gunsmoke, The Six Million Dollar Man* and *Lassie*.
>
> Today the tradition continues. Disney-Pixar made *John Carter* (2012) here and the new *Planet of the Apes* (2001) starring Mark Wahlberg was filmed at nearby Lake Powell.

Frontier Movie Town & Trading Post FILM LOCATION
(297 W Center St; ⊙ 7:30am-11pm Apr-Oct, 10am-5pm Nov-Mar) FREE Wander through a bunkhouse, saloon and other buildings used in Western movies filmed locally, including *The Outlaw Josey Wales* (1976), and learn some tricks of the trade (such as short doorways to make movie stars seem taller). This classic roadside attraction sells all the Western duds and doodads you could care to round up.

Best Friends Animal Sanctuary RESCUE CENTER
(☑ 435-644-2001; www.bestfriends.org; Angel Canyon, Hwy 89; ⊙ 9:30am-5:30pm; 🅿) FREE Kanab's most famous attraction is outside town. Surrounded by more than 33,000 mostly private acres of red-rock desert 5.5 miles north of Kanab, Best Friends is the largest no-kill animal rescue center in the country. The center shows films and gives facility tours four times a day; call ahead for times and reservations. The 1½-hour tours let you meet some of the more than 1700 horses, pigs, dogs, cats, birds and other critters on site.

Tours

★Dreamland Safari TOURS
(www.dreamlandtours.net; 3hr tour $90) Hikes with naturalist tour guides to gorgeous backcountry sites and slot canyons by 4WD. They also offer nature photography and multi-day backpacking trips.

Paria Outpost ADVENTURE TOUR
(☑ 928-691-1047; www.paria.com; half-day tour $125) Friendly, flexible and knowledgeable. Offers guided horseback rides in Grand Staircase-Escalante Monument, as well as 4WD tours and guided hikes.

Seldom Seen Adventures ADVENTURE TOUR
(☑ 888-418-9908; www.seldomseenadventures.net; day hike $129) Family-oriented, personalized tours of the national parks, GSENM and wilderness areas, with canyoneering, 4WD tours, super fat-tire biking and hiking. Also offers transfers.

✨ Festivals & Events

Western Legends Roundup FILM
(☑ 800-733-5263; www.westernlegendsroundup.com) The town lives for the annual Western Legends Roundup in late August. There are concerts, gunfights, cowboy poetry, dances, quilt shows, a film festival and more. Take a bus tour to all the film sites, or sign up for a Dutch-oven cooking lesson.

🛏 Sleeping

Hitch'n Post Campground   CAMPGROUND $
(📞800-458-3516, 435-644-2142; www.hitchn
postrvpark.com; 196 E 300 South; tent/RV sites
with hookups $18/29, camping cabins $32-36;
🛜🐾) Friendly 17-site campground near the
town center; has laundry and showers.

★Canyons Lodge   MOTEL $$
(📞435-644-3069, 800-644-5094; www.canyons
lodge.com; 236 N 300 West; r incl breakfast $89-
179; 🌐@🛜🐾) 🐾 A renovated motel
with an art-house Western feel. There's a
warm welcome, free cruiser bikes and good
traveler assistance. In summer, guests enjoy twice-weekly live music and wine and
cheese by the fire pit. Rooms feature original
artwork and whimsical touches. Recycles
soaps and containers.

Quail Park Lodge   MOTEL $$
(📞435-215-1447; www.quailparklodge.com; 125
N 300 W; r/ste $155/203; 🌐@🛜🐾) With
Schwinn cruiser bicycles and a postage-
stamp-size pool, retro pervades all 13 rooms
at this refurbished 1963 motel with surprisingly plush rooms. Mod cons include free
phone calls, microwaves, minifridges and
complimentary gourmet coffee.

Purple Sage Inn   B&B $$
(📞435-644-5377, 877-644-5377; www.purplesage-
inn.com; r incl breakfast $135-165; 🌐🛜) A for-
mer Mormon polygamist's home, this later
became a hotel, where Western author Zane
Grey stayed. Now it's a B&B with exquisite
antique details. Zane's namesake room –
with its quilt-covered wooden bed, sitting
room and balcony access – is our favorite.

Canyons Boutique Hotel   BOUTIQUE HOTEL $$
(📞435-644-8660; www.canyonshotel.com; 190
N 300 West; r incl breakfast $149-169; 🌐🛜🐾)
From the architecture to appointments, the
inn is a modern-day remake of period Vic-
toriana. Ethan Allen furnishings, gas fireplaces and jetted tubs grace every room, but
it all looks a little stiff in these parts. Look
for the new on-site restaurant.

Parry Lodge   MOTEL $$
(📞888-289-1722, 435-644-2601; www.parrylodge.
com; 89 E Center St; r $109-139; 🌐🛜🐾) The
aura of bygone Westerns is the best feature
of this rambling old classic motel. Some
rooms bear the names of movie stars who
stayed here, like Gregory Peck or Lana Turn-
er. If quality is your concern, opt for the

WORTH A TRIP

THE NORTH RIM

A solitary stunner, the North Rim of the
Grand Canyon is a very accessible day
trip, 81 miles south of Kanab on Hwy 89A.
This side of the park is higher (at 8200ft)
and sees far fewer visitors than the South
Rim, and yet the views are as good or
better. Note that services close from
mid-October through mid-May. Also,
Arizona does not observe daylight saving
time, so in summer it's one hour behind
Utah time. For a complete destination
rundown, pick up a copy of Lonely
Planet's *Grand Canyon National Park*.

L-shaped double queen room, nicely refurbished in cottage decor.

🍴 Eating

Honey's Marketplace   MARKET
(260 E 300 S; ⏱7am-10pm) Full grocery store.

Escobar's   MEXICAN $
(mains $7-12; ⏱11am-9:30pm Sun-Fri) Some-
times it feels like all of Kanab is stuffed
into this busy, family-run restaurant with
swift service and XL portions. Start with the
complimentary homemade chips and salsa
and move on to a green chile burrito and a
chilled mug of beer.

Jakey Leighs   CAFE $
(4 E Center St; sandwiches $4-8; ⏱7am-10pm Tue-
Sat, 7am-3pm Sun & Mon; 🛜) A quick fix for
breakfast and baked goods.

Fusion House   ASIAN $
(📞435-644-8868; www.fusionhousekanab.com;
18 E Center St; mains $9-15; ⏱10:30am-9pm Mon-
Sat, noon-9pm Sun; 🛜🍴) Casual Asian fusion
— think Japanese-style pork katsu curry, co-
conut shrimp, udon noodle soups, and fried
rice with spinach and pine nuts — served in
a diner-like setting on Kanab's main drag.

★Rocking V Cafe   AMERICAN $$
(www.rockingvcafe.com; 97 W Center St; lunch $8-
18, dinner $15-34; ⏱11:30am-10pm; 🍴) Fresh
ingredients star in dishes like hand-cut
buffalo tenderloin and chargrilled zucchini
with curried quinoa. Local artwork decorat-
ing the 1892 brick storefront is as creative as
the food. Off-season hours vary.

🛍 Shopping

Willow Canyon
Outdoor Co   OUTDOOR EQUIPMENT
(263 S 100 East; ☺7:30am-8pm) It's easy to spend hours sipping espresso and perusing the eclectic books here. Before you leave, outfit yourself with field guides, camping gear, USGS maps, hiking clothes and gas for your camp stove. Off-season hours vary.

ℹ Information

BLM Kanab Field Office (☎435-644-4600; 318 N 100 East; ☺8am-4pm Mon-Fri)
GSENM Visitor Center (☎435-644-1300; www.ut.blm.gov/monument; 745 E Hwy 89; ☺8am-4:30pm) Provides road, trail and weather updates for the Grand Staircase–Escalante National Monument.
Kane County Hospital (☎435-644-5811; 355 N Main St; ☺24hr) The closest medical facility to GSENM.
Kane County Office of Tourism (☎435-644-5033, 800-733-5263; www.visitsouthernutah.com; 78 S 100 East; ☺8:30am-6pm Mon-Fri, to 4pm Sat) The main source for area information; great old Western movie posters and artifacts on display.
Library (☎435-644-2394; 374 N Main St; ☺10am-5pm Mon & Fri, to 7pm Tue-Thu, to 2pm Sat) Free internet and wi-fi access.
Post Office (39 S Main St; ☺9am-4pm Mon-Fri, to 2pm Sat)

TRACKING DOWN DINOS

It's not uncommon to hear of experts locating dinosaur tracks in the vast wilderness expanse around GSENM – but they are usually prohibitively difficult to reach. Not so for the 185-million-year-old prints found at the **Moccasin Mountain Dinosaur Track Site**, 3 miles south of Coral Pink Sand Dunes State Park on freely accessible BLM land. The last 2.2 miles are deeply sandy, high-clearance 4WD track. Without the appropriate vehicle, you could park and hike the remaining distance. Six different dinosaurs, sized 1ft- to 20ft-long, left their tracks in a slickrock expanse the size of a football field.

Pick up a map and directions at the state park. If you see a beehives formation, you've gone too far. For more BLM track sites, see www.blm.gov/ut/st/en/prog/more/cultural/Paleontology.html.

Coral Pink Sand Dunes State Park

Restless winds shift giant Sahara-like sand dunes across half of this 3700-acre **state park** (☎435-648-2800; http://stateparks.utah.gov; Sand Dunes Rd; day use $8; ☺day use dawn-dusk, visitor center 9am-9pm Mar-Oct, 9am-4pm Nov-Feb). For lovers of the strange, it's worth the 24-mile, 90-minute round-trip off Hwy 89 to see the shocking coral-colored hills. The pinkish hue results from the eroding, red Navajo sandstone in the area. Note that 1200 acres of the park are devoted to ATVs, so it's not necessarily a quiet experience. The visitor center has displays and water. Follow the half-mile interpretive dune hike to the 265-acre conservation area that's closed to off-highway vehicles (OHV).

The same winds that shift the dunes can make tent camping unpleasant at the 22-site **campground** (☎800-322-3770; http://utahstateparks.reserveamerica.com; tent/RV sites $20/40); it has toilets and hot showers; no hookups. Reservations are essential on weekends when off-roaders come to play.

Paria Canyon-Vermilion Cliffs Wilderness Area

With miles of weathered, swirling slickrock and slot-canyon systems that can be hiked for days without seeing a soul, it's no wonder that this wilderness area is gold for seasoned trekkers, canyoneers and photographers. This is the home of the mesmerizing sculptural orange sandstone bowl known as the Wave, the Mona Lisa of the Southwestern desert. But that formation and others are far from easily accessible. This is the remotest of remote Utah lands, straddling the Arizona border, and permits are required for the most sought-after routes.

⊙ Sights & Activities

Toadstools   NATURAL FEATURE
About 1.5 miles east of the Paria contact station on Hwy 89, turn north and follow the dirt road to the rounded rock-tops you can see from the highway. The Toadstools are red hoodoos that are easily and freely explored on BLM land; they're less than a 1-mile hike from the end of the road. Slanting, late-afternoon light is best for catching the shape and depth of the eerie features.

Coyote Buttes North & the Wave   HIKING

(www.az.blm.gov/paria; permit $7) The golden ticket of hiking permits are the 20 coveted permits that are issued per day to explore the trail-less expanse of slickrock leading to the Wave. The 6.5-mile, five-hour round-trip hike is magical, in a setting of swirling, striped slickrock. At the time of writing, the permit system was under revision. In 2016 costs will increase, and the lottery will likely move to www.recreation.gov (no walk-in permits). Directions to the protected site are not divulged until you have a permit.

Note that overnight permits are also reserveable for Paria Canyons, four months in advance, but do not include access to Coyote Buttes North and the Wave.

Coyote Buttes South   HIKING

(permit $7) An alternative to Coyote Buttes North if you want to see related slickrock formations is to get a next-day permit for Coyote Buttes South. The permit is in much less demand (and not reserveable online), but a 4WD is absolutely required for the deep-sand access roads. Ask rangers for directions.

Wire Pass   HIKING

(day permit $6) Wire Pass (3.4 miles round trip) is a great slot-canyon day hike. The parking lot is 8 miles south along House Rock Valley Rd. You start out descending in a sandy wash and eventually the gorge slots up, narrowing to shoulder-width in places. You'll scramble down a few boulder-choked sections, and under logs jammed 50ft overhead, before reaching a wide alcove with what was likely an ancient granary ledge; look for the petroglyph panel on the far end.

Wire Pass dead-ends at the confluence with Buckskin Gulch. Stop here (1.2 miles along) or continue exploring the Buckskin slot canyon as far north or south as you like. Note that at times there may be water in one or both of the canyons.

Buckskin Gulch to White House   HIKING

(day permit $6) This 16-mile backpack hike starts at the Buckskin Gulch trailhead and ends at White House trailhead. Those overnighting must obtain a backcountry permit ($5 per night) online in advance.

🛏 Sleeping

Overnight backcountry camping permits can be reserved online and in person. Use of human-waste carryout bags is encouraged; the contact station provides them for free.

OFF THE BEATEN TRACK

BIG WATER

About 56 miles from Kanab, this small town with little more than a convenience store is known because of the dinosaur finds (and polygamist residents) in the area. The Big Water visitor center (p150) has great paleontology exhibits, which include a replica of a dig, various bones found in the monument (including the 13ft tail of a duckbill) and a spectacular 9ft-by-45ft mural by expert dinosaur painter Larry Felder. Dinosaur tracks are fairly common in the area; ask here about day hikes.

The south end of Smoky Mountain Road emerges at Big Water. The nearest town of consequence – Page, Arizona – is 17 miles southeast, and is the access point for Lake Powell and Antelope Canyon.

Stateline Campground   CAMPGROUND

(House Rock Valley Rd) FREE On the Utah/Arizona state line, this attractive, small campground is the most central for Wire Pass or Coyote Buttes North. It's first-come, first-served, with picnic tables, fire pits and pit toilets. It's 1 mile south of the Wire Pass trailhead, 9.3 miles south of Hwy 89. The clay road can be impassible when wet.

White House Campground   CAMPGROUND $

(Hwy 89, Paria Contact Station; tent sites $5) This primitive campground along the Paria River is frequently used as the endpoint of a Buckskin Gulch trip or the beginning of a Paria Canyon trip. The five walk-in sites have pit toilets, but no water and few trees. It's 2 miles down a dirt road behind the contact station, at the White House trailhead.

ℹ Information

Paria Contact Station (☎ 435-644-1200; www.blm.gov; Mile 21, Hwy 89; ⊙ 8:30am-4pm Mar 15–Nov 15) This seasonal information center can provide important weather and road updates and is the last place to fill up on water before your backcountry exploits. It's 44 miles east of Kanab.

ℹ Getting There & Away

Trailheads for most routes are along House Rock Valley Rd (4.7 miles west of the contact station). It's a rugged dirt road, passable only in dry weather.

Capitol Reef National Park

Best Views

→ Panorama Point (p170)

→ Sunset Point (p170)

→ Cohab Canyon trail overlooks (p165)

→ Rim Overlook (p166)

Best Places to Stay

→ Torrey Schoolhouse B&B (p174)

→ Lodge at Red River Ranch (p174)

→ Fruita Campground (p173)

Why Go?

In this forgotten fold of the Colorado Plateau, you'll find slot canyons that appear as cathedrals cut from the earth, and giant cream-colored domes that arc into perfectly blue skies that hold little fluffy clouds.

Capitol Reef doesn't make it onto many Utah national-park itineraries, lending it a carefree air that promises wide-open vistas, limited crowds (for now at least), and plenty of adventurous activities, from hiking through canyons and up to overlooks to dusty-bottoming your way out on rugged 4WD tracks. Or you can simply take in the history and geology that reveals itself in petroglyphs and early Mormon settlements, sandstone streaks and hoodoo towers, and a labyrinth of canyons that stretch back millions of years.

The park's centerpiece is the lazily curving Fremont River and the Waterpocket Fold, a 100-mile buckle in the earth's crust that stymied early explorers.

Driving Distances (miles)

	Capitol Reef National Park (Visitor Center)	Moab	Salt Lake City	Torrey
Moab	145			
Salt Lake City	225	235		
Torrey	10	155	215	
Zion National Park (Springdale Entrance)	190	345	310	180

Note: Distances are approximate

Entrances

The usual approach to Capitol Reef is to wind over Boulder Mountain on Hwy 12, then turn onto Hwy 24 near tiny Torrey. You'll pass scenic viewpoints, historic sites and hiking trailheads. South of the visitor center, the park's main scenic drive starts near Fruita, running 8 miles south.

Alternatively, the partly paved Burr Trail is a beautifully scenic back door to Capitol Reef's wonders and is easily accessed from the town of Boulder, and in the park via Notom-Bullfrog Rd.

Coming from Moab, you are likely to take I-70, turning southwest onto Hwy 24, where you pass the worthwhile Goblin Valley State Park.

Hwy 24 cuts through the central section of this long, thin national park, which was dubbed a reef by early explorers, as it blocked their way west like a reef blocks a ship's passage.

To the north of Fruita lies Cathedral Valley with its moonscape of towering monoliths. This is the least visited corner of the park. Several unpaved roads, accessible mainly by 4WD or high-clearance vehicle, go through the north. The easiest route is the Cathedral Rd.

DON'T MISS

Stay up late to watch the night sky. Summer ranger programs occasionally include star talks. And thanks to the remote location, with pitch-black skies cut only by the Milky Way and a confetti of a billion stars, the park was awarded the status of an 'International Dark Sky Park' by the International Dark-Sky Association.

When You Arrive

➡ Entrance to the park is $10 for motorized vehicles, $7 for cyclists.

➡ Pay at the self-service kiosk and save your receipt, which is valid for seven days.

➡ Unlike most national parks, there's no entrance station. Just follow Hwy 24 to the visitor center where you can pick up information, get tips on hikes, sit in on a quick ranger talk, fill your water bottles and watch a short orientation film.

➡ The nearest gas stations are in Torrey (11 miles west) and Hanksville (37 miles east).

➡ Always tell someone where you will be hiking and when you plan to return, watch out for flash floods, and bring a gallon of water per person per day.

PARK POLICIES & REGULATIONS

Capitol Reef's hiking, backpacking and back-country camping regulations are the same as for all of southern Utah's national parks. The park's pet policies are also the same as those of other parks in the area.

There's no public transportation in the park. Bicycles are only allowed on paved and dirt roads but can't go on hiking trails.

Fast Facts

➡ Total area: 381 sq miles

➡ Elevation: 5500ft

➡ Average high/low temperature (at Fruita) in July: 92°F/65°F (33°C/18°C)

Resources

➡ **Capitol Reef National Park** (www.nps.gov/care)

➡ **Capitol Reef Natural History Association** (www.capitolreefnha.org)

➡ **Canyoneering USA** (www.canyoneeringusa.com)

➡ **Utah.com** (www.utah.com)

➡ **Wayne County Tourism Office** (www.capitolreef.org)

CAPITOL REEF NATIONAL PARK

Capitol Reef National Park

N 0 —————— 20 km
0 —————— 10 miles

HICKMAN BRIDGE

Scuttle up red-rock cliffs and over slickrock to stand underneath this gorgeous natural bridge. (p164)

GOBLIN VALLEY STATE PARK

Head outside Capitol Reef for Gothic towers, wicked formations and amazing canyoneering in this off-the-beaten-track state park. (p175)

CAPITOL DOME

Capitol Reef is known for its enormous Navajo sandstone domes, one of which resembles the US Capitol building as it appeared to settlers in 1850. (p171)

PETROGLYPHS

Marvel at the evocative and rather expressionistic petroglyphs left by the Fremont and Ancestral Puebloan people throughout the park. Some of the best are along Hwy 24. (p171)

FRUITA

Pluck apples, peaches and cherries in this historic orchard right in the middle of the park. (p170)

COHAB CANYON

Scale the Waterpocket Fold in search of secret slot canyons and skyscraping lookouts. (p165)

Temple Mt Rd

Goblin Valley Rd

Goblin Valley State Park

Muddy Creek

Richfield (40mi); Hwy 89 & I-70 (40mi)

Upper Cathedral Valley Overlook

Cathedral Valley

Glass Mountain

Corral Canyon

(72)

Upper South Desert Overlook

Lower South Desert Overlook

Temple of the Sun
Temple of the Moon

(24)

Loa

Lyman

Fishlake National Forest

Capitol Reef National Park

The Hartnet

(24)

Fremont River

Hanks

Bicknell

Hickman Natural Bridge

Petroglyphs

Caineville

(95)

Panorama Point & Goosenecks Overlook

Capitol Dome

Orientation Pullout

Torrey

Visitor Center

Fruita

Cohab Canyon

(24)

Fremont River

Gifford Homestead

Slickrock Divide

The Tanks

Notom

(12)

Capitol Gorge

Dixie National Forest

Pleasant Creek

Oak Creek

Sandy Creek

(12)

Bitter Creek Divide (5650ft)

Boulder

Circle Cliffs

Upper Muley Twist Canyon

Waterpocket Fold

Strike Valley

King Bench

Strike Valley Overlook

Henry Mountains

Burr Trail Switchbacks

The Post

(12)

Escalante

Grand Staircase - Escalante National Monument

Tropic (30mi); Bryce Canyon National Park (38mi); Panguitch (58mi)

Escalante Canyons

Escalante River

Circle Cliffs

Lower Muley Twist Canyon

Halls Overlook

Halls Creek

Bullfrog Creek

Hansen Creek

Ticaboo

Moody Creek

Halls Creek Narrows

Lake Powell

Bullfrog

Peek-A-Boo Slot Canyon

Glen Canyon National Recreation Area

🚶 DAY HIKES

🚶 Grand Wash

Duration 45 minutes–1½ hours

Distance 2.2 miles one way

Difficulty Easy

Start/Finish Grand Wash trailhead, at end of 1.3-mile-long dirt spur road off Scenic Drive, 3.4 miles south of visitor center

Nearest Town Torrey

Transportation Private

Summary Capitol Reef's most dramatic canyon is worth visiting just to walk between the sheer walls of the Narrows. Avoid this hike if rain threatens, as the wash is prone to flash floods.

Start from the parking lot at the end of the Grand Wash spur road. It's an easy stroll up the packed-sand wash from the parking area. Look for seasonal wildflowers such as red-

dish Indian paintbrush, shrubby white-flowering Apache's plume and stalky, yellow-flowering prince's plume. The canyon's walls inch closer and closer together until, about 1.25 miles from the trailhead, you reach the Narrows, where the 80-story canyon is just 15ft wide – a thrilling sight. The canyon walls shrink and spread out again as the flat trail approaches Hwy 24. Return the way you came, or arrange for someone to pick you up on Hwy 24, around 4.5 miles east of the visitor center (look for a trailhead marker on the south side of the highway, where there's a small gravel pull-off).

🚶 Capitol Gorge

Duration 1–2 hours

Distance 2 miles

Difficulty Easy–moderate

Start/Finish Capitol Gorge trailhead, at end of 2.4-mile-long dirt spur road off Scenic Drive, 8 miles south of visitor center

Capitol Reef – Day Hikes

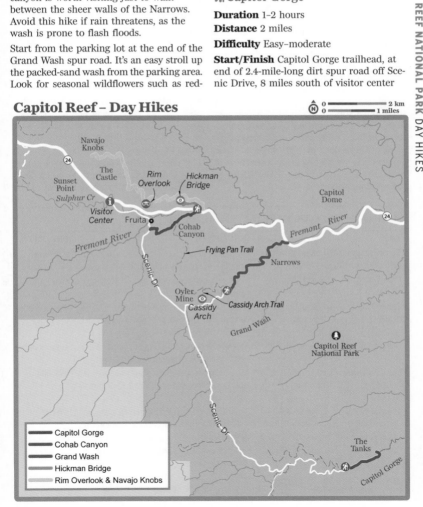

Nearest Town Torrey

Transportation Private

Summary Leave your car behind for an easy canyon ramble past historic petroglyphs, then scramble up to hidden water pockets. Avoid this flood-prone route if rain threatens.

Half a century ago, Capitol Gorge was the primary automobile route through the Waterpocket Fold. Pioneers first brought wagons through in the late 19th century, and the route remained in use until 1962. Today the sheer canyon walls are stained with desert varnish, which stands out in dramatic contrast to the red rock. Keep your eyes peeled for bighorn sheep, which have been successfully reintroduced in the park.

About 0.25 miles from the trailhead, you'll reach a scoured panel of ancient Fremont **petroglyphs**. A quarter-mile further, look up to see the **Pioneer Register**, a collection of carved names and dates that go back to the first pioneer passersby in 1871. Despite more recent graffiti, you can clearly make out many of the historic names and dates. Don't be confused by signatures on the right-hand wall, back closer to the petroglyphs. These date to 1911, when a USGS survey team lowered its leader over the wall to incise the party's names – vandalism by today's standards.

Just over 0.8 miles from the trailhead, bear left and follow signs to the **Tanks**, which lie atop a fairly steep 0.2-mile spur. These giant potholes, or water pockets, hold significant volumes of water much of the year. They were invaluable to early settlers and remain so for animals, so don't drink from or disturb them. When you're rested and ready, head back the way you came – the onward wash trail crosses park boundaries onto private land.

🥾 Hickman Bridge

Duration 1–2 hours

Distance 1.8 miles

Difficulty Easy–moderate

Start/Finish Hickman Bridge trailhead, off Hwy 24, 1.9 miles east of the visitor center

Nearest Town Torrey

Transportation Private

Summary If you've only got time for one hike, Capitol Reef's most popular trail is diverse, offering a canyon and desert-wash walk to a natural bridge, plus long sky views and spring wildflowers.

This popular hike is easy enough for anyone from kids to grandparents to enjoy. Since the route is largely exposed, it's best to hike

HIKING IN CAPITOL REEF NATIONAL PARK

NAME	START LOCATION	DESCRIPTION	DIFFICULTY
Cohab Canyon (p165)	Cohab Canyon trailhead	In a hidden canyon high atop Capitol Reef, sidle past slickrock to head-spinning overlooks	moderate
Grand Wash (p163)	Grand Wash trailhead	Flat trail passing between sheer 80-story-high canyon walls just 15ft apart	easy
Capitol Gorge (p163)	Capitol Gorge trailhead	Sheer-walled canyon wash featuring ancient petroglyphs, historical sites and secret watering holes	easy-moderate
Hickman Bridge (p164)	Hickman Bridge trailhead	Ascend over slickrock, past giant domes and a towering arch, ending with sweeping views	easy-moderate
Rim Overlook & Navajo Knobs (p166)	Hickman Bridge trailhead	Ascends from the Fremont River to an overlook, then climbs higher still for 360-degree panoramas	difficult
Lower Muley Twist Canyon (p169)	Lower Muley Twist Canyon trailhead	Scramble through a sky-high red-rock canyon just 10ft wide, then loop back through a gulch	difficult
Upper Muley Twist Canyon (p166)	Upper Muley Twist Canyon trailhead	Rugged backcountry loop featuring arches, sculpted sandstone narrows and long views of Waterpocket Fold	difficult

 Wildlife Watching   *Flush Toilets*   *Views*   *Great for Families*

it in the early morning. Cairns mark some of the route, which starts off the same way as the longer, more strenuous hike to the Rim Overlook and Navajo Knobs. Pick up a self-guided Hickman Bridge nature trail brochure at the trailhead, which corresponds to numbered signposts along the route.

Starting from the Fremont River – this is an agricultural-grade river, so you can swim here but be wary of depth and current and don't take any gulps – the trail ascends a red-rock cliff via a few easy switchbacks. As you cross an open area of desert vegetation strewn with volcanic black rocks, the highway vanishes behind giant white sandstone domes. A short spur leads to a tiny **archaeological site** where you can inspect the foundations of Fremont culture pit houses. During April and May look for scarlet claret cup and pink-flowering prickly pear cacti blooming beside the path.

The trail soon drops into a wash, where you can rest in a shady alcove before ascending over slickrock to **Hickman Bridge**, having gained 400ft in elevation from your start. While this chunky yellow arch can be tricky to spot from afar, the trail loops right beneath it for a marvelous appreciation of its mass. Hike counterclockwise and bear left beyond the arch to keep following the trail's loop. Pause to look over the rim and downriver to Fruita, an oasis of green.

🥾 Cohab Canyon

Duration 1-2 hours

Distance 1.7 miles one way

Difficulty Moderate

Start Cohab Canyon trailhead, off Scenic Drive, 1.2 miles south of the visitor center

Finish Hwy 24, 1.9 miles east of the visitor center

Nearest Town Torrey

Transportation Private

Summary Often overlooked, this trail deters crowds with a steep climb at the beginning, but exploring a hidden canyon and the views from atop Capitol Reef are worth every sweaty step.

If you're with people whose ability or interest in hiking isn't as great as yours, leave them to laze by the river or tour Fruita's historic sights while you tackle this climb with killer views. Starting across the road from Fruita Campground, just south of the Gifford Homestead, this trail makes a steep 0.25-mile initial ascent atop a rocky cliff. From there it levels out though a desert wash, beside which small slot canyons nestle. You'll pass more striking geologic features on your way through sheltered but windy Cohab Canyon itself, which protects piñon and juniper trees (and lizards!).

CAPITOL REEF NATIONAL PARK DAY HIKES

DURATION	ROUND-TRIP DISTANCE	ELEVATION CHANGE	FEATURES	FACILITIES
1-2hr	1.7 miles one way	400ft	🦌🚻	
45min-1½hr	2.2 miles one way	25ft	👪	
1-2hr	2 miles	125ft	🦌👪	
1-2hr	1.8 miles	400ft	🔭👪	🚻
4-6hr	9.4 miles	1600ft	🔭🪢	🚻
1-2 days	17 miles	1000ft	🔭🪢	⛺
1-2 days	15 miles	1100ft	🔭🪢	⛺

 Rock Climbing   *Backcountry Camping*

About 1.1 miles from the trailhead, a short but steep spur trail veers off left to climb to two **overlooks** of Fruita and the orchards. After about 0.25 miles of switchbacks, this spur trail splits into separate branches heading toward the southern and northern overlooks – visiting both before returning to the main trail adds just over a mile to this hike. This is a good turnaround point if you'd rather do just a 3.2-mile out-and-back hike, instead of a one-way shuttle hike over to Hwy 24.

The main trail continues threading its way through Cohab Canyon. It ascends to a junction with the **Frying Pan Trail**, a moderately difficult route that leads atop an escarpment for panoramic views, including of Cassidy Arch, before connecting with the Cassidy Arch Trail, which drops into the **Grand Wash** 4 miles from Cohab Canyon; add another mile if you take the worthwhile side trip to the arch. Otherwise, from the Frying Pan Trail junction, the main trail switchbacks down to Hwy 24, ending almost opposite the Hickman Bridge trailhead, around 2 miles east of the visitor center.

🚶 Rim Overlook & Navajo Knobs

Duration 4–6 hours

Distance 9.4 miles

Difficulty Difficult

Start/Finish Hickman Bridge trailhead, off Hwy 24, 1.9 miles east of the visitor center

Nearest Town Torrey

Transportation Private

Summary This slickrock route to twin bumps of Navajo sandstone perched on the precipitous western edge of Waterpocket Fold yields unsurpassed views. A steep, strenuous climb offers little shade and no water.

Start hiking from the **Fremont River** along the popular Hickman Bridge Trail, but after 0.3 miles, fork right at the signed junction – you'll leave most of the crowds behind. Follow cairns along much of this dry-wash and slickrock route, which sidles around Capitol Reef's giant white domes. Pause at the well-marked **Hickman Bridge Overlook**, south of the trail. Blending in amid the surrounding rock, this natural bridge is visible across a small canyon at eye level with the overlook.

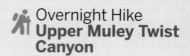

Overnight Hike
Upper Muley Twist Canyon

DURATION 1–2 DAYS
DISTANCE 15 MILES
DIFFICULTY DIFFICULT
START/FINISH UPPER MULEY TWIST CANYON TRAILHEAD, OFF BURR TRAIL
NEAREST TOWN TORREY
TRANSPORTATION PRIVATE

The upper canyon is less dramatic than the lower, but offers easier terrain and expansive views atop the fold. You'll pass arches and sculpted sandstone narrows along this hike, too.

Though you can approach Upper Muley as a long, difficult day hike, it's better to spend two days and enjoy the scenery. Most people camp near the Rim Trail junction, then hike the Rim Trail Loop without a pack.

Don't enter this flood-prone canyon if there is *any* chance of rain in the weather forecast.

To reach the trailhead, drive 3 miles west of the intersection with Notom-Bullfrog Rd on the Burr Trail, then turn right onto the signed side road to Strike Valley Overlook.

Alternatively, from Boulder follow the mostly paved Burr Trail, driving just over 2 miles on graded dirt to the turnoff above the switchbacks. With a high-clearance 4WD vehicle, you can usually drive the first 3 miles of this hike to the Strike Valley Overlook trailhead.

From the Upper Muley Twist Canyon trailhead, walk along the gravel wash and head generally northwest. The canyon is wide and the wash level for the 3-mile hike to the Strike Valley Overlook trailhead.

The 0.5-mile round-trip jaunt to the ❶ **overlook** is worth the energy, especially if you set down your pack at the trailhead.

Upper Muley Twist Canyon narrows 0.5 miles past the overlook, as steep red sandstone cliffs to the east turn in toward the wash.

About 1.2 miles further you'll see ❷ **Saddle Arch**, visible near the rim of the west wall. A sign on the east side of the wash marks the beginning of the Rim Trail Loop. Follow cairns up the canyon's east side, being prepared for some rock-scrambling and climbing uphill.

In about 15 or 20 minutes, you'll reach a broad bench capped with juniper trees and **③ camping spots**. Avoid treading on the crumbly cryptobiotic soil. If you want a view, but don't mind potentially high winds and not having any shade, camp at the saddle where the trail crests the fold. The Rim Trail Loop is slippery when wet, so use caution. From the potential campsites, follow cairns up to the east rim for spectacular views. A sign at the top points back down to the Canyon Route, which you'll be following later. You may find several sandy potential campsites nearby, too.

Follow the ridge north to a high point for views north along the fold to the grand white domes near the visitor center, 35 miles away as the turkey vulture flies.

After around 2 miles of roller-coaster ridge hiking, the trail plunges toward Muley Twist Canyon. Several cairned routes lead to the canyon floor, each requiring tricky scrambling. Turn down-canyon (south) and stay high, close to the east wall. After passing some wonderful hat-shaped formations, the trail swings east away from the **④ Narrows** below. Several deep potholes serve as water-storage tanks.

Beyond the gap in the west wall, the trail returns to the canyon floor. A quarter-mile down-canyon, the cairned trail climbs the east wall again, though in dry periods you may be able to continue along the canyon floor.

After about 2 miles you'll pass Saddle Arch, high on the west wall, soon after which a sign for the Rim Trail Loop signals the end of your loop. After closing the loop, the high, red canyon walls wax low and golden as you retrace your steps to the Strike Valley Overlook trailhead, 1.7 miles away, and another 3 miles south to the Upper Muley Twist Canyon trailhead.

Onward, the trail zigzags along the edge of a south-facing side canyon, a pattern that repeats for much of the remaining hike. As you continue climbing, you'll wind past the mouths of three more side canyons before reaching the **Rim Overlook**, 2.3 miles from the trailhead. Gorgeous views encompass a profile of the fold and its north end, along with mesas, domes, mountains and Fruita more than 1000ft below.

After climbing up and down more sandstone pitches, you'll pass between cliffs (on your right) and a radio repeater tower, and find yourself on a broad ledge that faces the **Castle**, a large, eroded, freestanding chunk of Waterpocket Fold. The trail rambles along this ledge to the northwest edge of a west-facing, W-shaped canyon. Following cairns, you'll climb the west rim of the W and soon spot the **Navajo Knobs** (6980ft), twin bumps that mark the high point on the next promontory. Watch your step as you clamber over loose rock to the double summit, then retrace your steps all the way back to the trailhead.

OTHER ACTIVITIES

Guided Tours

Hondoo Rivers & Trails   ADVENTURE TOUR
(☑ 435-425-3519; www.hondoo.com; 90 E Main St, Torrey) One of southern Utah's longest-operating backcountry guides, Hondoo specializes in horseback riding, but also offers 4WD tours, shuttles and guided hiking trips. Half-day trips (by horse, 4WD or foot) cost $120, full-day trips with lunch cost $150.

> ### ❶ OVERNIGHT HIKES
>
> Careful planning is essential for any backcountry trip.
>
> ➡ Be sure to get rangers' advice before setting out on any overnight hike.
>
> ➡ Pick up a free backcountry permit and check trail conditions at the visitor center.
>
> ➡ Ground fires are prohibited in the backcountry, so bring a camp stove.
>
> ➡ There are no established campgrounds in the backcountry.
>
> ➡ *Never* camp in a wash.
>
> ➡ Always stay on the trails, don't shortcut switchbacks and avoid stepping on cryptobiotic soil.

Earth Tours   HIKING
(☑ 435-691-1241; www.earth-tours.com; Boulder; day tours from $110; 🏠) Choose from half- and full-day area hikes and 4WD trips into the backcountry in and around Bryce, Escalante, Boulder Mountain and Capitol Reef. Keith will pick you up at your hotel in Torrey or Boulder.

Capitol Reef Backcountry Outfitters   ADVENTURE SPORTS
(☑ 435-425-2010; www.backcountryoutfitters.com; 875 E Hwy, junction Hwys 12 & 24, Torrey) In addition to 4WD and hiking packages, Backcountry Outfitters also rents bicycles ($40 per day) and ATVs ($150 per day). Shuttles and guided bike, ATV and horseback rides are available, too.

Cycling

The park's mostly paved **Scenic Drive** satisfies beginners and intermediates, while experienced mountain bikers love **Cathedral Valley**, though it becomes a muddy mess when wet. Capitol Reef Backcountry Outfitters rents bikes.

Horseback Riding & Pack Trips

If you're bringing your own stock, backcountry permits for horse-packing trips are free, but special use regulations apply. Reservations are required at least two weeks in advance to use the Post corral, off Notom-Bullfrog Rd.

Four-Wheel Driving

4WD roads crisscross Capitol Reef. To avoid bottoming out your precious Prius, rent an SUV (from $100 per day) at Thousand Lakes RV Park (p174).

Swimming

Only wade in wide, calm sections of a creek or river when there's no threat of a flash flood. Currents can be strong in bigger rivers. Across Hwy 24 from the Chimney Rock parking area, an easy, level trail leads to **Sulphur Creek**. Near the visitor center, you can hike a mile up Sulphur Creek to a large **wading pool** shaded by cottonwoods. You can also wade along **Pleasant Creek** from the end of the park's Scenic Drive. The **Freemont River** is an agricultural-grade river,

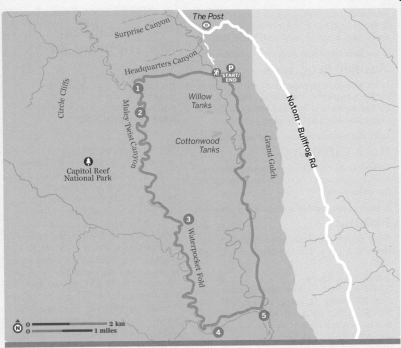

Overnight Hike
Lower Muley Twist Canyon

DURATION 1–2 DAYS
DISTANCE 17 MILES
DIFFICULTY DIFFICULT
START/FINISH LOWER MULEY TWIST CAN-YON TRAILHEAD, OFF NOTOM-BULLFROG RD
NEAREST TOWN TORREY
TRANSPORTATION PRIVATE

This loop follows the dramatic lower canyon through narrow red walls, then returns through grasslands broken up by colorful hills. The entire region must be relatively dry when you undertake this dangerously flood-prone hike.

Be sure to check with rangers about current conditions and the weather forecast before heading out. Less than 3 miles south of the Notom-Bullfrog Rd/Burr Trail junction, 35 miles south of Hwy 24, a well-signed road leads right from the Post. The trailhead is at the southwest edge of the parking lot.

The first mile is steep and exposed, with narrow drop-offs and ledges. From the parking area, follow the well-marked trail west up Waterpocket Fold's red, sloping back. After about an hour of steady climbing, the trail hits sand and the canyon's red walls come into view to the northeast. You'll level out and cross a ① **sandy area** strewn with vegetation. Leaving the wash, the trail bears south to lower ② **Muley Twist Canyon**, staying high on the canyon's east side, then cutting gently to the canyon floor, about 2 miles from the trailhead.

Sheer red Wingate sandstone walls tower 300ft on both sides. The hike now starts to follow a familiar pattern – from riverbed to high ground and back again – as the canyon twists south. Each alcove seems bigger, deeper and more graceful than the last. After passing two gaps in the west wall, you'll reach a ③ **big side canyon** to the northeast, home to several good campsites. Back in the main canyon, the trail soon turns from sand to sandstone and continues straight where the main canyon swings west. Mount a ④ **sandy plain** to more campsites amid sage and junipers.

Eventually you'll reach the canyon's narrows, where the 800ft walls are less than 10ft apart at points – narrow enough to 'twist a mule.' Soon afterward the canyon ends where its riverbed flows toward ⑤ **Halls Creek**. At this point, cairns mark the return route north to the Post trailhead. The Grand Gulch opens ever wider the further north you hike.

meaning there are pesticides etc running through it. It's safe for swimming, but you don't want to drink unfiltered water from it.

Ranger Programs

From May to September the park offers free public programs, including ranger talks, guided walks and evening shows at Fruita Campground's amphitheater.

Rock Climbing

Technical rock climbing is allowed, and you don't need a permit if you're not camping in the backcountry.

Fishing

You'll find surprisingly good fishing on the rivers and in the mountains around Capitol Reef.

Alpine Adventures   FISHING
(☑ 435-425-3660; www.alpineadventuresutah. com; 310 W Main St, Torrey; day/overnight trips from $225/850) Lake fishing and combination horse-pack trips.

Fremont River Guides   FISHING
(☑ 435-491-0242; www.flyfishingsouthernutah. com; PO Box 186, Biknell; trips from $225-350) Go fishing on the Fremont River or Boulder Mountain.

⊙ SIGHTS

Fruita Historic District

Offering welcome respite from the desert, Fruita (*froo*-tuh) is a shady green patch, a valley filled with mature, shade-giving cottonwoods and fruit-bearing trees. The first Mormon homesteaders arrived in the 1880s, and Fruita's final resident left in 1969.

The park now maintains more than 3000 mostly cherry, apricot, peach, pear and apple trees planted by early settlers, and if you visit between June and October you can eat ripe fruit straight from the trees for free (there's a nominal fee for any fruit taken from an orchard). To learn what's in season, ask at the visitor center or call the fruit hotline (☑ 435-425-3791).

You're welcome to pick fruit from any unlocked orchard during designated harvest times; just follow the ranger-posted instructions at the gates. Pick only mature fruit and leave the rest to ripen. You may not climb the

Driving Tour
Highway 24

DURATION 1–4 HOURS
DISTANCE 22 MILES ONE WAY
START TORREY
FINISH ORIENTATION PULLOUT
NEAREST TOWN TORREY

This easy, winding route gives you a taste of everything that Capitol Reef offers: striking geology, dramatic desert overlooks, ancient Native American petroglyphs, early Western settlers' sites, and hiking trails for stretching your legs.

From Torrey, head east into Capitol Reef on Hwy 24. There is no entrance station; driving this route is free. Be sure to stop at turnouts along the way to read interesting geologic interpretive panels. Then pull over at ❶ **Chimney Rock**, the towering reddish-brown rock formation 7 miles east of Torrey. If you're in great shape, consider hiking the strenuous 3.6-mile loop for wide-open clifftop views of Capitol Reef.

A half-mile east of Chimney Rock, turn right toward Panorama Point and drive 0.8 miles along a graded dirt road to the ❷ **Gooseneck Overlook**. An easy 0.1-mile walk from the parking area over rock slabs takes you to this viewpoint above Sulphur Creek, which twists through the canyon in elegant S-curves. Though the observation platform is fenced in, much of the area around it is open – watch your little ones!

From the parking area it's an easy 0.4-mile stroll to ❸ **Sunset Point**, where the ambient light on the cliffs and domes is best for photographers in the late afternoon.

Another 2.4 miles further east on Hwy 24, you'll arrive at the well-signed turnoff to Capitol Reef's ❹ **visitor center**, just north of the Fruita Historic District and the paved ❺ **Scenic Drive**.

Rising majestically just north of this junction is the snaggle-toothed ❻ **Castle**; an interpretive panel details its geologic history.

East of the visitor center, Hwy 24 skirts the Fremont River, the surrounding rock growing paler and more yellow as you approach the park's Navajo sandstone domes. Peer through the windows of the historic **7 Fruita school**, 0.8 miles east of the visitor center, before stopping at the **8 ancient petroglyphs** 0.2 miles further east. Created by the Fremont culture, these carvings helped convince archaeologists that the Fremont culture was distinct from that of Ancestral Puebloans. The boardwalk is wheelchair-accessible. Bring binoculars or a camera with a zoom lens.

Stop at the turnout 0.8 miles east of the petroglyphs for views of **9 Capitol Dome**, a giant sandstone dome that vaguely resembles the US Capitol, as it appeared in 1850. This parking area beside the Fremont River is where you'll find the trailheads for **10 Hickman Bridge** and the more strenuous Rim Overlook & Navajo Knobs route. On the south side of Hwy 24 is an alternate trail-head for **11 Cohab Canyon**, while 2.7 miles further east is the end of the Grand Wash.

About 4 miles east of Hickman Bridge, on your right, stop to peer through the window of the one-room 1882 **12 Behunin Cabin**, once home to a Mormon settler's family of 13. On the north side of the highway, 0.7 miles east of the cabin, you'll pass a waterfall. Swimming is not allowed here; numerous accidents and even drownings have occurred. At the park's eastern orientation pullout, just over 9 miles from the visitor center, are restrooms and an information kiosk. It's on the north side of the intersection with Notom-Bullfrog Rd.

trees, but ladders and handheld fruit pickers are available. Near the orchards is a restful **picnic area**, where deer roam and you'll hear birdsong in the trees, a rarity in the desert.

Displays at the **Gifford Homestead** (☉8am-5pm Mar-Oct), just over a mile south of the visitor center, reveal the day-to-day world of a typical Mormon settlers' homestead. At the small store you can buy ice cream, artisan breads and preserves made from the orchard fruit. Don't miss purchasing one of the famous pies – up to 13 dozen are sold daily, and they usually run out!

A short way back up the main road is the old **blacksmith shop**, though it's little more than a shed with period equipment inside (press a button to hear Dewey Gifford, the town's last resident, reminisce about life in Fruita). Nearby is the family-oriented **Ripple Rock Nature Center** (☉1-5pm Wed-Sun, late May-mid-Aug; 👪).

South of Fruita Campground the historic district ends, yielding to a trail alongside the Fremont River and the continuation of the park's **Scenic Drive**.

🛏️ SLEEPING & EATING

There's no lodging or food in the park, except for the pick-your-own fruit orchards and the baked goods sold at the Gifford Homestead, both in the Fruita Historic District. Eleven miles west of the visitor center, Torrey is the nearest place to sleep and eat.

Ask at the visitor center about current road conditions before heading out to the remote, primitive and little-visited Cathedral Valley and Cedar Mesa campgrounds.

Cathedral Valley Campground CAMPGROUND $
(☑435-425-3791; www.nps.gov/care; cnr Hartnet & Cathedral Rds; tent sites free; ☉year-round) The drive here (40 miles from the visitor centre) requires a high-clearance vehicle and may demand 4WD. Six first-come, first-served campsites have no water, but there are pit toilets, fire grates and picnic tables.

Cedar Mesa Campground CAMPGROUND $
(☑435-425-3791; www.nps.gov/care; Notom-Bullfrog Rd; tent sites free; ☉year-round) Five first-come, first-served sites lack water, but have

CAMPGROUNDS IN & AROUND CAPITOL REEF

CAMPGROUND	LOCATION	DESCRIPTION	NO OF SITES
Sunglow (www.fs.fed.us/r4/fishlake)	Forest Rd 143	Small USFS campground outside Bicknell, west of Torrey; can be a local hooligans' hangout.	7
Goblin Valley State Park (p175)	Goblin Valley Rd	Isolated campground with tin-roofed picnic shelters and showers but no hookups.	24
Cathedral Valley (p173)	cnr Hartnet & Cathedral Rds	Primitive backcountry campground near scenic rock formations; access road may require high-clearance 4WD vehicle.	6
Singletree (p174)	Hwy 12	Cooler, forested USFS campground high on Boulder Mountain; seasonal opening dates depend upon snowfall.	13
Sandcreek RV Park (p174)	Hwy 24	Small, family-run roadside RV park with log cabins near Torrey's town center; horse corral available.	24
Thousand Lakes RV Park (p174)	Hwy 24	Sprawling roadside RV park with above-average amenities including a playground, horseshoe pits and self-service laundry.	61
Cedar Mesa (p173)	Notom-Bullfrog Rd	Primitive backcountry campground; during dry season, dirt access road may be accessible by standard vehicle.	5
Fruita (p173)	Scenic Drive	Shady in-park campsites near fruit orchards and a river; often full, so arrive early.	71

 Drinking Water   Flush Toilets   Ranger Station Nearby   Great for Families   Dogs Allowed (On Leash)

pit toilets, fire grates and picnic tables, as well as great views east along the fold. It's 30 miles south of Hwy 24.

Fruita Campground CAMPGROUND **$**
(Scenic Dr; sites $20; ⊘year-round) This terrific 71-site campground sits under mature cotton-wood trees alongside the Fremont River, sur-rounded by orchards. First-come, first-served sites have access to water, but no showers. Spring through fall, sites fill up early.

ℹ Information

The park is open year-round. Just south of Hwy 24, the **visitor center** (☎ 435-425-3791; www. nps.gov/care; cnr Hwy 24 & Scenic Dr; ⊘ 8am-6pm Jun-Aug, 8am-4:30pm Sep-May) is also the park's headquarters. It's the only source for information in the park. Rangers and volunteer staff offer advice and can help you plan hikes and backcountry trips. The **Capitol Reef Natural History Association** (☎ 435-425-4106; www. capitolreefnha.org) runs the center's bookstore, which stocks topographic maps. Payphones and recycling bins are available at the visitor center

and Fruita Campground. Cell-phone reception is spotty to nonexistent throughout the park.

For all other tourist information and services, the gateway town of Torrey is about 11 miles west of the visitor center, near the intersection of Hwys 12 and 24. Hanksville (37 miles east) has restaurants, gas and lodging.

ℹ Getting Around

Capitol Reef has no public transportation sys-tem. In summer you can drive most dirt roads, including Notom-Bullfrog Rd and the Burr Trail, in a regular passenger car. In remote regions like Cathedral Valley, you'll likely need a high-clear-ance 4WD vehicle, although some sections of road may be passable by 2WD vehicles. The closest 24-hour gas stations are outside the park in Torrey (11 miles west) and Hanksville (37 miles east).

Bicycles are allowed on all park roads, whether paved or dirt, but are prohibited on all hiking trails. Cyclists and hikers can arrange drop-off/pick-up shuttle services (from $25) with Hondoo Rivers & Trails (p168).

ELEVATION	OPEN	RESERVATION REQUIRED?	DAY FEE	FACILITIES
7200ft	May-Oct	no	NA	
5100ft	year-round	yes	NA	
7000ft	year-round	no	NA	
8600ft	May-Sep	yes	NA	
6900ft	Mar-Oct	yes	NA	
6900ft	Apr-Oct	yes	NA	
5600ft	year-round	no	NA	
545ft	year-round	no	NA	

 Grocery Store Nearby   *Restaurant Nearby*   *Pay-phone*   *Summertime Campfire Program*   *RV Dump Station*

AROUND CAPITOL REEF NATIONAL PARK

Torrey
POP 187 / ELEV 6830FT

Torrey's primary money-making biz has shifted from logging and ranching to tourism. The town shuts down during winter, but in summer there's a whiff of counterculture in the air. If you're here during the third weekend in July, don't miss the Torrey Music Festival (www.torreymusicfestival.com), a one-day singer-songwriter jam, and traditional Torrey Apple Days (www.torreyutah.com), with live music, BBQ, pie-eating contests, a dance, derby and parade held around the July 4 national holiday.

SLEEPING

Sandcreek RV Park (☎435-425-3577; www.sandcreekrv.com; 540 Hwy 24, Torrey; tent sites $18, RV sites $25-30, cabins $35; ☺Mar-Oct; ☎✸) Friendly little campground with 12 pull-through spaces with full hookups, a horseshoe pit, horse pasture ($5 per night) and laundry. Nonguest showers are $5.

Singletree Campground (☎877-444-6777; www.recreation.gov; Hwy 12; sites $10-24) The Fishlake National Forest runs this basic 13-site tent and RV campground at an elevation of 8600ft on forested Boulder Mountain, 12 miles south of Torrey along Hwy 12. There's drinking water, vault toilets and an RV dump station.

Thousand Lakes RV Park (☎800-355-8995, 435-425-3500; www.thousandlakesrvpark.com; Hwy 24, 1 mile west of Torrey; tent/RV sites $18/33, camping cabins $35-95; ☺Apr-Oct; ☎✸) Twenty-two acres filled with facilities and services, including a heated swimming pool, playground, trading-post gift shop, 4WD rental and evening cook-out dinners ($15 to $23). Morning muffins and hot coffee included. RV sites have full hook-ups and pull-through spaces.

Austin's Chuckwagon Motel (☎435-425-3335; www.austinschuckwagonmotel.com; 12 W Main St, Torrey; r $61-91, cabins $147; ☺Mar-Oct; ✸☎✸✸) Rustic wood buildings ring the pool and shady grounds here at the town center. Good-value-for-the-money motel rooms have sturdy, basic furnishings; cabins also have kitchens. The on-site general store, deli and laundromat are a bonus.

★Torrey Schoolhouse B&B (☎435-633-4643; www.torreyschoolhouse.com; 150 N Center St, Torrey; r incl breakfast $115-145; ☺Apr-Oct; ✸☎) Ty Markham has done an exquisite job of bringing this rambling 1914 schoolhouse back to life as a B&B. Antiques and country elegance contrast with the fascinating black-and-white photos of classes starting from a century back. After a full gourmet breakfast you might need to laze in the garden a while before hiking.

Lodge at Red River Ranch (☎435-425-3322; www.redriverranch.com; 2900 West Hwy 24, Torrey; r $190-250, 2 night minimum; ℙ✸☎) This grand Western lodge sits on a 2000-acre ranch along the Fremont River, about 20 minutes from Capitol Reef. The log lodge features a vaulted common area, dining room, library nook and outside hot tub. Rooms are a well-conceived combination of antiques, native artifacts and Western art.

Capitol Reef Resort (☎435-425-3761; www.capitolreefresort.com; 2600 E Hwy 24, Torrey; r $150; ℙ✸☎✸) One of the closest resorts to the Capitol Reef National Park, this large motel complex offers well-put-together rooms with cowboy prints. It feels a bit corporate, but the views from the back rooms onto the red rocks are gorgeous.

EATING & DRINKING

Austin's Chuckwagon General Store (12 W Main St, Torrey; ☺7am-10pm Apr-Oct) Sells camping supplies, groceries, beer and deli sandwiches to go. There's an ATM, showers and laundromat too.

Mesa Farm Market (☎435-487-9711; www.mesafarmmarket.com; Hwy 24, Caineville; ☺7am-7pm Mar-Oct; ✸) ✿ Stop in Caineville at Mesa Farm Market for straight-from-the-garden organic salads, juices, goat cheese, and freshly baked artisan bread from an outdoor stone-hearth oven.

Royal's Foodtown (☑ 435-836-2841; www.royalsfoodtown.com; 135 S Main St, Loa; ☺ 7am-8pm Mon-Sat, 7am-7pm in winter) In winter, you'll have to drive 16 miles west of Torrey via Hwy 24 to Royal's Foodtown supermarket.

Slacker's Burger Joint (165 E Main St, Torrey; burgers $6-8; ☺ 11am-9pm Fri & Sat, 11am-8pm Mon-Thu) Order an old-fashioned burger (beef, chicken, pastrami or veggie), hand-cut fries (the sweet-potato version is delish) and thick milkshake (in a rainbow of cool flavors like cherry cordial), then enjoy – inside, or out at the picnic tables.

★ **Cafe Diablo** (☑ 435-425-3070; www.cafediablo.net; 599 W Main St, Torrey; lunch $10-14, dinner mains $22-40; ☺ 11:30am-10pm mid-Apr–Oct; ☑) One of southern Utah's best, with outstanding, highly stylized Southwestern cooking, including vegetarian dishes that burst with flavor. Think stuffed poblano peppers with quinoa and red chile mole (a spicy sauce), Mayan tamales and fire-roasted pork tenderloin on a cilantro waffle. Book ahead, you don't want to miss this one.

Rim Rock Restaurant (☑ 435-425-3398; www.therimrock.net; 2523 E Hwy 24, Torrey; mains $18-29; ☺ 5-9:30pm Mar-Dec) Grilled steaks, pasta and fish come with a million-dollar view of red-rock cliffs. Arrive before sunset for the best show. There's a full bar.

Robber's Roost Books & Beverages (www.robbersroostbooks.com; 185 W Main St, Torrey; snacks $2-5; ☺ 8am-4pm Mon-Sat, 1-4pm Sun May-Oct; ☎) Linger over a latte and a scone on comfy couches by the fire at this peaceful cafe-bookstore with bohemian bonhomie. Sells local-interest books and maps.

ENTERTAINMENT

Entrada Institute (www.entradainstitute.org; ☺ Sat Jun-Aug) This nonprofit has an artist-in-residence program and offers cowboy poetry and other performing art events, mostly at Robber's Roost bookstore.

Goblin Valley State Park

Melted rock formations from a Salvador Dalí fantasy fill the coliseum-like valley in this small, 3654-acre **park** (☑ 435-275-4584; www.stateparks.utah.gov/parks/goblin-valley; Goblin Valley Rd, off Hwy 24; per car $10; ☺ park 6am-10pm, visitor center 8am-5pm) in the San Rafael Desert. A couple of short canyon hiking trails let you roam around the eroded mushroom-shaped mounds of Entrada sandstone. If you stare at them for a while, they really do look like little goblins. An exposed 24-site **campground** (☑ 800-322-3770; http://utahstateparks.reserveamerica.com; tent & RV sites $23, yurt $80) provides covered picnic tables, drinking water, hot showers and an RV dump station. Campsites fill fast most weekends.

To get to Goblin Valley from Capitol Reef's visitor center, follow Hwy 24 east for about 38 miles to Hanksville. Fill your gas tank and grab lunch at **Duke's Slickrock** (☑ 435-542-3235; www.dukesslickrock.com; 275 E Hwy 24, Hanksville; mains $8-12; ☺ 7am-10pm), the friendliest cowboy grill this side of the swell. The food is straightforward and filling, the service is great, and there's a tipi tent site out back. From there, head north 19.5 miles.

Look for a signed turnoff on the west side of the highway, from where a paved road leads 5 miles west, then 7 miles south to the park's entrance station.

Little Wild Horse Canyon, 7 miles west of Goblin Valley, is a suitable hike for beginners, offering plenty of serpentine twists that can be combined with a return via Bell Canyon on an 8.2-mile circuit.

Some of Utah's most famous canyoneering routes are found in the area in and around Goblin Valley State Park. The **San Rafael Swell** and **Robber's Roost** areas are top spots for experts. Watch for flash floods, go with a guide if you're a novice, and try not to get lost.

On the west side of Canyonlands, Robber's Roost's Bluejohn Canyon is now one of the most famous canyoneering routes in the world. It gained infamy in 2003, when Aaron Ralston spent 127 hours here pinned to a boulder before finally amputating his arm. His ordeal has been captured in books and the media, as well as in the 2010 James Franco movie *127 Hours*. The biggest mistake he made: not telling anybody where he was going.

Canyonlands National Park

Best Hikes

➡ Grand View Point Trail (p183)

➡ Mesa Arch (p182)

➡ Upheaval Dome Overlook Trail (p183)

➡ Aztec Butte Trail (p180)

➡ Slickrock Trail (p183)

➡ Lathrop Canyon (p181)

Best Views

➡ Grand View at Island in the Sky (p183)

➡ Horseshoe Canyon's Great Gallery (p192)

➡ Dead Horse Point State Park (p190)

➡ The Maze (p191)

Why Go?

Rugged, otherworldly, untamed and at times impenetrable, Canyonlands offers up some of the most remote hiking, cycling and rafting in all of Utah's national parks. This is desert solitude at its best.

Scorched red rocks, resplendent layers of sandstone, buttes and sun-crested canyons shape the landscape's curves while, below, in the serpentine canyons of the Green and Colorado Rivers, you'll find a wonderworld of gleaming water, forgotten box canyons, foaming white water and delicate desert fauna that blooms ever so daintily with new spring rains.

Grand adventures here can last 10 days, while smaller-scale pursuits can be had from the main entrances at Needles and the aptly named Island in the Sky. Head to the edge of this tortuous rift in the Earth's crust and look hard enough and you might just see the curve of our firmament as it cascades with nonstop momentum to the West.

Driving Distances (miles)

	Canyonlands National Park (North Entrance)	Canyonlands National Park (South Entrance)	Capitol Reef National Park (Visitor Center)	Moab
Canyonlands National Park (South Entrance)	100			
Capitol Reef National Park (Visitor Center)	155	220		
Moab	30	75	145	
Zion National Park (East Entrance)	325	370	180	315

Note: Distances are approximate

Entrances

The Colorado and Green Rivers divide the park into three separate and distinct areas, called 'districts' by the National Park Service (NPS) – Island in the Sky, the Needles and the Maze.

Island in the Sky and the Needles feature visitor centers, developed campgrounds and paved roads to scenic overlooks, as well as dirt roads and hiking trails. The less-visited Maze and Horseshoe Canyon, an unconnected unit northwest of the Maze, offer only 4WD-accessible dirt roads, hiking trails and primitive campgrounds.

No roads cross the park. Instead, well-marked secondary spurs from two major highways access Canyonlands' districts.

Island in the Sky is the most developed district. To get there from Moab, drive north on Hwy 191 for about 30 minutes to Hwy 313; both roads are paved.

The Needles District lies about 75 miles (90 minutes) southwest from Moab via paved Hwys 191 and 211.

The Maze is about 130 miles from Moab, accessible along dirt roads off Hwy 24; take Hwy 191 north to I-70 then west to Hwy 24 south. Horseshoe Canyon also lies off of Hwy 24 via dirt roads.

DON'T MISS
....

Boating Canyonlands is a singular experience that will stay with you for a lifetime. The upper sections of the Green and Colorado Rivers offer flatwater that is perfect for kayaks, canoes and paddleboards. At their confluence, the rivers form Cataract Canyon, one of the gnarliest stretches of Class III to V white water in Utah.

When You Arrive

➡ Canyonlands is open year-round.

➡ Admission to the Island in the Sky and Needles districts, good for seven days, costs $25 per car, $15 per motorcycle or $10 per person arriving by bicycle or foot.

➡ There is no fee to enter the Maze.

➡ Consider purchasing a Local Passport ($50) for admission to Arches and Canyonlands National Parks and Natural Bridges and Hovenweep National Monuments for a year.

➡ Reserve your backcountry permit in advance through the Backcountry Permits Office (p184).

➡ No district in the park offers food, gas, firewood or ice.

➡ Water is limited, so bring your own.

➡ Arrange tours ahead of time with a Moab operator.

PARK POLICIES & REGULATIONS
....

Canyonlands follows most of the national park hiking and backcountry use regulations. A few rules to note:

➡ No ATVs allowed. Other 4WD vehicles, mountain bikes and street-legal motorbikes are permitted on dirt roads.

➡ Backcountry campfires are allowed only along river corridors; use a fire pan, burn only driftwood or downed tamarisk, and pack out unburnt debris.

➡ Free or clean-aid rock climbing is allowed, except at archaeological sites or on most named features marked on US Geological Survey (USGS) maps. Check with rangers.

➡ Bear-proof food canisters and human-waste removal is required in some backcountry areas; check with the park for details.

CANYONLANDS NATIONAL PARK

Fast Facts

➡ Total area: 527 sq miles

➡ Elevation: 5800ft

➡ Average high/low temperature in July: 118°F/51°F (48°C/10°C)

Resources

➡ **Canyonlands National Park** (www.nps.gov/cany)

➡ **Canyonlands Natural History Association** (www.cnha.org)

Canyonlands National Park

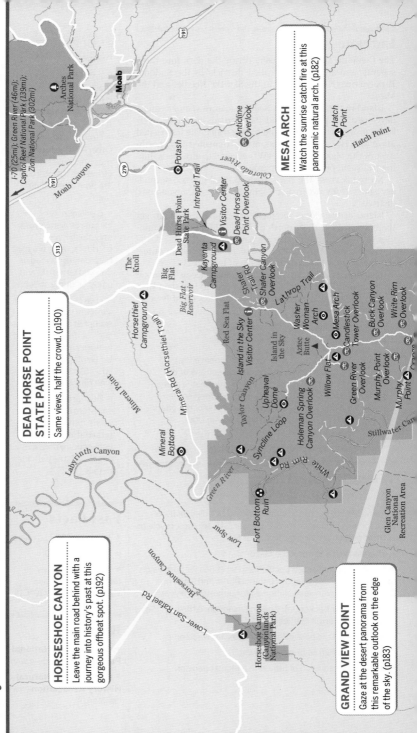

HORSESHOE CANYON

Leave the main road behind with a journey into history's past at this gorgeous offbeat spot. (p192)

DEAD HORSE POINT STATE PARK

Same views, half the crowd. (p190)

MESA ARCH

Watch the sunrise catch fire at this panoramic natural arch. (p182)

GRAND VIEW POINT

Gaze at the desert panorama from this remarkable outlook on the edge of the sky. (p183)

I-70 (25mi); Green River (46mi); Capitol Reef National Park (139mi); Zion National Park (302mi)

Arches National Park

Moab

Potash

Moab Canyon

Dead Horse Point State Park

Visitor Center

Dead Horse Point Overlook

Intrepid Trail

Colorado River

Antidline Overlook

Hatch Point

The Knoll

Big Flat

Big Flat Reservoir

Kayenta Campground

Shafer Trail Rd

Shafer Canyon Overlook

Lathrop Trail

Washer Woman Arch

Mesa Arch

Candlestick Tower Overlook

Buck Canyon Overlook

White Rim Overlook

Horsethief Campground

Mineral Rd (Horsethief Trail)

Red Sea Flat

Island in the Sky Visitor Center

Island in the Sky

Aztec Butte

Willow Flat

Green River Overlook

Murphy Point Overlook

Murphy

Mineral Point

Taylor Canyon

Upheaval Dome

Syncline Loop

Holeman Spring Canyon Overlook

White Rim Rd

Stillwater Can

Labyrinth Canyon

Mineral Bottom

Green River

Fort Bottom Ruin

Low Spur

Horseshoe Canyon

Lower San Rafael Rd

Horseshoe Canyon (Canyonlands National Park)

Glen Canyon National Recreation Area

Hatch Point

0   5 miles
0   10 km

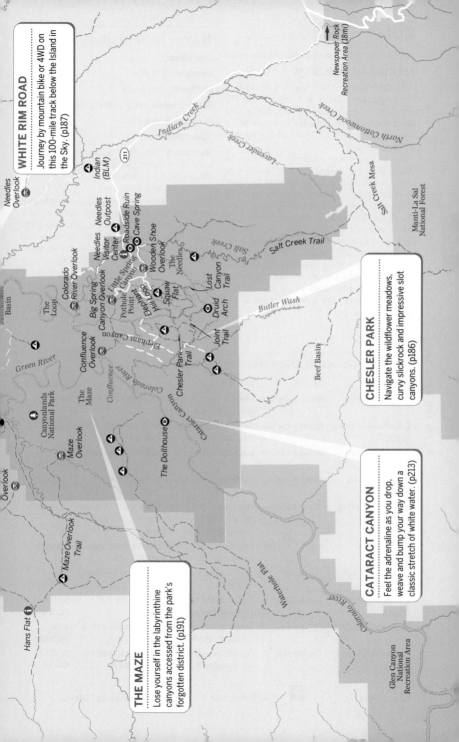

WHITE RIM ROAD

Journey by mountain bike or 4WD on this 100-mile track below the Island in the Sky. (p187)

Needles Overlook ⓡ

Basin

ⓧ

The Loop

Green River

Confluence Overlook ⓧ

Canyonlands National Park

ⓕ

Maze Overlook ⓡ

The Maze

ⓧ

ⓧ

The Dollhouse ⊙

ⓧ

Maze Overlook Trail

ⓧ

Overlook ⓡ

Hans Flat ❶

THE MAZE

Lose yourself in the labyrinthine canyons accessed from the park's forgotten district. (p191)

Indian Creek

211

Indian (BLM) ⓧ

Needles Outpost

Roadside Ruin ⊙

Cave Spring ⊙

Needles Visitor Center ❶

Little Spring Canyon Overlook

Colorado River Overlook ⓧ

Big Spring Canyon Overlook

Pothole Point

Elephant Hill

Elephant Canyon

Squaw Flat

Wooden Shoe Overlook

The Needles

Druid Arch ⊙

Joint Trail

Chesler Park Trail

ⓧ

ⓧ

ⓧ

Confluence

Colorado River

Cataract Canyon

Salt Creek

Lost Canyon Trail

Salt Creek Trail

Butler Wash

Beef Basin

Lavender Creek

North Cottonwood Creek

Newspaper Rock Recreation Area (18mi) ↑

Salt Creek Mesa

Manti-La Sal National Forest

CHESLER PARK

Navigate the wildflower meadows, curvy slickrock and impressive slot canyons. (p186)

CATARACT CANYON

Feel the adrenaline as you drop, weave and bump your way down a classic stretch of white water. (p213)

Colorado River

Waterhole Flat

Glen Canyon National Recreation Area

🚶 DAY HIKES

Island in the Sky

With the exception of trails that descend to the White Rim, hikes at Island in the Sky are short and moderately easy. For a hike along the mesa top, walk the first mile of the west-trending **Wilhite Trail**, off the road to Upheaval Dome.

For a longer hike, descend 1000ft to the White Rim. The easiest route is the **Murphy Loop**, but it's still an 11.3-mile, five- to seven-hour round trip. The **Gooseberry Trail** (5.4 miles, four to six hours) is for fit hikers only. Check conditions with rangers before long hikes. Where trails are indistinct, walk on rock or in sandy washes to avoid damaging fragile cryptobiotic crusts.

Canyonlands has a rep for serious hiking, but Island in the Sky offers a good selection of short trails with great vistas that are perfect for families. For a workout, do a few easy hikes in a day.

🚶 Aztec Butte Trail

Duration 1–1½ hours
Distance 2 miles
Difficulty Moderate
Start/Finish Aztec Butte trailhead
Nearest Town Moab
Transportation Private

Summary This short ascent of a Navajo sandstone dome yields stellar views; it's a steep hike over slickrock to the top. Check out the ancient granaries.

Be sure to wear rubber-soled shoes or hiking boots for traction. Stay on the trails, as fragile cryptobiotic crust is widespread atop the dome. In summer bring plenty of water and wear a wide-brimmed hat, as the exposed butte offers no shade. In winter the trail may be icy and impassable.

The first half-mile cuts across grassland to the base of the dome. Cairns mark the ascent. The second half-mile is moderately strenuous. The butte levels off at the top, revealing panoramic views and endless sky.

HIKING IN CANONLANDS NATIONAL PARK

NAME	REGION	DESCRIPTION	DIFFICULTY
Mesa Arch (p182)	Island in the Sky	Island in the Sky's most famous arch is gorgeous at sunrise	easy
Grand View Point Trail (p187)	Island in the Sky	No place in Canyonlands offers such a sweeping view; watch for passing condors	easy
Upheaval Dome Overlook Trail (p183)	Island in the Sky	Marvel at Island in the Sky's geologic mystery	easy-moderate
Aztec Butte Trail (p180)	Island in the Sky	Skitter up slickrock to an ancient Native American granary	moderate
Neck Spring (p181)	Island in the Sky	This solitary stream canyon attracts wildlife and fills with wildflowers in springtime; look for the remnants of pioneer ranching	moderate
Lathrop Canyon (p181)	Island in the Sky	Extensive canyon hike with stellar views; less trodden and perfect for solitude	moderate
Pothole Point Trail (p187)	The Needles	Stop by natural potholes to spot tiny swimming organisms	easy
Cave Spring Trail (p185)	The Needles	Past an abandoned cowboy camp, this trail climbs ladders up slickrock	easy-moderate
Slickrock Trail (p183)	The Needles	Semiloop trail with views of the Needles and La Sal and Abajo Mountains	easy-moderate
Chesler Park Loop & Joint Trail (p186)	The Needles	Popular trek passing grasslands and pinnacles and threading through narrow fractures	moderate-difficult

 Views   Wildlife Watching   Backcountry Camping

Look for the small, ancient **granary**, evidence of an Ancestral Puebloan culture, a likely precursor to modern-day Hopis and Zunis. A small spur trail leads to more ruins. This is the only archaeological site at Island in the Sky.

🏃 Neck Spring

Duration 2½ hours

Distance 6 miles

Difficulty Moderate

Start/Finish Shafer Canyon Overlook parking area

Nearest Town Moab

Transportation Private

Summary Good for solitude seekers, this stream canyon attracts wildlife and fills with wildflowers in springtime. Look for the remnants of pioneer ranching.

Perhaps because it isn't cliffside, this loop trail attracts fewer hikers. Following the sign in the **Shafer Canyon Overlook parking area**, it crosses the street and descends Taylor Canyon to Neck and Cabin Springs. The initial trail is an old roadbed built in the 1800s by ranchers to bring livestock to water. Hitching posts, water troughs and pipes are still visible (please leave them in place).

Descending slightly, the trail reaches **Neck Spring**. If you stay quiet here, you may see animals (mule deer, chipmunks and bighorn sheep) approaching for a drink. The moisture makes it an ideal climate for Gamble oak, maidenhair fern and Fremont barberry.

Leaving the alcoves, start to climb to white sand hills before reaching **Cabin Spring**, with a cabin, troughs and corrals near the site. A short, steep ascent climbs over sandstone. Follow the cairns to the mesa top, where the trail crosses the main road and continues 0.5 miles along the rim of Shafer Canyon to the parking lot.

🏃 Lathrop Canyon

Duration 2½ hours to 2 days

Distance 5 miles to rim, 22 miles to Colorado River

CANYONLANDS NATIONAL PARK DAY HIKES

DURATION	ROUND-TRIP DISTANCE	ELEVATION CHANGE	FEATURES	FACILITIES
30min	0.5 miles	100ft	🔭👪	
1-1½hr	2 miles	50ft	🔭👪	
1-1½hr	0.8-1.8 miles	50-200ft	🔭👪	⛴
1-1½hr	2 miles	225ft	🔭👪	
2½hr	6 miles	300ft	🦌	
2½hr-2 days	5-22 miles	2100ft	🔭	⛺⛴
45min	0.6 miles	20ft	🦌🔭	
30-45min	0.6 miles	50ft	🔭👪	
1½-2hr	2.4 miles	70ft	🔭	
1-2 days	11 miles	520ft	🔭	⛺

 Great for Families   *Picnic Facilities*

Island In The Sky – Day Hikes

Difficulty Moderate

Start/Finish Lathrop Canyon trailhead

Nearest Town Moab

Transportation Private

Summary An extensive hike into the canyon with stellar views. For an easy stroll, consider an out-and-back trip to the rim. Less trodden than other trails, it's perfect for solitude.

A ranger favorite, Lathrop Canyon is one of the few longer trails in this district. If short on time, hike out to the canyon rim for views of the Colorado River and La Sal Mountains.

Follow the level sandy single-track through the grasslands. It passes over undulating slickrock marked by cairns. Canyon views start here, including a glimpse of a gorgeous bend in the Colorado River.

The trail returns to sandy paths and twists along the canyon rim. It then descends steep switchbacks to a boulder-strewn wash that leads to White Rim Road. Hikers can follow the spur road down into Lathrop Canyon, a descent of 2100ft. Three at-large permits are available for camping below White Rim Rd.

Mesa Arch

Duration 30 minutes

Distance 0.5 miles one way

Difficulty Easy

Start/Finish Mesa Arch trailhead

Nearest Town Moab

Transportation Private

Summary This easy trail leads to Canyonlands' most photographed arch, one of the best places to watch the sunrise – though don't expect to be alone.

As you ascend, notice the trailside cryptobiotic soil, riddled with bubbly minicanyon systems. This is among the healthiest soil of its kind in the park.

A moderately easy walk up a gentle rise brings you to the arch, an elegant sweep of Navajo sandstone that dramatically frames the La Sal Mountains. A thousand feet below, the basin extends in layers of red, brown, green and tan. Look carefully in the near distance to spot a narrow green strip of the Colorado River. To your left, through the arch, search atop the red spires for Washer Woman Arch (so named for its resemblance to a crouching laundress).

Resist the temptation to climb on the arch. Climbing is prohibited on most features named on USGS maps. Anyway, the sheer drop below will surely give you a case of the butterflies. Scamper up the rocks for a look down on the arch.

🚶Upheaval Dome Overlook Trail

Duration 1–1½ hours

Distance 0.8–1.8 miles

Difficulty Easy–moderate

Start/Finish Upheaval Dome parking area

Nearest Town Moab

Transportation Private

Summary With views of a crater and upheaval canyon, this mysterious destination is debated to be the site of a meteor collision or just a strange geological feature.

This trail leads to overlooks of Upheaval Dome, one of the park's great geologic mysteries. Scientists disagree over how the feature formed – some suggest it's a collapsed salt dome, while others posit it was the site of a meteorite strike some 60 million years ago. Looking more like a mound of gray sand, the dome rests in a depression – one doesn't look up to it, but down on it, like a belly button.

It's an easy 0.4 miles to the first overlook. From the parking area, climb to the fork in the trail, bear right and ascend the slickrock to the **viewpoint**. If you find yourself on switchbacks, you've made a wrong turn.

To reach the second **overlook**, return to the fork in the trail and bear left, clambering over slickrock to a final steep descent. Here you'll have a broader panorama of the surrounding landscape. If you're pressed for time, skip the second vantage point. Otherwise, the afternoon light here is magnificent.

🚶Grand View Point Trail

Duration 1–1½ hours

Distance 2 miles

Difficulty Easy

Start/Finish Grand View Point parking area

Nearest Town Moab

Transportation Private

Summary Easily earned panoramic views from the cliff's edge to the broad mesa below and wide desert beyond; follow cairns and keep to the rocks.

After marveling at 100-mile views from the roadside observation area, take this easy stroll to the point itself for a better perspective of the massive mesa underfoot. Review the interpretive panels for interesting background. To the right of the panels, the trail descends stone steps to a fairly level, easy walk along the exposed rim – watch the little ones! To the south, scan the skies over Junction Butte for the peregrine falcons that nest atop it.

Scramble atop the rocks at trail's end for spectacular views. The Needles' namesake spires rise to the south, while off to the west lie the Henry Mountains (on Capitol Reef's eastern flank) and distant Boulder Mountain (eastern terminus of the Aquarius Plateau and top step of the Grand Staircase). Glance below to spot the chalky sandstone of White Rim and the placid Green River. If storm clouds start to roll in, particularly from the west, quickly return to your car.

The Needles

Taken collectively, these trails offer an overview of the region's human and geologic history. Unfortunately, none is wheelchair accessible, but you can take on most of them in a day. Cairns often mark sections across slickrock.

If you like long day hikes, the Needles also includes easily accessible backcountry treks you can do in a day.

One quick easy hike is the **Roadside Ruin Trail**, a 0.3-mile loop that takes 30 minutes to walk. It starts out across uneven gravel and finishes over slickrock. Look for a remarkably well-preserved Ancestral Puebloan granary tucked into a gap in the slickrock. If you're here in late spring, keep an eye out for blooming yucca. Otherwise, consider taking the Cave Spring or the Pothole Point trails.

🚶Slickrock Trail

Duration 1½–2 hours

Distance 2.4 miles

Difficulty Easy–moderate

BACKPACKING & OVERNIGHT TRIPS

The Needles is the top district for backpackers. Overnighters might also consider a river trip or a bike tour on the White Rim Rd. Intrepid adventurers can head off into the Maze, or might consider canyoneering near Robber's Roost.

Island in the Sky

Aside from White Rim Rd, which is mostly a biking route, there's just one major backpacking route in the district: the **Syncline Loop** (8.3 miles, five to seven hours), a primitive route requiring some navigational skills. If you're fascinated by Upheaval Dome, or would like a closer look at the Green River, this is a perfect route with lots of places to camp. Since the trail is largely exposed, it gets blazing hot in summer.

Rangers consider this a route and not a trail – the difference is that you will have to pay close attention in places to stay on the path. In fact, most park rescues occur along this stretch, primarily because day hikers underestimate the trail, get turned around and/or run out of water. Pay close attention to trail markers. You'll need a permit to stay overnight.

The Needles

The Needles is Canyonlands' top backpacking district, making it hard to get the backcountry permit necessary for an overnight hike.

In addition to the Chesler Park Loop and Joint Trail (p186), consider the **Confluence Overlook Trail**, a moderate four- to six-hour round-trip hike from the Big Spring Canyon trailhead, from where you can watch the Green River flow into the Colorado – one or the other river may be silty or muddy depending on recent rainfall. Many other hikes connect in a series of loops, some requiring route-finding skills. Among the best are the **Big Spring Canyon** and **Lost Canyon Trails**. For gorgeous scenery, the **Elephant Canyon Trail to Druid Arch** is hard to beat. Rock art along the **Salt Creek Canyon Trail** is very much worth a look.

Permits

Permits (currently $10 to $30) are required for overnight backcountry and mountainbiking camping, 4WD trips and river trips. Reserve online up to four months in advance through the **NPS Backcountry Permits Office** (https://canypermits.nps.gov/index.cfm; ☑ 435-259-4351; 2282 SW Resource Blvd, Moab; permits $10-30; ⊙ 8:30am-noon Mon-Fri). You can also just show up and inquire at the visitor center, although reservations are recommended in spring and fall. Try to book up to a year in advance.

If you don't have a reservation, you might be able to get a permit, depending on availability, the day before or the day of your trip from the visitor center in the district in which your trip begins, though it's hard to book at the last minute in fall and spring.

Safety Tips & Regulations

➡ Drink at least 1 gallon of water each day. Natural water sources are limited in the backcountry.

➡ Always carry a topographic map, adequate clothing and a flashlight.

➡ Always tell someone where you are going and when you expect to be back.

➡ Watch for flash floods.

➡ During a lightning storm avoid lone trees and high ridges.

➡ Protect cryptobiotic soil crusts by staying on trails and roads, or by walking on slickrock or washes.

➡ Permits are required for all overnight backcountry trips.

➡ Wood fires are prohibited.

➡ You have to tote your own poop from some campsites. In others, you'll bury it in a 6in hole at least 300ft from a water source.

Start/Finish Slickrock trailhead

Nearest Town Monticello

Transportation Private

Summary This ridgeline trail is high above the canyons with views below. After ascending gentle switchbacks to slickrock, you'll follow cairns. This semiloop trail is tricky to follow in places.

Brochures available at the trailhead describe four main viewpoints, each marked by a numbered signpost. Keep an eye out during your hike – bighorn sheep are occasionally seen here.

If you're short on time, at least visit Viewpoint 1 for a panorama you simply can't get from the road. Giant red cliffs hang like curtains below high buttes and mesas, the district's namesake needles touch the sky, and the La Sal and Abajo Mountains lord over the whole scene.

Bear right at the 'Begin Loop' signpost to reach Viewpoint 2, where hearty vegetation clings to the desert crust and lines the watercourses. Scamper up the rocks for a primo view. At Viewpoint 3 giant boulders ring Lower Little Spring Canyon, where purple and gray rock layers offer telltale evidence of an ancient shallow sea.

Viewpoint 4 is a high promontory that overlooks Big Spring Canyon, a vast rugged gorge. Watch overhead for birds soaring on thermals. To the north you'll spot Grand View Point at Island in the Sky, perched high atop the red Wingate sandstone cliffs.

On the return path you'll face the needles and spires to the south that define this district. The Abajo Mountains lie beyond.

Cave Spring Trail

Duration 30–45 minutes

Distance 0.6-mile loop

Difficulty Easy–moderate

Start/Finish Cave Spring trailhead

Nearest Town Monticello

Transportation Private

Summary Kids love this short hike for the cowboy artifacts, ladders and slickrock scampers. There are also prehistoric pictographs to view.

Pungent sagebrush marks this trailhead at the end of a well-maintained, mile-long dirt road. Hikers will first reach an abandoned cowboy camp with miscellaneous remnants left by cowboys in the 19th and 20th centuries. The trail continues beneath a

CANYONLANDS NATIONAL PARK DAY HIKES

The Needles – Day Hikes

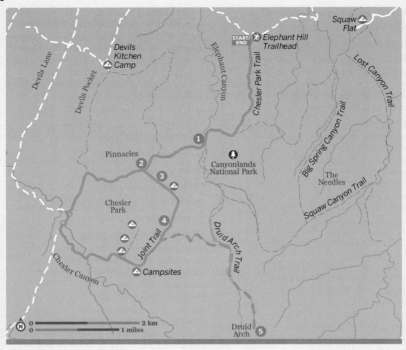

Overnight Hike
Chesler Park Loop & Joint Trail

DURATION 1–2 DAYS
DISTANCE 11-MILE LOOP
DIFFICULTY MODERATE OVERNIGHT HIKE, MODERATE–DIFFICULT DAY HIKE
START/FINISH ELEPHANT HILL TRAILHEAD
NEAREST TOWN MONTICELLO
TRANSPORTATION PRIVATE

With ample ups and downs, this loop gives great perspective on the Needles. Don't skip the Joint Trail, a narrow section that slips through deep fractures in the rock. A short segment follows a 4WD road.

Among Canyonlands' most popular backcountry treks, these combined routes cross desert grasslands, pass red-and-white-striped pinnacles and thread through tall hairline fractures. Though the trails aren't flat, elevation changes are mild and infrequent. You won't find any water. For most hikers, the *Trails Illustrated Needles District* map ($10) should suffice, but if you're inclined to wander, carry a 7.5-minute USGS map.

Park at the Elephant Hill trailhead, 3 miles from Squaw Flat Campground via a gravel 2WD road. From the parking area, the trail climbs to a bench, then undulates over slickrock toward rock spires. The next section is typically where people make a wrong turn. Cross the wash at the T-junction and follow signs to Chesler Park (*not* Druid Arch), descending 300ft along switchbacks into ❶ **Elephant Canyon**. Continue to follow signs along the canyon floor.

The final 0.2 miles to the ❷ **Chesler Park Viewpoint** climbs 100ft, topping out on the rocky pass amid spires 2.9 miles from the trailhead. This marks the beginning of the 5-mile ❸ **Chesler Park Loop**. Five campsites lie southeast of the junction.

The next morning, leave your backpack at the campsite and explore the claustrophobia-inducing ❹ **Joint Trail**, where the fractured rock narrows to 2ft across in places; the trail junction lies to the south, about midway around the Chesler Park Loop. Pause just east of the Joint Trail for stellar views of the towering pinnacles that ring Chesler Park. On the southwest section of the loop, you'll follow a half-mile stretch of a 4WD road. If staying two nights, take the side trip to ❺ **Druid Arch**.

protruding rock lip, then through 6ft sagebrush to **Cave Spring**, one of few perennial water sources in the Needles. Look for the rust-colored pictographs painted on these walls more than 1000 years ago.

From Cave Spring you'll climb **two ladders** up the slickrock for wraparound views of rock formations, steppes and mesas. The trail has awesome views of rock spires and the La Sal Mountains.

After crossing the undulating sandstone, the trail drops into a wash and returns to the trailhead.

🥾 Pothole Point Trail

Duration 45 minutes

Distance 0.6-mile loop

Difficulty Easy

Start/Finish Pothole Point trailhead

Nearest Town Monticello

Transportation Private

Summary This short loop across slickrock explores the microcosmic ecosystems of potholes. It features views of distant cliffs, mountains and rock formations similar to those along the Slickrock Trail.

The slickrock along this trail features naturally occurring dimples that collect water during rainstorms. To the naked eye, these potholes appear to be nothing more than mud puddles, but closer inspection reveals tiny organisms that must complete their life cycles before the water evaporates. Keep hands and feet out of the potholes, since these organisms are fragile. Though this is an excellent walk for contemplative souls and the scientifically inclined, it does lack drama, unless the potholes are teeming with life (which isn't always readily visible). Acrophobes, take heart: you won't have to stroll beside any cliffs.

🚗 DRIVING

Island in the Sky

Two main roads cross the mesa top at Island in the Sky, forming a Y. The visitor center and entrance station sit atop the northeast arm of the Y, Grand View Point is at the foot of the Y, and Upheaval Dome caps the northwest arm.

One primary 4WD route, the White Rim Rd, loops around the district about 1000ft below the mesa top.

🚗 Grand View Point Scenic Drive

Duration 50 minutes

Distance 12 miles

Start Visitor center

Finish Grand View Point

Nearest Town Moab

Summary This is a classic meander down the park's main road (paved) on a mesa top surrounded by cliffs and steep escarpments.

About 0.5 miles south of the visitor center, pull off to the left at the **Shafer Canyon Overlook**, where you can peer down 1000ft. Below is Shafer Trail Rd, the steep access route to the 4WD White Rim Rd.

A quarter-mile ahead you'll cross the **Neck** (slow down for great views), where the ridge narrows to 40ft across – eventually this strip will erode away, further isolating the mesa. The road levels out as it crosses **Grays Pasture**, where you might spot a bighorn sheep.

Just past Grays Pasture, take the left turn for **Mesa Arch**. This easy hike is worth every step – especially at sunrise when the arch's underside glows a fiery red. The road to Upheaval Dome bears right here.

A mile past the arch, pull off on the right to take in the sheer sandstone walls of **Candlestick Tower**. Visible to the southwest is the **Maze** and its many fins and canyons, all capped with white and orange horizontal lines.

Continue 1.5 miles to a turnout for the **Murphy Loop**. From the stunning overlook you'll see more of the Maze and the snaking Green River. The trail forks left just before the overlook.

Back on the road, 0.5 miles further on the left, take the paved walkway to the **Buck Canyon Overlook** for spectacular views of the La Sal Mountains. Another 1.8 miles south is the **White Rim Overlook**, a good picnic spot and starting point for the **White Rim Overlook Trail**, an easy, 1.2-mile round-trip hike.

CANYONLANDS NATIONAL PARK DRIVING

Grand View Pt & Upheaval Dome Scenic Drives

Three-quarters of a mile down the road, just before Grand View Point, the **Orange Cliffs Overlook** offers views west to the Henry Mountains, the last-charted mountain range in the Lower 48. The Orange Cliffs lie southwest, beyond the Maze. Come at sunset when the canyons glow orange in the waning light.

Five hundred feet ahead, the drive ends at **Grand View Point**, with one of the Southwest's most sweeping views, rivaled only by the Grand Canyon and nearby Dead Horse Point. In the foreground to the southeast, Monument Basin contains spires similar to those in the Needles; to see them, look south. To spot the Maze, follow the Green River from the northwest to the Confluence, where it meets the Colorado. West of the Confluence, the Doll House formations mark the edge of the Maze and the head of Cataract Canyon, one of North America's most intense stretches of white water.

Stand beside the interpretive panel at the overlook and look down at the rock – the south-facing gashes occurred when lightning struck a man here in 2003 (he lived). Off to your right is the **Grand View Point Trail**.

Upheaval Dome Scenic Drive

Duration 30 minutes

Distance 5 miles one way

Start Spur Junction, 6 miles south of visitor center

Finish Upheaval Dome

Nearest Town Moab

Summary In a few miles, this drive packs in the sights. Visit an ancient granary and peer down on the snaking Green River. Rock scrambling and crater gazing prove a hit with kids.

At the **Spur Junction** 6 miles south of the visitor center, turn northwest. A quarter-mile from the junction, turn left and drive to the **Green River Overlook** and **Willow Flat Campground**. Walk to the overlook for views of the Green River, Orange Cliffs and Henry Mountains. The small mesas in the foreground bear the marks of flash-flood erosion.

Large piñon trees around the parking area are 300 to 400 years old, while most of the blackbrush is more than 100 years old. The hardest thing for such desert plants is simply taking root. Nothing is growing on the parking-lot island, nor is anything likely to for another 50 years. Water and cryptobiotic crust make all the difference by providing nitrogen and a foothold for plants.

Back on the main road, half a mile further on the right, pull over at the **Aztec Butte Viewpoint and Trail**. Above the parking area is a **granary** built by Ancestral Puebloans.

About 2 miles ahead on the left (past a twisty section of road), you'll reach **Holeman Spring Canyon Overlook**, the only point along this drive that offers long views west across the Green River. A mile further, stop at the **Whale Rock Viewpoint and Trail**. Named for its smooth slickrock hump, Whale Rock lies at the end of an easy, mile-long round-trip hike that gains only 100ft. The path is exposed, so use the handrails.

Three-quarters of a mile ahead, the road ends at the **Upheaval Dome** parking lot and picnic area. To see the dome, stroll the short trail from the parking area.

The Needles

Be aware that storms wash out roads periodically and any road may be in poor condition. If the weather's been bad, check conditions at the visitor center before heading out.

🚗 Big Spring Canyon Overlook

Duration 30 minutes

Distance 6.4 miles

Start Visitor center

Finish Big Spring Canyon Overlook

Nearest Town Monticello

Summary Lovely at sunset, this short spurt goes by cool rock formations and slickrock to finish with gaping canyon views. The road is paved and well maintained. You can cycle it, but be careful as the shoulder of the road is narrow.

Stop first at the **Roadside Ruin** (a quarter-mile from the visitor center) and stroll the easy 0.3-mile loop trail to this ancient granary.

Unless you're bound for the 0.6-mile Cave Spring Trail, bear right at the fork in the road and pull over at the **Wooden Shoe Overlook**, on your left. Scan the cliffs overhead for the namesake rock formation with a tiny arch at its base.

Pass the turnoff for the campground and continue across the wide, even terrain of **Squaw Flat**. Two miles ahead on the left is a picnic area with shaded tables. The 0.6-mile **Pothole Point Trail** starts from the small parking lot just west of the picnic area. From here the road curls around the point to the moderately easy 2.4-mile **Slickrock Trail**.

Just past this trailhead, the road dead ends at the **Big Spring Canyon Overlook**. Park along the road and walk out on the rocks for a peek into the shallow canyons. Above the rocks rise 100ft formations that look as though they're made of whitish petrified sand dunes. To see the rock spires at Big Spring Canyon Overlook in the best light, visit in the morning – in the afternoon, the sun drops behind them.

OTHER ACTIVITIES

River rafting, kayaking and canoeing are also possible on the Green and Colorado Rivers. Book trips through Moab agencies.

Island in the Sky

Four-Wheel Driving & Mountain Biking

Blazed by uranium prospectors in the early 1950s, primitive **White Rim Road** circles Island in the Sky. Accessible from the visitor center via steep Shafer Trail Rd, the 70-mile route is the top choice for 4WD and mountain-biking trips. It generally takes two to three days to travel the loop in a 4WD vehicle, or three to four days by bike. As the route lacks any water sources, cyclists should team up with a 4WD support vehicle (there are 4WD rentals in Moab) or travel with an outfitter.

The park service limits the number of motorized vehicles. If you arrive without an overnight permit, call the visitor center about possible cancellations or no-shows. Rangers regularly patrol the route to check permits. Always stay on trails. No ATVs are allowed.

To learn more about the White Rim, pick up *A Naturalist's Guide to the White Rim Trail,* by David Williams and Damian Fagon.

Kids' Activities

When you arrive at the park, stop by the visitor center to pick up a **Junior Ranger Activity Guide**. Once kids complete certain activities, they can return to the visitor center to receive a special certificate and badge from a ranger.

Kids particularly like the Whale Rock and Mesa Arch trails, both easy walks with big payoffs. Keep an eye on your little ones, especially near overlooks, which are often unfenced.

Ranger Programs

For information about park attractions and insight on its human and geologic history, attend a ranger-led program. April through October, rangers give daily talks at Grand View Point at 10:30am and 11:30am. Talks are given daily at the visitor center at

10:30am and 1:30pm. For additions, check schedules at the visitor center.

The Needles

Four-Wheel Driving & Mountain Biking

Fifty miles of 4WD and mountain-biking roads crisscross the Needles. Stay on designated routes. Motorists and cyclists must obtain a permit for overnight trips, but not for day visits with the exception of Lavender and Horse Canyons, which require a $5 day-use permit fee; book in advance or check at the visitor center for cancellations, no-shows or leftovers.

All 4WD roads in the Needles require high-clearance vehicles (many off-the-lot SUVs do *not* have high clearance; AWD is not sufficient). Know what you're doing before you set out, or risk damaging your vehicle and/or endangering yourself. Towing fees can run to about $1000. If you're renting a 4WD vehicle, check the insurance policy; you might not be covered here. For more information, including 4WD routes and road conditions, check with a ranger when you book your permit. No ATVs are allowed.

Several 4WD and mountain-biking trails – formerly cattle roads – lead into the backcountry. Elephant Hill is the most technically challenging route in the district, with steep grades and tight turns. The route to the Colorado River Overlook is usually moderate in a vehicle and moderately easy on a mountain bike; check at the visitor center first since all conditions are possible. You will want to park and walk the final, steep 1.5-mile descent to the overlook. Following the district's main drainage, the Salt Creek Trail is moderately easy for vehicles, but sand makes it not recommended for bikes.

Kids' Activities

When you arrive at the park, stop by the Needles visitor center to pick up a Junior Ranger Activity Guide. Once kids complete certain activities, they can return to the visitor center to receive a special certificate and badge from a ranger.

DEAD HORSE POINT STATE PARK

The views at Dead Horse Point (www.stateparks.utah.gov; Hwy 313; park day use per vehicle $10, tent & RV sites $25; ☺ park 6am-10pm, visitor center 8am-6pm Mar-Oct, 9am-4pm Nov-Feb) pack a wallop, extending 2000ft below to the meandering Colorado River, 12,700ft up to the La Sal Mountains and 100 miles across Canyonlands' stair-step landscape. If you thrive on epic landscapes, you won't regret a side trip here.

The turnoff to Dead Horse is on Hwy 313, just 4 miles north of Island in the Sky (Moab is 30 miles away). Toward the end of the drive, the road traverses a narrow ridge just 30yd across. Ranchers once herded horses across these narrows – some were forgotten and left to die, hence the park name. A rough footpath skirts the point for views in all directions. To escape the small (but sometimes chatty) crowds, take one of the short hikes that rim the mesa. Visit at dawn or sunset for the best lighting.

The visitor center (http://stateparks.utah.gov/parks/dead-horse; ☺ 8am-6pm mid-Mar–mid-Oct, 9am-5pm mid-Oct–mid-Mar) features exceptionally good exhibits, shows on-demand videos and sells books and maps. Rangers lead walks and talks in summer. South of the visitor center, the 21-site Kayenta Campground (☎ 800-322-3770; www.stateparks.utah.gov; sites $28, yurts $88) provides limited water and a dump station, but no hookups. Reservations are accepted from March to October, but you can often secure same-day sites by arriving early. Fill RVs with water in Moab. Three yurts offer rad views of the surrounding wilderness.

Mountain bikers should check out the new Intrepid Trail, an excellent 9-mile single-track on the rim with great views. Rare for the Moab area, it's flat, so it's good for beginners, but its twists and turns keep riders on their toes. Another advantage – at 6000ft it can be cooler than riding in the bottom of a canyon on a hot day. The plateau is known to be 10°F cooler.

Pets are OK on a leash on all hiking trails but not on the Intrepid Trail for bikes.

Ask at the visitor center about renting a **Master Explorer Day Pack**, which contains binoculars, a magnifying lens and nature guide.

Kids especially like the Cave Spring Trail.

Ranger Programs

From March through October, rangers lead evening campfire discussions. Check schedules at the visitor center when you arrive in the park.

SIGHTS

Island in the Sky

You'll comprehend space in new ways atop the appropriately named Island in the Sky, a narrow, 6000ft flat-topped mesa that drops precipitously on all sides, providing some of the longest, most enthralling vistas of any park in southern Utah. The views far into the wilderness are punctuated to the west by the 11,500ft Henry Mountains near Capitol Reef, and to the east by the sky-punching 12,700ft La Sal Mountains, which remain snowcapped in early summer.

Offering paved roads and fine views, this is the park's most easily reached and popular district, welcoming about 260,000 visitors a year.

The small Island in the Sky Visitor Center (p193) sits atop the mesa about 2 miles beyond the park boundary and entrance station. From the visitor center, the road heads 12 miles south to Grand View Point. About halfway to the point, a paved spur leads northwest 5 miles to Upheaval Dome. A number of overlooks and trails line each road.

The Needles

Named for giant spires of orange-and-white sandstone that jut skyward from the desert floor, the Needles offers otherworldly terrain completely distinct from the scenery in Island in the Sky. Despite paved access roads, this district receives only half the number of visitors. Why? Perhaps because it's a 90-minute drive from Moab, and once you finally arrive, you have to work harder to appreciate its wonders – in short, you have to get out of the car and walk. But if you expend a little energy, payoffs include

DON'T MISS

NEWSPAPER ROCK
....

If you're fascinated by petroglyphs, head for **Newspaper Rock Recreation Area**. A single large sandstone face covered with images chipped out by various Native American groups and pioneers over a 3000-year stretch is beside Indian Creek on Hwy 211, about 12 miles west of Hwy 191. For more details contact the **BLM Monticello field office** (☑ 435-587-1510; 435 N Main St, Monticello; ⊙ 7:45am-noon & 1-4:30pm Mon-Fri).

peaceful solitude and an opportunity to experience, not just observe, the vast beauty of canyon country.

The Needles Visitor Center (p193) lies 2.5 miles inside the park boundary and provides drinking water. (If you've already visited Island in the Sky, be sure to bring your entrance receipt to avoid having to pay again.) From the visitor center, the paved road continues almost 7 miles to the Big Spring Canyon Overlook. Parking areas along the way access several sights, including arches, Ancestral Puebloan ruins and pictographs. About 3 miles past the visitor center, a side road leads to Squaw Flat Campground, with year-round water.

GPS has limited reception and is best used in conjunction with a map. Likewise, cell phones rarely have reception here. Credit card–operated pay phones outside the visitor center can be used at any hour.

The Maze

A 30-sq-mile jumble of high-walled canyons, the Maze is a rare preserve of true wilderness for hardy backcountry veterans. The colorful canyons are rugged, deep and sometimes inaccessible. Many of them look alike, and it's easy to get turned around. The district's name refers to one area within this sector. To visit the Maze, plan on spending at least three days, though a week may be ideal.

As the district lies west of the Confluence, the only way to reach it from Moab is to drive a 133-mile crescent-shaped route to the Hans Flat ranger station (p193), accessible by non-4WD vehicles. Take Hwy 191 north from Moab, to I-70 west, to Hwy 24 south. About 25 miles south of I-70, just past

CANYONLANDS NATIONAL PARK SIGHTS

the paved turnoff for Goblin Valley State Park, head southeast on the gravel road for 46 miles to Hans Flat. On the way, you'll cross the Glen Canyon National Recreation Area and Orange Cliffs Special Management Unit; if you plan to stop at either one, pick up a permit at Hans Flat.

There is no entrance fee or visitor center, but the ranger station sells books and maps (no food or water). The few roads into the district are very poor and can be closed by rain or snow; bring tire chains if visiting between October and April. You'll need a 4WD vehicle with a short wheelbase and high clearance. If you're inexperienced at four-wheel driving, stay away. You must also be prepared to repair your vehicle and, at times, the road. Those entering the Maze in a vehicle must reserve their backcountry campsite in advance.

If you don't have a 4WD, you can also leave your vehicle behind and hike into the district directly from the ranger station. For more advice and a full list of necessities, contact the ranger station in advance of your trip.

The Maze Overlook Trail requires that hikers carry at least a 25ft length of rope to raise and lower packs. Camping is at-large, and you'll find several reliable water sources (ask a ranger for locations). You can drive a 2WD vehicle to the North Point Rd junction, 2.5 miles south of Hans Flat, then hike 15 miles to the Maze Overlook.

Horseshoe Canyon

A separate unit of Canyonlands, west of the northern reaches of Island in the Sky, the little-known Horseshoe Canyon shelters millennia-old Native American rock art. The centerpiece is the Great Gallery, which consists of superb Barrier Canyon–style pictographs that date from between 2000 BC and AD 500. These heroic, life-size figures are nothing short of magnificent. Artifacts recovered in this district date back as far as 9000 BC. Damaging the rock art is a criminal offense: don't touch or disturb it in any way. Even the oils from your skin can harm the paintings.

The Great Gallery lies at the end of a 6.5-mile round-trip trail that descends 750ft from the main dirt road. Allow six hours. Rangers lead hikes here on Saturdays and Sundays from April through October; to arrange a group walk, contact the Hans Flat ranger station.

You can camp on BLM (Bureau of Land Management) land at the trailhead, though it's not a campground per se, but a parking lot. There is a single vault toilet, but no water or services. If you don't like primitive camping, try Moab (three hours away).

Shifting sand dunes can affect road conditions, so talk to a Canyonlands ranger before going. Take Hwy 191 north from Moab, to I-70 west, to Hwy 24 south. About 25 miles south of I-70, just past the turnoff for Goblin Valley State Park, turn east and follow the graded gravel road 30 miles to the Horseshoe Canyon unit.

🛏️SLEEPING

You won't find any rooms or restaurants in the park. For a hot meal and a warm bed, drive to Moab.

There is one developed campground at Island in the Sky and one developed front-country campground in the Needles. If they are full, check the campground at Dead Horse Point State Park and the Bureau of Land Management (BLM) sites on Hwy 313.

Island in the Sky

Willow Flat Campground   CAMPGROUND $
(www.nps.gov/cany/planyourvisit/islandinthesky. htm; tent & RV sites $10) Seven miles from the visitor center, the first-come, first-served, 12-site Willow Flat Campground has vault toilets but no water, and no hookups. Bring firewood and don't expect shade. Arrive early to claim a site during spring and fall.

The Needles

Store your food in your car or hang food in a stuff sack in the backcountry – campground ravens and small animals are notorious for getting into everything, including coolers.

BLM Campgrounds   CAMPGROUND $
(📞 435-259-2100; www.blm.gov/utah/moab; sites free-$6) There are several free BLM campsites outside the Needles entrance, including Superbowl and Bridger Jack. Hamburger Rock costs $6.

Squaw Flat Campground   CAMPGROUND $
(www.nps.gov/cany; tent & RV sites $15) This first-come, first-served, 26-site campground 3 miles west of the visitor center fills up every day from spring to fall. It has flush toilets and running water, but no showers and no hookups. Opt for side A, where many sites (12 and 14, for example) are shaded by juniper trees and cliffs. Maximum allowable RV length is 28ft.

ℹ Information

To start, pick up maps, guidebooks and information at the Moab Information Center (p222). For information only, call or visit the **Canyonlands NPS Headquarters** (☑ 435-719-2313; www. nps.gov/cany; 2282 SW Resource Blvd, Moab; ☺ 8am-4:30pm Mon-Fri). The **Canyonlands Natural History Association** (Map p208; ☑ 435-259-6003, 800-840-8978; www.cnha. org; 3031 S Hwy 191, Moab) has some good info on local history and runs the bookstore.

Hans Flat Ranger Station (☑ 435-259-2652; www.nps.gov/cany; Hans Flat Rd, Hwy 24; ☺ 8am-4:30pm) The station is 136 miles (3½ hours) from Moab, and has a few books and maps, but no other services.

Island in the Sky Visitor Center (☑ 435-259-4712; www.nps.gov/cany; Hwy 313, 1 mile after park entrance; ☺ 8am-6pm Mar-Oct, 9am-4:30pm Nov-Feb) Get books, maps, permits and campground information here. Schedules are posted daily for ranger-led lectures (10:30am and 11:30am most days) and hikes.

Needles Visitor Center (☑ 435-259-4711; Hwy 211; ☺ 8am-6pm Mar-Oct, 9am-4:30pm Nov-Feb) A small center with a few exhibits and curated sections, along with a Junior Ranger program for kids.

ℹ Getting Around

The easiest way to tour Canyonlands is by car. Traveling between districts takes two to six hours, so plan to visit no more than one per day. Speed limits vary but are generally between 25mph and 40mph. Beware of cattle on the road, particularly in winter and spring. They are frequently the cause of accidents. There are no gas stations within the park. Fuel up in Moab, and carry extra gas in the backcountry.

Many Moab tour operators guide rafting, hiking, cycling and 4WD tours in the park.

CANYONLANDS NATIONAL PARK INFORMATION

Arches National Park

Best Hikes

→ Balanced Rock (p201)

→ The Windows (p201)

→ Landscape Arch (p198)

→ Fiery Furnace (p198)

→ Delicate Arch (p200)

Best Views

→ Delicate Arch Viewpoint (p200)

→ The Windows (p201)

→ Landscape Arch (p198)

→ Courthouse Towers Viewpoint (p202)

→ La Sal Mountains Viewpoint (p202)

Why Go?

With the highest density of rock arches anywhere on earth, Arches National Park offers up a whimsical escape that pushes you to jump, gasp, leap and skip. Simply put, it's magic.

Located just a hop away from Moab, this diminutive park is quite user-friendly, making it a great spot for families, people with disabilities and hikers looking for big views. These views do sometimes come at a price, as the park can get downright overrun on weekends. Get up early, visit weekdays and consider some of the longer hikes to really explore the richness of this national treasure.

While there are more than 2000 arches here, top bucket-list sights include Delicate Arch, Balanced Rock and the Windows. Go further afield with canyoneering trips into the sandstone labyrinths of the Fiery Furnace or Devils Garden. Seeing the sun set or rise over these vainglorious arches, fins, bridges and spires is exhilarating and sublime.

Driving Distances (miles)

	Arches National Park	Bryce Canyon National Park	Canyonlands National Park (North Entrance)	Capitol Reef National Park (Visitor Center)	Moab
Bryce Canyon National Park	270				
Canyonlands National Park (North Entrance)	25	280			
Capitol Reef National Park (Visitor Center)	140	120	155		
Moab	5	270	30	145	
Zion National Park (East Entrance)	310	75	325	180	315

Note: Distances are approximate

Entrances

The park entrance and visitor center are accessed 5 miles northwest of Moab off Hwy 191. Most people drive it, but you can get here on a paved bike trail as well.

Past the visitor center, you climb into the park proper, where you'll find 22 miles of paved roads – most sights lie on or alongside the pavement. Crowds are often unavoidable. Parking areas overflow at peak times (weekends, spring through fall).

Every year the park takes new measures to handle the problem. The NPS may eventually institute a shuttle system if visitation increases. For now, to keep drivers from parking in dangerous or sensitive areas, rangers have stepped up ticketing for illegally parked cars. Always consider cycling, car pooling or taking a tour through the park to limit the congestion.

The best strategy is to arrive at the park by 7am, when crowds are sparse and the temperatures not so bad; or visit in the evening after 7pm. If you can't find a designated parking spot at one place, continue to the next. Also, drive carefully; accidents occur when drivers focus on the scenery, not the road – an easy trap to fall into at Arches.

DON'T MISS

A guided hike through the Fiery Furnace, one of the signature hikes of the park, takes you into a wild mousetrap of sandstone desertscapes. You need to be fit because you'll be clambering over rock, through canyons and around boulders. Access is extremely limited, so reserve ahead. If that just ain't your thing, make sure you check out both Landscape Arch, the longest arch in Arches National Park, measuring 306ft from base to base, and Delicate Arch.

When You Arrive

➡ Admission, good for seven days, is $25 per car, $15 per motorcycle and $10 per person on bike or foot.

➡ A Local Passport, good for admission to Arches and Canyonlands National Parks and Natural Bridges and Hovenweep National Monuments for a one-year period, costs $50.

➡ Arches is open year-round.

➡ Bring your own water and lunch. Expect to bring a gallon of water per person per day in the summer.

➡ The video at the visitor center gives an excellent (though slightly over-dramatized) view on the park's geological history.

PARK POLICIES & REGULATIONS

Most standard national parks policies apply here. Horses are only allowed in Arches National Park in very limited areas, including Salt Wash upstream from the Delicate Arch road and Courthouse Wash. Pets are not allowed on any of the hiking trails or in the visitor center. You can take them out on the leash at the campground, overlooks or pullouts along the paved scenic drive. Backcountry, climbing and canyoneering permits are available online and at the vistor center.

Fast Facts

➡ Total area: 119 sq miles

➡ Elevation: 4085ft

➡ Average high/low temperature (at the visitor center) in July: 100°F/87°F (31°C/38°C)

Resources

➡ **Arches National Park** (www.nps.gov/arch)

ARCHES NATIONAL PARK

Arches National Park

DEVILS GARDEN

Dance with the devil on the park's longest trail, stopping along the way to enjoy spectacular views of eight arches. (p199)

FIERY FURNACE

Head out on a ranger-guided trek through this perplexing and mind-defying sandstone maze. (p198)

DOUBLE O ARCH

Double your fun with a hike out to these twin arches. (p199)

LANDSCAPE ARCH

Tramp your way out for views of North America's longest natural arch at 93.3m. (p198)

Yellow Cat Flat

Salt Wash

Devils Garden Primitive Loop

Tin Canyon

Clover Canyon

Private Arch

Devils Garden

Wall Arch (fallen)

Pine Tree Arch

Navajo Arch

Partition Arch

Tunnel Arch

Landscape Arch

Dark Angel

Double O Arch

Skyline Arch

Devils Garden Campground

Broken Arch

Sand Dune Arch

Fiery Furnace

Fiery Furnace Viewpoint

Salt Valley Overlook

Wolfe Ranch

Delicate Arch (4829 ft)

Delicate Arch Viewpoint

Salt Valley

Arches National Park

Klondike Bluffs

Tower Arch

Marching Men

Panorama Point

Eye of the

Arches National Park

To (1mi); I-70 (16mi)

DELICATE ARCH

Clamber up slickrock for a sunset treat at this iconic rock formation. (p200)

BALANCED ROCK

Marvel at the power of wind and water beneath this 3577-ton balancing boulder. (p201)

NORTH WINDOW

Peer across the glory of the Colorado Plateau, taking in the rifts, fins and canyons that make this land great. (p201)

I-70

128

North Window

South Window

The Windows Section

Elephant Butte Arch (5653ft)

Double Arch

Cove Arch

Ham Rock

Turret Arch

Balanced Rock

Colorado River

128

Rock Pinnacle

The Great Wall

Rock Wall

Petrified Dunes Viewpoint

Petrified Dunes

Flats

Courthouse Wash

Tower of Babel

Courthouse Towers Viewpoint

The Organ

La Sal Mountains Viewpoint

Sheep Rock

Three Gossips

Park Ave

Park Avenue

Courthouse Towers

Visitor Center & Park Headquarters

Moab Canyon Pathway

Moab Canyon

River crossing, may not be through route

Moab

191

The Needles, Canyonlands National Park (75mi)

Mill Creek

279

Dry Fork

313

Island in the Sky, Canyonlands National Park (22mi)

🏃 DAY HIKES

Arches is geared more to drivers than hikers, with most of the main sights within a mile or two of paved roads. There are a few exceptions, but you won't find an extensive system of trails as at other national parks. Still, you can enjoy several hikes that will take you away from the sound of traffic, at least for a few hours.

Backpacking isn't popular at Arches National Park, but if you're determined, you can do so with a backcountry permit, available in person from the visitor center. There are neither designated trails nor campsites. Due to the fragility of biological soil crusts, the park discourages backcountry treks. The closest you'll come to an established backcountry route is the **Devils Garden Primitive Trail**.

If you're fit and would like to join a guided hike through the narrow sandstone labyrinth at the **Fiery Furnace** (adult/child \$10/5; ⊙Mar-Oct), you can make reservations up to six months in advance at www.recreation.gov. On rare occasions tours may be offered outside the reservation system. If so, tickets for these tours are sold in person on a first-come, first-served basis at the visitor center up to seven days in advance.

Buy tickets (in person only, adult/child \$10/5) at the visitor center. Walks run 2.5 to three hours and are generally offered twice daily (morning and afternoon) April through September.

While park rangers are discouraging it, accomplished hikers can explore the Fiery Furnace unguided. To do so, you must still pay a fee, watch a video and discuss with rangers how to negotiate this confusing jumble of canyons before they'll grant you a permit. Permits are limited to 50 a day, and usually sell out, so go early.

Arches is wildly popular and stays busy through Thanksgiving weekend. One tip is to try sunrise hiking (less popular than sunset).

🏃 Landscape Arch

Duration 30–60 minutes

Distance 2.1 miles

Difficulty Easy–moderate

Start/Finish Devils Garden trailhead

Nearest Town Moab

Transportation Private

Summary Among the world's longest natural stone spans, Landscape Arch is a spectacular ribbon of rock reached via a moderate gravel trail with spurs of interest.

Landscape Arch lies 0.8 miles along the Devils Garden trail at the northern end of the main park road. Along the trail, don't miss the short spurs (0.5 miles) to Tunnel and Pine Tree Arches. To make it more of a full-day hike, continue to Dark Angel spire or do the entire Devils Garden Primitive Trail. Before setting out, fill up with water at the trailhead parking lot. If you can, try to walk this trail in the morning, when it's much more pleasant than in mid-afternoon heat.

HIKING IN ARCHES NATIONAL PARK

NAME	START LOCATION	DESCRIPTION
Balanced Rock (p201)	Balanced Rock parking area	A precariously poised boulder perched atop a narrow rock spire
Delicate Arch (p199)	Wolfe Ranch	Arches' premier hike ascends slickrock to the iconic Delicate Arch
Landscape Arch (p198)	Devils Garden trailhead	Short walk to one of the world's longest spans, with side hikes to smaller arches
Sand Dune & Broken Arches (p200)	Sand Dune Arch parking area	Varied route that passes the Fiery Furnace fins and grasslands, threads through an arch and crosses slickrock
The Windows (p210)	The Windows trailhead	Gravel loop that goes beneath three massive arches that frame stunning views

 Views   Drinking Water   Backcountry Camping

From the trailhead, you'll thread through sandstone fins that stand on end like giant wedges. A third of a mile in, bear right at the fork and head downhill to **Tunnel Arch** (on your right) and the 45ft **Pine Tree Arch** (on your left). High on a cliff, aptly named Tunnel Arch looks like a subway tube through the Entrada sandstone. In contrast, Pine Tree Arch is meaty, with a bulbous frame around its gaping middle. Look for the gnarled namesake juniper, which juts from the base of the window.

As you approach **Landscape Arch** along the main trail, the terrain opens up, revealing long views to distant ridges and a vast expanse of sky. In the past visitors could hike right beneath the elegant 306ft sweep of desert-varnished sandstone, longer than a football field. But in 1991, a 60ft slab of rock fell from the arch, nearly killing several hikers. When you notice the cracks on the left side of the arch, it's easy to understand why the NPS closed the trail.

From here you can continue on a moderately difficult out-and-back hike to the trail's end at **Dark Angel** spire, adding about 3.4 miles to your journey. You can also add the difficult **Devils Garden Primitive Trail**, an additional stretch of 4.3 miles that includes cool views of sandstone fins. Both lead to **Double O Arch**, where you'll negotiate the narrow edge of a sandstone fin with a 20ft drop on either side. (This rocky route is not suitable for little ones.) Pick up a trail guide at the trailhead or ask a ranger for route details.

Sand Dune & Broken Arches

Duration 15–30 minutes to Sand Dune Arch, 30–60 minutes to Broken Arch, 2 hours for complete loop

Distance 0.4 miles (Sand Dune Arch), 1.2 miles (Broken Arch), 2.4 miles (complete loop)

Difficulty Easy–moderate

Start/Finish Sand Dune Arch parking area

Nearest Town Moab

Transportation Private

Summary A varied walk that leads though rock fins (giving a taste of the Fiery Furnace), cool sand dunes and slickrock, this is a good place to take the kids.

From the Sand Dune Arch parking area, follow the trail through deep sand between narrow stone walls that are the backmost fins of **Fiery Furnace**. In less than a quarter-mile you'll arrive at **Sand Dune Arch**, which looks something like a poodle kissing a polar bear. Resist the temptation to climb or jump off the 8ft arch.

From here you can bear left to return to your car or bear right across open grassland en route to 60ft Broken Arch. At the next fork (the start of the loop trail), grasses give way to piñon pines and junipers along a gentle climb to **Broken Arch**. The treat here is the walk *through* the arch atop a slickrock ledge. Wear rubber-soled shoes or boots, or you may have trouble climbing to the arch.

ARCHES NATIONAL PARK DAY HIKES

DIFFICULTY	DURATION	DISTANCE	ELEVATION CHANGE	FEATURES	FACILITIES
easy	15–20min	0.3 miles	20ft		
moderate-difficult	2–3hr	3 miles	480ft		
easy-moderate	30min–1hr	2.1 miles	50ft		
easy-moderate	2hr	2.4 miles	140ft		
easy	30min–1hr	0.6 miles	140ft		

 Great for Families   *Picnic Sites*   *Restrooms*

Arches National Park – Day Hikes

N
0 — 4 km
0 — 2 miles

Balanced Rock
Delicate Arch
Landscape Arch
Sand Dune & Broken Arches
The Windows

Wall Arch
Landscape Arch
Clover Canyon
Salt Wash
Broken Arch
Devils Garden Trailhead
Sand Dune Arch
Fiery Furnace
Arches National Park Rd
Delicate Arch (4829 ft)
Wolfe Ranch
Arches National Park
(4WD Only)
Willow Flats
Willow Flats Rd
Rock Pinnacle
The Great Wall
Balanced Rock
Windows Rd
Elephant Butte (5653 ft)
North Window
Turret Arch
South Window
Colorado River
128

When you're ready, return to the parking area or continue north to Devils Garden Campground. The route follows cairns over slickrock, passing through stands of desert pines. Watch for new arches forming near the trail. If you're staying at the campground, you can join the loop trail there. From the campground spur it's another half a mile back to the start of the loop trail.

This is a good trail for kids, especially the first section, though savvy adult hikers may find it too tame.

Delicate Arch

Duration 2–3 hours

Distance 3 miles

Difficulty Moderate–difficult

Start/Finish Wolfe Ranch

Nearest Town Moab

Transportation Private

Summary This is a shadeless ascent to a bowed sandstone arch that Edward Abbey likened to cowboy chaps. Follow rock cairns on slickrock and mind yourself on exposed heights.

The trail to Delicate Arch may seem interminable on the way up, but the rewards are so great that you'll quickly forget the toil – provided you wear rubber-soled shoes or boots and drink a quart of water along the way (there is no shade). You won't be alone – this is the most popular long hike at Arches.

Start out behind **Wolfe Ranch**, where a short spur trail leads to a small **petroglyph panel**. The trail is wheelchair-accessible to the petroglyph panel. Illustrations showing people on horseback were probably authored by the nomadic Utes, who adopted riding after the arrival of the Spanish.

Past the panel, the trail climbs a series of small switchbacks, soon emerging onto a long, steady slickrock slope. (This hill is visible from the trailhead, as are the tiny figures trudging up the slickrock like pilgrims.) Take your time on this stretch, especially on hot days. If you keep a steady pace, plan on making it to the top in 45 minutes.

As you approach the arch, the trail skirts a narrow slickrock ledge that may be daunting for those afraid of heights – yet it's worth pushing on to round the final corner. To your right, a broad sandstone amphitheater opens up below, and Delicate Arch crowns its rim, framing the 12,700ft La Sal Mountains in the distance. Circle the rim to the base of the arch, which sits atop a saddle that drops precipitously on either side. (If you bypass the bowl and bear left, it's possible to clamber high atop large flat rocks for a different perspective – and fewer people.)

Balanced Rock

Duration 15–20 minutes

Distance 0.3 miles

Difficulty Easy

Start/Finish Balanced Rock parking area

Nearest Town Moab

Transportation Private

Summary The draw is a boulder as big as a naval destroyer, teetering on a spindly pedestal. Loop around the formation to have a good look at the forces of erosion at work.

A 3577-ton boulder atop a leaning pedestal, Balanced Rock shoots from the earth like a fist. The pedestal is made of soft Dewey Bridge mudstone, which erodes faster than the rock above. Eventually, this pedestal will snap, and the boulder will come crashing down.

While you can see the formation clearly from the trailhead, the loop allows you to grasp its actual size (55ft to the top of the pedestal, 128ft to the top of the rock). On the outside of the trail look for yucca, an important desert species that can provide food, soap, needles and rope.

There is wheelchair access to the viewpoint.

The Windows

Duration 30–60 minutes

Distance 0.6 miles

Difficulty Easy

Start/Finish The Windows trailhead

Nearest Town Moab

Transportation Private

Summary A gravel loop trail makes an easy climb to three massive arches (North and South Windows and Turret Arch). Take the alternative, slightly longer return for a back view of the two windows.

One of the park's most heavily trodden paths, this trail leads directly to North and South Windows and offers a terrific view of Turret Arch. Rangers lead interpretive talks here from spring through fall; if you're interested, check the bulletin board at the parking area. The trail forks about 500ft from the lot. Bear right for a close look at Turret Arch along a short loop that rejoins the main trail.

The left fork climbs to the North Window. Stand beneath this arch for one of the park's best views, taking in red-rock cliffs and Castle Valley in the distance. Above you is the giant smooth sweep of the mature arch, supported by a base of lumpy Dewey Bridge mudstone. South Window sits higher than North Window. Though tempting, keep off the arch (climbing or walking on any arch with an opening of 3ft or more is prohibited).

Two trails lead back to the parking lot from here: the wide, graded main trail and the narrow primitive trail. The latter heads east and then north, with great views and a brief respite from the crowds. Follow the cairns.

OTHER ACTIVITIES

Arrange guided climbing, hiking and canyoneering trips through Moab tour operators.

Rock Climbing

Rock climbing is permitted at Arches, but can only be done on established routes. Most routes require advanced techniques. Climbing permits can be obtained online through the Arches Canyoneering & Climbing Permits webpage (https://arches permits.nps.gov/) or self-register at the visitor center. Before you set out, ask at the visitor center about current regulations and route closures.

Ranger Programs

Rangers lead several activities from spring through fall, most notably the **Fiery Furnace guided hike** (by reservation) in summer; you can also reserve online. Ask when you get here about other ranger talks and programs.

Kids' Activities

When you arrive at the park, stop by the visitor center and pick up a **Junior Ranger Activity Guide**. Once kids complete certain activities, they can return to the visitor center to receive a special certificate and badge from a ranger. Kids can also get an **Explorer Pack** on loan with stuff to do throughout the park. Keep kids on trails to protect the delicate desert ecosystem.

⌂ SLEEPING

Arches offers one developed campground, but no rooms or restaurants. Drive the 5 miles to Moab for all services and further accommodation options (p215).

Devils Garden Campground   CAMPGROUND **$**
(☑ 877-444-6777; www.recreation.gov; tent & RV sites $20) Surrounded by red rock and scrubby piñons, the park's only campground is 19 miles from the visitor center. From March to October, sites are available by reservation. Book months ahead.

ⓘ Information

There are no places in the park to buy prepared food, groceries or supplies. For all services, drive to Moab.

The **visitor center** (www.nps.gov/arch; 7-day pass per vehicle/motorcycle/bike $25/15/10; ⊕9am-4pm) has educational exhibits and a bookstore. Rangers are on hand to answer questions and help you plan your visit; ask about ranger-led activities. You can also pick up your reserved tickets for the Fiery Furnace guided walk. If you arrive after hours, stop at the parking lot and read the information panels. Potable water faucets are located at the entrance. Stock up on water while you're here; the next water source is 18 miles up the road, at Devils Garden.

ⓘ Getting Around

Currently the only way to see Arches is by bicycle or private vehicle, on foot or through an organized tour.

Driving Tour
Arches Scenic Drive

START VISITOR CENTER
END VISITOR CENTER
LENGTH 43 MILES, INCLUDING SPURS; 2½ HOURS

Hitting all the highlights, this paved drive visits Arches' strange forms and flaming desert landscapes. It's packed with photo ops and short walks to arches and iconic landmarks.

From the ❶ **visitor center**, the steep road ascends Navajo sandstone, once ancient sand dunes. Stop at the ❷ **Moab Fault Overlook**. Interpretive panels explain the geology. A mile ahead, stop at ❸ **Park Avenue**, where you can take a walk past a giant rock fin that calls to mind a row of New York City skyscrapers.

Half a mile past Park Avenue, stop at the ❹ **La Sal Mountains Viewpoint**. This laccolithic mountain range developed underground during volcanic activity, then rose to the surface, fully formed, some 24 million years ago. If the scenery looks familiar, many of the driving scenes in the film *Thelma & Louise* were shot in Arches.

As you descend toward the ❺ **Courthouse Towers Viewpoint**, look left for the ❻ **Three Gossips**, towers that resemble three figures sharing a secret. From the viewpoint turnout, look up at the monoliths. These walls were probably once connected by arches since fallen away, particularly at ❼ **Sheep Rock**. Just ahead in ❽ **Courthouse Wash**, stands of bright-green cottonwood trees offer dramatic proof of how water can transform the parched desert into an oasis. About 1.5 miles further, on the right, the undulating landscape at ❾ **Petrified Dunes** was once a vast sweep of sand dunes. (Technically, the dunes aren't 'petrified,' as they contain no carbon, the determining element in petrification.)

After a 3-mile ascent, you'll arrive at the 3577-ton ❿ **Balanced Rock**, which teeters precariously atop a narrow stone pedestal. Pull over and take the 15-minute loop trail, then turn right onto Windows Rd, a 5-mile round-trip spur. You'll find pit toilets beside the parking lot at road's end.

Take the easy, short walks to ⑪ **North** and ⑫ **South Windows** and to ⑬ **Double Arch**. It's hard to grasp the immensity of these gigantic marvels until you're beside them. If you want a long view of the vast surrounding landscape but are short on time, head to North Window and stand right beneath it.

Back on the main road, stop at ⑭ **Panorama Point**. The 360-degree view includes an overlook of ⑮ **Salt Valley**, a onetime salt dome that collapsed when water washed away the salt. Interpretive panels explain the geology.

Two-and-a-half miles past the Windows spur, turn right on the signed spur to ⑯ **Wolfe Ranch** and Delicate Arch. Pull into the first parking lot (which includes pit toilets) and take the short, easy walk to the primitive 1907 cabin, with its juniper-log walls and shale roof. ⑰ **Salt Wash**, which is wet year-round, runs from the cabin to the Colorado River. If you're lucky, you may spot a river otter. Cross the footbridge for a surprisingly close look at a small petroglyph panel, incised by Ute people sometime after the year 1600 (look but don't touch, as oils from fingers deteriorate the rock). If you're up for a strenuous hike, climb the trail to ⑱ **Delicate Arch**, the park's premier hike. Otherwise, continue driving to the ⑲ **Delicate Arch Viewpoint**, 1 mile beyond the Wolfe Ranch turnout.

Two short trails lead to views of the arch, which has also been nicknamed the 'School-marm's Breeches' and the 'Cowboy Chaps.' Follow the crowds to the right for an easy 50yd walk to the lower view, or bear left for a moderately strenuous 0.5-mile hike and 200ft ascent to the better view.

Return to the main road, turn right and drive 3 miles to the ⑳ **Salt Valley Overlook** for a perspective down to Wolfe Ranch and Salt Valley, then pull off again at the ㉑ **Fiery Furnace**. A short walk between split-rail fences leads to the overlook, from where you can peer between the giant fins of Entrada sandstone – at sunset they resemble flames in a furnace.

From here the main road skirts past the Fiery Furnace and the ㉒ **Sand Dune Arch trailhead** to road's end at the ㉓ **Devils Garden trailhead**. Refill your water bottle and picnic before taking the moderately easy walk to ㉔ **Landscape Arch**, the span of which is longer than a football field. Drive out the way you came, omitting the spur roads.

Moab

Best Hikes & Bikes

➜ The Whole Enchilada (p205)

➜ Klondike Bluffs Trail (p207)

➜ Corona Arch Trail (p207)

➜ Fisher Towers Trail (p207)

➜ La Sal Mountains (p207)

➜ Moonflower Canyon (p208)

Best Places to Stay

➜ BLM Campgrounds (p215)

➜ ACT Campground (p215)

➜ Sunflower Hill Inn (p217)

➜ Sorrel River Ranch (p220)

Why Go?

Perfectly located in a little scrub brush valley amid some of grandest scenery in the American West, Moab is the pivot for adventures into Arches and Canyonlands National Parks.

It's also an adrenaline-seeker's paradise, with amazing access to some of the sickest single-track mountain-biking trails in the world, river-rafting and jetboating on nearby rivers, plus climbing, canyoneering, four-wheeling and hiking on an astro-fantastic desertscape that make this the best place on earth to play on Mars.

The town on its surface is little more than a strip of classic Americana motels, cheesy T-shirt shops, tour operators and bike outfits. Pull back the curtain and you'll discover hometown treats such as softball games, arts councils and fun-loving locals, brewpubs and bistros, and about a million visitors a year to create traffic mix-ups in a former uranium outpost that has a permanent population hovering around 5000.

Driving Distances (miles)

	Arches National Park	Bryce Canyon National Park	Canyonlands National Park (North Entrance)	Capitol Reef National Park (Visitor Center)	Moab
Bryce Canyon National Park (Park Entrance)	270				
Canyonlands National Park (North Entrance)	25	280			
Capitol Reef National Park (Visitor Center)	140	120	155		
Moab	5	275	30	145	
Zion National Park (East Entrance)	310	75	325	180	315

Note: Distances are approximate

History

Moab was founded by Mormon ranchers and farmers in the late 1870s after years of resistance from the Native American peoples of the region.

Nothing much changed until the Cold War of the 1950s, when the federal government subsidized uranium mining, and Moab's population tripled in three years. In search of 'radioactive gold,' miners bladed a network of primitive roads, laying the groundwork for the region to become a 4WD mecca half a century later. The miners also left ponds of radioactive tailings, residue from the mineral extraction process. Though uranium mining bottomed out in the 1980s when the feds quit paying premiums for the stuff, salt and potash mining continue, as does drilling for natural gas in the surrounding area, a contentious issue.

Hollywood loves Moab and has shot hundreds of Westerns in the surrounding countryside, mostly from the 1950s to the 1970s. But neither the mining boom nor Hollywood has had as much influence on Moab's current character as the humble mountain biker. In the mid-1980s, an influx of fat-tire enthusiasts discovered the challenging and scenic slickrock desert and triggered a massive surge in tourism that continues unabated.

◉ Sights

Moab Giants AMUSEMENT PARK
(www.moabgiants.com; Hwys 213 & 219; entrance from $20; 🚼) About to open at the time of research, this new paleo-amusement park features giant lifesize replica dinosaurs, walking trails, 3-D videos that might even bring you to a fourth dimension in some sections, information on dino tracks and more. It might be garish for some, but with a $10 million initial investment, it will certainly be entertaining.

Museum of Moab MUSEUM
(www.moabmuseum.org; 118 E Center St; adult/child $5/free; ⊙10am-6pm Mon-Sat Apr-Oct, noon-5pm Mon-Sat Oct-Apr) Regional exhibits feature everything from paleontology and geology to uranium mining and Native American art.

Moab Museum of Film & Western Heritage MUSEUM
(☑435-259-2002, 866-812-2002; www.redcliffs lodge.com/museum; Mile 14, Hwy 128; ⊙8am-10pm) **FREE** Head out to the Moab Museum of Film & Western Heritage, based at Red Cliffs Adventure Lodge, 15 miles north of town, to see Hollywood memorabilia from films shot locally; there are also historical displays on area ranches.

Hole 'n the Rock HOUSE
(www.moab-utah.com/holeintherock; 11037 S Hwy 191; tours adult/child $6/3.50; ⊙9am-5pm; 🚼) An unabashed tourist trap 12 miles south of Moab, Hole 'n the Rock is a 5000-sq-ft home-cum-cave carved into sandstone and decorated in knockout 1950s kitsch.

🏃 Activities

Mountain Biking

Local trail coalitions have added a bunch of new trails in the last five years. The basic rating systems follows skiing designations of green for easy, blue for moderate, black for difficult and double-black diamond for insane-experts-only-need-apply. It's important to protect the surrounding desert. Avoid all off-trail riding, and pack out everything you pack in. The busiest seasons are spring and fall. In summer, start riding by 7am at the latest – after that, it's too hot. In winter, snow might cover trails, but you can bike the roads. Check at local bike shops for guided trips, trail maps ($2 per map), route info, rentals and shuttles.

★ The Whole Enchilada MOUNTAIN BIKING
Accessed from the top of Geyser Pass at 10,600ft, this masterpiece combines the Burro Pass, Hazzard County, Jimmy Keen, UPS, LPS and Porcupine Rim Trails, offering everything from high-mountain descents to slickrock. It's a full-day affair for advanced riders with 7000ft of vertical drop and 26.5 miles of trails.

Bar-M Loop MOUNTAIN BIKING
Bring the kids on this easy, 8-mile loop skirting the boundary of Arches, with great views and short slickrock stretches. Connect from here to more advanced **Moab Brands** trails.

Klonzo MOUNTAIN BIKING
Accessed from Willow Springs Rd, this area offers a mix of flowing beginner, intermediate and advanced terrain.

MOAB SIGHTS

MOAB FAST FACTS

➡ Population: 5130

➡ Elevation: 4026ft

➡ Average high/low temperature in July: 100°F/87°F (37°C/30°C)

Moab Region

â ⊗
0 _____ 5 miles
0 _____ 10 km

FISHER TOWERS
Take in the inspired views of Castle Valley as you hike through canyons to these eroded sandstone monoliths caked in the region's red mud. (p207)

WHOLE ENCHILADA MOUNTAIN BIKE TRAIL
Bust your butt on a gargantuan feast for adrenaline gluttons. (p205)

MAIN STREET
Grab a pint of local beer and relax in the fun restobars after a long day's adventure. (p220)

BLM HWY 128 CAMPGROUNDS
Go rustic at a low-key campsite shaded by canyon walls while the Colorado River rushes nearby. (p215)

MATHESON WETLANDS PRESERVE
Check out flocks of over 200 species of shore birds, raptors and waterfowl, as well as aquatic mammals like beaver, muskrat and river otters. (p209)

THE COLORADO RIVER
Honor the sun and river gods atop a paddleboard, kayak or raft on this main artery of the region. (p211)

Capitol Reef National Park (131mi);
Grand Staircase-Escalante
National Monument (196mi);
Bryce Canyon National Park (251mi);
Zion National Park (299mi)

Manti-La Sal National Forest

Manti-La Sal National Forest

Manti-La Sal National Forest

Dome Plateau

Fisher Valley

Fisher Mesa

Fisher Towers Rd

Fisher Towers

Onion Creek

Colorado River

Adobe Mesa

Castle Creek

Castle Valley

Placer Creek

Porcupine Rim

Sand Flats Rd

128

Dry Mesa

Placer Creek

Negro Bill Canyon

North Fork Mill Creek

Mill Creek

Pack Creek

Spanish Valley

Elephant Butte

The Windows Section

Petrified Dunes

The Organ

The Great Wall

Courthouse Wash

Courthouse Towers

Moab Canyon Pathway

Arches National Park

Moab

Moab Valley

Matheson Wetlands Preserve

Colorado River

Moab Canyon

Arths Pasture

128

191

279

279

191

Main St

Zion National Park (372mi);
Bryce Canyon National Park (419mi);
Grand Staircase-Escalante

The Knoll

313

313

Canyonlands

Gemini Bridges   MOUNTAIN BIKING
A moderate, full-day downhill ride past spectacular rock formations, this 13.5-mile one-way trail follows dirt, sand and slick-rock. Located about 7 miles north of Moab on Hwy 191.

Moonlight Meadow Trail   MOUNTAIN BIKING
Beat the heat by ascending La Sal Mountains to 10,600ft on this moderate 10-mile loop among aspens and pines (take it easy: you will get winded).

Sand Flats Recreation Area   MOUNTAIN BIKING
(Slickrock; www.utah.com/playgrounds/sand_flats. htm; car/cyclist $5/2) Iconic slickrock trail that's way harder than you'd think – and way too crowded.

Klondike Bluffs Trail   MOUNTAIN BIKING
Intermediates can learn to ride slickrock on this 15.6-mile round-trip trail, past dinosaur tracks to Arches National Park. Mostly blue and black trails. Get here by going on Hwy 191 to Mile 148, exiting to Klondike Bluff.

Magnificent 7   MOUNTAIN BIKING
Accessed north of Moab on Hwy 313 (13 miles in from the turnoff), some of the most exposed terrain in Moab is found on the 20 miles of advanced trails.

Navajo Rocks   MOUNTAIN BIKING
By the north entrance to Canyonlands, this intermediate area has good sandstone terrain that even rides well in rainy season. There are seven trails, connecting over 22 miles.

Park to Park Trail   CYCLING
A paved-road bike path travels one way from Moab into Arches National Park (30 miles), or you can turn off and follow the Hwy 313 bike lane to the end of Canyonlands' Island in the Sky park (35 miles). On Hwy 128, it follows the Colorado River to Negro Bill Canyon.

Poison Spider Bicycles   MOUNTAIN BIKING
(☑435-259-7882, 800-635-1792; www.poisonspider bicycles.com; 497 N Main St; rental per day $45-75) Friendly staff are always busy helping wheel jockeys map out their routes. Well-maintained road and suspension rigs for rent.

Rim Tours   BICYCLE TOUR
(☑435-259-5223; www.rimtours.com; 1233 S Hwy 191) Well-organized and well-supported half-day, full-day and multiday bike trips cover territory all across southern Utah. Trips start at $90 for a half-day, costing around $800 to $950 per person for a four-day sup-ported trek, including rental of sparkling Santa Cruz full-suspension 29ers. Day trips depart at 7am; reserve ahead.

Moab Cyclery   MOUNTAIN BIKING
(☑435-259-7423, 800-451-1133; www.moabcyc lery.com; 391 S Main St) Good half-, full-, multi-day and multisport tours. Rental and sales; biker shuttles available.

Chile Pepper Bike Shop   MOUNTAIN BIKING
(☑435-259-4688, 888-677-4688; www.chilebikes. com; 720 S Main St) This shop rents bikes for $48 to $68 per day; checking bikes out at 4:30pm with returns the next day at 1pm means you could potentially get two rides in. It also repairs bikes, dishes out local trail information and has plenty of maps.

Western Spirit Cycling Adventures   TOUR
(☑435-259-8732, 800-845-2453; www.western spirit.com; 478 Mill Creek Dr) Canyonlands White Rim, Utah and nationwide multiday tours.

Day Hikes
In the BLM and national forest land surrounding Moab, there are remarkable hikes, with a fraction of the visitors of the big walks in the national parks. Carry plenty of water, stick to trails, and wear insect repellent between spring and early summer to repel aggressive gnats.

Corona Arch Trail   HIKING
To take in petroglyphs and two spectacular, rarely visited rock arches, hike the moderately easy Corona Arch Trail, the trailhead for which lies 6 miles up Potash Rd (Hwy 279). Follow cairns along the slickrock to Bowtie and Corona Arches. You may recognize Corona from a well-known photograph in which an airplane is flying through it – this is one big arch! The 3-mile walk takes two hours.

Fisher Towers Trail   HIKING
The Fisher Towers Trail takes you past these towering sandstone monoliths, the tallest of which rises 900ft. The west-facing monoliths get quite hot in the afternoon, so wait for sunset, when rays bathe the rock in color and cast long shadows. (Bring a flashlight; many lingering hikers have ended up stuck on the trail in the dark.) The moderate–difficult 2.2-mile (one-way) trail lies off Hwy 128, 21 miles northeast of Moab; follow signs.

La Sal Mountains   HIKING
(www.fs.usda.gov; La Sal Mountain Loop) To escape summer's heat, head up Hwy 128 to the Manti–La Sal National Forest lands, in the mountains east of Moab, and hike through white-barked aspens and ponderosa pines.

MOAB ACTIVITIES

Moonflower Canyon   HIKING

If you're short on time, take the easy 1-mile round-trip hike along Moonflower Canyon, a shaded stroll on mostly level ground that ends at a sandstone bowl beneath hanging gardens. A perennial stream makes this hike a cooler, less dusty alternative. The trailhead lies 1.2 miles from town along Kane Creek Rd. Look for petroglyphs at the parking area.

Negro Bill Canyon Trail   HIKING

(Hwy 128, trailhead 3 miles north of Moab) The moderately easy trail includes a 2.5-mile walk along a stream. (The politically incor-

Moab

Portal RV Resort (1mi); Moab Rafting & Canoe Co (0.9mi);
Slickrock Campground (1mi); Canyonlands by Night (1.6mi);
Arches National Park (5mi); Red Cliffs Lodge (16.3mi);
Sorrel River Ranch (19mi); Castle Valley Inn (19.6mi); Archview Resort

Moab Information Center

Canyonlands Natural History Association

Moab Regional Hospital (160yd)

Swanny City Park

See enlargement

bike path

Adobe Abode (0.3mi);
Matheson Wetlands Preserve (0.3mi);
BLM Kane Creek Campgrounds (1.1mi);
Moonflower Canyon (1.2mi)

Grand Ave

bike path

Sand Flats Recreation Area (2.4mi);
Slickrock Bike Trail (2.4mi)

BLM Office

Pack Creek

Bittle Ln

Canyonlands Field Institute (0.1mi); ACT Campground (0.7mi); Sheri Griffith Expeditions (1.4mi);
O.A.R.S (1.7mi); Canyonlands NPS Headquarters (2mi); Karen's Canine Campground (2mi);
Hole 'n the Rock (12mi); Pack Creek Ranch (12.7mi); Canyon Rims Recreation Area (30mi);
Needles District, Canyonlands National Park (70mi)

MOAB ACTIVITIES

rect canyon name refers to a prospector who grazed his cows here in the 1800s.) Scoot down a shaded side canyon to find petroglyphs, then continue to the 243ft-wide **Morning Glory Natural Bridge**, at a box canyon. Plan on three to four hours.

Matheson Wetlands Preserve BIRD-WATCHING
(☑435-259-4629; www.nature.org; 934 W Kane Creek Blvd; ☺dawn-dusk) **FREE** The Nature Conservancy oversees the 890-acre preserve just west of town. You can spot over 200 species of bird in this wetlands area. Also chances of seeing beaver, muskrat and river otter.

Canyonlands Field Institute TOUR
(☑435-259-7750; www.cfimoab.org; 1320 S Hwy 191; ☺May-Oct) This nonprofit operation uses proceeds from guided tours to create youth outdoor-education programs and train local guides. It offers occasional workshops and seminars throughout the summer. Top tours include the Rock Art Tour ($80, 8am Friday to Sunday), the geology-focused Arches Sunset Tour ($80, 4pm Friday to Sunday) and customized river trips.

Overnight Hikes

For backpacking hikes, Canyonlands National Park is your best bet. Or consider the Canyon Rims Recreation Area, where backpacking trails crisscross the Dark Canyon Primitive Area.

Hidden Valley Trail HIKING
For a moderate–difficult rim hike above Moab, try this trail, which meanders through a pristine hanging valley in the Behind the Rocks Wilderness Study Area. The trailhead is on BLM land at the end of Angel Rock Rd. Plan on taking four to six hours. Following a series of switchbacks, you'll emerge on the level grassy valley for a mellow 2-mile walk. Expect shade in late afternoon.

Driving

People come from around the world to drive in Utah, using Moab as their hub. From paved desert highways for retirees in RVs

---

Moab

◉ **Sights**
- 1 Museum of Moab C3

➕ **Activities, Courses & Tours**
- 2 Adrift Adventures B2
- 3 Canyon Voyages Adventure Co B2
- 4 Chile Pepper Bike Shop B5
- 5 Cliffhanger Jeep Rental C2
- 6 Desert Highlights D2
- 7 Gear Heads Outdoor Store B4
- 8 Moab Adventure Center B4
- 9 Moab Cyclery B4
- 10 Moab Desert Adventures B2
- 11 Moab Rafting & Canoe Co B4
- 12 Navtec Expeditions B2
- 13 Poison Spider Bicycles B2
- 14 Rim Cyclery B3
- 15 Rim Tours D6
- 16 Tag-A-Long Expeditions B2
- 17 Western Spirit Cycling
     Adventures D4

🛏 **Sleeping**
- 18 3 Dogs and a Moose B3
- 19 Adventure Inn B2
- 20 Best Western Canyonlands Inn C2
- 21 Big Horn Lodge B4
- 22 Cali Cochitta C3
- 23 Canyonlands Campground B5
- 24 Gonzo Inn B3
- 25 Inca Inn B1
- 26 Kokopelli Lodge B3
- 27 Lazy Lizard Hostel D6
- 28 Moab Valley Inn C5
- 29 Redstone Inn B4
- 30 Sunflower Hill Inn C2
- 31 Up the Creek Campground B4

🍴 **Eating**
- 32 City Market & Pharmacy B4
- 33 Crystal's Cakes and Cones C1
- 34 Desert Bistro B3
- 35 Eddie McStiff's D2
- 36 EklectiCafé B2
- 37 Jailhouse Café B3
- 38 Jeffrey's Steakhouse B2
- 39 Love Muffin B3
- 40 Milt's C4
- 41 Moab Brewery B5
- 42 Moab Farmers Market B2
- 43 Moonflower Market B3
- 44 Pantele's Deli D2
- 45 Pasta Jay's C2
- 46 Sabaku Sushi D2
- 47 Singha Thai D2
- 48 The Spoke on Center C1

🍷 **Drinking & Nightlife**
- 49 Dave's Corner Market C4
     Ghost Bar .... (see 38)
- 50 Woody's Tavern B3

🎭 **Entertainment**
- 51 Moab Arts & Recreation Center B3
- 52 Slickrock Cinemas 3 .... B5

🛍 **Shopping**
- 53 Back of Beyond Books B3

MOAB ACTIVITIES

to vertical slickrock trails for four-wheeling adrenaline junkies, you'll find scenic drives for every taste.

Colorado River Scenic Byway (Hwy 128)
DRIVING TOUR

This curvy 31-mile drive follows the winding Colorado River through gorgeous red-rock country of mesas, rock walls, alfalfa fields and sagebrush. Extend the trip with the La Sal Mountain Loop Rd.

Drive north on Main St/Hwy 191 and turn right (east) onto Hwy 128. The road winds through red-rock canyons along the Colorado River's serpentine course, which is why it is known in the area as 'the river road.' Arches National Park lies on the north side of the river for the first 15 miles.

Six miles from Hwy 191 you'll reach Big Bend Recreation Site, where you can picnic by the river; climbers will enjoy the low-key bouldering here.

Eleven miles further on, you'll pass the La Sal Mountain Loop Rd turnoff and Castleton Tower, a narrow 400ft spire that rises above Castle Valley, and is one of the area's most iconic rock climbs. Across from Castleton,

WORTH A TRIP

DETOUR TO MONUMENT VALLEY

From Moab, skirt south on Hwy 191 for stellar desert scenery. Two hours, or 100 miles, south of Moab, the pinprick-sized **Bluff** (www.bluff-utah.org), a historic town surrounded by red rock, makes a good base. From here, motor the rugged hairpin turns of the **Moki Dugway** (30 miles) or visit **Natural Bridges National Monument** (www.nps.gov/nabr; Hwy 275; 7-day pass per vehicle $6, tent & RV sites $10; ⊙ 24hr, visitor center 8am-6pm May-Sep, 9am-5pm Oct-Apr), a white-sandstone canyon with a scenic, paved 9-mile loop perfect for pedaling. But nature's grand slam is **Monument Valley Navajo Tribal Park** (☑ 435-727-5874; www.navajonationparks.org; per 4-person vehicle $20; ⊙ drive 6am-8:30pm May-Sep, 8am-4:30pm Oct-Apr, visitor center 6am-8pm May-Sep, 8am-5pm Oct-Apr), where a 17-mile unpaved driving loop circles reddish mesa formations that sprout like earthen giants. A favorite for Hollywood shots, it's in the Navajo Indian Reservation, 47 miles south of Bluff. Camping is $10 per site.

the Nuns and Priests Pinnacles shoot up in a graceful line.

At mile marker 21, the Fisher Towers rise almost as high as the Eiffel Tower (at 900ft, Titan is the tallest).

Ten miles ahead, you'll reach the Dewey Bridge site. Built in 1916, it was among the first spans across the Colorado. The bridge was destroyed by accidental fire in 2008 and its future is currently in limbo due to the high cost of reconstruction. Park near the site to watch rafters running downriver.

When ready, return to Moab or double back to the La Sal Mountain Loop Rd. I-70 lies 13 miles north.

La Sal Mountain Loop Road
DRIVING TOUR

This 67-mile route through Manti-La Sal National Forest runs from the scorching desert into cool green woodlands. Though paved, it's narrow and lacks any guardrails.

When the desert gets too hot to handle, take this route through Manti–La Sal National Forest and let it whisk you to where you can camp, cycle, hike or sit by a stream and listen as wind ruffles the aspens. Snow closes the road between November and March. Allow three to four hours off-season.

About 15 miles northeast of Moab, off Hwy 128, the La Sal Mountain Loop Rd (aka Castle Valley Rd) climbs southeast into the national forest, up switchbacks (a problem for large RVs) into the forest. Four miles from the turnoff, look to your left for the spires known as the Priest and Nuns, as well as Castle Rock. The route winds past junipers and piñon pines, followed by scrub oaks and, finally, alpine slopes of majestic pines, firs and white-barked quaking aspens, the leaves of which turn a brilliant yellow-gold in autumn. Here, high above canyon country, you'll gain a fresh perspective on the vastness of the Colorado Plateau.

At the crest, you can turn left on a dirt spur road and climb 5 miles further to the picnic area and developed campground at Warner Lake. For information on hiking and camping, check with national forest rangers. From the Warner Lake spur junction, the loop road descends to Hwy 191, 8 miles south of Moab.

Potash Road
DRIVING TOUR

This 15-mile scenic desert drive passes mining remnants on the way into dry country with rock walls and solitude. Petroglyphs, dinosaur tracks and arches are highlights.

Three miles north of Moab, off Hwy 191, the paved Potash Rd (Hwy 279) skirts south along the Colorado River. It's named for a potash extraction plant at road's end. Just past the turnoff you'll pass a radioactive tailings pond from Moab's uranium-mining days, while midroute, stunning natural beauty abounds. Such are the region's contradictions.

Highlights include Wall Street (for rock climbers), Native American petroglyph panels (look for signs), dinosaur tracks (bring binoculars for a better look), a 1.5-mile hiking trail to Corona Arch, and Jug Handle Arch, 3ft wide but 45ft high. Also find the Potash Dock put-in for float trips down the Colorado River. Past the potash plant, the road continues as a rough 4WD track into Canyonlands' Island in the Sky district, linking with Shafer Trail Rd.

Hurrah Pass   DRIVING TOUR
The 33-mile Hurrah Pass offers jaw-dropping vistas of the Colorado River, Dead Horse Point and Grand View Point. Drivers can continue on but the road gets rougher and is best for 4WD vehicles; 4WD is mandatory beyond the pass.

This route starts out west along paved Kane Creek Rd, off Hwy 191 in Moab, soon passing petroglyph sites and a rock climbing area. The pavement yields to gravel as you enter Kane Springs Canyon. About 10 miles in you must ford the creek, which, depending on the weather, may be impassable; 4WD is recommended.

After 15 miles you'll reach 4470ft Hurrah Pass. The stupendous scenery includes views up to Dead Horse and Grand View Points. South of the pass the road descends toward the Colorado River, with views of the potash plant on the opposite bank (look for the fields of blue). Explore the desert, and when ready, double back to Moab or continue south on Lockhart Basin Rd toward Canyonlands' Needles district.

From Lockhart Basin Rd the road is much more difficult (4WD is mandatory) and often confusing, eventually emerging about 50 miles south on Hwy 211, just east of the Needles. Contact the BLM for maps and information if you want to do the whole route.

Canyon Rims   DRIVING TOUR
A lovely out-of-the-way 54-mile drive to the Needles and Anticline Overlooks, with great views of the Needles and Hurrah Pass, this route is accessible by cars and buses.

The BLM-administered Canyon Rims Recreation Area lies south of Moab, west of Hwy 191 and east of Canyonlands National Park. If you've already visited the area's other major overlooks (eg Dead Horse and Grand View Points) and have time, this byway makes a good day trip. It's also a fine detour on the way to or from the Needles. Don't fret if you miss it, however. The area is especially popular with hikers, campers and all-terrain-vehicle (ATV) enthusiasts. For more information, contact the BLM or stop by the Moab Information Center.

Turn west off Hwy 191, 32 miles south of Moab. The paved road leads 22 miles west to the Needles Overlook, a great panorama of the national park. About two-thirds of the way to the overlook take the spur, where a gravel road stretches 16 miles north to the Anticline Overlook, a promontory with awesome views of the Colorado River, Meander Canyon and Hurrah Pass Rd below.

River Running
More than a dozen outfitters run a variety of float trips on the Colorado and Green Rivers. Though permits limit the number of people on the water, favorite takeout beaches can get pretty crowded, and for good reason: this is fun – *really* fun! Whatever your

MOAB ACTIVITIES

ℹ CHOOSING A BOAT & RIVER

Outfitters ply the rivers in a variety of boats. Resembling a rowboat, an **oar rig** is a rubber raft that a guide rows downriver. Also made of rubber, a **paddle boat** is steered by a guide and paddled by passengers. Not technically a raft, a **motor rig** is a large boat driven by a guide (**jet boats** fall into this category). While this is the quickest way downriver, speed isn't so conducive to slowly soaking up desert landscapes. You can also float in a **kayak, inflatable kayak, paddleboard** or **canoe**.

Rapids are rated on a scale from one (I) to six (VI), with Class I being still water and Class VI an unnavigable waterfall. Class II rapids are good for novices and families with little kids. Class III are thrilling, while Class IV are borderline scary, depending on your perspective. Class V rapids are technical and dangerous.

Top white-water runs include Cataract Canyon and Westwater. Labyrinth Canyon, Meander Canyon and the Colorado River from Dewey Bridge to Takeout Beach are top flat-water paddles.

interest – be it bashing through rapids or studying canyon geology – rafting, kayaking, canoeing or paddleboarding may well prove the highlight of your vacation.

Rafting season runs April to September; jet-boating season lasts longer. Water levels usually crest in May and June. Most flat-water rafting day trips cost $55 to $79, while longer full-day trips cost around $160 for Westwater and $375 for Cataract Canyon. Two- to five-day excursions run from about $350 to more than $800 per person. Jet-boat trips cost about $89. Paddleboard trips start at around $75. Discounts often apply to children accompanying parents. Many companies combine rafting trips with hiking, canyoneering, 4WD or mountain-biking trips.

Do-it-yourselfers can rent canoes, inflatable kayaks or rafts. Rates run $40 a day for canoes and kayaks, and $95 to $200 a day for rafts, depending on size (all come with life jackets and paddles). Advance permits are required for trips within the national parks and certain areas outside them.

While guided half- and full-day trips are often available on short notice, you should book overnight trips well ahead.

Pick up Belknap's indispensable water-proofed *Canyonlands River Guide*.

RAFTING TOURS

Outfitters on guided tours take care of everything, from permits to food to setting up camp and shuttling you back to town.

Canyon Voyages Adventure Co   ADVENTURE SPORTS
(☑800-733-6007; www.canyonvoyages.com; 211 N Main St) In addition to half- to five-day mild white-water and kayaking trips, Canyon or-ganizes multisport excursions that include options like hiking, biking, paddleboarding and canyoneering. Kayak, canoe and outdoor equipment rental available.

Navtec Expeditions   ADVENTURE SPORTS
(☑435-259-7983; www.navtec.com; 321 N Main St) Comprehensive rafting excursions, including Cataract Canyon, combo hiking and 4WD trips.

O.A.R.S   TOUR
(☑435-259-5919, 800-346-6277; www.oars.com; 2540 S Hwy 191) Has a permit for Canyonlands National Park and guides single- or multiday combination hiking and rafting tours.

Sheri Griffith Expeditions   RAFTING
(☑800-332-2439; www.griffithexp.com; 2231 S Hwy 191) Operating since 1971, this rafting specialist has a great selection of river trips on the Colorado, Green and San Juan Rivers – from family floats to Cataract Canyon rapids, and from a couple of hours to a couple of weeks.

Adrift Adventures   ADVENTURE TOURS
(☑435-259-8594, 800-874-4483; www.adrift.net; 378 N Main St) Rafting, jet-boat rides, sportboat rides, 4WD land excursions and multisport packages, plus Arches National Park bus tours.

Tag-A-Long Expeditions   ADVENTURE SPORTS
(☑800-453-3292; www.tagalong.com; 452 N Main St) This rafting outfitter offers a little of everything: flat-water jet-boat rides, white-water rafting, land safaris, horseback riding, scenic flights, skydiving and more. Ask about jet-boat-return support for Cataract Canyon trips.

THE SCOURGE OF THE COLORADO

As you float down the Colorado, notice the dense stands of wispy-looking trees. Tamarisk, also called salt cedar, is an ornamental tree imported to the US in the 19th century and later planted along the river for erosion control. It has since taken over the banks of the Colorado and is choking the waterway.

A single large tamarisk transpires 300 gallons of water *a day*. Some estimates place the species' combined water consumption as high as one-third of the river's overall flow. If that water were returned to the river, the Colorado might again reach the sea. They also increase alkaline levels in water, making it harder for other native species to survive.

The good news? In Death Valley, California, land managers have almost entirely eradicated tamarisk stands, and once-threatened wetlands are rebounding. As you cross the bridge into Moab, and elsewhere along the Colorado, look for charred tree stumps and scorched riverbanks – evidence of the local eradication effort by fire (and herbicides). Biologists are now introducing beetles to eat the tamarisks, a risky move that could reduce tamarisk stands by 70% to 80%. To learn more, visit Living Rivers at Restoration Creamery.

Moab Rafting & Canoe Co KAYAKING
(☑ 435-259-7722; www.moab-rafting.com; 420 Kane Creek Blvd) Small company with guided and self-guided canoe and raft trips.

RAFTING WITHOUT A GUIDE

Good outfitters provide complete information to help you plan a self-guided trip. Reserve equipment, secure permits and book shuttles far in advance. Without a permit, you'll be restricted to several mellow stretches of the Colorado and Green Rivers, but if you want to run Class III and IV rapids in Westwater Canyon or enter Canyonlands on either river, you'll need a permit.

Permits may be solicited a year in advance. Check the river permits link on www.discovermoab.com, or contact the **BLM** (Bureau of Land Management; ☑ 435-259-2100; www.blm.gov/utah/moab; ⊙ 7:45am-4:30pm Mon-Fri) or the NPS (p184) directly. Backcountry permits are issued at the appropriate visitor center. Strict rules govern sanitation and fires, depending on where you raft; confirm regulations with the appropriate agency.

To rent a raft, canoe or kayak, contact Canyon Voyages. For canoe rentals, call Moab Rafting & Canoe Co. For shuttles to or from the rivers, call Roadrunner Shuttle (p222). To get back from the Confluence, you must book a jet-boat shuttle in advance; try Tag-A-Long Expeditions.

Colorado River Northeast of Moab Boating the 36 miles of river northeast of Moab from Westwater Canyon to Takeout Beach takes two to five days. This section is divided into three distinct stretches. All fall within the jurisdiction of the BLM. Take Hwy 128 from Moab, which roughly parallels the river, making put-in and takeout a breeze.

If you're seeking serious white water, **Westwater Canyon** is the place. The first canyon along the Colorado in Utah, Westwater boasts Class III and IV rapids through the oldest exposed layer of rock on the planet. Most people make the 17-mile trip in one long day (10 hours) from Moab, though some choose to camp and make it a two-day trip. Most outfitters offer both options. A BLM permit is required.

Like mellow water and just want to float along? **Dewey Bridge to Hittle Bottom** is a 7-mile section of flat water with great scenery and wildlife-watching. One stretch passes through a bird sanctuary. No permit required.

Also known as Fisher Towers, or simply as the Daily, **Hittle Bottom to Takeout Beach** is the most popular stretch of river near Moab, perfect for novices who aren't ready for Westwater. Families can safely bring small children without boring their teens. The Daily offers mostly Class I and II rapids, with one short section of Class III known as White's Rapid (Class IV at high water, when it's not recommended for kids). Camp at riverside BLM campgrounds. No permit is required.

Colorado River Southwest Moab (Meander Canyon) This 48-mile section takes three to five days, starting at Potash Dock and ending at Spanish Bottom. The flat-water trip from Potash Dock to the Confluence (where the Green and Colorado Rivers meet) moves slowly on the wide river. It's a scenic trip, good for mellow souls or novice boaters. You can put in at Moab Dock to lengthen the trip by 15 miles, but since it parallels the highway this section is usually skipped.

A mile and a half north of the Confluence, you'll reach the **Slide**, a moderate rapid that you can portage. In the 4-mile stretch from the Confluence to Spanish Bottom, eddies and whirlpools kick in as you approach Cataract Canyon (*do not* miss the takeout). An NPS permit is required to enter Canyonlands. (For a half-day flat-water paddle, put in at Moab and take out at Gold Bar; for a full day, take out at Potash.)

Cataract Canyon The Class V rapids of Cataract Canyon are legendary. Twenty-six rapids churn and roil over this 14-mile stretch where the Colorado squeezes through narrow canyons. Trips down the Cat are extremely technical and dangerous; there's no room for error. Though a jet boat can do it in a day, it is well worth taking your time, camping on beautiful beaches and finding harmony with the natural pace of the river.

This 112-mile trip takes from three days to a week, starting at Moab and ending in Hite. The intensity of the rapids fluctuates hugely, depending on snowmelt and drought. Many fail to realize that you have to float on flat water quite a ways to reach the canyon (rafts put in at Potash or Mineral Bottom), and once through the rapids, you'll wind up on flat Lake Powell – though you'll be so high on adrenaline, you probably won't even notice. Peak flow runs mid-May to mid-June. An NPS permit is required; reserve through the NPS.

Green River (Labyrinth & Stillwater Canyons) 'Discovered' by John Wesley Powell during his famed expeditions, this flat-water stretch down the Green is ideal for canoes. You'll pass rock art along the scenic route. Start at Green River State Park and end at Mineral Bottom (68 miles) or Spanish Bottom (124 miles); the trip takes between three and nine days.

Take out at the Confluence or use extreme caution en route to Spanish Bottom, lest you get sucked into Cataract Canyon. An NPS permit is required south of Mineral Bottom.

Four-Wheel Driving

Four-wheelers should always be sensitive to the fragile desert environment and respect other users on the trail by passing at reasonable speeds.

For experienced drivers only, the best-known 4WD road in Moab is Hell's Revenge. In the BLM-administered Sand Flats Recreation Area east of town, it follows an 8.2-mile route up and down shockingly steep slickrock. Also for experts, the shared-use Moab Rim Trail loops high on the rim rock southwest of town.

Avoid unsigned roads in BLM Wilderness Study Areas, and never drive off-road, which could irreparably damage fragile cryptobiotic soil. The consequences are evident all around the area, where tire tracks and grazing cows have trampled the cryptobiotic soil. Without this living crust, the desert sands blow free. Without protection, what only seems barren now could turn into a veritable wasteland.

For more details about routes, pick up a pamphlet from the Moab Information Center, ask a tour operator or inquire at a 4WD rental agency. Also consider *Moab Utah Backroads & 4WD Trails* by Charles Wells.

ATVs, Jeep and Razors are popular for off-road expeditions, and are rented out by many local agencies.

If you rent a 4WD vehicle, *read the insurance policy* – it may not cover damage from off-road driving and will likely carry a $2500 deductible. Check when you book. Whenever possible, rent a relatively new vehicle.

The week before Easter the annual Jeep Safari takes place.

Cliffhanger Jeep Rental   DRIVING TOUR
(☑435-259-0889; www.cliffhangerjeeprental.com; 40 W Center St) TeraFlex suspension Jeeps ($195), Rhino two-seaters and four-wheelers ($129 to $169) for rent.

Dan Mick's Jeep Tours   DRIVING TOUR
(☑435-259-4567; www.danmick.com) Private Jeep tours and guided drive-your-own-4WD trips with good ol' boy Dan Mick. A highly regarded local operation.

Moab Adventure Center   ADVENTURE SPORTS
(☑435-259-7019, 866-904-1163; www.moabadventurecenter.com; 225 S Main St) The open-air, canopy-topped land safaris offered here are popular. This megacenter also arranges, alone or in combination, rafting trips, Jeep rental, horseback riding, rock climbing, guided hikes, scenic flights and even Arches National Park bus tours.

Horseback Riding

Rates for horseback riding generally range from $80 for a three-hour ride to $100 for a four-hour outback ride. Kids must be eight years old or older.

Red Cliffs Lodge   HORSEBACK RIDING
(☑435-259-2002, 866-812-2002; www.redcliffslodge.com; Mile 14, Hwy 128; half day $79-99) In Castle Valley, 14 miles north of town, Red Cliffs Lodge provides horseback trail rides (March to November), offered mornings and evenings. If you book a multisport rafting trip that includes horseback riding, you'll still be coming here.

Rock Climbing & Canyoneering

Moab offers solid rock climbing. West of town, off Potash Rd, Wall Street gets crowded on weekends and is an excellent spot to meet other climbers. It's about the only sport-climbing area nearby. Traditional climbers should check out BLM-administered Indian Creek, off Hwy 211 on the way to Canyonlands' Needles district, for the best crack climbing. Castle Valley serves up a number of classic desert towers on the solid Wingate Sandstone layer. Canyoneering expeditions offer chances to rappel into slickrock canyons and hike through cascading water. For a guidebook to climbs, we recommend Fred Knapp's *Classic Desert Climbs*.

★**Moab Desert Adventures**   ROCK CLIMBING
(☑804-814-3872; www.moabdesertadventures.com; 415 N Main St; half/full day from $165/265) Top-notch climbing tours scale area towers and walls; the 140ft arch rappel is especially exciting. Canyoneering trips also available ($165).

Desert Highlights   ADVENTURE SPORTS
(☑800-747-1342, 435-259-4433; www.deserthighlights.com; 50 E Center St; 5hr canyoneering from $95) Canyoneering and combo raft trips here are big on personal attention. Offers trips to some worthy, little-known destinations.

Gear Heads
Outdoor Store   OUTDOOR EQUIPMENT
(☑888-740-4327, 435-259-4327; www.moabgear.com; 471 S Main St) Stock up on all the outdoor gear you need, including climbing ropes,

route guides, books and water-jug refills. The knowledgeable staff are quite helpful.

Skydiving & Air Tours

Redtail Aviation   SCENIC FLIGHTS
(☑435-259-7421; www.redtailaviation.com; 30min $123) Fly high above Arches, Canyonlands, Lake Powell, San Rafael Swell, Monument Valley and more.

Skydive Moab   ADVENTURE SPORTS
(☑435-259-5867; www.skydivemoab.com; tandem 1st jump $225) Skydiving and base-jumping.

Winter Activities

From December through February, there's snowfall in the desert parks. Trails may be icy and route finding becomes more difficult. Manti–La Sal National Forest receives tons of light, dry Utah powder, perfect for cross-country skiing, but bad for avalanches. For current information on weather and road conditions and the avalanche risk, call ☑435-259-7669 or visit www.avalanche.org.

The La Sals provide a hut-to-hut ski system, which you can access via snowmobile. To reserve a self-guided trip and book the huts, contact Tag-A-Long Expeditions (p212). **Rim Cyclery** (☑435-259-5333; www. rimcyclery.com; 94 W 100 N) rents ski equipment, while Gear Heads rents snowshoes and stocks gear.

🎆 Festivals & Events

Moab loves a party and throws a pretty good one. For calendars, contact the Moab Area Travel Council (www.discovermoab.com).

Skinny Tire Festival   SPORTS
(www.skinnytirefestival.com) Road cycling festival; first weekend in March.

Jeep Safari   SPORTS
(www.rr4w.com) The week before Easter, about 2000 Jeeps (and thousands more people) overrun the town in the year's biggest event. Register early; trails are assigned.

Moonshadows in Moab   SPORTS
(☑435-259-2698; www.moonshadowsinmoab. com) Biking by July moonlight.

Moab Music Festival   MUSIC
(☑435-259-7003;   www.moabmusicfest.org) World-class classical musicians converge on the landscape of the Utah Canyonlands region in September.

Moab Folk Festival   MUSIC
(www.moabfolkfestival.com) 🍃 Folk music and environmental consciousness combine. This festival is 100% wind-powered, venues are easily walkable and recycling is encouraged.

🛌 Sleeping

For a small town, Moab offers a lot of lodgings. Unfortunately they fill up fast during busy holiday weekends and in high season. Book well ahead. Listed rates are generally for double occupancy; high season is from March through October. Keep in mind that some places close in winter.

Cyclists should ask whether a property provides secure bike storage (ie only one person holds the key – 'bike storage' isn't the same thing). Most lodgings provide coffeemakers, many include refrigerators and some have microwaves; ask when you book.

Vacation condo and home rentals are big here. Check out aggregators to save big on condos mostly located south of town. Many include pools, kitchens and living rooms. **Moab Utah Lodging** (www.moabutahlodging. com) and **Moab Condo Rentals** (www.moab condorentals.com) are good local sources for vacation rentals.

Camping

Make reservations when possible. On busy holiday weekends all of the campgrounds around Moab are full. For more information and options, visit the Moab Information Center or check online links at www.moab -utah.com and www.discovermoab.com.

BLM Hwy 128 Campgrounds   CAMPGROUND $
(☑435-259-2100; www.blm.gov/utah/moab; Hwy 128; tent sites $15; ⊙year-round) The best place to stay to beat the heat (other than in the La Sals) is along the Colorado River on Hwy 128. Vegetation and the canyon walls provide shade at these 12 BLM campgrounds along a 28-mile stretch of the river. Each includes fire rings and vault toilets but not water. Only group reservations are accepted.

ACT Campground   CAMPGROUND $
(☑435-355-0355; www.actcampground.com; 1536 S Mill Creek Dr; tent site $25, RV $39-44, r $49-59; ⊙year-round; 🅿❄🛜🐕) 🍃 Check out the first commercial straw-bail building in

---

DOG LODGINGS
....

Moab's best kennel is **Karen's Canine Campground** (☑435-259-7922; 2781 Roberts Dr), where Fido is another one of mom's brood. It has a kiddie pool, shade canopies and a play area. Call ahead.

the state of Utah at this roadside RV park, campground and learning center, all in one. There's a very cool community kitchen and learning center, where the owners hope to put on presentations on desert ecology and biology. We only wish it were a little further from the road.

The 21 RV sites include electricity, water, sewer and cable TV, while the nine rooms share exquisite new bathrooms (bring your own linens). There are 19 tent sites that edge a treed drainage, plus a patio area and grill.

Up the Creek Campground　CAMPGROUND $
(☑435-260-1888; www.moabupthecreek.com; 210 E 300 South; tent sites 1/2 people $25/32; ☺Mar-Oct) There's something about this shady, tent-only grove with flower beds, lush lawns and recycling that fosters a sense of community. The 20 sites are within walking distance of downtown. Showers are included, but are also available to nonguests for $6; no fires.

Archview Resort & Campground　CAMPGROUND $
(☑435-259-7854, 800-813-6622; www.moab-utah. com/archview/archview.html; Hwy 191; tent site $27, RV site from $43; ☺ Mar-Nov; 🛜) Near the Hwy 191/313 junction, Archview includes a pool, gas station and grocery store. Be forewarned: it's completely exposed and bakes in summer.

Canyonlands Campground　CAMPGROUND $
(☑435-259-6848; www.canyonlandsrv.com; 555 S Main St; tent sites $27-34, RV sites with hookups $40-47, camping cabins $65; ☺year-round; ▩🛜▩) Old-growth tree-shaded sites, right in town but still quiet. Includes showers, laundry, store,

---

MOAB SLEEPING

BOOKS, MAPS & GEAR

Moab is the best spot in the region to replenish gear and grab maps or a regional read. For camping items hit **Gear Heads** (p214).

Locally owned **Back of Beyond Books** (www.backofbeyondbooks.com; 83 N Main St; ☺9am-6pm; 🛜) carries a comprehensive selection of regional guides, histories, political nonfiction, news and magazines. Staff show regional expertise and are happy to help.

Canyon Voyages (p212) rents camping and backpacking gear, while **Tag-A-Long Expeditions** (p212) rents tents and sleeping bags. Otherwise, many tour outfitters will rent gear only to their trip participants.

---

small pool and playground. Rates are slightly higher for events and holidays.

Slickrock Campground　CAMPGROUND $
(☑800-448-8873, 435-259-7660; www.slickrock campground.com; 1301½ N Hwy 191; tent sites $26-34, RV sites with hookups $38-42, cabins $59; ☺Mar-Nov; ▩🛜▩▩) North of town. Tent sites have canopies; RV sites have 30-amp hookups only. Nonguest showers $3; also has hot tubs, heated pool and a store.

Portal RV Resort　CAMPGROUND $
(☑435-259-6108; www.portalrvresort.com; 1261 N Hwy 191; tent sites $24, RV sites with hookups $36-42; ☺year-round; 🛜▩) The best place for luxury RVers, with long pull-throughs. Has showers, spa, laundry, store and dog run.

Sand Flats Recreation Area　CAMPGROUND $
(www.blm.gov/ut/st/en/fo/moab/recreation/camp grounds/sand_flats_recreation.html; Sand Flats Rd; tent & RV sites $15; ☺yaer-round) At the Slickrock Bike trailhead, this mountain-biker special has 120 nonreservable sites, fire rings and pit toilets, but no water and no hookups.

BLM Kane Creek Campgrounds　CAMPGROUND $
(www.blm.gov/ut/st/en/fo/moab/recreation/camp grounds.html; Kane Creek Rd; tent sites $15) Just west of Moab, five first-come, first-served campgrounds, with 105 sites total, are found along Kane Creek. Sites have vault toilets and fire rings.

Warner Lake Campground　CAMPGROUND $
(☑435-587-2041, 888-444-6777; www.reserveam erica.com/camping/warner-lake; off La Sal Mountain Loop Rd; tent sites $10; ☺Apr-Oct) When it's 100°F (38°C) in Moab, the La Sals may be a balmy 75°F (24°C) by day and downright chilly at night. Warner Lake Campground sits up high at 9400ft and is one of several developed campgrounds that provides water.

Horsethief Campground　CAMPGROUND $
(☑435-259-2100; www.blm.gov/utah/moab; Hwy 313, Mile 11; tent sites $15) If you are headed to Dead Horse Point or Island in the Sky, this attractive campground is a great option, and cooler than lower-elevation spots. There are 55 sites with picnic tables, vault toilets and grills. Bring water. It's first-come, first-served. RVs are OK. Just up the road, **Cowboy Camp**, has seven walk in tent sites (Mile 18).

Canyon Rims Recreation Area　CAMPGROUND $
(☑435-259-2100; www.blm.gov/utah/moab; Hwy 191; day/week pass per car $5/10, tent sites $15) This oft-overlooked recreation area lies 30 miles south of town, just west of Hwy 191.

It's remote but well toward the Needles. Two developed campgrounds have well-spaced sites in desert vegetation.

Moab Under Canvas CAMPGROUND $$$
(☎801-895-3213; www.moabundercanvas.com; Hwy 191, Mile 138; teepee $79-89, tent $175-350, site tent $400-450; ☺Mar-Oct) This new 'glamping' option gives you rustic canvas tents with some laudable creature comforts - the pimped-out suites even have flush toilets and sitting areas – just like a Victorian explorer (kinda). There's a community bonfire at night and you have excellent views onto Arches from the 40-acre compound. All in all, it's still got a ways to go. It's too close to the road and the appointments and service do not deserve this sky-high pricepoint.

Lodging

Kokopelli Lodge MOTEL $
(☎435-259-7615; www.kokopellilodge.com; 72 S 100 East; r $79-149; ❀⚡☎) Retro styling meets with desert chic at this great-value budget motel. Amenities include a hot tub, barbecue grill and secure bike storage.

Lazy Lizard Hostel HOSTEL $
(☎435-259-6057; www.lazylizardhostel.com; 1213 S Hwy 191; dm/s/d $11/30/34, cabins $35-41; ℗❀@⚡) This hippie hangout is popular with European travelers and the non-car set. Located behind A-1 storage, it has frayed couches, worn bunks, a small kitchen and a peaced-out patio. The little cabins out back are the way to go.

Adventure Inn MOTEL $
(☎435-259-6122; www.adventureinnmoab.com; 512 N Main St; r $69-105; ☺Mar-Oct; ❀⚡) Go for the economy rooms at this great little indie motel, which sports spotless rooms (some with refrigerators) and decent linens, as well as laundry facilities. There's a picnic area on site and the owners prove helpful.

Inca Inn MOTEL $
(☎435-259-7261; www.incainn.com; 570 N Main St; r $100; ☺Feb-Nov; ❀⚡☎) This small mom-and-pop motel has old and slightly dark rooms with small double beds that are plenty clean. There's a teeny-tiny pool out front.

★Sunflower Hill Inn INN $$
(☎435-259-2974; www.sunflowerhill.com; 185 N 300 East; r $175-250; ❀⚡☎) This is one of the best bets in town. A top-shelf B&B, Sunflower Hill offers 12 rooms in a quaint country setting. Grab a room in the cozier cedar-sided early-20th-century home over the annex rooms. All rooms come with quilt-piled beds and antiques – some even have jetted tubs.

The staff are eager to please and the hot tub works magic.

Cali Cochitta B&B $$
(☎435-259-4961, 888-429-8112; www.moab dreaminn.com; 110 S 200 East; cottages $140-180; ❀⚡) Charming and central, these adjoining brick cottages offer snug rooms fitted with smart decor. A long wooden table on the patio makes a welcome setting for communal breakfasts. You can also take advantage of the porch chairs, hammock or backyard hot tub in the zen garden.

3 Dogs and a Moose B&B $$
(☎435-260-1692; www.3dogsandamoosecottages. com; 171 W Center St; cottages $125-285; ❀⚡☎) Lovely and low-key, these four downtown cottages make an ideal base camp for groups and families who want a little socializing in situ. The style is French country meets playful modern. You can pick your own tomatoes in the landscaped yard, where there are also hammocks, bike wash, grill and hot tub.

Gonzo Inn MOTEL $$
(☎435-259-2515, 800-791-4044; www.gonzo inn.com; 100 W 200 South; r $169, ste $215-255; ❀@⚡☎) Less an inn than a chain-style motel spruced up with retro-70s steel accents and sleek cement showers, the Gonzo Inn is friendly, and we love the location off the main drag. No fear and loathing here, it caters well to cyclists, with a bicycle wash and repair station as well as a laundry. Rooms have refrigerators and coffeemakers.

Castle Valley Inn B&B $$
(☎435-259-6012; www.castlevalleyinn.com; 424 Amber Lane, off La Sal Mountain Loop; r & cabins $115-230; ❀) For tranquility, it's hard to beat this top option off La Sal Mountain Loop Rd, 15 miles north of Moab. With cozy quilts and handmade Aspen furniture, rooms (in the main house or new bungalows) sit amid apple, plum and apricot orchards. Bungalows offer full kitchen and grill; there's also an outdoor hot tub. Ideal for cycling Castle Valley.

Best Western Canyonlands Inn MOTEL $$
(☎435-259-2300; www.canyonlandsinn.com; 16 S Main St; r $219-259; ❀☎) A comfortable choice at the central crossroads of downtown, this independently owned hotel features ginormous rooms, fitness center, laundry, playground and outdoor pool. It's a little removed from Main St, but you still get a hint of noise.

Big Horn Lodge MOTEL $$
(☎435-259-6171; www.moabbighorn.com; 550 S Main St; r from $129; ☺❀⚡☎) With a kitschy Southwestern-style facade and cozy interiors

CAMPGROUNDS IN & AROUND MOAB, CANYONLANDS & ARCHES

CAMPGROUND	LOCATION	DESCRIPTION
Arches National Park		
Devils Garden (p202)	Arches National Park	Trailside, with picnic tables & grills but few amenities; extremely popular, book far in advance
Canyonlands National Park		
Needles Outpost (Map p179)	Hwy 211	Dusty, private campground outside Needles; hot showers but lagging service
Squaw Flat (p193)	The Needles	Popular, exceptionally pretty sites located trailside with some shade & slickrock
Willow Flat (p192)	On a dirt road close to Island in the Sky	On a dirt road near the Green River Overlook, close to trails; the Sky has few amenities; popular
Moab		
ACT Campground (p215)	S Mill Creek Dr	Sustainable, forward-thinking campground right in town, with hookups, showers, shared kitchen & fire rings
Archview Resort & Campground (p216)	Hwy 191	Shadeless but has wi-fi, grills & pool, 10 minutes from downtown
Canyonlands Campground (p216)	Main St	RV village complete with pool & playground, shade for tents; central
Portal RV Resort (p216)	Hwy 191	Upscale RV resort, with pool, wi-fi and grassy tent sites; borders golf course
Slickrock (p216)	Hwy 191	Well maintained, with air-conditioned cabins, tent canopy
Up the Creek Campground (p216)	E 300 South	Nice tent-only campground with picnic tables & shade; in center of town
Around Moab		
BLM Campgrounds (p215)	Hwy 128	10 popular campgrounds along Colorado River, buggy if without breeze
BLM Kane Creek Campgrounds (p216)	Kane Creek Rd	Just west of Moab, with fire rings & toilets
Hatch Point Recreation Area (Map p178)	Canyon Rims	Dirt-road campground with fire rings and pit toilets, by Anticline Overlook
Horsethief Campground (p216)	off Hwy 313	Mesa-top sites that are open but well spaced, attractive; bring water
Kayenta (p190)	Dead Horse	Near trails, good sites with picnic tables, fire rings & grills
Moab Under Canvas (p217)	Hwy 191	Skip the tent & set up in this luxury spot just north of town, with fire rings, toilets, canvas tents
Sand Flats Recreation Area (p216)	Sand Flats Rd	Sandstone setting with pit toilets, near Slickrock Bike Trail; bring water
Warner Lake Campground (p216)	off La Sal Mountain Loop Rd	High-altitude lake sites with picnic tables in national forest
Wind Whistle	Canyon Rims Recreation Area (p216)	Dirt-road access, scenic & less crowded, with picnic tables & pit toilets

   Drinking Water   Flush Toilets   Ranger Station Nearby Great for Families   Dogs Allowed (On Leash)

NUMBER OF SITES	ELEVATION	OPEN	RESERVATIONS AVAILABLE?	FACILITIES
52	5200ft	year-round	yes	
20	5100ft	Apr-Nov	yes	
26	5100ft	year-round	no	
12	6000ft	year-round	no	
40	5100ft	year-round	yes	
77	4026ft	Mar-Nov	yes	
140	4026ft	year-round	yes	
80	4026ft	year-round	yes	
200+	4026ft	Mar-Nov	yes	
20	4026ft	Mar-Nov	yes	
n/a	4000ft	year-round	groups only	
105	5100ft	year-round	yes	
10	5900ft	year-round	groups only	
56	5800ft	year-round	no	
21	6000ft	year-round	Mar-Oct	
n/a	5100ft	Mar-Oct	yes	
120	4500ft	year-round	no	
20	9500ft	Apr-Oct	no	
17	6000	year-round	groups only	

MOAB SLEEPING

 Grocery Store Nearby   *Restaurant Nearby*   *Pay-phone*   *Summertime Campfire Program*   *RV Dump Station*

paneled with knotty pine, this two-story motel is a strong bet. Service is taken seriously and there are loads of extras (including a heated swimming pool inches from the road, refrigerators and coffeemakers).

Redstone Inn   MOTEL **$$**
(📞800-772-1972, 435-259-3500; www.moabredstone.com; 535 S Main St; r $105-110; ❄️🛜🐾) The small pine-paneled rooms here are decorated with rustic wood furniture, lending a cozy feel to their otherwise utilitarian boxiness. The walls are thin, though. It has a bike wash area and storage, guest laundry, on-site hot tub and pool privileges across the street.

Moab Valley Inn   MOTEL **$$**
(📞435-259-4419; www.moabvalleyinn.com; 711 S Main St; r from $109; ❄️🛜🐾) Kids will love the swimming pool, half-shaded by awnings. Rooms are nondescript but pets are allowed.

Adobe Abode   B&B **$$**
(📞435-259-7716; www.adobeabodemoab.com; 778 W Kane Creek Blvd; r $159-169; ❄️) On the upper outskirts of town, this modern adobe pays homage to pioneer style with a mix of antlers, bear rugs and antique guns. The grounds are xeriscaped and rooms comfortable.

Pack Creek Ranch   LODGE **$$**
(📞888-879-6622; www.packcreekranch.com; off La Sal Mountain Loop; cabins $175-235; 🛜🐾) This hidden Shangri-la's log cabins are tucked beneath mature cottonwoods and willow trees in the La Sal Mountains, 2000ft above Moab. Most feature fireplaces; all have kitchens and gas grills (bring groceries). No TV or phones. Edward Abbey is among the artists and writers who came here for inspiration. Amenities include horseback riding and an indoor hot tub and sauna.

Sorrel River Ranch   LODGE **$$$**
(📞877-317-8244; www.sorrelriver.com; Mile 17, Hwy 128; r $429-779; ❄️@🐾) Southeast Utah's only full-service luxury resort and gourmet restaurant was originally an 1803 homestead. The lodge and log cabins sit on 240 lush acres, with riding areas and alfalfa fields along the Colorado River. Details strive for rustic perfection, with bedroom fireplaces, handmade log beds, copper-top tables and Jacuzzi tubs.

Red Cliffs Lodge   LODGE **$$$**
(📞435-259-5050; www.redcliffslodge.com; Mile 14, Hwy 128; ste/cabin $240/340; ❄️🐾🛜) Dude ranch meets deluxe motel. These comfortable rooms feature vaulted knotty-pine ceilings, kitchenettes with dining tables, and private (though cramped) patios, some over-looking the Colorado River. Larger rooms are ideal for families. Also offers horseback riding and a hot tub, an on-site movie museum for Western buffs and wine tasting. Pets are allowed and horse boarding is available.

 # Eating

Most midrange places have full bars. Some close in winter. Make reservations for top-end places.

⭐ **Milt's**   BURGERS **$**
(356 Mill Creek Dr; dishes $4-9; ⏰11am-8pm Mon-Sat) Meet greasy goodness. A triathlete couple bought this classic 1954 burger stand and smartly changed nothing. Heaven is one of their honest burgers, jammed with pickles, fresh lettuce, a side of fresh-cut fries and creamy milkshake. Be patient: the line can get long. It's near the Slickrock Bike Trail.

EklectiCafé   ORGANIC **$**
(352 N Main St; breakfast & sandwiches $5-10; ⏰7am-2:30pm Mon-Sat, to 1pm Sun; 🛜) Soy-ginger-seaweed scrambled eggs anyone? This wonderfully quirky cafe lives up to its eclectic name with its food choice and decor. Come for organic coffee, curried wraps and vegetarian salads. Dinner served some weekend evenings.

Pantele's Deli   DELI **$**
(📞435-259-0200; 98 E Center St; sandwiches $8-10; ⏰11am-4pm Mon-Sat) Doing a brisk business, this deli makes everything fresh and it shows. Salads come in heaping bowls and high-piled sandwiches are stuffed with fresh roasted turkey or roast beef cooked in-house. The wait is worth it.

Love Muffin   CAFE **$**
(www.lovemuffincafe.com; 139 N Main St; mains $6-8; ⏰7am-2pm; 🛜) Early-rising locals buy up many of the daily muffins – like the Breakfast Muffin, with bacon and blueberries. Not to worry, the largely organic menu at this vibrant cafe also includes creative sandwiches, breakfast burritos and inventive egg dishes such as the Verde, with brisket and slow-roasted salsa.

Moab Brewery   AMERICAN **$**
(www.themoabbrewery.com; 686 S Main St; mains $8-14; ⏰11:30am-11pm) Choosing from the list of microbrews made in the vats just behind the bar area may be easier than deciding what to eat off the vast and varied menu. Be aware that service isn't a strong suit.

Crystal's Cakes and Cones   ICE CREAM **$**
(26 Center St; ice cream $2-5; ⏰noon-9pm) For a little piece of Americana, queue up at this

popular spot where farm-fresh local teenagers serve ever-growing lines with a smile.

Sabaku Sushi
SUSHI **$$**

(☎435-259-4455; www.sabakusushi.com; 90 E Center St; rolls $6-9, mains $13-17; ☺5pm-midnight Tue-Sun) The ocean is about a million miles away, but you still get a creative selection of fresh rolls, catches of the day and a few Utah originals at this small hole-in-the-wall sushi joint. Stick with the status quo with traditional sashimi and *nigiri* offerings or get adventurous with the lip-smacking Elk Tataki and Devil's Garden Roll (topped with a pineapple habanero sauce).

The Spoke on Center
AMERICAN **$$**

(☎435-260-7177; www.thespokemoab.com; 5 N Main St; mains $12-18; ☺11am-10pm) This burger joint sprawling over two stories of semi-industrial open-concept dining space is earning local accolades for its skillet-plated burger combos and substantial sides. Come dinner, check out the big-dog entrée options like chicken alfredo or grilled salmon with quinoa salad.

Singha Thai
THAI **$$**

(92 E Center St; mains $13-18; ☺11am-3pm & 5-9:30pm Mon-Sat, 5-9:30pm Sun; ☝) Ethnic food is as rare as rain in these parts, so locals pile into this authentic Thai cafe for curries and organic basil chicken. Service is sleepy and the ambience generic, but if you're hot for spice, it delivers. No bar.

Pasta Jay's
ITALIAN **$$**

(☎435-259-2900; www.pastajays.com; 4 S Main St; mains $13-17; ☺11am-9pm) With shady outdoor patio seating and a kids' menu, Jay's serves heaping portions of garlicky pasta served with hot homemade bread. Lunch specials are a bargain.

Eddie McStiff's
AMERICAN **$$**

(www.eddiemcstiffs.com; 59 S Main St; mains $10-20; ☺11:30am-midnight, to 1am Fri & Sat; ☝) Though it's as much taproom-bar as restaurant, the burgers and pizzas (gluten-free available) are almost as popular as the beer here. Occasional live music brightens the night.

Jailhouse Café
BREAKFAST **$$**

(101 N Main St; breakfast $11-14; ☺7am-noon Mar-Oct) Eggs Benedict here is hard to beat but the line goes deep on weekends. Waffles and ginger pancakes are other temptations. In a former jailhouse, with patio seating.

★ Desert Bistro
SOUTHWESTERN **$$$**

(☎435-259-0756; www.desertbistro.com; 36 S 100 West; mains $22-42; ☺5:30-11pm Wed-Sun) Stylized preparations of game and fresh, flown-in seafood are the specialty at this welcoming white-tablecloth restaurant inside an old house. Think smoked elk in a huckleberry glaze, pepper-seared scallops and jicama salad with crisp pears. Everything is made on-site, from freshly baked bread to delicious pastries. Great wine list, too.

Jeffrey's Steakhouse
STEAK **$$$**

(☎435-259-3588; www.jeffreyssteakhouse.com; 218 N 100 West; mains $22-40; ☺5-10pm) In a historic sandstone house, Jeffrey's is serious about beef, which comes grain-fed, wagyu-style and only sometimes in generous cuts. If the night is too good to end, head upstairs to the upscale Ghost Bar. Reservations advised.

Sorrel River Grill
MODERN AMERICAN **$$$**

(☎435-259-4642; Mile 17, Hwy 128, Sorrel River Ranch; breakfast $10-12, lunch $12-15, dinner $24-40; ☺7am-3pm & 5-10pm Mar-Oct, 8-10am & 5:30-7:30pm Nov-Feb) For romance, it's hard to beat the wraparound veranda overlooking redrock canyons outside Moab. The New American menu changes seasonally, but expect seared steaks, succulent rack of lamb and the freshest seafood flown in.

Self-Catering

Moonflower Market
HEALTH FOOD **$**

(39 E 100 N; ☺8am-8pm) Nonprofit health-food store with loads of community info.

Moab Farmers Market
MARKET **$**

(www.moabfarmersmarket.com; 400 N 100 West; ☺5-8pm Thu May-Oct) Local farms vend their summer produce in Swanny City Park.

City Market & Pharmacy
MARKET **$**

(425 S Main St; ☺6am-11pm) Moab's largest grocery store, with sandwiches and salad bar to go.

🍷 Drinking & Nightlife

Woody's Tavern
BAR

(www.worldfamouswoodystavern.com; 221 S Main St; ☺11am-midnight) Full bar with great outdoor patio; live music Friday and Saturday in season.

Ghost Bar
BAR

(218 N 100 West; ☺7-11pm) A loungey, dime-sized jazz nook serving wine and a full list of cocktails; upstairs at Jeffrey's Steakhouse.

Dave's Corner Market
COFFEE SHOP

(401 Mill Creek Dr; ☺6am-10pm) Sip shade-grown espresso with locals at the corner convenience store.

☆ Entertainment

Moab Arts & Recreation Center   CONCERT VENUE
(www.moabrecreation.com; 111 E 100 N) The rec center hosts everything from yoga classes to contra dance parties and poetry gatherings.

Canyonlands by Night & Day   DINNER SHOW
(☑ 435-259-5261, 800-394-9978; www.canyon landsbynight.com; 1861 N Hwy 191; adult/child $69/59; ⊙ Apr-Oct; 🎫) Start with dinner riverside, then take an after-dark boat ride on the Colorado, with an old-fashioned light show complete with historical narration.

Slickrock Cinemas 3   CINEMA
(☑ 435-259-4441; 580 Kane Creek Blvd) First-run movies.

❶ Orientation

Hwy 191 becomes Main St through Moab. The town follows a fairly typical Mormon grid, in which numbered streets radiate from the intersection of Main and Center Sts. Compass points indicate where you are in relation to that hub: thus, 100 E 300 South is one block east and three blocks south of Main and Center. It's easy once you get used to it.

❶ Information

Cell phones work in Moab but not in river canyons.

EMERGENCY

Moab Regional Hospital (☑ 435-259-7191; 719 W 400 N) For 24-hour emergency medical care.
Police (☑ 911; 217 E Center St)

INTERNET ACCESS

Grand County Public Library (www.moab library.org; 257 E Center St; free internet; ⊙ 9am-8pm Mon-Fri, to 5pm Sat) Easy 15-minute internet; register for longer access.

ESSENTIALS

For fresh spring water, take Hwy 191 north to Hwy 128 east and continue 100yd to **Matrimony Springs** (Hwy 128), on the right. **Gear Heads** (p214) offers free filtered water.

You can wash your whites at **Moab Laundry Express** (471 S Main St, Desert Plaza; ⊙ 24hr; 🛜). **Up the Creek Campground** (p216) has tidy and clean showers, also available at **Archview Campground** (p216), **Canyonlands Campground** (p216) or **Poison Spider Bicycles** (p207).

MEDIA

Canyon Country Zephyr Iconoclastic free newspaper.
Moab Community Radio Tune in (89.7 FM and 106.1 FM) for alternative local programming, from folk to funk.
Moab Happenings A free newspaper geared to visitors.

POST

Post Office (☑ 435-259-7427; 50 E 100 North; ⊙ 8am-5pm Mon-Fri, 9am-1pm Sat)

TOURIST INFORMATION

Moab Information Center (www.discover moab.com; cnr Main & Center Sts; ⊙ 8am-7pm; 🛜) Excellent source of information on area parks, trails, activities, camping and weather. Extensive bookstore and knowledgeable staff. Walk-in only.

USEFUL WEBSITES

BLM (☑ 435-259-2100; www.blm.gov/utah/ moab) Online and phone assistance only.
Manti-La Sal National Forest Moab Ranger Station (☑ 435-259-7155; www.fs.fed.us/r4/ mantilasal) No walk-in visitors, but provides information online and by phone.
Moab Area Travel Council (www.discover moab.com) Excellent for pretrip planning.
Utah Mountain Biking (www.utahmountainbik ing.com) Descriptions of all major biking areas.

❶ Getting Around

At **Canyonlands Field airport** (CNY; www. moabairport.com; off Hwy 191), 16 miles north of town via Hwy 191, **Enterprise** (☑ 435-259-8505; Mile 148, N Hwy 191; ⊙ 8am-5pm Mon-Fri, to 2pm Sat) has cars and SUVs.

You'll find several gas and service stations in town – don't forget to top off the tank. Obey speed limits, or police will ticket you.

Several companies operate shuttle services to Arches, Canyonlands and environs, plus the town of Green River; some will also shuttle your private vehicle to meet you at a trailhead.

Coyote Shuttle (☑ 435-260-2097; www. coyoteshuttle.com) On-demand Canyonland airport and river shuttles. Biker/hiker shuttles cost $25 one way.

Roadrunner Shuttle (☑ 435-259-9402; www. roadrunnershuttle.com) On-demand Canyonland Airport, hiker-biker and river shuttles.

Elevated Transit (☑ 888-353-8283; www. elevatedtransit.com) Daily service from Blanding and Richfield in the south to Salt Lake City. The Blanding line stops in Monticello, Moab and Green River, continuing to Price, Spanish Fork, Provo and the Salt Lake City Terminal and airport. Moab to Salt Lake City Airport one way costs $70.

Understand Utah's National Parks

The Parks Today

These cathedrals of sand and stone are a living hallmark to the vast open space and wide-open views that define the American West and its independent people. With five national parks and millions more acres of protected wilderness, the Colorado Plateau is one of the last great stands of virgin wilderness in America. This desolate promised land has given rise to middle-of-America political sensibilities, a wholesome serving of religious zeal and just enough old-school new-agers and lifestyle escapists to keep things real.

Best on Film

Thelma and Louise (1991) This road-trip story of the enduring female spirit was shot in Arches and Monument Valley.

127 (2010) This James Franco film recounts the gruesome real-life story of Aron Ralston's ordeal in the Utah backcountry, where he was trapped by a boulder for 127 hours, eventually cutting off his own arm to save his life.

Big Love (2006–11) Starring Bill Paxton, this HBO drama examines the true romance and intimate humanity of Utah's polygamists.

The Greatest Story Ever Told (1965) The sermon on the Mount was filmed in Canyonlands in this epic bible tale.

Best in Print

Desert Solitaire (Edward Abbey, 1968) Provocative and hilariously cranky, this tale chronicles the author's experience as a ranger at Arches.

Under the Banner of Heaven (Jon Krakauer, 2003) Perhaps the most high-profile book ever written on Utah. It's a compelling exposé of extremist polygamist groups and a provocative look at the state's oft-troubled history.

Refuge: An Unnatural History of Family and Place (Terry Tempest Williams, 2001) This story explores the intimate and sensual landscapes of Utah's land and people.

Land Use

Over 60% of Utah's land is controlled by the federal government under the Bureau of Land Management, the US Forest Service, the US Fish and Wildlife Service, the National Park Service and the Department of Defense – no wonder land use and stewardship are contentious issues. Open a newspaper or listen to the chatter at the local diner and you'll see that this is the singular thread that dominates the political and environmental debates seen across the state – and across much of the Inner-Mountain West.

The current debate looks beyond the pie-in-the-sky protections the Red Rock Wilderness Act (p235) would afford, focusing instead on states' rights. In 2012, Utah passed the Utah Transfer of Public Lands Act, calling for the feds to hand over control of around 31 million acres of public lands, arguing that Utahans were better placed to manage their own resources, and should benefit from the taxes and development rights that would come with it.

The protections for the national parks were not threatened by this move, but the purportedly energy-rich terrain of the Grand Staircase-Escalante National Monument would be transferred into state hands. Opponents called foul, saying the law was unconstitutional and cooked up to bypass environmental protections, adding that there's no way Utah could foot the bill to manage such large swaths of land. The law gave the feds a deadline of December 31, 2014, to hand over the lands. That date came and went, with no handover. But cost-benefit studies have been undertaken (showing that with aggressive resource extraction, Utah could make it work financially). Litigation and grand compromises are possible as the state continues its fight to assert control over its lands – perhaps setting precedents for land-use and maintenance in neighbouring states.

What will happen in the waning days of the Obama presidency also weighs heavily on local minds in this steadfastly 'red' state, which largely espouses conservative values. Some environmentalists are speculating that

Obama will follow Bill Clinton's Grand Staircase initiative and leverage the Antiquities Act to protect another large chunk of Utah – another hit against state control.

Visitation

The National Park Service (NPS) celebrates its 100th anniversary in 2016. The centennial will bring a great deal of media attention to southern Utah's parks, at a time when increased visitation and limited budgets are pushing officials and infrastructure to the limits.

A highly successful media campaign called the Mighty Five, low gas prices and a strong US economy combined to spur record visitation across Utah's parks and public lands in 2014 and 2015. In some cases, it was too much to handle, with the Utah Highway Patrol closing off access to Arches National Park over the Memorial Day Weekend in 2015 after a traffic jam extended out of the park and onto the highway.

Mitigating the impact of tourist traffic to protect the parks and ensure their enjoyment by future generations is a top priority for the NPS. Shuttles serving Zion Canyon and the gateway town of Springdale, as well as part of Bryce Canyon's scenic drive, encourage visitors to get out of their cars and reduce traffic. Zion Canyon's visitor center is a model of green architecture, using evaporative cooling, solar panels and other energy-saving measures. All southern Utah's parks have extensive recycling programs and free ranger-led activities that promote visitor awareness of climate change and the importance of wilderness conservation.

On a larger level, the parks service faces mounting economic challenges. There's a reported maintenance backlog of $9.5 billion. Energy development around the parks on BLM land (including a proposed coal mine near Bryce and oil extraction near the San Rafael Swell) pose continued environmental risks.

New Trends

On the social front, while Utah retains its Mormon roots, there seems to be an opening up in the state. Drinking laws were relaxed with the 2002 Salt Lake Olympics. Mormonism was front and center in 2008, when Mormon candidate Mitt Romney gained the Republican nomination for president.

A snapshot from a 2012 Census Bureau Report indicates that most Utahans are married couples with children, are overwhelmingly white, and have the second-highest fertility rate in the country. But it also shows that fertility rates are declining, the population is becoming more diverse (especially among young people), and there are fewer stay-at-home moms than in the past. The number of Utahans self-identifying as Mormon dropped from 70% in 1990 to 60% in 2013. According to a recent study by Yale University, 60% of Utahan believe climate change is happening, while only 45% believe it's caused by human activities, lagging behind national changes in attitudes (63% and 48% respectively). An estimated 61% of Utahans oppose same-sex marriage.

UTAH POPULATION: **2.9 MILLION**

UTAH AREA: **82,169 SQ MILES**

VISITORS: **40 MILLION (COLORADO PLATEAU)**

NATIONAL PARKS VISITORS: **7 MILLION**

MEDIAN HOUSEHOLD INCOME: **UTAH $58,821**

if 100 people come to Zion...

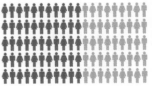

55 would use the South Zion Canyon entrance
33 would use the East (tunnel) entrance
12 would use the Kolob Canyons (Northwest) entrance

seasonal visitation – Zion (% of annual visitors)

Jan-Mar 11 | Apr-Jun 34.5 | Jul-Sep 36 | Oct-Dec 17.5

population per sq mile

UTAH | USA

🚶 ≈ 20 people

History

The human history of southern Utah and its vast public lands entangles itself in a cryptic knot of exploitation, conservation, compassion and avarice. This desolate desert plateau gave rise to dinosaurs and ancestral Native American civilizations, Mormon settlers and cowboy outlaws, uranium prospectors and new-era conservationists driven to protect this unique corner of the American wilderness. The history of the US and the West has left an imprint, but it's the traces of Utah's indigenous peoples and original mavericks that resonate today.

First Peoples

Traces of Fremont: Society and Rock Art in Ancient Utah (2010), written by Steven R Simms, with beautiful photographs by François Gohier, heralds an often-overlooked ancient indigenous people's legacy by examining evidence they left behind.

It's not definitively known when humans first arrived in the Southwest. Most likely, nomadic peoples migrated from Asia across a land bridge between Siberia and Alaska, making their way south between 23,000 and 10,000 years ago. Some models posit subsequent migrations by boat. We know that they arrived by 10,000 BC, as archaeologists have dated spearheads found among the remains of woolly mammoths and other ice-age mammals. However, Native American creation stories say that the people have always been here, or that they descended from the spirit world.

However they arrived, these early groups were primarily skilled hunters. By 8500 BC, most large prehistoric mammals were extinct – some possibly hunted to that fate, though many were unable to adapt to the drying glacial climate. This led to what scholars call the Desert Archaic period, which lasted roughly from 6500 BC to AD 200. The term 'Desert Archaic' refers as much to the period's hunter-gatherer lifestyle as it does to an ecosystem or block of time.

As a survival method, hunting and gathering proved remarkably adaptive and resilient in the Southwest. Early Desert Archaic peoples lived nomadically in small, unconcentrated groups, following the food supply of seasonal wild plants and such small animals as rabbits. Shelters were temporary, and caves were often used. These people became skilled at basketry, a functional craft for groups on the move.

Eventually, late Desert Archaic peoples established semiregular settlement patterns and started to cultivate crops such as primitive corn, beans and squash. By AD 200 several distinct cultures had emerged. An-

TIMELINE	250 million BC	60 million BC	23,000 BC–10,000 BC
	Triassic Period of the Mesozoic Era, dinosaurs evolve, southern Utah's plateau country is a shallow sea off the western edge of the Earth's giant supercontinent known as Pangaea.	Beginning of the Cenozoic Era – or Age of Mammals. Seismic activity and the movement of continental plates uplifts the entire Colorado Plateau, creating the Grand Staircase and Rocky Mountains.	Made up of nomadic hunters and gatherers, groups of indigenous peoples migrate from Asia over the Bering Strait land bridge to North America. Competing theories suggest continual migration by boat.

cestral Puebloans dominated the Colorado Plateau, which encompasses southern Utah, southwest Colorado and northern portions of Arizona and New Mexico. They were once called the Anasazi – a Navajo word meaning 'ancient enemy' – by archaeologists, but Ancestral Puebloans is now the preferred term, since contemporary tribes believe they are descended from these ancient peoples.

Ancestral Puebloans dominated the Colorado Plateau from around 200 BC to AD 1500; in southern Utah they left a few centuries earlier, around AD 1200. There's no consensus over why Ancestral Puebloans abandoned the area when they did. It was likely a combination of drought, soil erosion, disease and conflict with other groups over dwindling resources.

Ancestral Puebloans adopted irrigated agriculture, became highly accomplished basket-makers and potters, and believed in a complex cosmology. They are best known for their cliff dwellings, pueblo villages

Guide to Rock Art of the Utah Region (2000), by Dennis Silfer, is an overview of current scientific knowledge about prehistoric indigenous cultures, offering detailed, if dated, descriptions and explanations of sites.

HISTORY FIRST PEOPLES

WRITTEN ON THE LAND

Anywhere in southern Utah you may encounter it: the pecked outlines of human figures and animals, painted handprints, squiggled lines etched into desert varnish. Rock art is mysterious and awesome and always leaves us wondering: who did this and why? What were they trying to say? Dating from at least 2000 BC to as late as the 19th century AD, rock art in Utah was once called 'a wilderness Louvre' by *National Geographic*. The rock art found in southern Utah has been attributed to every known ancestral and modern people, from ice-age hunters and Desert Archaic nomads to contemporary Native American tribes. One way archaeologists track the spread of ancestral cultures is by studying their distinctive rock-art styles, which tend to be either abstract or representational, both zoomorphic and anthropomorphic. Representational rock art is usually more recent, while abstract designs appear in all ages.

The top spot to view rock art is the Great Gallery at Horseshoe Canyon (p192) in Canyonlands. Other fine examples are found in every national park and across BLM and public lands.

Preservation

⇒ Do not disturb or remove any artifacts or features at the site.

⇒ Do not trace, repaint, remove graffiti or otherwise touch or apply any materials to the rock art.

⇒ Stay back at least 10ft from all rock-art panels, using binoculars or a zoom lens for better views.

⇒ Do not climb the cliffs above rock-art sites, as that could let loose a rockslide that would damage the site.

⇒ Minimize the number of vehicles you bring to rock-art sites, and do not hike off-trail or build campfires nearby.

6500 BC–AD 200	200 BC–AD 1200	1100	1776
Desert Archaic cultures occupy southern Utah. These nomadic hunter-gatherers become adept at catching small game and adapting desert plants to new uses, including making baskets.	Ancestral Puebloans develop a vibrant culture, with pueblos, cliff dwellings and ceremonial centers across the Colorado Plateau; distinct Fremont Culture arises contemporaneously.	Southern Paiute tribes emerge in the Colorado Plateau region, spreading all the way to present-day California, flourishing for the next 700 years until the arrival of explorers and settlers.	In search of a shortcut from Santa Fe to California, the Domínguez-Escalante expedition sees the first non–Native Americans explore the Colorado Plateau.

and kivas (ceremonial underground chambers). While southern Utah contains far fewer of these ancient structures than surrounding states, it does boast abundant Ancestral Puebloan rock art. Hovenweep National Monument and Cedar Mesa are your best bet to see these dwellings.

Living in southern Utah concurrently were the Fremont people, who migrated from the north and continued a seminomadic existence, preferring hunting and gathering to farming and villages. They abandoned the area around the same time as the Ancestral Puebloans, and their distinctive rock art is also widespread.

Southern Paiutes & Spaniards

Southern Paiute tribes began emerging around AD 1100. Comprising a dozen or so distinct bands, Paiute territory extended from California's deserts east to Colorado, and from Utah's Great Basin south to Arizona's Painted Desert. The Kaibab Paiutes lived near what is now Zion National Park. Today, their tribal reservation surrounds Pipe Spring National Monument on the northern Arizona Strip.

Generally speaking, Southern Paiutes followed the same survival strategy as Desert Archaic peoples – migrating with the seasons, hunting small animals, gathering wild plants and tending a few modest crops. A staple of their diet was the piñon, or pine nut, and they continued the tradition of fine basketry. Their shelters and even their clothes often weren't made to last more than a season. Southern Paiutes lived largely in peace for more than 500 years. No one coveted the unyielding land they called home, yet they found abundance in it. Deer were plentiful, the winters around present-day St George were mild, and in summer they fished mountain lakes. Ever-growing numbers of Europeans on the continent didn't know of them, and gold-hungry 16th-century Spanish conquistadors like Coronado never penetrated the Colorado Plateau's rugged territory.

Then, in 1776, the same year the US declared its independence from Britain, the Domínguez-Escalante expedition encountered the Kaibab band of Southern Paiutes while skirting the western edge of the Colorado Plateau. In the first recorded European impressions of them, Silvestre Vélez de Escalante, a Franciscan friar and Spanish Catholic missionary, described 'a large number of people, all of pleasing appearance, very friendly and extremely timid.'

The Spanish expedition had two goals: to open a communication route from Santa Fe to California and to spread Christianity among indigenous peoples. But the expedition never made it further west, nor did Spain fund the establishment of any Utah missions. Afterward, the Southern Paiutes were left mostly, but not entirely, alone. Some of the Spanish Trail trading route had been cut, and occasional trappers wandered through, as did strange diseases and even Ute and New Mexican slave traders, who often kidnapped Paiute children to sell for horses and goods elsewhere.

Stephen Trimble's hefty tome *The People: Indians of the American Southwest* (1993) stitches together tribal histories and modern realities by letting Native Americans, including Utah's Southern Paiutes and Colorado River tribes, speak for themselves.

To learn more about the 1776 Domínguez-Escalante expedition and read excerpts from Escalante's own diary, track down *Pageant in the Wilderness* (1972), by Herbert Bolton; it's one of the first authoritative accounts.

1839	1844	1847	1848
After fleeing arrest in Missouri, Mormon founder Joseph Smith leads his followers to Nauvoo, Illinois, where a temple and town are built beside the Mississippi River.	An armed mob of 200 men storms the jail in Carthage, Illinois, where Joseph Smith is imprisoned, shooting and killing the Mormon leader and self-confessed polygamist.	Mormons fleeing religious persecution in the east start arriving in Salt Lake City. Over the next two decades, more than 70,000 Mormons will migrate to Utah.	The Mexican-American War ends with the 1848 Treaty of Guadalupe Hidalgo; Mexico cedes much of the present-day Southwest, including parts of Utah, to the USA.

By the early 19th century, the Southern Paiutes could weather the passing wagon trains, which trampled grasses and crops, but smallpox and measles were decimating them. By mid-century, before they'd ever had to fight or strike a deal with a Mormon missionary settler, some Southern Paiute populations had dwindled by two-thirds.

Paiute, Ute, Goshute, Shosone and Navajo people all live in modern-day Utah. The Uintah and Ouray Reservation is in the Northeast, and is the second-largest Native American reservation in the United States. In the southeast, don't miss a day of horseback riding, hiking or shopping in the Navajo Nation, the largest Native American reservation in the US. Festivals celebrating Native American traditions mostly happen in the summer.

Arrival of the Mormons

In 1847 Brigham Young and party reached a point near Utah's Great Salt Lake. Fleeing persecution for their beliefs back east, the Mormons were charged by their prophet Joseph Smith to find a place out west where they could build a heavenly city on earth. They were looking, in other words, for what Southern Paiutes had long enjoyed – the solitude and freedom from interference this harsh land provided. As the story goes, Young sat upright out of his sickbed long enough to say, 'This is the right place. Drive on.'

The Mormons were not your average pioneers, and Young was not an average leader. The plan was to build an independent nation, a theocracy outside the boundaries of the USA. Within a year, however, the rapidly expanding country caught up with them. The 1848 Treaty of Guadalupe Hidalgo turned the Mexican territory into a US possession, and the concurrent discovery of gold in California attracted streams of passing miners, and with them, Manifest Destiny, the nationalistic belief that the US was ordained by God to stretch from 'sea to shining sea,' from the Atlantic to the Pacific Oceans. Utah would not remain isolated for long.

In 1850 the Territory of Utah was established, with Young as territorial governor. If Young despaired over the political fate of his State of Deseret, he didn't let on. Instead, he aspired to settle an empire larger than Texas as fast as he could. He sent Mormon pioneers in all directions to plow, irrigate and farm the desert into submission, which they did. The Mormons succeeded because they were zealously dedicated to their faith, tempered by their journey to Utah along the Mormon Trail, and organized. They attacked the land as a cohesive group, fired by visions of God, not gold.

Everywhere they went in southern Utah, Mormons displaced Paiutes, appropriating water sources and the most desirable land. In an apparent contradiction, the Mormons also 'adopted' the Paiutes and gave them practical support, which they came to depend on. The *Book of Mormon* claims that Native Americans are one of Israel's lost tribes, so bringing them back into the fold was considered an important Mormon mission, even as racist attitudes toward indigenous peoples prevailed.

The University of Utah Press (www.uofpress.com) and the national parks' cooperative natural history associations are your best sources of new history books, covering eras from indigenous tribes to Spanish explorers and Mormon settlers.

With spare prose and uncommon insight, Western writer Wallace Stegner captures the early history of Utah and the Mormons in *The Gathering of Zion: The Story of the Mormon Trail* (1964) and *Mormon Country* (1942).

HISTORY ARRIVAL OF THE MORMONS

1850	1854–58	1861	1863
US federal government establishes the Territory of Utah after denying Latter-Day Saints leader Brigham Young's proposal for a more expansive State of Deseret (Mormon for 'honeybee').	The Mormons send missionaries to convert the Southern Paiutes; a Mormon militia group massacres 120 immigrants. Mormon missionary Nephi Johnson becomes the first non–Native American to enter Zion.	Nicknamed Utah's Dixie, the experimental farming community of St George is founded during the Mormon church's Cotton Mission days; scarce drinking water makes life difficult. The Civil War kicks off.	Isaac Behunin and his sons are the first Mormons to settle Zion Canyon, building a cabin and clearing some farmland. Behunin is credited with naming Zion Canyon.

The end result for the Paiutes turned out to be much the same as for Native American tribes elsewhere in the Southwest – that is, cultural disenfranchisement, the loss of traditional hunting grounds and access to water sources, and a population decimated by foreign diseases and indentured servitude.

A Massacre, a War & Statehood

In *Massacre at Mountain Meadows* (2008), Ronald Walker and Richard Turley unflinchingly examine one of the darkest incidents in Mormon pioneer history. For another viewpoint, read journalist Jon Krakauer's *Under the Banner of Heaven* (2003).

With their modern-day prophets, the practice of 'celestial marriage' (that is, polygamy) and theocratic territorial government, Mormons were perceived as a threat by federal authorities and everyday US citizens, whom the Mormons called Gentiles. In the 1850s, tensions ran high, and minor clashes were common. On September 11, 1857, in the mountains outside St George, building religious hysteria and fear of a federal invasion led a Mormon militia – possibly with the enlisted help of local Paiutes – to slaughter 120 innocent California-bound pioneers. Details of the Mountain Meadows Massacre are still debated today, but the incident confirmed the government's worst fears, prompting the US Army to surround and subdue Salt Lake City that same year.

No one was killed and hardly a shot fired in the so-called Mormon War, which had two main repercussions: it instituted a secular government in Utah, beneath which the religious hierarchy continued to operate for a decade or more; and it curtailed territorial ambitions, reducing the size of Utah. Through the Civil War and beyond, the territory petitioned for

---

LATTER-DAY SAINTS

Self-proclaimed prophet Joseph Smith was born in Vermont in 1805. The child of mystics, Joseph came of age just as a widespread religious revival movement, called the Second Great Awakening, was feverishly beginning to take hold of the country. Religious revival camp meetings were a common sight, especially in rural towns and on the Western frontier.

Smith claimed to have received his first heavenly visit at age 18, when the angel Moroni revealed to him the location of golden tablets buried in the woods near his home in New York. This was three years after God told him in a vision that all churches currently in existence were false. The angel Moroni returned three more times, once a year. After the fourth visit, Smith was allowed to take the golden tablets home and, using 'stone spectacles' provided by the angel, read and transcribe the indecipherable word of God.

Three years later, in 1830, these revelations were published as the *Book of Mormon*, and the Church of Jesus Christ of Latter-Day Saints was established, with Smith as its charismatic leader. There's much more to the story of the Mormon faith – which thanks to globe-trotting missionaries is one of the world's fastest-growing religions, with over 15 million members. If you're curious, just open the *Book of Mormon;* there's one in every hotel room in Utah. St George in Southwest Utah is a great town in which to explore Mormonism in greater depth.

1865–67	1869	1870	1872
Utah's Black Hawk War reaches its peak, with fighting between Mormon settlers and Ute, Paiute and Navajo tribespeople; Native American resistance does not end until 1872.	First transcontinental railway line is completed north of Salt Lake City. John Wesley Powell successfully descends the Colorado River and begins a geologic survey of southern Utah.	Mormon pioneer Ebenezer Bryce and his family settle near Bryce Canyon, which he famously calls 'a hell of a place to lose a cow.'	John Wesley Powell returns to southern Utah and explores Zion Canyon, calling it Mukuntuweap, which he believed was a Paiute word for 'straight canyon.' Yellowstone National Park is formed.

statehood, but it was continually denied, even as states around it were accepted. Animosity between Mormons and the federal government lingered, with polygamy as the sticking point. Finally, in 1890 the Mormon church officially repudiated polygamy and asked its followers to do the same. Six years later Utah won statehood.

A Tale of Two Explorers

In their efforts to be self-sufficient, the Mormons established several missions in southern Utah in the 1850s and '60s: the Iron Mission, centered around Cedar City, mined ore and smelted iron for construction; while the Cotton Mission, centered around St George, grew cotton for Mormon use and export. Neither mission was ultimately successful. However, the Mormons also sent missionaries south to convert the Southern Paiutes, and its success was largely due to Jacob Hamblin, who arrived in 1854.

Hamblin gained the respect and trust of some Native American tribes across the Southwest. He said he believed that if he always told the truth, listened and never shed Native American blood, he would be safe. Hamblin became a peacemaker who negotiated important treaties and, with Native American assistance, explored the Colorado Plateau as no non–Native American had before him, serving as an ambassador of the Mormon church, including to the Hopi mesas and the Navajo Nation.

In 1869 one-armed Civil War veteran and geologist John Wesley Powell became famous for being the first to descend the length of the Colorado River through the Grand Canyon. Powell's motivation was not religious, but to survey and explore the land and peoples of southern Utah for science. Powell and his survey teams' geologic and ethnological work largely forms the basis of what we know about early southern Utah today. In 1870 Hamblin secured Powell's second expedition a welcome among Southern Paiutes. As Hamblin had done, Powell demonstrated respect and earned both safe passage and practical assistance from the Southern Paiutes. You can track Powell's expeditions in Canyonlands, Zion, Staircase-Escalante National Monument and Lake Powell National Recreation Area.

Taming Zion's Wilderness

Earlier indigenous peoples undoubtedly knew and entered Zion Canyon, for they left evidence on the rocks, but to the Kaibab Paiutes it was a place to be avoided, particularly after sunset. Mysterious and foreboding, the canyon was seen as inhabited by trickster gods who were capricious, even willfully malicious. The first non–Native American to enter Zion Canyon was Nephi Johnson, a Mormon pioneer who came south with Jacob Hamblin on a mission. In 1858, at the behest of Brigham Young, Johnson explored the upper reaches of the Virgin River, looking for good places to settle. One can only imagine what he must have felt as he entered Zion Canyon alone, his Paiute guide waiting safely behind.

Curious about the lives of early Mormon settlers? Immerse yourself in the anthology *Pioneer Voices of Zion Canyon* (2006), by Eileen M Smith-Cavros, or *I Was Called to Dixie* (1979), by Andrew Karl Larson, a cotton missionary.

HISTORY A TALE OF TWO EXPLORERS

For more historical context on John Wesley Powell and his groundbreaking work, read Wallace Stegner's fascinating book *Beyond the Hundredth Meridian: John Wesley Powell and the Second Opening of the West* (1953).

1878	1889	1890	1896
Mormons permanently settle in the Moab region. (Ute tribespeople violently thwarted a previous effort in the 1850s.) Agriculture and grazing quickly become the economic mainstays.	Wild West outlaw Butch Cassidy, the son of Mormon immigrants, flees to southern Utah to hide out after robbing a bank in Telluride, Colorado.	Mormon president Wilford Woodruff signs a manifesto that officially ceases the practice of polygamy; plural marriage is still practiced today among fundamentalist groups in rural Utah.	Utah is admitted to the Union as the 45th state after territorial politicians agree to explicitly ban the practice of polygamy in the new state constitution.

Mormons didn't settle in the canyon until 1863, when Isaac Behunin and his sons built the first cabin and cleared some farmland. Behunin is credited with naming Zion Canyon, saying 'A man can worship god among these great cathedrals as well as in any man-made church.' When Brigham Young visited in 1870, he disagreed. Whether due to the arduous journey or the forbidden tobacco Behunin was growing, Young proclaimed it 'Not Zion,' a name that stuck among Mormons for years.

After his first famous Colorado River expedition, John Wesley Powell explored Zion Canyon in 1872. He called it Mukuntuweap, which he believed was a Paiute word for 'straight canyon.' But it was Clarence Dutton, a poet-geologist in Powell's employ, who captured its grandeur. On seeing the canyon in 1875, Dutton wrote: 'In coming time it will, I believe, take rank with a very small number of spectacles, each of which will, in its own way, be regarded as the most exquisite of its kind which the world discloses.'

In a 1908 official report, a government surveyor first suggested preserving Zion Canyon as a monument. President Taft signed the proclamation creating Mukuntuweap National Monument in 1909. Methodist minister Frederick Vining Fisher toured the canyon in the company of a Latter-Day Saints bishop in 1916, giving names to many of the famous rock formations, including Angels Landing and the Great White Throne. In 1919 the monument's name and designation were officially changed by Congress, and thus Zion National Park was born.

Within a year, park visitation doubled to about 3700 people. To better facilitate tourism to southern Utah, a railroad spur was extended to Cedar City in 1923. Zion Lodge opened two years later, accommodating railway tourists following the 'Grand Circle' route around the Southwest. In 1930 the Zion–Mt Carmel Hwy and its tunnel were completed, offering a paved route into and through Zion, bringing in over 55,000 tourists that year.

Beneath These Red Cliffs: An Ethnohistory of the Utah Paiutes (2006), by Ronald L Holt, with a foreword by tribal chairwoman Lora Tom, is an unflinching tale of indigenous survival, from Western occupation to tribal restoration.

Bryce Canyon

Bryce Canyon nestles alongside the Paunsaugunt Plateau, the latter's name derived from a Paiute word meaning 'home of the beavers.' Fur trappers like Jedediah Smith who roamed the area in the early 19th century made no mention of Bryce's striking scenery, and nor did Spanish traders. During his 1869 survey, John Wesley Powell stuck to the rivers and passed right by. Captain Sutton, a member of Powell's survey, described the distant terrain as seeming 'traversable only by a creature with wings.'

Mormons scouts arrived at Bryce Canyon in the 1850s as they searched the entire Paunsaugunt Plateau for arable land. In the mid-1870s a small group settled in the adjacent valleys, which seemed well suited for grazing livestock. Among the latter was Ebenezer Bryce, who stayed in the area for five years, building an irrigation ditch and a road into the canyon. Bryce moved his family south to Arizona in 1880, but left behind in the canyon his name and the now famous epithet, 'It's a hell of a place to lose a cow.'

An expansive, well-researched history is *The Proper Edge of the Sky: High Plateau Country of Utah* (2002), by Edward Geary, who stitches together in telling detail the ongoing relationship of people and the land.

1916	1919	1923	1927
President Woodrow Wilson authorizes the establishment of the National Park Service (NPS); Methodist minister Frederick Vining Fisher visits Zion Canyon. The US enters WWI a year later.	Already national monuments, both Zion and the Grand Canyon officially become national parks; a dirt road to the Grand Canyon's North Rim is built from Kanab, Utah.	Union Pacific Railroad is extended to Cedar City; building begins on Bryce Canyon Lodge, made of local timber and stone and designed by Gilbert Stanley Underwood.	Laborious and often-dangerous construction starts on the Zion–Mt Carmel Hwy, which opens three years later, bringing more tourists to southern Utah.

Like Zion Canyon, Bryce was popular among railway tourists and conservationists at the turn of the 20th century, though it was more difficult to reach. It wasn't until 1915, when JW Humphrey became the founding supervisor of Utah's Sevier National Forest, that Bryce's fate would be sealed. In 1916 Humphrey brought in photographers to take the first pictures of the spectacular canyon for a promotional article that appeared in a Union Pacific Railroad publication. Word got out.

In 1919, the same year Zion became a national park, the state legislature recommended that Bryce also be protected. Four years later President Harding established Bryce Canyon National Monument. In 1928 Bryce became Utah's second national park. In the 1920s, construction of Bryce Canyon Lodge, another Union Pacific Railroad 'Grand Circle' Southwest touring stop, was carried out using locally quarried stone and harvested timber.

The History of Southern Utah and its National Parks (1950), by AM Woodbury, is as much a period piece as a source of reliable history written by a man who lived through the parks' founding.

A Capital Wonderland

Capitol Reef's European-American history dates back to 1872, when Mormon settlers first planted fruit trees along the banks of the Fremont River near the town of Junction. Once their trees flourished, the settlers renamed the town Fruita. Over the next decades, Torrey resident Ephraim Pectal sought to promote interest in 'Wayne Wonderland,' a nickname given to the Waterpocket Fold, which lies in Wayne County. Soon after being elected to the state legislature in 1933, Pectal lobbied President Franklin D Roosevelt to establish what he dubbed 'Wayne Wonderland National Monument.' In 1937 President Roosevelt signed a proclamation creating the mercifully renamed Capitol Reef National Monument.

Despite Depression-era improvements completed by the Civilian Conservation Corps, Capitol Reef was mostly neglected by the federal government for the next two decades. The first official park ranger didn't arrive until 1958. But the nationwide 'Mission 66' national parks renewal project brought a host of new tourist facilities to serve over 145,000 annual visitors by 1967. In 1971, Congress made Capitol Reef a national park.

The Making of Moab

It wasn't until 1878 that Mormons permanently settled in the Moab region. (Ute tribespeople had violently thwarted a previous effort in the 1850s.) Agriculture and grazing quickly became the economic mainstays, although the new railroad that bypassed Moab in 1883 dealt a serious blow to this frontier community. Ranchers used much of the land in what is now Canyonlands National Park as winter pasture for grazing herds, a practice that continued through to 1975.

In the early 20th century, local residents, including the editor of Moab's first newspaper, touted southern Utah's geologic wonders, finally attracting the attention of the Rio Grande Western Railroad. Recognizing the potential of Arches as a tourist destination, the railroad lobbied the

Famous Western novelist Zane Grey used southern Utah as a backdrop for many of his romanticized cowboy tales; *Riders of the Purple Sage* (1912) is his best-known story. It's a galloping read.

1928	1933	1936	1941–45
Named after Mormon settler Ebenezer Bryce, Bryce Canyon becomes Utah's second national park; more than 25,000 tourists arrive that year, often en route to and from the Grand Canyon.	During the Great Depression, President Roosevelt creates the Civilian Conservation Corps in Utah, who plant more than three million trees in Utah over the next decade.	After five years of arduous construction, Boulder (Hoover) Dam is finished at the Nevada–Arizona state line near Las Vegas, with serious implications for the flow and volume of the Colorado River.	During WWII, Utah becomes an important state for defense operations, including military bases, mineral mining and arms manufacturing.

government for federal protection. In 1929, President Hoover established Arches as a national monument.

In the Cold War era of the 1950s, when the federal government subsidized uranium mining, Moab's population tripled in three years. By the early '60s, Arches superintendent Bates Wilson started lobbying for further protection of southeastern Utah's natural resources, calling for the establishment of a 'Grand View National Park.' In 1964, President Johnson established Canyonlands National Park. In 1971, Congress declared Arches a national park too, and expanded the boundaries of Canyonlands.

Rock climbers, hippies, rafters, mountain bikers and off-road enthusiasts have shaped the surrounding desert over the years, making this an adrenaline-sports capital.

Exploitation vs Conservation

The amount of arable land in Utah is less than 5%, and in southern Utah that figure is less than 1%. What farmland there is and towns there are depend entirely on rivers. The rain that falls in the desert is hardly enough to work up a good spit. Twentieth-century development has been slow to recognize and adapt to these facts, however. Politicians have dammed countless rivers across the Southwest to try to control and divert their flow and create power: the Colorado River has been dammed twice, by Hoover Dam in 1936 and Glen Canyon Dam, among the world's largest, in 1963. Public works projects have repeatedly failed, often spectacularly and expensively, and yet the attempts continue. And still no Eden.

Throughout the busy Beehive State, mining has experienced various heydays – from the great silver mines of the 19th century to modern coal, oil and mineral mining, especially to support WWII military operations. In the 1950s the federal government subsidized uranium exploration, spurring more Cold War–era mining operations in southern Utah, especially around Moab. Though these efforts unearthed little of the radioactive element, mining roads further opened this once-remote landscape to recreational tourism and encouraged settlement. At the same time, all of this extraction has exacted a high toll on the slow-healing desert.

Today, southern Utah's desert settlements are well established, and politics demands that they be supported, even as the economic and environmental costs keep growing. At the same time, many people – both outsiders and those who have made their homes in this seemingly inhospitable place – have long recognized the rare beauty of these lands and made efforts to preserve them. In fact, the first paintings of such Western landmarks as the Grand Canyon and Zion Canyon, by Albert Bierstadt and Thomas Moran, were instrumental in sparking the US conservation movement during the late 19th century, which in turn brought about the establishment of the National Park Service (NPS) in 1916.

Those Who Came Before: Southwestern Archaeology in the National Park System (1993), by Robert and Florence Lister, puts Capitol Reef, Canyonlands and Arches in the greater context of the Colorado Plateau, with striking photographs.

Roadside History of Utah (1999), by Cynthia Larsen Bennett, is an informative, thought-provoking if weighty companion for history buffs, covering both major interstates and rural highways throughout the state, including southern Utah's 'Forgotten Corridor.'

1950s	1962	1963	1964
After getting a master's degree in philosophy, writer and political activist Edward Abbey works as a seasonal ranger at Arches National Monument, laying the groundwork for his memoir *Desert Solitaire*.	Utah's all-weather state Hwy 24 through the Fremont River canyon is finally finished and paved, opening up the Capitol Reef region to burgeoning tourism.	Controversial Glen Canyon Dam is finished and artificial Lake Powell begins to form, eventually covering up ancestral Native American sites and stunning rock formations.	Canyonlands National Park is set aside by Congress, after a lobbying and public-opinion campaign jump-started by Arches National Monument superintendent Bates Wilson. In 1971, both are designated national parks.

Not everyone wants to see southern Utah's remaining wilderness protected. Established by President Clinton in 1996 and administered by the Bureau of Land Management (BLM), Grand Staircase-Escalante National Monument is southern Utah's most controversial federal land grab. Many of Utah's Republican majority believed the president was 'appeasing his Sierra Club constituents' by establishing a monument in a state that had not supported him in either election. Counties in southern Utah sued the federal government, claiming the executive branch lacked jurisdiction to declare a national monument. In 2004 a federal court ruled that the president had acted within his bounds under the authority of the 1906 Antiquities Act. Given ever-growing regional tourism, Grand Staircase-Escalante is likely not the last part of southern Utah's vast wilderness to be set aside 'for the enjoyment, education, and inspiration of this and future generations,' as the NPS mission statement promises.

HBO's hit cable TV drama *Big Love* is a fictional depiction of fundamentalist Mormons and the contemporary practice of 'plural marriage' (ie polygamy) in Utah.

HISTORY EXPLOITATION VS CONSERVATION

THE RED ROCK WILDERNESS ACT: A CITIZENS' PROPOSAL

Any attempt to conserve land in the Southwest stirs intense passions, and the Red Rock Wilderness Act is a doozy. If passed, it would set aside over 9 million acres of southern Utah desert as congressionally designated wilderness area, the most restrictive type of public lands. This restricted use prohibits motorized vehicles, resource extraction, road building and infrastructure development. Indeed, members of the public are only permitted to enter such areas on foot, horse or non-motorized boat, and the act would prohibit mountain bikers (a big sore point for some).

Nearly 80% of Utah's land already lies in public hands, 65% of which is owned by the federal government. The Red Rock Wilderness Act would change the status of about 15% of these existing federal lands. Opponents of the act frequently say that Utah has already done enough. Putting even more land off-limits to resource extraction and road building is unfair. Why not, they say, focus conservation efforts on other Western states – they have plenty of land, right?

Land, yes. Wilderness, no. And there's the rub. Precious little land in the US remains pristine enough to qualify as wilderness. Southern Utah, the last US region to be settled by non-native peoples and mapped, has more than most. Much of Utah is already federally protected to some degree, but proponents say the amount and the protections aren't enough.

In 1985 the BLM itself identified more than 3 million acres for further possible wilderness designation in southern Utah, but a citizens' group did its own inventory and suggested that nearly 6 million acres could be added to that total. In 1989 it formalized its plan as a congressional bill dubbed 'The Citizens' Proposal' – which was eventually renamed America's Red Rock Wilderness Act. The bill has since been reintroduced into every new session of Congress, before which it still sits – at least, for the time being.

To learn more or take action yourself, contact the **Southern Utah Wilderness Alliance** (SUWA; www.suwa.org). For opposing views, head to Facebook for Utahans Against the Red Rock Wilderness Act.

1989	1996	2000	2009
Introduction of the Red Rock Wilderness Act, controversial landmark legislation that sees over 9 million acres of Utah designated wilderness. The act has yet to pass.	President Bill Clinton establishes Grand Staircase-Escalante National Monument, allowing for some land uses (eg hunting and grazing by permit) not allowed in national parks. Mountain biking continues its rise.	Zion Canyon institutes a mandatory seasonal shuttle system to relieve car congestion and reduce air pollution, eliminating over 5 million pounds of carbon-dioxide emissions annually.	Zion National Park celebrates its centennial, themed 'A Century of Sanctuary.' Over 2.7 million visitors arrive in the park that year.

Geology

Home to all of Utah's national parks, the Colorado Plateau is one of the geologic features that defines the West. No wonder this land of canyons, desert towers and hoodoos so often sits center stage in Hollywood Westerns and Willy E Coyote cartoons. The rise of the plateau, coupled with the effects of a million years of erosion by sand, wind and rivers, is fundamental to understanding the striated geologic history of Utah's national parks.

An Overview of the Colorado Plateau

A technical and colorful overview of the region's rocks is provided in *Geology of Utah's Parks & Monuments* (2003), published by the Utah Geological Association, and edited by Douglas Sprinkel and a team of specialists.

The Colorado Plateau extends for 337,000 sq km through portions of Utah, Colorado, New Mexico and Arizona. Evidence of its long-term stability is readily apparent in the horizontal layers of sediment that have changed little from the day they were laid down. But to the west, the thinning and stretching of the Earth's crust has been so vigorous that mountain ranges have collapsed onto their sides and entire valleys have fallen thousands of feet. To the east, colliding forces have crumpled the land to form the Rocky Mountains.

Starting out as a shallow basin collecting sediment from nearby mountains, the entire Colorado Plateau was uplifted some 60 million years ago. At that time, the plateau split along deep cracks called faults. Over hundreds of thousands of years, these cracks have eroded to form stupendous cliffs that subdivide the Colorado Plateau into several smaller plateaus. Along the western edge, for example, a line of high, forested plateaus tower 3000ft above desert lowlands and valleys. Nicknamed the High Plateaus by geologist Clarence Dutton in 1880, the term encompasses the flat-topped mesas of Zion and Bryce Canyon National Parks and also Cedar Breaks National Monument.

From an aerial perspective, these lofty plateaus and cliffs form a remarkable staircase that steps down from southern Utah into northern Arizona. Topping this so-called 'Grand Staircase' are the Pink Cliffs of the Claron Formation extravagantly exposed in Bryce Canyon. Below them jut the Gray Cliffs of various Cretaceous formations. Next in line are the White Cliffs of Navajo sandstone that make Zion Canyon justly famous. These are followed by the Vermilion Cliffs near Lees Ferry, Arizona, and finally come the Chocolate Cliffs abutting the Kaibab Plateau and Grand Canyon.

Challenging *Basin & Range* (1981), by Pulitzer Prize–winning writer John McPhee, is as much about the journey through, as the geology of, the Great Basin, which covers much of western Utah, Nevada and eastern California.

Another way of understanding the Grand Staircase is to visualize that the top layers of exposed rock at the Grand Canyon form Zion's basement, and that Zion's top layers in turn form the bottom layers of Bryce Canyon National Park. Geologically speaking, one can imagine the parks as being stacked on top of each other. Hypothetically, a river cutting a canyon at Bryce would eventually form another Zion Canyon, and then, over time, create another Grand Canyon.

A Four-Act Play

Perhaps the simplest way to approach the geologic story of the Colorado Plateau is to think of it as a four-act play. The first act features sedimentation, followed by lithification, then uplift and, finally, erosion. While this is an oversimplification, and there's overlap between the scenes, it offers a framework for understanding the region's geologic history.

More than 250 million years ago, the Colorado Plateau country was a shallow sea off the west coast of the young North American continent (which at the time was merged with other continents into a giant supercontinent known as Pangaea). This time period, known as the Paleozoic Era, marked the dramatic transition from primitive organisms to an explosion of complex life-forms that spread into every available niche – the beginning of life as we know it. Fossils, limestone and other sediments from this era now comprise nearly all exposed rocks in the Grand Canyon, and they form the foundation that underlies all of the Colorado Plateau.

At the close of the Paleozoic Era, the land rose somewhat and the sea mostly drained away, though it advanced and retreated numerous times during the Mesozoic Era (250 million to 65 million years ago). Sedimentation continued as eroding mountains created deltas and floodplains, and as shallow seas and tidal flats left other deposits. Meanwhile, the rise of an island mountain chain off the coast apparently blocked moisture-bearing storms, and a vast Sahara-like desert developed across the region, piling thousands of feet of sand atop older floodplain sediments. Zion's monumental Navajo sandstone cliffs and Arches' soaring spans of Entrada sandstone preserve evidence of mighty sand dunes.

Over millions of years the weight of the accumulated layers (more than 2 miles thick) compacted loosely settled materials into rocks cemented together with mineral deposits – a process called lithification. Sandstone, siltstone and mudstone are each cemented together with calcium carbonate. Variations in particle size and quantities of cement account for these layers' differing strengths – weakly bonded rocks crumble relatively easily in water, while more durable rocks form sheer cliffs and angular blocks.

Then came the uplift. About 60 million years ago North America began a dramatic separation from Europe, sliding west over another part of the earth's crust and leaving behind an ever-widening gulf in the Atlantic Ocean. This movement caused the continent's leading edge to uplift, forever transforming the face of the continent by raising the Colorado Plateau more than a mile above sea level. Though the plateau avoided the geologic turmoil that deformed much of western North America, the forces of uplift did shatter the plateau along fault lines into stair-step subplateaus. Furthermore, the creation of the Rocky Mountains provided headwaters for great rivers that would chisel their way through the newly risen plateau in their rush to the sea, forming the great canyons we see today.

In fact, nearly every aspect of the Colorado Plateau landscape is shaped by erosion. Several factors make the forces of erosion particularly dramatic in the Southwest. First are the region's colorful rock layers themselves. As these layers rose, gravity enabled watercourses to gain momentum and carve through stone, while sporadic rainfall and an arid climate ensured the soft layers would otherwise remain intact. These factors have remained consistent over millennia, enabling fragile hoodoos, fins and arches to develop.

Water is by far the most dramatic shaping force. Flash floods tear through soft rock with immense power, tumbling house-sized boulders down narrow slot canyons and scooping out crumbling sediments like pudding. Those who witness summer thunderstorms will notice how quickly desert waters turn rust-red with dissolving sedimentary rock. Zion's Virgin River has been described as 'a red ribbon of liquid sandpaper' due to its relentless downward gouging.

GEOLOGY A FOUR-ACT PLAY

Among the piles of slick picture books, *Water, Rock & Time* (2005), by Robert L Eves, stands out. It pairs colorful illustrations and photos with eloquent writing and clear descriptions of Zion's geology, accessible for everyone.

Armchair explorers can take a virtual field trip to southern Utah, or learn where to find dinosaur tracks, on the Utah Geological Survey's website (http://geology. utah.gov).

Roadside Geology of Utah (1990), by Halka Chronic, is an invaluable companion for geology buffs, aspiring and otherwise. By the end of your trip, you'll never confuse your Navajo and Entrada sandstones again!

Iconic Formations of Southern Utah

With arches, buttresses, hoodoos, fins, narrows, canyons and spindly wind-whipped towers, Utah offers up iconic glimpses into the earth's violent and fascinating geological history. Here you can travel through time as you journey past layer upon layer of sandstone, gape at delicate arches or just sit and wonder how a river could carve a canyon so deep and so elegant.

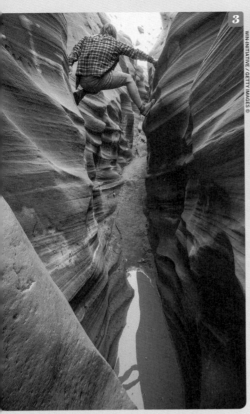

1. Landscape Arch (p199)
At 306ft, this elegant sweep of sandstone in Arches National Park is longer than a football field.

2. Grand View Point (p187)
The mesa stretches out from this Canyonlands spot, one of the most stunning vistas in the Southwest.

3. Slot Canyon (p142)
There are miles of undulating orange walls in Grand Staircase-Escalante National Monument.

4. Delicate Arch (p201)
A narrow slickroad ledge leads hikers up to this sandstone archway.

5. Goblin Valley State Park (p175)
Hiking trails in this small desert park lead past mushroom-shaped mounds of Entrada sandstone.

As the rocks' calcium-carbonate cement dissolves in rainwater, it releases sand particles and flows down rock faces, then hardens again as it dries, leaving drippings that look like candle wax – a common feature on rock faces in both Zion and Bryce Canyons. Over time, this leaching away of the cement also widens cracks and creates isolated fins that further split and dissolve into hoodoos, windows, arches and other fantastic forms, as seen in all of southern Utah's parks.

In winter, storm erosion works in tandem with another equally powerful force. As rainfall seeps into cracks, it freezes and then expands with incredible pressure (sometimes over 20,000lb per square foot), pushing open crevices and prying loose blocks of stone. At higher elevations such as Bryce Canyon, this freeze-thaw cycle is repeated more than 200 times each year, exacting a tremendous but ultimately beautiful toll on the natural landscape.

Reading the Parks

It's a complex geologic tableau that characterizes the national parks of southern Utah, from Arches to Zion. In a sense it's a remarkably homogenous region, but at the same time, the forces of erosion have carved an amazingly intricate and diverse landscape that's difficult to comprehend. Each park and national monument reveals an astonishing geologic story that goes far beyond the scope of this brief introduction.

Zion National Park

Part of southern Utah's High Plateaus district, Zion sits on the southwest corner of the Colorado Plateau, marking the transition from relatively stable plateau country to the more tectonically active Great Basin. Separating these distinct regions is a long line of cliffs along the Hurricane Fault.

In Zion Canyon, massive cliffs expose more than 2000ft of Navajo sandstone, formed by ancient sand dunes. Nowhere else in the world do these rock formations reach such grand heights. Meanwhile, in the park's Kolob Canyons area, sheer cliffs jut abruptly from the Hurricane Fault as if they rose out of the ground just yesterday. The reddish coloration of all of these cliffs is caused by iron oxides. In the more freshly exposed rocks of Kolob Canyons, the red is evenly distributed. More oxides have leached out of Zion Canyon's ancient weathered cliffs, however, leaving the uppermost layers whitish.

Bisecting the national park, the Virgin River continues its steady march – cutting downward about 1000ft every million years – so rapidly, in fact, that side tributaries can't keep up and are left as hanging valleys high on cliff faces. The dynamic interplay between Navajo sandstone and the underlying Kayenta Formation largely shapes Zion Canyon. Through the Narrows, for example, the Virgin River flows entirely between sandstone walls, but where it cuts deeply enough, the river readily erodes the softer shale underneath the sandstone cliffs and dramatically widens the canyon.

Bryce Canyon National Park

Bryce is not a canyon at all, but a series of amphitheaters gouged from the gorgeous Pink Cliffs. The park's central Claron Formation results from soft siltstone and mudstone that settled to the bottom of a giant freshwater lake 60 million years ago. Traces of manganese and iron account for this layer's fetching pink and orange hues. About 15 million years ago, the lakebed lifted, cracking from the stress along countless parallel joints, while further east the Aquarius Plateau rose even higher. The significant valley between the plateau and Bryce was carved by the

---

Zion's soaring cliffs were once humongous sand dunes – look closely for fine diagonal lines of cross-bedding, the marks of ancient winds that once swept the dunes.

Glen Canyon was flooded in 1963, forming Lake Powell. The Sierra Club had blocked the creation of the dam in nearby Dinosaur National Monument, paying less attention to Glen Canyon.

Paria River, which over the past million years has begun to nip at the park's cliffs.

Bryce features dramatic formations at all stages of development, from newly emerging fins to old weathered hoodoos beaten down into colorful mounds. Runoff along joints on the canyon rim forms parallel gullies with narrow rock walls, or fins, which ultimately erode into the isolated columns known as hoodoos. The layers are so soft that in heavy rains they would quickly dissolve into muddy little mounds, except that siltstone layers alternating with resistant limestone bands give the layers strength as they erode into towering hoodoos. Many hoodoos end up with a cap of harder limestone at their apex, protecting the softer material beneath.

Grand Staircase-Escalante National Monument

This vast, complex region contains examples of nearly every rock type and structural feature found in the Colorado Plateau country. Revealed here are more than 200 million years of geologic history and one of the world's most exceptional fossil records of early vertebrate evolution. The entire period that dinosaurs ruled the earth is preserved in remarkable detail. Grand arches, waterfalls, slot canyons, sculpted sandstone cliffs and challenging terrain make this a memorable place to visit.

The monument encompasses its namesake feature, the Grand Staircase, on its western edge. Over a dozen different geologic layers document Mesozoic seas, sand dunes and slow-moving waters that once teemed with abundant ancient life. Examples range from the lavender, rose, burgundy and peach colors of volcanic ash and petrified forests of the Chinle Formation to the ancient sand dunes preserved in the bluffs of Wingate sandstone at Circle Cliffs.

Few other features characterize this place like the celebrated slot canyons of the Escalante River, carved by fast-moving waters entrenched in resistant sandstone channels that cut downward rather than spreading outward. At their upper ends these canyons modestly wind through the slickrock like tiny veins before feeding into increasingly larger arteries that eventually empty into the Colorado River.

Capitol Reef National Park

Here, along a narrow, 100-mile stretch, the earth's surface is bent in a giant wrinkle, exposing multiple rock formations in tilted and upended strata. It's a unique geological feature of the region, in that the relatively stable Colorado Plateau was twisted and pulled here. This type of step-up feature is known as a monocline, and the Waterpocket Fold is one of the longest contiguously exposed monoclines in the world. Incredibly, the rock layers on the west side have been upended more than 7000ft higher than those to the east. Dubbed a reef by early explorers, who found it a barrier to travel, the fold is capped with bare rounded domes of Navajo sandstone reminiscent of the US Capitol building from the 1850s – hence the name Capitol Reef.

While just a few major canyons cut across the Waterpocket Fold, a baffling maze of side canyons crisscrosses the park in myriad directions. All formed along clefts and other weak points in the rock, where moisture collects (natural pools of water atop the fold account for its name) and eventually scours out ever-expanding gullies. Another sandstone layer, the Wingate Formation, gives the Waterpocket Fold a line of distinctive sheer red cliffs on its west side. A third sandstone layer, Entrada sandstone, forms the freestanding pinnacles and walls of Cathedral Valley.

Other formations add so much color and structural diversity that this park is considered without equal in a region chock-full of geologically impressive parks.

GEOLOGY READING THE PARKS

One of the best views of the Grand Staircase lies along Hwy 89A between Kanab, Utah, and Jacob Lake, Arizona, where the steps rise dramatically.

Singing Stone: A Natural History of the Escalante Canyons (1999), by Thomas Fleischner, brings the geology of Grand Staircase-Escalante National Monument into understandable, human terms as it examines the land controversies of the New West.

Capitol Reef has lots to interest amateur paleontologists, including North America's oldest pre-dinosaur megatrack site.

Canyonlands National Park

Canyonlands is defined by the mighty Colorado and Green Rivers. Although the rivers have already carved through 300 million years of the Earth's history, only the oldest 125 million years' worth of rock layers remain – a staggering testament to the power of erosion. When you gaze into the canyon depths from Grand View Point at the Colorado River, you're only looking at the middle slices of a giant geologic cake, with the top layers eaten away and the bottom layers still unseen.

Canyonlands is even more diverse than the Grand Canyon, possessing not just two converging river canyons, but intervening high mesas and a complex landscape of slickrock canyons, spires and arches. Cradled between the Green and Colorado Rivers, the Island in the Sky Mesa is a tableland of Wingate sandstone topped with scattered buttes and domes of Navajo sandstone. Below the mesa, slopes plunge 2000ft to the rivers past a shelf of White Rim sandstone partway down. The rivers twist and turn along meandering paths inherited from the Miocene epoch (about 10 million years ago), when the land was still a flat plain.

To the south, you'll find the Needles, where colorful red and white bands showcase a complicated, 250-million-year-old history of retreating and advancing shallow seas. The red layers formed in river flooding after the sea's retreat, while white layers represent ancient beaches and coastal dunes. To the west lies the Maze, an almost incomprehensibly convoluted landscape explored by backcountry adventurers.

In many parts of Utah, red cliffs appear to be stained black by a thick coating of desert varnish. Composed of clay minerals, oxides and hydroxides of manganese and iron, this patina is formed very slowly (even for geological time) and is instrumental in dating rock formations. It also provides the canvas on which many of southern Utah's petroglyphs have been carved.

Dive deeper into Utah's geology, with history, hiking and interactive map features on www.utahgeology.com.

Arches National Park

Compared to the other parks, Arches' geologic makeup is relatively easy to understand. Ancient rock layers rose atop an expanding salt dome, which later collapsed, fracturing layers along the dome's flanks. These cracks then eroded along roughly parallel lines, leaving fins of freestanding Entrada sandstone. In the last 10 million years, erosion has removed roughly a vertical mile of rock, carrying away all older materials save for the freestanding fins. This process continues today: even as brittle arches occasionally collapse, new ones are always in the making.

An arch formation is more a matter of happenstance than a predictable pattern, as people pay scant attention to the countless 'almost' arches that crumble into oblivion. But in a few lucky cases, rock slabs flake from the sides of fins in just the right way to create small openings that grow into arches as water seeps into cracks, freezes and dislodges more pieces.

At times the rock itself assists by releasing tremendous internal pressures stored within its layers, which causes more slabs to pop off. The uniform strength and hard upper surfaces of Entrada sandstone are the perfect combination for creating such beautiful arches, and today this park has the world's greatest concentration of natural stone arches.

Arches National Park has 2000 known arches within its boundaries, ranging in size from just 3ft to over 300ft wide; the largest is Landscape Arch.

Wildlife

The Colorado Plateau's harsh and arid landscape asks a lot of the plants and animals that make their homes here. Rains are few and far between, habitable terrain is limited, smaller washes evaporate quickly while rivers are separated by hundreds of miles, and the temperature shifts are dramatic. This said, many specialized plants and animals have found remarkable ways to survive and adapt to life on the plateau.

Animals

Wildlife in southern Utah's parklands ranges from nimble bighorn sheep and speedy raptors to scampering lizards and nosy ringtail cats, all scattered across a vast and wild region. Only rarely do animals congregate in large or conspicuous numbers, however. During the hottest days of summer, most animal activity takes place in the early evening or at night, when temperatures drop. Bird-watching is a particularly rewarding activity in southern Utah.

A Field Guide to Desert Holes (2002), by Pinau Merlin, is a quirky look at underground critters most visitors usually won't notice in the desert, unless you know where and how to look for them.

Large Mammals

Mountain Lions

Even veteran wildlife biologists rarely see a mountain lion, though a fair number reside in canyon country. Like their favorite prey, mule deer, mountain lions mostly inhabit forested areas. Reaching up to 8ft in length and weighing as much as 175lb, these solitary animals are formidable predators that rarely bother humans. A few attacks have occurred in areas where human encroachment has pushed hungry lions to their limits, mainly around rapidly growing towns and cities.

Mule Deer

Forests and meadows are the favored haunts of mule deer, which typically graze in the early morning and evening. Uncommon when settlers first arrived, and soon hunted out, mule deer nearly vanished around the turn of the 20th century, then quickly rebounded as their predators were eliminated.

Bighorn Sheep

Like solemn statues, desert bighorn sheep often stand motionless on distant cliff faces or ridgelines, distinguished by their distinctive curled horns. During the late-fall and early-winter breeding season, males charge each other at 20mph and ram horns so loudly that the sound can be heard for miles.

Small Mammals

Chipmunks & Squirrels

Several species of small, striped chipmunks and ground squirrels are ubiquitous in the parks. The white- and brown- or black-striped Uinta chipmunk is especially common along the canyon rim in Bryce and on Zion's forested plateaus. Though it resembles a chipmunk, the golden-mantled ground squirrel lacks facial stripes. Both species scamper through the forest, searching for nuts and seeds. They also beg for handouts – and occassionally run off with unattended sandwiches – but resist the urge to feed them.

On open desert flats you're more likely to see the white-tailed antelope squirrel, one of the few mammals active during the daytime. Look for its white tail, which it carries over its back like a reflective umbrella, shielding it from the sun as it darts between shady patches. True to its name, the speckled gray rock squirrel nearly always inhabits rocky areas. This large, bold squirrel often visits campgrounds.

To learn more about Bryce Canyon's prairie-dog community, download the ranger podcast from the park's official website at www.nps.gov/brca/photos multimedia/podcasts.htm.

Beavers

Some of the first Western explorers to wander across the Colorado Plateau came in search of prized beaver pelts. Limited to the few large rivers, beavers have never been common in southern Utah, but they are frequently sighted, because most visitors flock to the parks' rivers. In Zion their persistent nocturnal gnawing on large cottonwood trees presents something of a quandary. Wire mesh protects the base of some trees, but the park must still address the bigger question of how to restore the original balance of beavers, spring floods and cottonwoods that existed before humans forced the river into its current channel.

Porcupines

Looking much like an arboreal pincushion, the porcupine spends its days sleeping in caves or the hollows of trees in piñon-juniper woodlands. It's easy to overlook this strange creature, though on occasion you might encounter one waddling slowly through the forest. It's most active at night, when it gnaws on the soft inner wood of trees or pads around in search of flowers, fruit, nuts and berries.

Ringtail Cats

One of southern Utah's most intriguing creatures is the nocturnal ringtail cat, which looks like a masked chihuahua with a raccoon tail. It preys on mice and squirrels, but will eat lizards, birds or fruit in a pinch. Fairly common in rocky desert areas, ringtails may appear around campsites at night, though they are generally timid and secretive.

POTHOLES

A miracle of life unfolds wherever desert rains accumulate in what seem like lifeless, dusty bowls among the rocks. Hiding in the dust are the spores and eggs of creatures uniquely evolved to take advantage of ephemeral water. Within hours of rainfall, crustaceans, insects, protozoa and countless other organisms hatch and start swimming in this brew of life. Though most are microscopic or very small, there are also oddly shaped, 1in to 2in tadpole shrimp that resemble prehistoric trilobites.

Toads and frogs arrive the night after a rain and lay eggs that hatch quickly. Unlike amphibians in other areas, which can take months or years to develop, these tadpoles are champion athletes that emerge from the water in two to three weeks. No matter how productive a pothole may seem, however, its lifespan is limited by evaporation. All too soon, water levels drop, and everything turns to dust again. By then all the organisms have retreated into dormancy to wait for the next drenching rainstorm, which may be years or even decades away.

Because each pool is a fragile ecosystem, hikers should exercise special care when they find a pothole. If necessary, remove only a little water, and don't jump or swim in the water, because body oils, sunscreens and insect repellents can harm resident life. These creatures have nowhere else to go! Even when dry, these pools need our attention because the 'lifeless' dust is actually full of eggs and spores waiting to spring into life again.

Wood Rats

Although they bear a superficial resemblance to city rats, wood rats are extraordinary, gentle creatures. The Colorado Plateau's species all share a maddening propensity for stealing small shiny objects like watches or rings and leaving bones, seeds or other small objects in exchange – hence the animal's common nickname, the pack rat. Wood rats build massive stick nests (middens) that are used by countless generations. Upon dismantling these middens and examining their contents, biologists have been able to document more than 50,000 years of environmental prehistory in the region.

Birds

Small Birds

The first birds many people encounter are white-throated swifts, which swoop and dive in great numbers along cliff faces and canyon walls. Designed like sleek bullets, these sporty 'tuxedoed' birds seem to delight in riding every wind current and chasing each other in noisy, playful pursuit. Flying alongside the swifts are slightly less agile violet-green swallows, a familiar sight around campgrounds and park buildings. Both species catch their food 'on the wing.'

One bird with a unique call is the blue grouse. This resident of mountain forests vocalizes from the ground and has such a deep call that you almost feel it in your bones. Most sightings occur when a startled grouse erupts from your feet into flight. On rare occasions you may spot a male as it puffs up its chest and drums to attract a female.

The stirring song of the canyon wren is, for many people, the most evocative sound on the plateau. So haunting is the song it hardly seems possible that this tiny rust-red rock-dweller could produce such music. Starting as a fast run of sweet tinkling notes, the song fades gracefully into a rhythmic cadence that may leave you full of longing.

In contrast, the garrulous call of the Steller's jay can grate on your nerves like a loud rusty gate. But this iridescent blue mountain bird makes up for it with wonderfully inquisitive and confiding mannerisms. It often seems to have no fear of humans and eagerly gathers around picnic tables and campsites, hoping for leftovers – keep these birds wild by not giving them handouts or any other encouragement to beg.

Another common forest dweller is Clark's nutcracker, a grey bird with black wings and tail. Its highly specialized diet consists almost entirely of pine nuts, which it pries out of thick pine cones using its downturned bill like a crowbar. These birds may deposit up to 1000 ground caches of nuts in a single year, making its feeding habits integral to the survival and propagation of mountainous pine forests.

Rafters and riverside hikers will almost certainly meet the brilliant blue grosbeak, with its loud, long musical warbles. This migratory bird scours dense thickets for tasty insects and grubs, and males often ascend to high perches to defend their territory. The American dipper is often seen bobbing its head to snap up underwater insects, especially in Zion's Virgin River. This medium-sized gray fellow is North America's only true aquatic songbird, ably swimming in rapidly rushing rivers (without webbed feet!) to feed.

Large Birds

Of the various owls that reside on the Colorado Plateau, none is as familiar as the common and highly vocal great horned owl, which regularly fills the echoing canyons with its booming 'hoo-hoo hooo hooo' calls. This is among the largest and most fearsome of all raptors, and when one moves into the neighborhood, other owls and hawks hurry on to

Discover Utah's birds and the best spots to sight them on the extensive www.utahbirds.org website.

Once threatened by extinction – and still a species of special concern in Utah – some bald eagles spend their winters in Zion and Bryce's canyon country, with an estimated 1000 wintering across the state.

more favorable hunting grounds or run the risk of being hunted down as prey themselves. This bird's glaring face and prominent 'horns' (actually erect tufts of feathers) may startle hikers as it peers down at them from a crevice or dark cavity.

Scientists have documented 16 native species of bats in Canyon-lands National Park, accounting for nearly 90% of all bat species found in the entire state.

The threatened Mexican spotted owl has garnered considerable media coverage over the years. In California and the Pacific Northwest, this owl nests solely in old-growth forests, which are being logged, and climate change is affecting its habitat in the Southwest. The subspecies that lives on the Colorado Plateau makes its home in Utah's rugged canyons and mountain forests. Sightings are rare – there are only 2000 left in the US – but thrilling.

Commanding vast hunting territories of some 60 sq miles, powerful golden eagles are typically observed in passing as they travel widely in search of jackrabbits and other prey (up to the size of an adult deer). Watch for the characteristic golden tint on the eagle's shoulders and neck. Boasting a 7ft wingspan, it is among the area's largest birds, second in size only to reintroduced California condors. California condors are often confused with common turkey vultures. You can tell these fellow scavengers apart by the coloration on the undersides of their wings. Turkey vultures (or 'TVs') have black wings, with white tips. California condors also have black wings, but with white triangular-shaped patches on their undersides.

Despite their endangered status in recent decades, peregrine falcons thrive throughout the region, especially in Zion Canyon. There they find plenty of secluded, cliffside nesting sites, as well as one of their favorite food items, white-throated swifts, which they seize in midair. Look for the falcon's long, slender wings and dark 'moustache.'

Visitors may be surprised to see wild turkey. Formerly hunted out, this flashy game bird has been making a slow comeback in areas where it's protected, particularly in Zion Canyon. In the spring mating season, males fan out their impressive tails and strut around to impress females.

Amphibians & Reptiles

Amphibians

Bleating choruses of common canyon tree frogs float up from boulder-strewn canyon streams each night. Gray-brown and speckled like stone, these tiny frogs dwell in damp crevices by day, emerging at night (and sometimes late afternoon) to sing beside rocky pools. Occupying a similar habitat is the aptly named red-spotted toad, a small species with red-tipped warts covering its body. Its nighttime song around breeding pools is a high, persistent musical trill.

In *Desert Solitaire,* Edward Abbey recounts how a gopher snake that lived beneath his trailer in Arches National Park seemed to keep the rattlesnakes away.

More secretive, and thus rarely encountered, is the tiger salamander, the region's only salamander. Spending the majority of its life in a burrow, this creature emerges when abundant water triggers its breeding cycle. In order to fully develop, a larval salamander requires a water source, although some larvae never change into the adult form and become sexually mature while still in the larval stage. Coloration varies by region, but most are blackish all over.

Lizards

Perhaps the region's most abundant and widespread reptile is the eastern fence lizard, a small creature you'll probably see perched atop rocks and logs or scampering across the trail. During breeding season, males bob enthusiastically while conspicuously displaying their shiny blue throats and bellies. Females have dark, wavy crossbars on their backs and only a pale bluish wash underneath.

Bold in comparison is the greenish collared lizard, a large-headed species with striking black bands around its neck. This fearsome lizard eats just about every small animal it can overpower. Because it has little to fear, it often perches conspicuously atop large boulders, scanning for movement in all directions. Like most of southern Utah's lizards, it's inactive during the coldest winter months.

You may also encounter the curiously flattened horned lizard, which looks like a spiny little pancake. This lizard's shape is an adaptation to its exclusive diet of ants. In order to survive on this nutrient-poor diet, the horned lizard must eat lots of ants and consequently has an extremely large stomach that lends it its short, round appearance. Its shape also makes it harder for predators to grasp its body.

Snakes

The Colorado Plateau is excellent habitat for snakes, though visitors seldom encounter more than a few resident species. Most common is the gopher snake, easily mistaken for a rattlesnake because it hisses and vibrates its tail in dry leaves when threatened. Sporting a tan body with dark brown saddles, this 6ft to 8ft constrictor preys upon rodents, small birds, lizards and even the offspring of other snakes.

Nothing compares to the jolt of terror and adrenaline prompted by the angry behavior of a rattlesnake. Both humans and wild animals react with instinctive fear, even though rattlesnakes rarely strike unless provoked. These mild-mannered creatures would rather slide away unharmed than provoke a confrontation. A few species reside in the region, but only rarely does a visitor get close enough to tell them apart.

Another snake that keeps its distance is the striped whipsnake. This extremely slender 3ft to 6ft snake moves like lightning when alarmed and can climb into trees and bushes so quickly it seems like it's falling away from you. The snake uses this speed to capture lizards and rodents.

Fish

The Colorado River and its tributaries were once home to at least 14 native fish species, nearly all of them unique to these waters and highly adapted to extreme conditions. After the introduction of grazing, dams and other artificial changes to the landscape, dozens of introduced species are now outcompeting these native fish.

One representative native species is the threatened Colorado pikeminnow, North America's largest minnow (it can weigh up to 25lb and reach over 3ft in length). Once so abundant that it was pitchforked out of irrigation canals, the pikeminnow is in drastic decline, as many artificial dams block its 200-mile migration route. Three other endangered fish, the humpback chub, bonytail and razorback sucker, suffer similar fates. It's unclear whether they will survive the changes being made to the rivers.

Plants

The Colorado Plateau's complex landscape supports an equally diverse mix of plant species. Many are specific to the plateau, while others are drawn from adjacent biological zones such as the Great Basin, Mojave Desert and Rocky Mountains. Each park and monument boasts a list of hundreds of species, and no two places are alike.

Most species are adapted in some way to the Southwest's arid environment, either lying dormant until rains arrive or toughing it out through dry spells. If you arrive in wet season or after a drenching rain, you may be lucky enough to witness the region in its full splendor, when flowers carpet the landscape in all directions.

Wondering what flower you just saw? Use Arches National Park's online flower database, searchable by month, color and name, or download free plant-finder keys from www.nps.gov/arch/learn/nature/wildflowers.htm.

Wildlife Spotter's Guide

Head out into the desert wilderness for glimpses of this unique and delicate ecosystem that includes blooming cacti and living soils, tadpole shrimp, owls and peregrine falcons, lizards, snakes and bugs aplenty, plus a few larger mammals like bighorn sheep, mountain lions and mule deer.

1. Mule Deer
Mule deer frequent park campgrounds and developed areas, often moving upslope to avoid summer heat and returning down-slope as winter approaches.

2. Pronghorn Antelope
Pronghorn antelope are North America's fastest land mammals, running at speeds of up to 60mph. Catch them if you can – in a photo, that is – at Bryce Canyon.

3. Bighorn Sheep
Thanks to reintroduction efforts throughout southern Utah, bighorns are making a slow recovery after hunting and diseases introduced by domestic sheep drove their populations to record lows. Bring binoculars to spot theses sure-footed, cliff-climbing animals. Close sightings are rare and typically brief.

4. Raptors
Rare but beautiful California Condors sometimes are seen soaring through the canyons. Other top raptors include the great horned owl, golden eagle (pictured) and peregrine falcon.

5. Chipmunks and Squirrels
Small mammals are more abundant than their larger cousins, and many types of squirrels (pictured), chipmunks and small carnivores can be spotted around park campgrounds and picnic areas and along hiking trails.

6. Big Birds
The most ubiquitous large bird is the common raven (pictured), which seems to delight in making a noisy scene with its raucous calls and ceaseless play. This bird is an especially common sight along roadsides, where roadkill provides it with a steady supply of food.

7. Small Birds
Whether you get a thrill from watching the high-speed dives of white-throated swifts or from hearing the bright songs of canyon wrens (pictured) echoing across the plateau, there's no question that southern Utah's 250-plus bird species are among the region's top highlights.

8. Amphibians and Reptiles
Amphibians and reptiles are uniquely adapted to desert life, and a surprising variety of beautiful and unique species call southern Utah home. Fast-moving lizards (pictured: common collared lizard) skitter and snakes slither throughout the region, while frogs and toads are commonly found around water sources.

KWIKTOR / GETTY IMAGES ©

SUMIKOPHOTO / GETTY IMAGES ©

NORBERT KURZKA · PHOTOGRAPHY / GETTY IMAGES ©

PHOTO BY ANDREW REDING / GETTY IMAGES ©

CAROL POLICH PHOTO WORKSHOPS / GETTY IMAGES ©

What you'll witness more often, however, is the plodding life of plants that struggle to conserve every molecule of precious liquid. Many plants sport hairy or waxy leaves to prevent evaporation, while others bear tiny leaves. At least one common plant, Mormon tea, has done away with water-wasting leaves altogether and relies on its greenish, wiry stems for photosynthesis. Most species have long taproots to penetrate the soil in search of water.

The rapid rate of erosion on the Colorado Plateau also has a profound effect on the area's ecosystems. Unlike other regions, where eroded materials accumulate and cover vast areas with homogenous soils, erosion on the plateau carries sediments away. Plants have nowhere to live except on freshly exposed bedrock, and because each rock layer has its own distinctive composition and chemistry, this profoundly limits the species that can grow there.

Biological soil crust (p254) is the living groundcover that forms the foundation of high desert plant life across the plateau. This black crust is dominated by cyanobacteria, but also includes lichens, mosses, green algae, microfungi and bacteria. It's the web that keeps the desert from eroding. Never step on these delicate living features.

LIFE ZONES

Dominating southern Utah's parks, desert scrub is the hot, dry zone below 4000ft where scraggly shrubs cling to life on sandy flats. The most common are low-growing blackbrush, shad scale, Mormon tea and sagebrush. Annual precipitation is likely to average less than 8in, a number that includes winter snows as well, so it isn't very much rain, and most of it ends up running over bare rocks and washing away before plants can even use it.

Another widespread habitat is the open woodland of piñon pine and Utah juniper. Piñon-juniper woodland ('P-J' for short) grows mostly between 4000ft and 7000ft. Due to competition for water, trees are spaced widely here, though they still provide shade for many understory plants, as well as food and shelter for many animals. In some areas the trees grow in distinct lines, following cracks in the rock where water gathers after rain.

Growing in a narrow band between 7000ft and 8500ft, ponderosa pine forest indicates the presence of increased rainfall at higher elevations. In Zion, however, ponderosa pines grow at lower elevations, because porous Navajo sandstone is full of water, demonstrating once again how water dictates where plants can grow in this region. Ponderosa pines thrive in Zion and Bryce Canyon (with a few stands in Grand Staircase-Escalante) but are absent in lower-elevation Capitol Reef, Canyonlands and Arches.

Boreal forest above 8500ft has much in common with Rocky Mountain forests, even supporting many of the same plants and animals. This is a zone of cool, moist woodland and rainfall that exceeds 20in a year, conditions that favor trees like spruce, Douglas fir and quaking aspen. This forest populates a few high mesas in Zion, but the best examples are found at higher elevations in Bryce Canyon, particularly at road's end near Rainbow Point, where stands of ancient bristlecone pines survive.

Due to intensive grazing, the grassland that once covered much of this region has been largely replaced by desert scrub and alien weeds. Early Western explorers' journals describe a lush grassy landscape, though you'd hardly know it today. In areas of deeper sand and soil, where shrubs don't grow well, it's still possible to find pockets of galleta and Indian ricegrass.

Readily available water supports another set of unique habitats, ranging from hanging gardens clustered around cliffside seeps to riparian woodland lining perennial creeks and rivers. The presence of water attracts many plants and animals to these habitats. Monkeyflowers, columbines and ferns mark spots where springs flow from sandstone cliffs. Riverbanks that were once home to majestic cottonwood and willow stands are more likely today to harbor highly invasive tamarisk.

Trees

Piñon pines are well known for their highly nutritious and flavorful seeds. These same seeds have long been a staple for Native Americans, and many animals also feast on the seeds when they ripen in the fall. Piñons bear stout rounded cones and short single needles. Together with Utah junipers, piñon pines form a distinctive plant community that covers millions of acres of Southwestern desert. Blue, berrylike cones and diminutive scalelike needles distinguish junipers.

Mingling with piñons and junipers in some canyons is the beautiful little Gambel oak, with its dark green leaves turning shades of yellow and red in autumn and adding to the palette of color, particularly in Zion Canyon. Often growing in dense thickets, the oaks produce copious quantities of nutritious, tasty acorns long favored by Native Americans and used to make ground meal, breads, cakes and soups.

To identify the stately ponderosa pine, look for large spiny cones, needles in clusters of three, and yellowish bark that smells like butterscotch or vanilla. Between 20,000 and 12,000 years ago, the Douglas fir was one of the region's dominant species, though today they are restricted to isolated mountaintops and north-facing slopes. This relict of an earlier time dramatically demonstrates how the region's vegetation has changed since the ice age. It's identified by its single needles and cones with three-pronged bracts on each seed.

Found amid damp mountain meadows, quaking aspen is immediately recognizable by its smooth, white bark and circular leaves. Every gust of wind sets these leaves quivering on their flattened stems, an adaptation for shaking off late snowfalls that would otherwise damage fragile leaves. Aspen groves comprise genetically identical trunks sprouting from a common root system that may grow to more than a hundred acres in size. By budding repeatedly from these root systems, aspens have what has been called 'theoretical immortality' – some aspen roots are thought to be more than a million years old.

Rivers and watercourses in this harsh desert landscape are lined with thin ribbons of water-loving plants that can't survive anywhere else. Towering prominently over all others is the showy Fremont cottonwood, whose large, vaguely heart-shaped leaves rustle wildly in any wind. Hikers in the canyons' scorching depths find welcome respite in the shade of this tree. In spring, cottonwoods produce vast quantities of cottony seed packets that fill the air and collect in every crack and crevice. Box elder is another common streamside plant. It issues winged, maplelike seeds and bears trifoliate leaves that resemble those of poison ivy.

Since 1920 the aggressive weedy tamarisk (salt cedar) has largely replaced native streamside plant communities. Though this delicately leaved plant from Eurasia and Africa sports a handsome coat of soft pink and white flowers through the summer, its charm ends there, for it robs water from the soil and completely overwhelms such native species as cottonwood and willow.

A special treat is a visit to the fruit orchards (p170) of Capitol Reef, where you can pick apples, peaches and cherries.

Shrubs

Blackbrush covers large tracts of Southwestern deserts. This dark shrub reaches great ages and is only rarely replaced by young seedlings. With wiry stems, shrunken leaves and yellowish-red petal-less flowers blooming only after heavy spring rains, it may look more dead than alive.

Also triggered by spring rains, the common cliff rose (or desert bitterbrush) paints rocky slopes with its white blossoms surrounding yellow stamens. You're likely to 'hear' this plant before you see it, as bees and

The common desert shrub nicknamed Mormon tea is a species of Ephedra plant, which Native Americans also used for medicinal purposes, including as a stimulating brew.

Ancient bristlecone pines may be slow growing, but they're believed to be the oldest living single organisms on Earth, with some possibly 5000 years old.

insects swarm to its acrid-smelling flowers. Though its resinous, leathery leaves taste bitter, deer still munch on the plant in winter.

Narrowleaf yucca is a stout succulent related to agave and century plants. Yuccas favor sandy sites, while blackbrush predominates on thin gravelly soils. Growing in a dense rosette of thick leaves, this plant sends up a 5ft stalk of creamy flowers. A night-flying moth pollinates these flowers; in exchange, the caterpillars eat some seeds. Native Americans used yucca fibers to weave baskets and sandals.

Ripening in summer, the juicy black canyon grape is a tart favorite food of many different kinds of mammals and nearly 100 species of birds. Its vines snake over bushes and rocks in damp canyons, particularly in Zion Canyon, where its maplelike leaves turn yellow, orange and red in the fall.

Another distinctive shrub is greenleaf manzanita, which flourishes in ponderosa pine forests along the rim of Bryce Canyon. It bears reddish-brown bark and equally smooth, quarter-sized leaves. Bees alight on its pale pinkish flowers, while mammals and birds feed on its dark-red fruit.

Wildflowers

A surprisingly large variety of wildflowers thrive in the Colorado Plateau's arid, rocky landscapes. While late-winter precipitation and spring snowmelt trigger some plants to flower, many others bloom following midsummer thunderstorms or when temperatures cool in early autumn.

Seeps, springs and stream banks host some of the most dramatic flower displays. The brilliant flash of monkeyflowers amid greenery comes as something of a shock for hikers who've trudged across miles of searing baked rock. These red, yellow and purple flowers with widely flared 'lips' are very tempting to hummingbirds.

Columbines are also common at the seeps and springs, though some species range up into forested areas as well. The golden columbine and crimson-colored Western columbine are most common in wet, shaded canyon recesses. Rock columbine grows amid Bryce Canyon's hoodoos, where its vivid blue flowers stand out against red-rock cliffs. The flowers of both species hold pockets of nectar that attract large numbers of butterflies and hummingbirds.

The showy prince's-plume boldly marks selenium-rich desert soils with a 2ft to 3ft stalk of dainty yellow flowers. By using selenium in place of sulfur to manufacture its amino acids, this plant renders itself poisonous to herbivores and grows in soils that other plants can't tolerate. Prospectors once thought of this plant as an indicator of places to dig for uranium, as selenium deposits may naturally occur near uranium. Other wildflowers that do well on dry, gravelly slopes include stalky penstemon and paintbrush varieties, all with bright, showy tubular flowers in a rainbow of colors.

In peak years, evening primroses are so abundant that it looks like someone scattered white tissues over the sandy desert. Turning from white to rosy pink, the small flowers open at sunset and close by morning, thus avoiding the day's heat and conserving water. At night, large sphinx moths dart from flower to flower, collecting nectar and laying eggs.

Blooming in late spring and early summer, the three-petaled sego lily is another white flowering plant that is also Utah's state flower. Native Americans and early Mormon settlers once harvested the plant's walnut-sized bulbs for food. Don't confuse its small, delicate blooms with the large, showy white flowers of sacred datura, which blooms from spring through fall. This poisonous plant was traditionally used by some indigenous tribes during religious rituals as a potent hallucinogenic, but it can be deadly.

Take a sneak peek at Zion's comprehensive plant library – a virtual botanical treasure chest for researchers and park rangers – online at www. nps.gov/zion/naturescience.

Wildflowers of Zion National Park (1999), by Stanley Welsh, is an excellent pocket-sized guide that covers the most common wildflowers that hikers and visitors will encounter along the park's trails, blooming from spring through autumn.

Conservation

Here under the desert stars and up by the devilish hoodoos, the dance of nature is profound, intricate and delicate. The uniquely adapted ecosystems here are intimately tied to water, and even the smallest of environmental impacts can create huge change for one of North America's largest intact wildernesses.

With the highest concentration of protected lands in the continental US, plus protective management by a variety of governmental agencies, it seems that most of the damage to this landscape could be a thing of the past. But much work remains, and top conservation challenges today are increased visitation, mining and resource extraction, land-use and management, climate change, invasive species and man-made dams.

Increased Visitation

An estimated 40 million people will travel through the Colorado Plateau this year – a lot of boots on the ground, paddles in the water, and wheels on the trail. And the five national parks are seeing an unprecedented spike in visitation, with recent statistics indicating seven million annual visitors.

In a region where life hangs by a fragile thread, the heavy trampling of feet and off-road vehicles leaves lasting impressions. Desert crusts, wet meadows and riverside campsites are slow to recover from such use, and repeated visits can cause permanent damage. The effects may accumulate so gradually they almost go unnoticed. Scientists at Bryce Canyon estimate that 3% of the vegetation disappears each year from people wandering off-trail among the hoodoos – just tiny little bites that build up over time. Human artifacts like petroglyphs are also at risk from idiots leaving graffiti.

The parks are acutely aware of this and actively try to mitigate visitor impacts wherever possible. Both Zion and Bryce Canyon have developed free public-transit systems and a growing network of pedestrian and bicycle trails as a way of reducing traffic congestion and air pollution. All of southern Utah's parks and concessionaire businesses now encourage and facilitate recycling. And Zion's visitor center is a model of smart, sustainable ecobuilding practices.

But visiting national parks is good for the environment right? Sure it is. More visitation means more visibility and awareness for protecting Utah's wild lands, it means an educated citizenry and it means more funds for the National Park Service (NPS).

To minimize the impacts of your trip, consider riding bikes into the parks or at the very least carpooling, staying on trails, picking up litter and, of course, leaving no trace. Consider this: the challenge of visitation is not just about air pollution and littering, it's also about noise pollution, light pollution that affects dark skies and habitat encroachment.

Land Use

Grazing, mining, oil and gas extraction, and military exercises still create scars around southern Utah's parks and monuments, and land use in Utah has become a hot-button environmental issue in the US West today (p224).

Cadillac Desert: The American West and Its Disappearing Water (1993), by Marc Reisner, is an exhaustively researched, compelling account of the West's most critical issue: balancing development with its most precious resource.

Edward Abbey is arguably Utah's most famous environmentalist. Check out *The Monkey Wrench Gang* (1975), a mostly fictionalized, raucous tale of 'ecowarriors' and their plan to blow up Glen Canyon Dam, along with the dreamy classic *Desert Solitaire* (1968).

To learn more about the great land debate, check out the Southern Utah Wilderness Alliance (www.suwa.org), a grassroots political organization that's been critical in the land-conservation fight.

Desert vegetation grows so slowly that even effects from early Western prospectors, ranchers and explorers may look fresh, and protected parklands remain damaged by long-ago visitors. Cows have had such a devastating impact on the desert that it no longer functions as the same ecosystem. Only on a few inaccessible mesa tops do fragments of ancestral plant communities survive. Today's dry, brushy desert hardly resembles the landscape that existed even half a century ago, and it's not likely to recover for centuries to come.

Plants that adapt best seem to be invasive weeds, which have quickly overtaken areas damaged by cows and human activities. Introduced plants such as tamarisk, Russian thistle (tumbleweed) and cheatgrass pose a serious problem, as they can force out native plants and animals, creating extensive monocultures. Cheatgrass even alters the chemistry of the soil, possibly rendering it unusable to other plants. And many invasive plants are nearly impossible to remove once they gain a foothold.

Construction of dams and reservoirs throughout the Southwest has radically changed the delicate balance that has sustained life here for millennia. In place of floodplains that once richly nourished riparian and aquatic food chains, dams now release only cold water in steady flows that favor introduced fish species and invasive weeds. In populated areas, the draining of underground aquifers is shrinking the water table and drying up desert springs and wetlands that animals have long depended on during the dry season.

Lyrical and evocative of a beautifully sere landscape, *The Secret Knowledge of Water: Discovering the Essence of the American Desert* (2001), by Craig Childs, is required reading for anyone heading out into southern Utah's backcountry wilds.

Climate Change

The EPA estimates that temperatures in the US Southwest have risen by 1.5°F over the last century. Over the next 100 years, the NPS expects the Colorado Plateau will become hotter and more arid – a recent BLM report said temps could rise by as much as two degrees by 2060 – causing even more extreme droughts. This affects where plants grow, where animals eat, where wildfires burn, and even where people play. Across the Southwest, piñon pines are dying off at an alarming rate as a result of an ongoing drought, animals are changing habits to adapt to changing ecosystems, and the tourism industry is adjusting approaches as changing rain patterns affect river levels, sandstorms affect watersheds, and ski areas and even tourism seasons change as winter temperatures rise.

BIOLOGICAL SOIL CRUSTS

One of the desert's most fascinating features is also one of its least visible and most fragile. Only in recent decades have biological soil crusts begun to attract attention and concern. These living crusts cover and protect desert soils, gluing sand particles together so they don't blow away. Cyanobacteria, among Earth's oldest living life forms, start the process by extending mucous-covered filaments that wind through the dry soil. Over time these filaments and the sand particles adhering to them form a thin crust that is colonized by microscopic algae, lichens, fungi and mosses. This crust absorbs huge amounts of rainwater, reducing runoff and minimizing erosion.

Unfortunately, this thin crust is instantly fragmented under the heavy impact of human footsteps, not to mention bicycle, motorcycle and car tires. Once broken, the crust can take up to 50 years to repair itself. In its absence, the wind and rains erode desert soils, and much of the water that would otherwise nourish desert plants is lost. Many of these soils formed during the wet climates of the Pleistocene and may be irreplaceable in today's arid conditions. Tragically, as soon as the crust is broken and soil is lost, grasses will be permanently replaced by shrubs, whose roots fare better in the thinner soils.

Visitors to the Southwest bear a special responsibility to protect these living soil crusts by staying on established trails. Look closely before you walk anywhere – intact crusts form a rough glaze atop the soil, while fragmented crusts have sharp edges. At all costs, avoid walking or camping on these ancient soils.

Survival
Guide

Clothing & Equipment

CLOTHING

Modern outdoor garments made from new synthetic fabrics (which are breathable and actively wick moisture away from your skin) are better for hiking than anything made of cotton or wool. The exception to this is if you're hiking out of the canyon in midsummer, when cotton is a godsend. Soak cotton shirts or bandannas with water at every opportunity, and allow the evaporative cooling effect to ease your journey.

To cope with changing temperatures and exertion, layering your clothing is a good way to regulate your body temperature.

For the upper body, the base layer is typically a T-shirt made of synthetic fabric. The second layer can be a lightweight, breathable long-sleeve shirt for sun protection or a synthetic fleece sweater that will keep you insulated. The outer shell consists of a weatherproof jacket that also protects against strong cold winds.

For the lower body, shorts will probably be most comfortable in midsummer, although some hikers prefer long pants – light, quick-drying fabric (eg nylon) is best. Thermal 'long john' type underwear can't be easily removed, and it is not recommended except when conditions are expected to remain very cold all day. Waterproof overpants are an outer shell for the lower body.

Hikers in southern Utah should always carry a windproof and waterproof rainjacket and pants that are properly seam-sealed. The jacket should have a hood to keep the rain and wind off your head.

Trail-running or walking shoes with good traction and soft soles are fine over most terrain. If you have bad ankles, consider higher-ankle hiking boots. Make sure your shoes are broken in. Consider synthetic socks to wick away moisture.

MAPS

If you're driving or taking the shuttle and hiking on frontcountry trails, the glossy fold-out, full-color map and seasonal park newspaper available at national park entrance stations and visitor centers is usually enough to get around. **Bureau of Land Management** (BLM; www. blm.gov) and **United States Forest Service** (USFS; www. fs.fed.us) offices give away or sell maps that cover lands under their jurisdiction. They may not be great maps for general use, but they're indispensable for exploring outside the national parks, where public recreation lands can be a patchwork of different agencies' jurisdictions and private landholdings.

The **United States Geological Survey** (USGS; ☑888-275-8747; www.usgs. gov) publishes the standard 1:24,000 (7.5-minute) topographical quadrangle maps, available as free downloads online in PDF format. The level of detail is more than most visitors will need, unless you're planning a backcountry trip. Keep in mind that some USGS map survey information may be outdated, and buying these maps can quickly become expensive if your route extends across multiple quads. You can order print copies ($8 per quad) directly from the website or look for them at southern Utah's national-park bookstores, outdoor outfitters and public lands information offices (see the USGS website for a complete list of local retailers).

National Geographic (☑800-437-5521; http://shop. nationalgeographic.com) publishes the Trails Illustrated series of waterproof, tear-resistant topographic maps (scale varies from 1:35,000 to 1:70,000), which collectively cover all of southern Utah's national parks, as well as other wilderness areas, including around Moab. Based on USGS maps, but often helpfully marked up with more details for outdoor recreation, these foldable maps ($10 to $12 each) are widely available at national-park visitor centers and elsewhere. If you're traveling with a handheld GPS, or want to customize trail maps to print out yourself at home, National Geographic's TOPO! mapping software is a good investment; the Utah state series costs $50.

For driving maps, the *Utah* state highway map is perfectly adequate. It's available free from many tourist information offices. In addition to more detailed regional driving maps, the American Automobile Association also publishes an *Indian Country Guide Map* ($5), which covers southern Utah, northern Arizona and the Four Corners area. AAA maps are free for auto-club members. For a handy driving and motorcycling road atlas, Benchmark Press' *Utah Road* *& Recreation Atlas* ($23) shows every road in the state, along with land and water features, outdoor recreation areas, campgrounds, trailheads and hundreds more points of interest.

NAVIGATION EQUIPMENT

Maps & Compass

Carry a good map of the area you are hiking in, and know how to read it. Before setting off on your hike, ensure that you understand the contours and the map symbols, plus the main ridge and river systems in the area. Familiarize yourself with the true north–south directions and the general direction in which you are heading. On the trail, try to identify major landmarks (eg mountain peaks) and locate them on your map. This will give you a better grasp of the region's geography.

Buy a compass and learn how to use it. The attraction of magnetic north varies in different parts of the world, so compasses need to be balanced accordingly. Compass manufacturers have divided the world into five zones. Make sure your compass is balanced for your destination zone. There are also 'universal' compasses on the market that can be used anywhere in the world.

This is a very basic introduction to using a compass and will only be of assistance if you are proficient in map reading. For simplicity, it doesn't take magnetic variation into account. Before using a compass we recommend you obtain further instruction.

Hold the compass flat in the palm of your hand. Rotate the bezel so the red end of the needle points to the N on the bezel. The bearing is read from the dash under the bezel.

To orient the map so that it aligns with the ground, place the compass flat on the map. Rotate the map until the needle is parallel with the map's north–south grid lines and the red end is pointing to north on the map. You can now identify features around you by aligning them with labeled features on the map.

To take a bearing from the map, draw a line on the map between your starting point and your destination. Place the edge of the compass on this line with the direction-of-travel arrow pointing towards your destination. Rotate the bezel until the meridian lines are parallel with the north–south grid lines on the map and the N points to north on the map. Read the bearing from the dash.

To follow a bearing, rotate the bezel so that the intended bearing is in line with the dash. Place the compass flat in the palm of your hand and rotate the base plate until the red end points to N on the bezel. The direction-of-travel arrow will now point in the direction you need to walk. To determine your bearing, rotate the bezel so the red end points to the N. Place the compass flat in the palm of your hand and rotate the base plate until the direction of travel arrow points in the direction in which you have been hiking. Read your bearing from the dash.

GPS

The cheapest handheld GPS receivers now cost less than $100 (although these may not have a built-in averaging system that minimizes signal errors). Other important factors to consider when buying a GPS receiver are its weight and battery life. Remember that a GPS receiver is of little use to hikers unless used with an accurate topographical map. The receiver simply gives your position, which you must then locate on the map.

GPS receivers will only work properly in the open. The signals from a crucial satellite may be blocked (or bounce off rock or water) directly below high cliffs, near large bodies of water or in dense tree cover, and give inaccurate readings. GPS receivers are more vulnerable to breakdowns (including dead batteries) than the humble magnetic compass – a low-tech device that has served navigators faithfully for centuries – so don't rely on them entirely. Smartphone GPSs can be helpful for navigation on major roads, but with limited cell service in the parks, don't rely on the old iThing for your location.

EQUIPMENT

Packs

For day hikes, a day pack will usually suffice, but for multiday hikes you'll need a backpack.

Day packs with built-in hydration systems (such as Camelbak) eliminate the hassle of toting unwieldy water bottles.

Backpacks with a relatively large capacity (between 2500 and 5500 cub in, or 40L to 90L) are best for overnight backcountry hiking.

A backpack that weighs on your shoulders as you hike is not just uncomfortable, it may be doing permanent injury to your back. You should look for backpacks with robust, easily adjustable waist belts that can comfortably support the entire weight carried, effectively transferring the load from your shoulders onto your hips. Shoulder straps should serve only to steady your backpack.

Tents

A three-season tent will suffice for most backpacking trips in southern Utah. Ultralight backpackers may opt to ditch the tent and use just the rainfly and footprint (ground tarp). If you're planning a backcountry trip during winter, then you'll need a four-season tent to keep you sheltered from the snow and harsh windy, wet and freezing conditions.

The floor and the outer shell, or rainfly, should have taped or sealed seams and covered zips to stop leaks. Most hikers find tents of around 4.5lb to 6lb a comfortable carrying weight. Dome- and tunnel-shaped tents handle windy conditions better than flat-sided tents.

Sleeping Bags

As with tents, three-season sleeping bags will suffice for most campers in southern Utah. Cooler seasons and higher elevations, for example at Bryce Canyon, call for both sleeping bag and a sleeping pad (mat) for insulation from the cold ground.

During the summer, lower desert elevations are usually hot enough to forego a sleeping bag altogether; backcountry campers might consider bringing just a sleeping bag liner or a sheet. Some campers soak a sheet in a nearby river for the evaporative cooling effect to ensure a more soothing sleep.

Down fillings are warmer than synthetic for the same weight and bulk but, unlike synthetic fillings, do not retain warmth when wet. Mummy bags are the best shape for weight and warmth. The given figure (23°F, for instance) is the coldest temperature at which a person should feel comfortable in the bag (although the ratings are notoriously unreliable).

An inner liner helps keep your sleeping bag clean, as well as adding an insulating layer. Silk liners are lightest, but they also come in cotton or polypropylene.

Self-inflating sleeping mats put an air cushion between you and the ground. More importantly they insulate from the cold. Foam mats are a low-cost but less comfortable alternative.

Stoves & Fuel

The type of fuel you'll use most often will help determine what kind of camp stove is best for you. The following types of fuel can be found in the US, and local outdoor outfitters and camping supply stores can help you choose an appropriate camp stove if you aren't traveling with your own.

Butane, propane and isobutane are clean-burning fuels that come in nonrecyclable canisters and tend to be more expensive. These fuels are best for camping in warmer conditions, as their performance markedly decreases in below-freezing temperatures. Check airline regulations before you bring fuel. You can buy all types of fuel in Utah.

Inexpensive white gas is reliable in all temperatures. It's more volatile than other types of fuel, but overall it's the most efficient and clean-burning type of fuel available in the US.

The most sustainable alternative is renewable denatured alcohol, which burns slowly but also extremely quietly. Lower temperatures mean longer cooking times, so you'll have to carry more fuel with you.

It doesn't matter how lightweight or efficient your stove is if you forget to bring a way to ignite it. Waterproof matches are a smart idea.

Other Sports

For **cycling**, you can either rent the latest bikes or bring your own. Full-suspension mountain bikes are recommended for most beginners – they're just easier. If you have them, bring cycling shorts and top, repair kits and pumps. Most riders use a small hydration day pack. A good bike lock is nice for overnights in Moab.

If you're **paddling**, it gets cold on rivers. Don't forget warm dry clothes (in a drybag – your guide has one if you don't). River sandals are useful when fording waterways or doing water sports. Outside of summer, consider a wetsuit or drytop.

If you're **climbing** or **canyoneering**, with long cracks, you'll need a massive rack of protection gear with multiple same-size cams. Some canyoneering routes require rappelling equipment, ropes and harnesses. Always check rental climbing equipment for frays. Some national parks require earth-colored climbing chalk.

EQUIPMENT CHECKLIST

Backpackers will have a longer list than this, but try to pack light. If you forget something, southern Utah has camping supply stores and outdoor outfitters to fix you up; they are usually found in gateway towns, but not inside the parks themselves, where concessionaires sell only limited supplies. In addition to the following, optional items include analtimeter, bandanna, binoculars, camera, film/charger and batteries, candle, cell phone, drybag for river trips, emergency distress beacon, GPS receiver and spare batteries, groundsheet, fire pan (required for some backcountry fires), hiking poles, mosquito net and swimsuit.

Clothing

⇒ broad-brimmed sun hat; winter cap

⇒ hiking boots, or sturdy trail-running shoes; river sandals or flip-flops

⇒ shorts and lightweight trousers or skirt; socks and underwear; sweater or fleece; thermal underwear; T-shirt and long-sleeved shirt with collar; warm hat, scarf and gloves; waterproof jacket; waterproof pants

Equipment

⇒ backpack with waterproof liner or cover

⇒ first-aid kit

⇒ high-energy food and snacks and one day's emergency food supplies

⇒ insect repellent

⇒ lighter or matches (consider wrapping duct tape around the lighter)

⇒ map, compass and guidebook

⇒ map case or clip-seal plastic bags

⇒ pocket knife

⇒ sunglasses

⇒ sunscreen and lip balm

⇒ survival blanket or bag

⇒ toilet paper and trowel

⇒ flashlight or headlamp, spare batteries and bulb

⇒ watch

⇒ water containers (you need a gallon of water per person per day)

⇒ whistle

⇒ helmet for cycling, paddling, canyoneering or climbing

Overnight Hikes

⇒ animal-proof food container – in some areas

⇒ biodegradable soap

⇒ cooking, eating and drinking utensils

⇒ sewing/repair kit

⇒ sleeping bag and/or liner

⇒ sleeping pad (and, if inflatable, patch kit)

⇒ spare cord for hanging things and supporting tents

⇒ stove, fuel and lighter/matches

⇒ tent, pegs, poles and guy lines

⇒ toiletries

⇒ water-purification filter or tablets

⇒ plastic bags to bring out trash

⇒ portable toilet – aka groover – for some trips

Directory A–Z

Accommodations

→ Only Zion and Bryce Canyon have in-park lodges, but all of southern Utah's national parks and monuments have campgrounds. You'll find other accommodations in gateway towns and cities just outside the parks, especially in St George, Cedar City, Springdale and Moab. Good options also exist in towns along Hwy 12, including Torrey, Boulder, Escalante and Tropic, and Kanab on Hwy 89.

→ Weekends and big festivals are the busiest times, filling every room and campsite. At any time, make reservations if park proximity or a certain standard of quality is important. Some campgrounds, motels and B&Bs, a few hotels and the Bryce Canyon Lodge all close during the off-peak winter season (roughly November through March). Walk-in customers can try politely bargaining over room rates during slow months. Prices are now largely set through aggregators, with large fluctuations from weekend to midweek and off-peak rates.

→ The air-con icon ❄ denotes properties where in-room air-conditioning is available (not just fans). The swimming pool icon ☰ denotes either an indoor or outdoor pool. Look for the family-friendly icon 👪 and pet-friendly icon 🐾.

→ Many accommodations in Utah are entirely nonsmoking. Cleaning fees of over $100 may be charged if there's any evidence of someone having smoked in your room.

B&Bs & Inns

B&B rates often include a home-cooked breakfast. Minimum stays are common in high season and on weekends. Amenities vary widely, but rooms with TV and telephone are the exception; the cheapest units share bathrooms.

Camping & Cabins

A few campgrounds are open year-round; most generally open in March, April or May and stay open until the first snowfall, usually between late October and mid-November.

Campgrounds in state and national parks tend to have flush toilets and

sometimes hot showers and RV dump stations. Private campgrounds cater more to the RV crowd, with water and electricity hook-ups, wi-fi, showers and even cable TV. In national forests (USFS) and Bureau of Land Management (BLM) land, expect more basic campsites with fire pits, picnic benches, vault toilets and possibly no drinking water. USFS and BLM lands may allow free, dispersed roadside camping, although campfires may require a permit.

The most popular campgrounds fill up fast, especially at national and state parks and everywhere in summer. Some accept reservations, while others are strictly first-come, first-served (show up early in the day to claim a site, especially on weekends and holidays). For camping reservations in national parks, national forests and other federal recreation lands (eg BLM), contact the **National Recreation Reservation Service** (☎877-444-6777, 518-885-3639; www.recreation.gov). For Utah state-park campgrounds, contact **Reserve America** (☎800-322-3770, 518-885-3639; www.reserve america.com; reservation fee $8).

Hotels & Motels

Just about every hotel and motel offers air-conditioned, nonsmoking rooms with a TV and phone. Rooms are often priced by the size and number of beds; rates are usually

---

BOOK YOUR STAY ONLINE

For more accommodation reviews by Lonely Planet authors, check out http://lonelyplanet.com/hotels/. You'll find independent reviews, as well as recommendations on the best places to stay. Best of all, you can book online.

SLEEPING PRICE RANGES

The price categories are for double rooms with private bathrooms. Unless otherwise stated, room rates do not include breakfast or taxes (10.2% to 13.6%). If you're traveling with children, some places advertise that 'kids sleep free' in the same room as their parents, but an extra fee may be charged for a rollaway bed or cot.

$ under $100

$$ $100 to $250

$$$ over $250

the same for single or double occupancy, with a surcharge for a third and fourth person. 'Suites' may simply be oversized rooms, not necessarily two separate rooms.

Lodges

Of the national parks in the area, only Zion, Bryce Canyon and the Grand Canyon's North Rim have lodges.

Ranch Resorts

Luxury resorts and guest ranches ('dude ranches') are often destinations in themselves. You'll find a few ranch resorts scattered outside Zion's east entrance and around Capitol Reef and Moab.

Vacation Rentals

Vacation rentals (a condo or private home with kitchen, living room and multiple bedrooms) are popular around Moab and Zion, and a great option for families.

Activities

Hiking is the activity of choice, but it's just one of many pursuits possible in and around southern Utah's parks. Rock climbing and canyoneering

are also huge, while horseback trail rides and 4WD roads are popular activities back down closer to earth. Although the parks aren't great for mountain biking, there are miles of fat-tire trails outside Moab, also a jumping-off point for river-rafting and paddling trips. Winter brings snow play, cross-country skiing and snowshoeing to the mountains.

Climate

The weather in southern Utah can vary wildly from one park or town to the next, even from one day to the next, especially during the unpredictable shoulder seasons of spring and fall. Then there's the summer heat, which routinely hovers above 90°F (32°C). Winter brings snowstorms. Altitude makes a difference in temperature year-round: hikers in Zion Canyon may be sweat-soaked at noon, but campers at Bryce Canyon will shiver in their sleeping bags later that night.

Courses

Southern Utah's parks offer a range of outdoor education opportunities, from naturalist-guided hikes and photography walks to extended learning vacations and college-credit courses.

➡ Associated with Zion National Park, the nonprofit **Zion Canyon Field Institute** (📞435-772-3264, 800-635-3959; www.zionpark.org; programs $45-85) offers year-round educational field trips, such as archaeology programs and wildlife-watching, as well as volunteer opportunities and photography workshops (eg wildflowers, fall foliage, winter scenes).

➡ Associated with Canyonlands and Arches National Parks, nonprofit **Canyonlands Field Institute** (📞435-259-7750; www.cfimoab.

org; 1320 S Hwy 191; ⊙May-Oct) offers some field trips and programs to the public, although it primarily caters to school groups, summer youth camps and corporate retreats.

➡ Mostly for the academic community, the institute run by the **Bryce Canyon Natural History Association** (📞435-834-4600; www.bryce canyon.org) provides in-depth studies of Bryce's unique geology, along with a few courses, such as photography, that are geared for the general public. Call or check the website.

Discount Cards

Park Passes

The **America the Beautiful Annual Pass** (📞888-275-8747; http://store.usgs.gov/pass; $80) is valid for free admission to all national parks and federal recreation lands for 12 months from when you buy it. Each pass admits four adults and all accompanying children under age 16. Buy the pass online or from any participating federal agency, including at national park entrance stations. Upon entry, be prepared to present your pass along with a photo ID (eg driver's license).

With the **America the Beautiful senior pass** (lifetime fee $10), US citizens and permanent residents 62 or older receive free admission to all national parks and federal recreation lands, plus 50% off select activity fees (eg camping in national parks). The lifetime **America the Beautiful access pass** (free) is for US citizens or permanent residents with a permanent disability; bring documentation if your disability is not readily visible. These discount parks passes must be obtained in person.

Automobile Clubs

Members of the **American Automobile Association** (AAA; 📞877-428-2277, emergency roadside assistance 800-222-4357; www.aaa.com; annual membership from $52) and its foreign affiliates (eg Canada's CAA) qualify for small discounts (usually 10%) on hotels and motels, Amtrak trains, car and RV rentals, chain restaurants and shops, tours and more.

Senior Cards

People over the age of 65 (sometimes 55, 60 or 62) often qualify for the same discounts as students; any ID showing birth date should suffice as proof of age. Members of the **American Association of Retired Persons** (AARP; ☎800-566-0242; www. aarp.org; annual membership $16), for those 50 years of age and older, often get discounts (usually 10%) on hotels, car rentals and more.

Student Cards

For international and US students, the **Student Advantage Card** (www.student advantage.com; $23) offers 15% savings on Amtrak train and Greyhound bus fares, plus discounts of 10% to 20% at some motels, hotels, chain stores and airlines.

Electricity

120V/60Hz

120V/60Hz

Food & Drink

Meals are often an afterthought on a trip to southern Utah's national parks, but gateway towns do provide a decent variety of options, from basic cafeteria eats to upscale Southwestern cuisine. Zion and Bryce Canyon's park lodges offer filling, but just-OK food; their top-end prices and historical atmosphere make them better for a special occasion than everyday dining. The other parks do not offer food (and water is occasionally limited) so bring it in.

Groceries & Self-Catering

➡ Small grocery stores in park gateway towns usually stock only a limited selection of items, such as canned goods, bread, milk, ice and other staples. If you're driving to southern Utah, you may want to stop off in larger towns and cities like St George and Moab to stock up on groceries – it'll cost less than buying supplies in smaller park gateway towns.

➡ To fill up your cooler, ice is sold at almost every convenience store and gas

station, but they may run out on hot summer days. In-room refrigerators are not always a standard amenity at motels and hotels, and they're not available inside park lodges. In all of southern Utah's national parks, you'll find picnic areas and campsites with picnic tables; the latter may have fire pits or grates for cooking.

Insurance

➡ Getting travel insurance to cover any theft, loss or medical problems you may encounter is highly recommended. Some travel insurance policies do not cover 'risky' activities such as motorcycling, skiing or even trekking, so read the fine print. Make sure the policy covers hospital stays and an emergency flight home.

➡ Paying for your airline ticket or rental car with a credit card may provide limited travel accident insurance. If you already have private health insurance or a homeowners' or renters' policy, find out what they will cover and only get supplemental insurance. If you have prepaid a large portion of your vacation, trip cancellation insurance may be a worthwhile expense.

➡ Worldwide travel insurance is available at www.lonely planet.com/travel_services. You can buy, extend and claim online at anytime – even if you are already on the road.

EATING PRICE RANGES
....

The following price ranges refer to a main course on the dinner menu.

$ under $15

$$ $15 to $25

$$$ over $25

Internet Access

➡ We use an internet icon @ where there's an online terminal available for use and the wi-fi icon 🛜 when wireless internet access is offered, whether free or fee-based. Many hotels, motels and private RV campgrounds have either a public computer terminal or offer wi-fi (sometimes free, or costing $10 or more per day); ask when reserving.

➡ In the national parks, wi-fi hot spots are rare (look for unsecured networks near visitor centers and lodges). Pay-as-you-go self-service internet terminals are rarely available and can also be slow, unreliable and/or expensive.

➡ Nearby towns and cities usually have at least one coffee shop, cybercafe or copy center offering online terminals (typically $5 to $12 per hour) and wi-fi. Some cybercafes may let you upload your photos and/or burn them onto CDs.

➡ Public libraries usually offer internet terminals (though these may have time limits and require advance sign-up or waiting in line) and sometimes wi-fi. Out-of-state residents may be charged a small fee for internet terminal use.

Maps

The maps in this book provide good reference for shorter hikes. However, if you are on a serious backcountry hike, you should use a topographic map, compass and/or GPS (p257).

Money

Prices are listed throughout the book in US dollars. Foreign currency is not accepted anywhere.

ATMs

ATMs are available 24 hours, seven days at many banks,

LIQUOR LAWS

Utah has some of the oddest liquor laws in the country. As with everywhere in the US, you must be aged 21 to drink legally. But that's where the similarities end.

In Utah, grocery stores sell near-beer (which doesn't exceed 3.2% alcohol content) seven days a week. State-run liquor stores and package agencies sell beer, wine and spirits Monday through Saturday (closed Sunday). In southern Utah you'll find licensed liquor stores and package agencies in St George, Hurricane, Cedar City, Kanab, Panguitch and Moab.

Lounges and taverns only serve near-beer. Stronger drinks are served at restaurants with liquor licenses between 10am and 1am daily, as well as at 'dining or social clubs' that are open to the general public. At restaurants, servers aren't permitted to offer alcoholic drinks or show you a drink menu unless you specifically ask. When you order a drink, you must also order food, but a snack or appetizer will do. Wherever you're doing your drinking, you can only order one drink for yourself at a time. A pitcher of margaritas? Fuhgeddaboutit.

Alcohol is legally prohibited on Native American reservations and cannot be transported on tribal lands, even if you're just passing through.

shopping malls, gas stations and grocery and convenience stores. You may also find them at park bookstores, concessionaire shops, and lodges. Expect a surcharge of at least $2 per transaction, on top of any fees applied by your home banking institution. Most ATMs are connected to international networks and offer fairly good exchange rates. Avoid ATMs inside Las Vegas casinos, which tack on exorbitant surcharges and fees of $5 or more per transaction.

Credit Cards

Credit cards are almost universally accepted. In fact, you'll find it next to impossible to rent a car, book a hotel room or order tickets over the phone without one. Visa, MasterCard and American Express are most common.

Most ATMs will dispense cash if you use your credit card, but that can be expensive because, in addition to steep service fees, you'll be charged interest immediately. Ask your credit-card

company for details and a four-digit PIN number.

Moneychangers

If you're arriving from abroad, exchange money at the airport or in the nearest city, for example, at a major bank or currency-exchange office such as American Express. In smaller park gateway towns, exchanging money may be impossible. There are currently no currency-exchange services inside the parks, so make sure you have plenty of US cash and a credit card.

Tipping

Tipping is *not* optional. Only withhold tips in cases of outrageously bad service.

Airport & hotel porters Per bag $2, minimum per cart $5.

Bartenders Per round 10% to 15%, minimum per drink $1.

Guides Not required, but recommended. A good start is $20 per day.

Hotel maids Per night $2 to $5, left under the card provided.

Restaurant servers Tip 15% to 20%, unless a gratuity is already charged on the bill.

Taxi drivers Tip 10% to 15%, rounded up to the next dollar.

Opening Hours

Regular business hours are from 9am until 5pm weekdays. In bigger towns, supermarkets may stay open until 8pm or later. In Utah, many restaurants are closed on Sunday; if you find one open, snag a seat and be happy.

Unless otherwise noted within reviews, standard opening hours are as follows.

Banks 9am to 5pm Monday to Friday; some will also open 9am to 1:30pm Saturday.

Post offices 8:30am to 4.30pm, and also may be open Saturday morning, usually 9am to noon.

Shop hours 10am to 5:30pm Monday to Saturday and noon to 5pm Sunday; malls stay open later.

Restaurants Breakfast is usually served from 7am to 10am, lunch

from 11:30am to 2:30pm and dinner from 5pm to 9pm daily. Some restaurants stay open throughout the day, while others close between meals.

Bars Usually open from 5pm to 1am daily.

Seasonal hours In summer many businesses, especially in park gateway towns, keep longer hours. In winter most keep shorter hours and a few even close (depending on seasonal demand and the weather, but typically from November through March).

INTERNATIONAL VISITORS

All travelers should double-check current visa and passport requirements *before* coming to the USA. For the latest entry requirements and eligibility, consult the Visa section of the **US Department of State website** (http://travel.state.gov) and the Travel section of the **US Customs & Border Protection website** (www.cbp.gov). If you're still in doubt, contact the nearest US embassy or consulate in your home country (visit www.usembassy.gov for a complete list).

Entering the Country

➡ Under the US Department of Homeland Security (DHS) registration program, **US-VISIT** (www.dhs.gov/us-visit), almost all visitors (excluding, for now, most Canadian and many Mexican citizens) will be digitally photographed and have their electronic (inkless) fingerprints scanned upon arrival; the process typically takes less than a minute.

Passports

➡ Under the Western Hemisphere Travel Initiative (WHTI), all travelers (including returning US citizens) must have a valid machine-readable passport (MRP) when entering the US by air, land or sea. An MRP has two lines of letters, numbers and <<< at the bottom of the data page.

➡ MRPs issued or renewed after October 26, 2006 must be e-passports (ie have a digital photo and integrated chip with biometric data). MRPs issued or renewed between October 26, 2005 and October 25, 2006 must have a digital photo or integrated chip on the data page.

➡ The only exceptions to these MRP requirements are for select US, Canadian and Mexican citizens who are able to present other WHTI-compliant documents (eg pre-approved 'trusted traveler' cards).

➡ For full details, visit www.getyouhome.gov.

Visas

➡ Currently, under the US Visa Waiver Program (VWP), visas are not required for citizens of 36 countries for stays up to 90 days (no extensions) if you have an MRP. If you don't have an MRP, you'll need a visa to enter the USA.

➡ Citizens of VWP countries *must* register with the Electronic System for Travel Authorization (ESTA) online (https://esta.cbp.dhs.gov/) at least 72 hours before their trip begins. Once approved, ESTA registration is valid for up to two years.

➡ Citizens from all other countries need to apply for a visa in their home country. The process costs a nonrefundable $131, involves a personal interview and can take several weeks, so apply as early as possible.

Post

The **US Postal Service** (USPS; ☏800-275-8777; www.usps.com) is inexpensive and reliable. You won't find any post offices inside the parks, but visitor-center bookstores, concessionaire shops and lodges may sell stamps. Outside the parks, gateway towns usually have at least one post office, while cities have multiple branches.

Public Holidays

On holiday weekends, especially Memorial Day, Fourth of July and Labor Day in summer, expect the parks to be ridiculously busy, with campgrounds full and all nearby accommodations booked out weeks, if not months, in advance.

On national holidays, banks, schools and government offices (including post offices) close, and transportation, museums and other services operate on a Sunday schedule. Holidays falling on a weekend are usually observed the following Monday.

New Year's Day January 1

Martin Luther King Jr Day Third Monday in January

Presidents' Day Third Monday in February

Memorial Day Last Monday in May

Independence Day July 4 (aka the Fourth of July)

Labor Day First Monday in September

Columbus Day Second Monday in October

Veterans' Day November 11

Thanksgiving Day Fourth Thursday in November

Christmas Day December 25

Telephone

➡ Cell (mobile) phone and data reception is sketchy at best in southern Utah's national parks and wilderness areas, and varies depending on your exact location and service provider. In most park gateway towns, cell-phone reception is usually decent, though again it depends on where you are.

➡ Please be considerate of other park visitors when using your cell phone. Being woken up by phones ringing in a neighboring campsite, or listening to someone conduct a loud conversation at a scenic viewpoint, can really tarnish the outdoor experience for everyone in the immediate vicinity.

➡ Public payphones are found in southern Utah's national parks at campgrounds, lodges and visitor centers. Local payphone calls cost 50¢ minimum, the cost increasing with the distance and length of call. Increasingly, in-park payphones are not coin-operated and will only accept credit cards or prepaid calling cards. You're usually better off using a prepaid phonecard, typically sold at park bookstores and concessionaire shops and lodges. Be sure to read the fine print for hidden costs, such as activation fees or connection surcharges for making calls from payphones.

Time

➡ Utah is on Mountain Standard Time (GMT minus seven hours). When it's noon in Salt Lake City, it's 11am in Los Angeles, 3pm in New York, 8pm in London and 5am (the next day) in Sydney.

➡ Daylight Saving Time (DST) starts on the second Sunday in March, when clocks are set one hour ahead, and ends on the first Sunday in November.

➡ If you're driving to Utah, beware that the state of Arizona (including Grand Canyon National Park) does not observe DST, but the Navajo Nation does. Confused yet? We thought so.

Tourist Information

National park visitor centers and regional public lands information offices are your best bets for parks travel information once you arrive in southern Utah.

The state's official tourism agency, **Utah Travel Council** (☏801-538-1030, 800-200-1160; www.utah.com), offers loads of free information to help plan a vacation, including downloadable travel e-guides and website sections dedicated to national and state parks, outdoor recreation, annual festivals and events, and more. You'll find a **Utah Welcome Center** (☏435-673-4542; http://travel.utah.gov; 1835 S Convention Center Dr, Dixie Convention Center; ⊙8:30am-5:30pm) in St George. County and other regional travel bureaus are also helpful:

Capitol Reef Country Travel Council (☏435-425-3365, 800-858-7951; www.capitolreef.org) Covers Capitol Reef and Hwy 12.

Cedar City & Brian Head Tourism & Convention Bureau (☏800-354-4849, 435-586-5124; www.scenicsouthernutah.com; 581 N Main St; ⊙8:30am-5pm Mon-Sat) Area-wide info and free internet use.

Escalante Chamber of Commerce (☏435-826-4810; www.escalante-cc.com) Covers Grand Staircase-Escalante National Monument and Boulder.

Garfield County Office of Tourism (☏435-676-1160, 800-444-6689; www.brycecanyoncountry.com) Covers Bryce Canyon and Hwy 12.

Kane County Office of Tourism (☏435-644-5033, 800-733-5263; www.visitsouthernutah.com; 78 S 100 East; ⊙8:30am-6pm Mon-Fri, to 4pm Sat) The main source for area information; great old Western movie posters and artifacts on display.

Moab Area Travel Council (www.discovermoab.com) Comprehensive online resource.

Zion Canyon Visitors Bureau (☑888-518-7070; www.zion park.com) Offers comprehensive accommodations listings of family-friendly motels and hotels, as well as boutique inns and B&Bs, in the gateway town of Springdale, on UT 9 west of the park.

Travelers with Disabilities

➡ The national parks exist for the enjoyment of all, offering opportunities for those in wheelchairs or with hearing, visual or other physical or mental disabilities to experience the wilderness. It may also be possible to obtain a free lifetime 'America the Beautiful' entry pass.

➡ The **National Park Service** (NPS; ☑800-877-8339; www.nps.gov/accessibility.htm) publishes *National Parks: Accessible to Everyone,* a free online, downloadable and printable large-type guide with helpful info and details about facilities at specific parks.

➡ Also check individual park websites or ask at park visitor centers for up-to-date accessibility guides, details of which are often printed in the parks' free newspaper guides.

➡ All of southern Utah's national parks have wheelchair-accessible visitor centers, at least one accessible campsite in their main campground and a few viewpoints and/or trails that are wheelchair-accessible. Some parks also offer ranger programs for the hearing impaired.

➡ Service animals (ie guide dogs) may accompany visitors on park shuttles, inside museums and visitor centers, and on hiking trails and in the backcountry (check current regulations to see if permits are required at visitor centers). Ensure your service animal wears its official vest at all times, to avoid any misunderstandings with park rangers or other visitors.

➡ In Zion and Bryce Canyon, park shuttles are wheelchair-accessible and lodges offer ADA-compliant wheelchair-accessible rooms.

➡ Accommodations outside the parks are required to have at least one wheelchair-accessible room, though few are fully ADA-compliant. More often, these are ground-floor rooms with wider doorways, less furniture, and handles around the tub and toilet. Always ask exactly what 'accessible' means when making reservations.

➡ Some car-rental agencies offer hand-controlled vehicles and vans with wheelchair lifts at no extra charge, but you must reserve them well in advance.

➡ **Access Utah Network** (☑801-533-4636, relay line 711; www.accessut.org) is a state agency that provides accessibility information for all Utah parks and referrals to other helpful organizations. The nonprofit, Salt Lake City–based **Splore** (☑801-484-4128; www.splore.org) specializes in providing outdoor activities (eg river rafting, canoeing, rock climbing) for those with special needs.

Volunteering

There are many opportunities to volunteer in and around southern Utah's parks, from one-day projects to longer-term endeavors. Volunteers can do trail maintenance, pull invasive plants, train to be an interpretive ranger or work with youth organizations.

Bureau of Land Management (www.blm.gov/ut/st/en/res/volunteer.html) Apply online or contact the nearest BLM office.

National Park Service (www.nps.gov/volunteer) Apply for the Volunteer in Parks (VIP) program and search for opportunities by park name or state online.

Sierra Club (www.sierraclub.org) Day or weekend service projects and volunteer vacations, including for families, focus on conservation (annual membership $25).

Student Conservation Association (www.thesca.org) Nonprofit organization offers conservation internships that earn academic credit, as well as summer trail-crew work.

Volunteer.gov (www.volunteer.gov) Online searchable database of volunteers for all public lands agencies, including NPS and the US Forest Service (USFS).

Zion Canyon Field Institute (☑435-772-3264, 800-635-3959; www.zionpark.org; programs $45-85) Arranges day-long service projects, typically in the Narrows of the Virgin River during summer and fall.

Work

Nearly everyone who works inside the parks is employed by the National Park Service (NPS), the parks' cooperating nonprofit organizations or by park concessionaire businesses. Most employment opportunities are low-paying seasonal jobs that are mostly filled by young people, teachers or retirees. Planning ahead is essential, whether you are applying with NPS or park concessionaires – applications for summer jobs are typically due around December. Getting work for non-US citizens without a work visa is nearly impossible, though under-the-table arrangements may be found.

Transportation

GETTING THERE & AWAY

Most travelers to Utah arrive by air or car, with bus and train running a very distant third and fourth place. Major transportation hubs are Las Vegas and Salt Lake City. You can also fly into Denver or Phoenix, though both are a bit further away.

Flights, tours and rail tickets can be booked online at www.lonelyplanet.com/bookings.

Air

Airports

Denver International Airport (www.dia.com) Denver is 5½ hours from both Arches and Canyonlands.

Grand Junction Regional Airport (www.gjairport.com) Small regional airport in western Colorado. Two hours from Arches and Canyonlands.

McCarran International Airport (www.mccarran.com) Las Vegas' airport is three hours from Zion and 4½ hours from Bryce.

Phoenix Sky Harbor International Airport (https://skyharbor.com) Six hours from Zion.

Salt Lake City International Airport (www.slcairport.com) Three to four hours from all of Utah's main parks.

St George Municipal Airport (www.flysgu.com) Small airport one hour from Zion. Closer than the main hubs, but less likely to have good airfare deals.

Land

Bus

➡ Long-distance buses can get you to major points within the region, but you'll still need to rent a car to get around as public transportation to the parks is nonexistent.

➡ **Greyhound** (☎800-231-2222; www.greyhound.com), the main long-distance bus company, doesn't serve many smaller towns, including traveler hubs such as Moab.

➡ Private shuttles do sometimes connect parks with nearby towns, such as Green River to Moab or St George to Zion.

➡ To save money, plan seven days in advance, buy tickets online, travel on weekdays and travel with a companion.

➡ You can take bus tours (p271) of the park, a good alternative if you don't have a car.

Car, Motorcycle & RV

➡ While the quickest way to get to the Utah is by plane, the best way to get around is with your own private vehicle. Most destinations cannot be reached with public transportation.

Train

➡ **Amtrak** (☎800-872-7245; www.amtrak.com) operates

CLIMATE CHANGE & TRAVEL

Every form of transport that relies on carbon-based fuel generates CO_2, the main cause of human-induced climate change. Modern travel is dependent on aeroplanes, which might use less fuel per kilometre per person than most cars but travel much greater distances. The altitude at which aircraft emit gases (including CO_2) and particles also contributes to their climate change impact. Many websites offer 'carbon calculators' that allow people to estimate the carbon emissions generated by their journey and, for those who wish to do so, to offset the impact of the greenhouse gases emitted with contributions to portfolios of climate-friendly initiatives throughout the world. Lonely Planet offsets the carbon footprint of all staff and author travel.

two major routes through the area. Use them to reach to reach the region, but not for touring.

➡ The *California Zephyr* runs between the San Francisco Bay Area and Chicago with stops at Green River (50 miles northwest of Moab, no car rental), Grand Junction (western Colorado, with car rental) and Salt Lake City.

➡ The *Southwest Chief* runs from Chicago to Los Angeles, with stops at Albuquerque in New Mexico, and Flagstaff in Arizona.

GETTING AROUND

Regardless of how you got to Utah, once you've arrived the best way to get around is with a private vehicle.

Bicycle

➡ Touring southern Utah by bike is a hardy endeavor and best done with the support of an outfitter or tour operator. The **Adventure Cycling Association** (☎800-755-2453; www.adventurecycling.org) provides info on cycling routes, sells bicycle maps and arranges tours. For emergency roadside assistance, join the Better World Club.

➡ Zion Canyon, Bryce Canyon and Capitol Reef have scenic drives open to recreational cyclists. Although national park trails are off-limits to bicycles (except for Zion's Pa'rus Trail), bicycles are usually allowed on any paved or dirt park road.

➡ Bicycle rentals are readily available. Expect to spend $25 to $50 per day for a cruiser or basic mountain bike.

➡ Moab is generally considered the mountain-biking capital of the Southwest. Grand Staircase-Escalante and the Zion area are also good mountain-biking destinations.

Bus

➡ There is no bus service to or between southern Utah's national parks. However, both Zion and Bryce Canyon offer free seasonal park shuttles that are handy for seeing the main sights and avoiding traffic headaches.

➡ In Zion, the mandatory park shuttle runs from spring through fall, when the canyon's main scenic drive is closed to private vehicles. Another free shuttle route runs through the gateway town of Springdale, connecting with the Zion

shuttle. Both routes run frequently. Shuttles do not serve Hwy 9 east of Canyon Junction through the Zion–Mt Carmel Tunnel or the park's more remote Kolob Terrace and Kolob Canyons Roads.

➡ In Bryce Canyon, an optional park shuttle runs from May through September. Although this free shuttle connects the dots between the park's most popular sightseeing spots, as well as the lodge, visitor center, campground and Ruby's Inn tourist complex just north of the park, it does not travel all the way down the canyon's scenic drive, except on twice-daily guided shuttle-bus tours (free).

Car & Motorcycle

There are usually no restrictions on travel by private vehicle in the national parks, although Zion Canyon is only accessible to park shuttle buses from spring to fall. Otherwise, cars and motorcycles are allowed on all public paved and dirt roads inside and outside the parks.

Automobile Associations

For 24-hour emergency roadside assistance, free maps and travel discounts on lodging, attractions, car rentals and more:

American Automobile Association (AAA; ☎800-874-7532, roadside assistance 800-222-4357; www.aaa.com) Has a walk-in office in St George and reciprocal agreements with some international auto clubs (eg Canada's CAA); bring your membership card from home.

Better World Club (☎866-238-1137; www.betterworldclub.com) Ecofriendly alternative auto club that supports environmental causes and offers optional emergency roadside assistance for cyclists. Annual membership (from $60) gets

---

ARE WE THERE YET?

Judging how long it will take to drive from point A to point B in southern Utah is an art form. Some highways drive like dirt roads, some dirt roads like highways, and slow-moving trucks and RVs can impede your progress for miles uphill. While we try to provide accurate driving times, most southern Utah road savvy is only gained through hard-won experience. When in doubt, always plan for it to take longer than you think.

As a rule, if a dirt road is noted as 'good' and passable to passenger cars, you can usually drive an average of 30mph on it, but numerous rough sections and washes will force you to slow to 20mph or even 10mph. The speed limit on state highways is 55mph to 65mph; on the interstates it's 75mph to 80mph.

you two 24-hour emergency roadside pickups and transport within a 5-mile radius.

Good Sam RV Club (☎866-205-7451; www.goodsamclub.com) Emergency roadside assistance and towing services for RVs, online route planner and 10% discounts at participating campgrounds.

Driver's License
➡ Visitors may legally drive a car in Utah for up to 12 months with their home driver's license.

➡ If you're from overseas, an International Driving Permit (IDP) will have more credibility with police and simplify the car-rental process, especially if your license doesn't have a photo or isn't written in English.

➡ To legally ride a motorcycle, you'll need a valid US state motorcycle license or a specially endorsed IDP.

Fuel & Repairs
➡ Always start out with a full tank of gas and extra gallons of drinking water, plus food and blankets in case of emergencies.

➡ Gas stations are few and far between in southern Utah. There are no gas stations inside any of the parks, and gas can be expensive in gateway towns. Try to fill up in bigger cities and along interstate highways, where gas is cheaper and stations are often open 24 hours.

➡ For emergency roadside assistance and towing services, join an auto club. In case of any roadside emergencies, keep in mind that cell phones work in most towns and cities, but only in very limited areas of the national parks.

➡ Just outside Bryce Canyon, **Ruby's Inn American Car Care Center** (☎435-834-5232; www.rubysinn.com; 105 S Main St, Bryce Canyon City; ⊙7am-11pm May-Sep, 8am-6pm Oct-Apr)

offers full-service repairs for cars, trucks and RVs, although parts are limited and you may have to wait quite a while for all but the simplest of repairs. It also sells standard auto supplies and decently priced gas, and offers a car wash and 24-hour, AAA-approved towing services. Otherwise, your best bets for faster car repairs and finding auto supplies are in St George and Moab.

Insurance
For rentals, always first check your auto-insurance policy from home to see if you're already covered.

➡ Utah law requires all drivers to carry proof of liability insurance, which covers damage to any property or people you might hit.

➡ Insurance against damage to the car itself, called collision damage waiver (CDW) or loss damage waiver (LDW), costs another $30 or so per day; it may also require that you pay the first $100 to $500 for any repairs. Some credit cards offer reimbursement for collision damage if you pay for the entire rental with that card. There may be exceptions for rentals longer than 15 days, exotic models or 4WD vehicles.

➡ Many rental companies stipulate that any damage a car sustains while being driven on unpaved roads is not covered by the insurance they offer. A few companies prohibit driving off paved roads entirely, even when renting a 4WD vehicle. Clarify this ahead of time if you plan on doing any off-road driving.

Rental
➡ To rent your own wheels, you'll need to be at least 25 years old, hold a valid driver's license and have a major credit card, *not* a check or debit card. A few companies may rent to drivers between 21 and 25

years of age for a surcharge (about $25 per day).

➡ With advance reservations, you should be able to get an economy-size vehicle for around $30 per day, excluding insurance, taxes and fees. Some major car-rental companies, including Avis, Budget and Hertz, now offer 'green' fleets of hybrid rental cars; expect to pay significantly more for these models.

➡ Renting a 4WD vehicle such as a Jeep costs more (from $45 per day). The cheapest places to rent 4WD vehicles are Las Vegas and Salt Lake City, but then you'll be stuck with a higher-priced, fuel-inefficient vehicle for your entire trip. Renting a 4WD locally in southern Utah is more expensive on a daily basis (easily over $100), but may work out cheaper overall if you only need a 4WD for a couple of days.

➡ Car-rental rates usually include unlimited mileage, but hefty surcharges apply for additional drivers and one-way rentals. Child or infant safety seats are required by law (reserve when booking), renting from $10/50 per day/week.

➡ Most companies have rental desks at Salt Lake City, McCarran (Las Vegas) and Denver international airports and Grand Junction regional airport. St George, Cedar City and Moab also have rental locations.

➡ Motorcycle rentals and insurance are not cheap, especially if you have got your eye on a Harley-Davidson. Depending on the model, it costs $100 to $250 per day plus taxes. Rental rates usually include helmets, unlimited miles and liability insurance, but collision insurance (CDW) costs extra.

Road Conditions
➡ For highway driving conditions, visit the website of the **Utah Department**

of Transportation (UDOT; ☎801-965-4000; www.udot. utah.gov). Every national park provides updates on roads within its boundaries; either visit the park website or call the visitor information numbers. For road conditions outside the national parks, contact the federal agency in charge of that area – most often it's the BLM or USFS.

➡ Overall precipitation is low, but when it does rain, it can wreak havoc. Most common during July and August, short, heavy thunderstorms cause flash floods and turn dirt roads into impassable mud slicks, though they dry quickly. Even the lightest rain can leave desert slickrock and hard clay roads treacherously slippery and too dangerous for any vehicle (including 4WDs) for at least a day or two afterward.

➡ Always check with rangers before driving dirt roads, and watch the skies. Never park your vehicle in a desert wash, where it could possibly get swept away by a flash flood.

➡ In winter, higher elevations have snow, while lower elevations see freezing rain, occasional snow and nighttime temperatures that can turn blacktop roads icy. High-elevation mountain roads may be closed completely from the first snowfall in late October or early November until the snow melts away, usually between April and June.

Road Hazards

Be extra cautious while driving in Utah. It may be tempting to put your vehicle into cruise control and zip down the highway at 80mph without a care in the world, but there is no shortage of hazards, from dust storms and rainstorms to livestock and wildlife.

➡ Be particularly vigilant any time you see a wildlife-crossing road sign, especially at dusk. While hitting a deer

is bad enough, hitting an elk, which weighs anywhere from 500lb to 900lb, may very well result in serious injury or death.

➡ Driving too slowly or erratically can be a hazard in the parks. Maintain a reasonable speed on crowded scenic drives. Do not block traffic by suddenly stopping in the middle of the road to take a photo. All of the rules of the road still apply in national parks.

➡ If you're driving an RV or other oversized vehicle, be courteous and don't hog the road – use signposted pullouts to let faster traffic pass.

➡ National park parking lots are renowned for accidents: overloaded vehicles with poor visibility, screaming children causing a distraction, pedestrians who pop up out of nowhere and aggressive drivers trying to snag precious parking spots make for a particularly high collision rate. If you are at fault in an accident within a national park, not only are you responsible for all damages, but you will also be issued a ticket. Take it slow.

Road Rules

➡ Drive on the right-hand side of the road. The use of seat belts is required for drivers, front-seat passengers and anyone under age 20. Children under eight years old are required to sit in a car seat or booster, unless they are taller than 57in (145cm). Motorcycle helmets are not required for adults over age 18.

➡ The maximum speed limit on major Utah highways is 80mph, but it can be much lower on back roads.

➡ You may make a right turn on a red light after first coming to a full stop, unless signs say otherwise. U-turn laws vary by city; look for posted signs.

➡ It is permissible to talk on your cell phone while driving,

but illegal to 'manipulate' your phone (ie dial or text). Get a hands-free setup if you don't already have one.

➡ Strict penalties for driving under the influence (DUI) of drugs or alcohol in Utah include steep fines and jail time. Police can give roadside sobriety checks to assess if you've been drinking or using drugs. You'll fail if your blood-alcohol is over the legal limit (0.08%). Refusing to be tested can result in immediate suspension of your driver's license. It is illegal to carry open containers of alcohol inside a vehicle, even when they're empty; store them in the trunk instead.

RVs

RVs remain a popular way to travel around southern Utah. Although the larger models can be cumbersome to navigate and guzzle gas at an alarming rate, they solve transportation, accommodation and cooking needs in one fell swoop.

➡ After the size of the vehicle, consider the impact of gas prices, gas mileage, additional mileage costs, insurance and refundable deposits; these can add up quickly. It pays to shop around and read the fine print.

➡ Rental rates vary by size, model and mileage. The base rate for a four-person vehicle can be anywhere from $420 to $1800 weekly in summer, plus 34¢ for each additional mile not included in your package. Get out a good map and calculator to determine if it's practical.

➡ Before heading out, consult http://gorving.com or www.rvtravel.com for tips galore.

➡ Visit **Woodall's** (www. woodalls.com) for a thorough RV campground guide.

➡ Some roads in southern Utah are not appropriate

for RVs, and a few roads expressly forbid travel by RVs (or sometimes only for models over a certain length). For further details, consult seasonal park newspapers or ask the staff at visitor centers.

➡ RV dump stations and electrical hookups are found at private campgrounds outside the parks. Inside the parks, dump stations may only be available seasonally (if at all) and generator use is usually restricted to certain hours at NPS campgrounds, which may not have pull-through sites and may restrict RV camping to vehicles of a certain length only.

➡ Be aware that if you're planning on driving an RV or other oversized vehicle through the Mt Carmel–Zion Tunnel inside Zion National Park, you'll need to pay an escort fee and time your trip during specific hours.

Rental

Adventure Touring RV Rentals (☎877-778-9569; www.adventuretouring.com) Serving Las Vegas and Denver.

Cruise America (☎800-671-8042; www.cruiseamerica.com) Rents RVs and trailers in Salt Lake City, Las Vegas, Denver and other major gateway cities.

Jucy Rentals (☎800-650-4180; www.jucyrentals.com) Green and purple pop-up camper vans; located in Las Vegas.

Zion Trailer Rentals (☎435-275-4470; www.rentrvutah.com) Rents trailers and RVs in the Zion and Bryce region.

Tours

Most ranger-guided walking, hiking and shuttle-bus tours of the parks are free; ask at park visitor centers about what's currently being offered. The parks' natural-history associations also offer excellent guided tours and field trips.

Region-wide tour operators include the following:

Adventure Bus (☎888-737-5263, 909-633-7225; www.adventurebus.com) Offers sleep-aboard bus tours of southern Utah's national parks and the Grand Canyon, departing from Salt Lake City.

Backroads (☎510-527-1555, 800-462-2848; www.backroads.com) Offers walking, hiking, cycling and multisport trips for all ages (including families with children) at Zion, Bryce Canyon and the Grand Canyon's North Rim.

Green Tortoise (☎800-867-8647; www.greentortoise.com) Youth-oriented backpacker trips utilize converted sleeping-bunk

buses to visit southern Utah's national parks, departing from Las Vegas.

Road Scholar (☎800-454-5768; www.roadscholar.org) This nonprofit organization offers learning trips, including bus, walking and hiking tours, and group-oriented outdoor activities.

Southern Utah Scenic Tours (☎435-867-8690, 435-867-8690; www.utahscenictours.com) Offers Grand Circle tours of the Southwest and southern Utah backroads trips (including the Grand Canyon's North Rim and Monument Valley) by bus, van or SUV, departing from Las Vegas.

Hitchhiking

Hitchhiking is never entirely safe anywhere in the world, and we don't recommend it. That said, hitchhiking is sometimes the only way to get between trailheads after an end-to-end hike, if you don't happen to have two cars to shuttle. The rules for hitchhiking in each national park change every year, so ask at the visitor center before you stick your thumb out. Keep in mind that hitchhiking is usually only allowed at designated roadside pull-outs within the parks.

Health & Safety

The keys to health and safety are good predeparture preparations and common sense while traveling. While the potential problems may seem frightening, few visitors experience anything worse than a skinned knee. Much of this information covers worst-case scenarios, which can be avoided or at least dealt with more effectively if you're well prepared.

BEFORE YOU GO

If you're planning on doing any hiking, start getting regular physical exercise a few weeks prior to your trip. When possible, visitors from lower elevations and cooler climes should allow at least a day or two to acclimatize before undertaking any strenuous activity in southern Utah's deserts or mountains. And remember the golden rule: if you're going into the backcountry, always let someone know where you are going and how long you plan to be gone. There's even an app for that: www.hiker alert.com.

Further Reading

Hikers, climbers, backpackers, paddlers and other off-road explorers may want to stuff one of these excellent first-aid guides into their packs.

➡ *Backcountry First Aid and Extended Care*, by Buck Tilton (2007). Pocket-sized guide is compact and lightweight, but info-packed for situations when medical help is over an hour away.

➡ *Wilderness 911*, by Eric A Weiss (2007). A step-by-step guide to first aid and advanced care in remote areas when you have limited medical supplies.

➡ *Medicine for the Outdoors*, by Paul S Auerbach (2009). Hefty layperson's reference gives explanations of wilderness medical problems and practical treatment options.

IN THE PARKS

➡ While crime is not a particular problem in any of the national parks, you should still lock your car, and place any valuables you don't carry with you in the trunk, especially when you park at less-visited trailheads.

➡ For casual park visitors, staying safe and healthy is usually a matter of hydrating properly, being aware of the weather forecast (eg watch for flash floods) and not goofing around near precarious cliffs and canyon rims. Many emergencies arise when visitors overestimate their own physical abilities or underestimate the power of Mother Nature.

➡ When visiting southern Utah, you'll need to be more self-sufficient and prepared for the unexpected than usual. The desert offers innumerable ways to come to a bad end, and people discover new ways all the time.

Medical Assistance

➡ In any emergency, dial ☑911. Unfortunately, if you're injured in rural areas or inside the parks, calling may not be an option; cell phones often don't work outside the major interstate corridors, and canyon walls block signals. Satellite phones and personal locator beacons (PLBs) are your best options in the backcountry.

➡ Park rangers with medical training can help visitors who get into trouble, free of charge for basic first aid. For more serious ailments, drive to the nearest hospital emergency room or clinic. Search-and-rescue (SAR) and helicopter evacuations are only for truly life-threatening emergencies. Emergency operations are costly and also put the lives of rangers and other staff at risk.

Infectious Diseases

Rabies

➡ Rabies is a viral infection of the brain and spinal cord that is almost always fatal. The rabies virus is carried in the saliva of infected animals and is typically transmitted through an animal bite, though contamination of any break in the skin with infected saliva may result in rabies. In the US, most cases of human rabies are related to exposure to bats. But rabies may be contracted from any mammal, including squirrels, raccoons and unvaccinated cats and dogs.

➡ If there is any possibility, however small, that you have been exposed, you should seek preventative treatment, which consists of rabies immune globulin and rabies vaccine and is quite safe. In particular, any contact with a bat should be discussed with health authorities, because bats have small teeth and may not leave obvious bite marks. If you wake up to find a bat in your room, especially if you have small children, rabies prophylaxis may be necessary.

Environmental Hazards

Altitude

The rim at Bryce Canyon ranges in altitude from 8000ft to 9000ft above sea level, while Cedar Breaks rises above 10,000ft. A common complaint at high elevations is altitude sickness, characterized by shortness of breath, fatigue, headaches, dizziness and loss of appetite. It sounds benign, but it can actually be quite serious – drink plenty of water and take a day or two to acclimatize before attempting anything strenuous. If symptoms persist, return to a lower elevation. Ibuprofen helps.

Bites & Stings

ANIMAL BITES

➡ Do not attempt to pet, handle or feed any wild animal, no matter how cute and cuddly it may look. Most injuries from animals in the parks are directly related to people trying to do just that. For example, squirrels on Zion's Riverside Walk are notoriously aggressive because so many park visitors have illegally fed them.

➡ Any bite or scratch by a mammal, including bats and squirrels, should be promptly and thoroughly cleansed with large amounts of soap and water, followed by application of an antiseptic such as iodine or alcohol. Local health authorities should be contacted for possible rabies treatment, whether or not you've already been vaccinated against rabies. It may also be advisable to start an antibiotic, because wounds caused by animal bites and scratches frequently become infected.

SNAKES

➡ Despite southern Utah's abundance of venomous snakes, fatalities are rare. Snakebites can usually be prevented by giving the animal space – when you encounter a snake, back away slowly. Most reported snakebites result from people picking up the snake, either out of bravado or mistakenly assuming the animal is dead.

➡ If you're bitten by a snake, seek immediate help. Snakebites don't cause instantaneous death, and medical centers usually stock the necessary antivenins.

➡ If you're bitten on a limb, a light constricting band above the bite can help. Keep the affected area below the level of the heart, and move as little as possible. What you should *not* do is wrap the limb in a tight tourniquet, slash or suck the wound, put ice on it or take any alcohol or drugs. Simply stay calm and get to a hospital.

SPIDERS & SCORPIONS

➡ There are no particular first-aid techniques for spider or scorpion bites. Some (like tarantula bites) are merely painful, while others (like black widow and scorpion bites) contain venom. Doses are generally too small to kill adult humans, but children face a risk of serious complications.

➡ Cool the wound using cold water or ice, and if you're hiking, return immediately; reactions can be delayed for up to 12 hours, and you may want to call Utah Poison Control (📞800-222-1222) and seek medical help.

Cold

HYPOTHERMIA

➡ While generally associated with winter hiking at altitude, hypothermia is a real danger in the desert in any season. Even a sudden rain shower or high winds can rapidly lower your body temperature. Symptoms of hypothermia include exhaustion, numbness, shivering, stumbling, slurred speech, dizzy spells, muscle cramps and irrational or even violent behavior.

PREHYDRATION

Because your body can only absorb about a quart of water per hour, it's beneficial to prehydrate before embarking on a long hike. To get a head start on hydration, drink plenty of water the day and evening before your hike, and avoid diuretics like caffeine and alcohol.

WATER PURIFICATION

All groundwater in the desert, whether a river, seasonal stream or sandstone seep, should be considered unsafe to drink and treated accordingly.

Giardiasis and cryptosporidiosis are common intestinal diseases that stem from drinking untreated water. Giardiasis can be treated, but there is no effective treatment for cryptosporidiosis. Both can last for anywhere from a few weeks or months to several years, though neither is typically life-threatening.

The most reliable way to destroy the offending organisms is to boil water. Water purification tablets and portable water filters (0.5 microns or smaller) are good options outside meal times; ultraviolet purifiers are the newest gadget on the market, though they are battery dependent. Drinking water provided at national park visitor centers and campgrounds is reliably safe, unless posted notices indicate otherwise.

➡ Hypothermia often strikes people hiking narrow canyons, where they must wade or swim in pools that are frigid even in summer. One such place is Zion's Narrows, where hikers spend most of their time immersed in the Virgin River. Hypothermia is also a danger for campers from fall to spring, when overnight temperatures routinely drop near or below freezing, even in the desert or following mild days in the mountains.

➡ To help avoid hypothermia, don't wear cotton clothes (which dry slowly and provide no insulation when wet). Instead wear synthetics or woolen clothing that retain warmth even when wet. Always carry waterproof layers and high-energy, easily digestible snacks like chocolate, nuts and dried fruit. Canyoneers should wear a wet- or dry-suit when advised.

➡ To treat hypothermia, take shelter from bad weather and change into dry, warm clothing. Drink hot liquids (no caffeine or alcohol) and snack on high-calorie food. In advanced stages, carefully put hypothermia sufferers in a warm sleeping bag cocooned inside a windproof and waterproof outer wrapping. Do not rub victims, who must be handled gently.

Heat

DEHYDRATION & HEAT EXHAUSTION

➡ You don't need to do much to become dehydrated in the desert – just stand around. If you do engage in an activity, expect water and salts to leave your body at a vastly accelerated rate.

➡ It's very important to both drink water and eat salty foods when hiking in the desert. The minimum is a gallon of water a day per person, or 16 ounces every hour while active. Though that may sound like a lot, you'll drink that and more if you're active. Keep a few extra gallons of water in the car. Eating is just as important, however, and is the half of the equation many people forget. Always carry high-energy bars or trail mix.

➡ Dehydration (lack of water) or salt deficiency can cause heat exhaustion. Signs and symptoms of heat exhaustion, which occurs when you lose water faster than your body can absorb it, include nausea, vomiting, fatigue, headaches, dizziness, muscle cramps, heavy sweating and/or cool, clammy skin.

➡ Treat heat exhaustion by drinking, eating, resting in the shade and cooling the skin with a wet cloth and fanning yourself.

HEATSTROKE

➡ Heatstroke, which can be fatal, occurs when your internal cooling mechanism breaks down and your body temperature rises dangerously.

➡ Symptoms include flushed, hot and dry skin (ie sweating has stopped), severe throbbing headaches, hyperventilation and a rapid pulse. Some victims may act in an uncharacteristically bizarre manner, display a lack of coordination and eventually go into convulsions.

➡ Immediate hospitalization is essential. In the meantime, move the victim into the shade, remove clothing and cover with a wet cloth or towel, fan vigorously and seek immediate help. Ice packs can be applied to the neck, armpits and groin.

HYPONATREMIA

➡ Hyponatremia (low sodium blood level) occurs when you drink a lot of water but don't eat. The excess water essentially flushes electrolytes and nutrients from your body.

➡ Prevention is key: add electrolyte powder or a pinch of sea salt to drinking water.

➡ Symptoms are similar to heat exhaustion (and can become life-threatening if left untreated), including nausea, muscle cramps, headache and vomiting.

➡ Treatment is to rest in the shade and eat salty foods until the blood's sodium-level balance is reestablished. Rapidly evacuate if the victim's mental status changes.

Sunburn

➡ You can sunburn quickly in the desert, sometimes in less than an hour, even on a cloudy day. Apply sunscreen (SPF 30 or higher) religiously every morning and reapply throughout the day. Always wear a hat, preferably one with a wide brim.

SAFE HIKING

➡ Hiking into a desert means taking extra precautions (p256) to make sure you return safely. This is true whether you plan to be gone an hour or a week. The desert has a way of compounding simple errors in judgment very quickly, and consequences range from unpleasant to grave.

➡ If you do run into trouble, don't panic – sit down (if possible) and regain your cool before making any important decisions.

➡ One little-talked-about risk facing hikers is their own enthusiasm. Respect your limits. Remember that even in the middle of a national park, you're in a remote, wild place. Don't act foolishly by tackling a trail that's above your skill level. Twisting an ankle or breaking a leg is surprisingly easy.

➡ Depending on where you are when you're injured, it could take several hours or even days before a SAR team can find you and get you to a hospital. Needless to say, if no one knows where you are, or what time to expect you back, they won't even come looking.

Getting Lost

➡ Getting lost is always a danger. Always bring a map (preferably a topographical map) and a compass (p257), and be familiar with prominent landmarks. Handheld GPS units can be helpful, but remember that batteries fail and sometimes it's impossible to get a clear satellite signal when you're inside a canyon.

➡ Always stay on the trail; don't take shortcuts. Not only does this help avoid

---

COMMON AILMENTS

Plaguing hikers of all ages in southern Utah, the following may not pose problems if you're prepared.

Blisters

To avoid blisters, make sure your shoes are well worn in before you hit the trail. Your footwear should fit comfortably with enough room to move your toes; shoes that are too big or too small will cause blisters. The same goes for socks: be sure they fit properly and ideally are specifically made for hikers. But take into consideration Utah's extreme temperatures – you don't want to be wearing thick hiking socks if it's hot out. Wet and muddy socks can cause blisters, so even on a day walk, pack a spare pair. Keep your toenails clipped but not too short. If you do feel a blister coming on, treat it sooner rather than later by applying a bit of moleskin (or duct tape).

Fatigue

A simple statistic: more injuries happen toward the end of the day than when you're fresh. Although tiredness can simply be a nuisance on an easy walk, it can be life-threatening on narrow exposed ridges or in bad weather. You should never set out on a walk that is beyond your capabilities on the day. If you feel below par, have a day off or hop on a park shuttle. To reduce the risk of accidents, don't push yourself too hard – take rests every hour or two and build in a good half-hour or hour-long lunch break. Toward the end of the day, take down the pace and increase your concentration. Also eat properly throughout the day; nuts, dried fruit and chocolate are all good, energy-giving snack foods.

Knee Strain

Many hikers will feel the burn on long, steep descents, especially in southern Utah's canyon country. Although you can't eliminate strain on knee joints when dropping steeply, you can reduce it by taking shorter steps that leave your legs slightly bent and ensuring that your heel hits the ground before the rest of your foot. Lightweight hiking poles are effective in taking some of the weight off your knees. Compression bandages may also help.

accidents and injuries from steep drop-offs and hidden hazards, but it makes it easier for potential rescuers to find you. If you do get lost, stay calm and stay put, making your location as visible as possible (eg spread out brightly colored clothing or gear in an exposed place). Use a signal mirror or whistle to alert other hikers that you need help.

Falls & Jumping

➡ Nothing focuses one's attention like the edge of a 2000ft-high crumbling sandstone cliff. The consequences of a fall are self-evident and keep most people from taking unnecessary risks. Yet people fall to their deaths every year in southern Utah. Cliff edges are sheer and trails along them very exposed. Rocks can be loose and slickrock, when wet, is indeed slick.

➡ There are no guardrails along the parks' hiking trails; watch your children carefully at all times.

➡ The more pernicious danger is carelessness. Most park rescues involve young men who are canyoneering and have fractured their legs while bouldering, leaping off rocks, or jumping into shallow, murky pools.

Flash Floods

➡ Flash floods are an ever-present danger in the desert, as flash floods that drowned seven hikers in Zion's Keyhole Canyon in September 2015 sadly demonstrated. No matter how dry a streambed looks, or how sunny it is overhead, a sudden rainstorm miles away can cause a stream or dry wash to 'flash' in minutes, sending down a huge surge of rock- and log-filled water that sweeps away everything in its path. Flash floods will

kill hikers caught in creeks, dry riverbeds and narrow canyons, unless there is an escape route.

➡ Never park or camp in dry washes.

➡ Always check the flash-flood warnings at park visitor centers or with the national weather service; this is especially crucial if you're planning on hiking through any slot canyons.

➡ Flash floods are most common during the summer monsoon season (roughly July through mid-September), but they can happen anytime a storm drops heavy rain.

➡ Telltale signs of an impending flash flood include sudden changes in water clarity (eg the stream turns muddy), rising water levels and/or floating debris, and a rush of wind, the sound of thunder or a low, rumbling roar. If you notice any of these signs, immediately get to higher ground (go as high as you can) – the water level doesn't usually increase all at once with one large wave, so you should have a minute or two to escape. If that's not possible, get behind a rock fin.

➡ Do not run down canyon – you can't beat a flash flood. Instead, wait it out; water levels usually drop within six to 24 hours.

Crossing Rivers & Streams

➡ On some backcountry trails, especially popular canyoneering routes, you may have to ford a river or stream swollen with snowmelt that is fast-flowing and cold enough to be a potential risk. Before stepping out from the bank, ease one arm out of the shoulder strap of your pack and unclip the belt buckle and chest compression straps. That way, if you lose

your balance and are swept downstream, it will be easier to slip off your pack.

Flora & Fauna

➡ Southern Utah is awash in critters that, if bothered, can inflict a fair bit of pain, including rattlesnakes, scorpions, tarantulas, black widows, wasps and even centipedes. Spiders rarely bite unless harassed, which is also true of rattlesnakes, which like to warm themselves on trails or rock ledges, particularly in the late afternoon.

➡ Avoid shoving your hand beneath logs and rocks or into piles of wood, and never reach blindly over ledges or beneath boulders.

➡ Always shake out your hiking boots before putting them back on.

➡ If you encounter a mountain lion while hiking (extremely unlikely), maintain eye contact and do not look away. Wave your arms or hiking poles above your head to make yourself appear larger, and therefore possibly a threat. Gather young children to your side and stick together. Back away slowly, but resist the urge to run, which makes you look like prey. If the lion approaches you, yell loudly, throw rocks and sticks, and fight back by whatever means possible.

➡ Learn to identify poison ivy: serrated leaves that grow in clusters of three and waxy white berries. This toxic plant grows in thickets, preferring moisture-laden canyons. If you think you've been exposed, immediately wash the affected area with soap and water.

Lightning

➡ If a thunderstorm is brewing, avoid exposed ridges or summits. Never seek shelter under objects that are isolated or higher than their surroundings, such as a lone tree. In open areas where there's no safe shelter, find a dry depression in the ground and take up a crouched-squatting position with your feet together; do not lie on the ground. Keep a layer of metal-free insulation, such as a camping pad, between you and the ground. Avoid contact with metallic objects, including backpack frames or hiking poles.

➡ If you're hiking with a group, spread out, keeping at least 50 feet between each person. If anyone is struck by lightning, immediately begin first-aid measures such as checking their airway, breathing and pulse, and treat any burns. Prolonged rescue breathing may be necessary, due to respiratory arrest. Evacuate and get medical help as quickly as possible.

Rockfall

➡ Always be alert to the danger of rockfall, especially after heavy rains. If you accidentally let loose a rock on a trail, loudly warn other hikers below. Bighorn sheep, deer and other large animals sometimes dislodge rocks, another reason to be especially vigilant while hiking.

SAFE CYCLING

➡ Newcomers to desert road cycling and mountain biking should pay particular heed to safety. Wear a helmet, carry lots of water and bring high-energy foods. Also pack a map and keep track of your route. Don't start out on rough trails – first get your bearings on easier rides. The vibration from rougher trails can loosen headsets, so be sure to check your fittings.

➡ Expect the best, but prepare for the worst. In addition to extra water and food, carry a windbreaker, a wide-brimmed hat, sunscreen, sunglasses, a patch kit, tools and matches. Avoid riding alone, and always tell someone where you're going. The desert is unforgiving and should never be underestimated.

➡ Road cyclists must adhere to traffic regulations and should use caution along heavily trafficked roads, especially during the busy summer season. On Zion Canyon's Scenic Drive, cyclists must pull over and allow park shuttle buses to pass.

➡ Although not required by Utah law, always wear a helmet as well as bright colors to improve your visibility to drivers. Emergency roadside assistance for cyclists is offered by the Better World Club.

Behind the Scenes

SEND US YOUR FEEDBACK

We love to hear from travelers – your comments keep us on our toes and help make our books better. Our well-traveled team reads every word on what you loved or loathed about this book. Although we cannot reply individually to postal submissions, we always guarantee that your feedback goes straight to the appropriate authors, in time for the next edition. Each person who sends us information is thanked in the next edition – the most useful submissions are rewarded with a selection of digital PDF chapters.

Visit **lonelyplanet.com/contact** to submit your updates and suggestions or to ask for help. Our award-winning website also features inspirational travel stories, news and discussions.

Note: We may edit, reproduce and incorporate your comments in Lonely Planet products such as guidebooks, websites and digital products, so let us know if you don't want your comments reproduced or your name acknowledged. For a copy of our privacy policy visit lonelyplanet.com/privacy.

AUTHOR THANKS

Greg Benchwick

Thanks to the team of amazing rangers at the national parks. Jennifer at the BLM offered great insights on backcountry life, while Stacey at Poison Spider gave me all the beta I'd ever need to mountain-bike Moab. Michele Hill at the Moab Travel Council was instrumental in identifying new businesses. A lot of people have shared life-changing experiences with me in the Utah backcountry. Thanks for not letting me fall Ryan Taylor, Rob Ickes, Julian Tonsmeire, Dave Elsner, James Klapps, The Squirrel, Reba The Dog, Mom and George, Daddio, Tia Boo, Kesslove and Violeta.

Carolyn McCarthy

Many thanks go to those who helped me in my travels, especially the rangers of GSENM. Appreciation goes out to Meg Simone for her fine company on the trail, Jessica Haynie, for joining in, and my co-authors Chris and Greg for their collaboration. Lastly, thanks to the ancient ones who once lived here for continuing to intrigue and inspire us.

Christopher Pitts

Huge thanks to all of Zion's rangers and especially the helpful folks at the Wilderness Desk. Aly Baltrus provided stats and facts and put me in touch with ranger Carolyn Finnerty, who answered more than her fair share of questions and provided super-useful feedback on errors and omissions. Ben Rhinesmith was a font of area knowledge, a great canyoneering guide and even took some memorable photos to boot. Thanks are also due to co-authors Carolyn and Greg for insider tips and all-around sage words of advice on our second book together. Here's to another project! Back at home, big hugs to the Scotts and Trampedachs for hosting an extended sleepover while certain irresponsible parents lost money in Vegas. Or did we win? Finally love to my dearest partners in crime: Perrine, Céleste and Elliot.

ACKNOWLEDGMENTS

Climate map data adapted from Peel MC, Finlayson BL & McMahon TA (2007) 'Updated World Map of the Köppen-Geiger Climate Classification', Hydrology and Earth System Sciences, 11, 163344.

Cover photograph: Zion Canyon from Angel's Landing, Michele Falzone/AWL

THIS BOOK

This 3rd edition of Lonely Planet's *Zion & Bryce Canyon National Parks* guidebook was researched and written by Christopher Pitts, Greg Benchwick and Carolyn McCarthy. This guidebook was produced by the following:

Destination Editor
Alexander Howard
Product Editors
Kate James, Kate Mathews
Assisting Editors
Carolyn Bain, Helen Koehne, Kirsten Rawlings, Erin Richards, Simon Williamson
Senior Cartographer
Alison Lyall

Book Designer
Katherine Marsh
Cover Researcher
Marika Mercer

Thanks to Brent Anderson, Melanie Dankel, Katie O'Connell, Luna Soo, Angela Tinson, Lauren Wellicome, Clifton Wilkinson

Index

NOTES

Map Legend

Sights
- Beach
- Bird Sanctuary
- Buddhist
- Castle/Palace
- Christian
- Confucian
- Hindu
- Islamic
- Jain
- Jewish
- Monument
- Museum/Gallery/Historic Building
- Ruin
- Shinto
- Sikh
- Taoist
- Winery/Vineyard
- Zoo/Wildlife Sanctuary
- Other Sight

Activities, Courses & Tours
- Bodysurfing
- Diving
- Canoeing/Kayaking
- Course/Tour
- Sento Hot Baths/Onsen
- Skiing
- Snorkeling
- Surfing
- Swimming/Pool
- Walking
- Windsurfing
- Other Activity

Sleeping
- Sleeping
- Camping

Eating
- Eating

Drinking & Nightlife
- Drinking & Nightlife
- Cafe

Entertainment
- Entertainment

Shopping
- Shopping

Information
- Bank
- Embassy/Consulate
- Hospital/Medical
- Internet
- Police
- Post Office
- Telephone
- Toilet
- Tourist Information
- Other Information

Geographic
- Beach
- Gate
- Hut/Shelter
- Lighthouse
- Lookout
- Mountain/Volcano
- Oasis
- Park
- Pass
- Picnic Area
- Waterfall

Population
- Capital (National)
- Capital (State/Province)
- City/Large Town
- Town/Village

Transport
- Airport
- BART station
- Border crossing
- Boston T station
- Bus
- Cable car/Funicular
- Cycling
- Ferry
- Metro/Muni station
- Monorail
- Parking
- Petrol station
- Subway/SkyTrain station
- Taxi
- Train station/Railway
- Tram
- Underground station
- Other Transport

Note: Not all symbols displayed above appear on the maps in this book

Routes
- Tollway
- Freeway
- Primary
- Secondary
- Tertiary
- Lane
- Unsealed road
- Road under construction
- Plaza/Mall
- Steps
- Tunnel
- Pedestrian overpass
- Walking Tour
- Walking Tour detour
- Path/Walking Trail

Boundaries
- International
- State/Province
- Disputed
- Regional/Suburb
- Marine Park
- Cliff
- Wall

Hydrography
- River, Creek
- Intermittent River
- Canal
- Water
- Dry/Salt/Intermittent Lake
- Reef

Areas
- Airport/Runway
- Beach/Desert
- Cemetery (Christian)
- Cemetery (Other)
- Glacier
- Mudflat
- Park/Forest
- Sight (Building)
- Sportsground
- Swamp/Mangrove

OUR STORY

A beat-up old car, a few dollars in the pocket and a sense of adventure. In 1972 that's all Tony and Maureen Wheeler needed for the trip of a lifetime – across Europe and Asia overland to Australia. It took several months, and at the end – broke but inspired – they sat at their kitchen table writing and stapling together their first travel guide, *Across Asia on the Cheap*. Within a week they'd sold 1500 copies. Lonely Planet was born.

Today, Lonely Planet has offices in Franklin, London, Melbourne, Oakland, Beijing and Delhi, with more than 600 staff and writers. We share Tony's belief that 'a great guidebook should do three things: inform, educate and amuse'.

OUR WRITERS

Greg Benchwick

Capitol Reef National Park, Canyonlands National Park, Arches National Park, Moab Greg has been drifting across the high plains of the Colorado Plateau for most of his life – he calls it a 'true spiritual home'. As a kid, he canoed desolate river canyons with his family, while in his wilder college days he pushed the limits on classic rock-climbing routes like Castleton Tower and the Moonlight Buttress. He's backpacked lost canyons, hitchhiked to Zion, mountain-biked Moab, and found solitude and peace in the lost corners of this desert wonderworld. Greg also wrote the Understand section, Clothing & Equipment and Directory A–Z .

Read more about Greg at:
http://auth.lonelyplanet.com/profiles/gbenchwick

Carolyn McCarthy

Bryce Canyon National Park, Around Bryce Canyon National Park, Grand Staircase-Escalante National Monument, Around Grand Staircase-Escalante National Monument The red-rock desert of Utah is a favorite destination for Carolyn. She has contributed to more than 30 titles for Lonely Planet, including *Panama*, *Trekking in the Patagonian Andes*, *Argentina*, *Chile*, *Colorado*, *Southwest USA* and national parks guides. She has also written for *Outside*, *BBC Magazine*, *National Geographic* and other publications. Follow her on Instagram @masmerquen and Twitter @RoamingMcC. For more information, see www.carolynmccarthy.pressfolios.com.

Christopher Pitts

Zion National Park, Around Zion National Park Chris first drove West on a family road trip across the country and immediately fell in love with the star-studded nights. Four years at Colorado College gave him plenty of opportunities to hitch-hike to Utah and lug around gallons of water during not-always-sunny spring breaks in the Canyonlands. Fifteen years, several continents and two kids later, he's back in Colorado, traveling I-70 with the rest of the family whenever the opportunity arises. Visit him online at www.christopherpitts.net. Chris also wrote the Plan section, Transportation and Health & Safety.

Published by Lonely Planet Publications Pty Ltd
ABN 36 005 607 983
3rd edition – Apr 2016
ISBN 978 1 74220 201 3
© Lonely Planet 2016   Photographs © as indicated 2016
10 9 8 7 6 5 4 3 2 1
Printed in China

Although the authors and Lonely Planet have taken all reasonable care in preparing this book, we make no warranty about the accuracy or completeness of its content and, to the maximum extent permitted, disclaim all liability arising from its use.

All rights reserved. No part of this publication may be copied, stored in a retrieval system, or transmitted in any form by any means, electronic, mechanical, recording or otherwise, except brief extracts for the purpose of review, and no part of this publication may be sold or hired, without the written permission of the publisher. Lonely Planet and the Lonely Planet logo are trademarks of Lonely Planet and are registered in the US Patent and Trademark Office and in other countries. Lonely Planet does not allow its name or logo to be appropriated by commercial establishments, such as retailers, restaurants or hotels. Please let us know of any misuses: lonelyplanet.com/ip.